The Bolsheviks and the Chinese Revolution

1919–1927

Chinese Worlds

Chinese Worlds publishes high-quality scholarship, research monographs, and source collections on Chinese history and society from 1900 into the next century.

"Worlds" signals the ethnic, cultural, and political multiformity and regional diversity of China, the cycles of unity and division through which China's modern history has passed, and recent research trends toward regional studies and local issues. It also signals that Chineseness is not contained within territorial borders – overseas Chinese communities in all countries and regions are also "Chinese worlds". The editors see them as part of a political, economic, social, and cultural continuum that spans the Chinese mainland, Taiwan, Hong Kong, Macau, South-East Asia, and the world.

The focus of Chinese Worlds is on modern politics and society and history. It includes both history in its broader sweep and specialist monographs on Chinese politics, anthropology, political economy, sociology, education, and the social-science aspects of culture and religions.

The Literary Field of Twentieth-Century China
Edited by *Michel Hockx*

Chinese Business in Malaysia
Accumulation, Ascendance, Accommodation
Edmund Terence Gomez

Internal and International Migration
Chinese Perspectives
Edited by *Frank N. Pieke* and *Hein Mallee*

Village Inc.
Chinese Rural Society in the 1990s
Edited by *Flemming Christiansen* and *Zhang Junzuo*

Chen Duxiu's Last Articles and Letters, 1937–1942
Edited and translated by *Gregor Benton*

Encyclopedia of the Chinese Overseas
Edited by *Lynn Pan*

New Fourth Army
Communist Resistance along the Yangtze and the Huai, 1938–1941
Gregor Benton

A Road is Made
Communism in Shanghai 1920–1927
Steve Smith

The Bolsheviks and the Chinese Revolution 1919–1927
Alexander Pantsov

Chinatown, Europe
Identity of the European Chinese Towards the Beginning of the Twenty-First Century
Flemming Christiansen

Birth Control in China 1949–1999
Population Policy and Demographic Development
Thomas Scharping

The Bolsheviks and the Chinese Revolution

1919–1927

Alexander Pantsov

UNIVERSITY OF HAWAI'I PRESS
HONOLULU

For
Katya, Nina, and Dasha

© 2000 Alexander Pantsov

Published in North America by
University of Hawai'i Press
2840 Kolowalu Street
Honolulu, Hawai'i 96822

First published in the United Kingdom
by Curzon Press
Richmond, Surrey
England

Printed in Great Britain

Library of Congress Cataloging-in-Publication Data

Pantsov, Alexander, 1955-
  The Bolsheviks and the Chinese revolution 1919-1927 / Alexander Pantsov.
      p. cm. – (Chinese Worlds)
  Originally published: Richmond, Surrey, England : Curzon Press, 2000.
  Includes bibliographical references and index.
  ISBN 0-8248-2319-2 (cloth : alk. paper). – ISBN 0-8248-2327-3
(pbk. : alk. paper)
      1. Communism–China–History. 2. China–History–Warlord period,
      1916-1928. 3. Trotsky, Leon, 1879-1940. 4. Stalin, Joseph, 1879-1953. 5.
      Communism–Soviet Union–History. I. Title. II. Series.
  HX418.P36 2000
  951.04'1–dc21   99-049835

Contents

Acknowledgements

This work was made possible by financial support from the Chiang Ching-kuo Foundation for International Scholarly Exchange (Taipei, Taiwan), to which I express my deep gratitude. In addition to the Foundation, I would like to thank the Kennan Institute for Advanced Russian Studies (USA) and the British Academy, from whom I received short-term grants in 1991 and 1992.

This study was originally written in Russian in 1993 when I was working in the Moscow Institute of Comparative Political Science at the Russian Academy of Sciences, but due to some peculiar circumstances it has not been published in Russia. I am indebted to a group of my closest colleagues and friends from the United Kingdom and the USA who made it possible for my book to appear in English. Their contribution to my translation, editing and polishing the manuscript are invaluable. My sincere thanks go to Professor Emeritus Morris Slavin of Youngstown State University; Professor Gregor Benton of the University of Leeds; Professor Steven Levine of the University of Montana; Professor Woodford McClellan of the University of Virginia, Charlottesville; Professor William Pelz of Elgin Community College; Professor Donald Raleigh of the University of North Carolina at Chapel Hill; Mr. Eric Schuster of DePaul University; Mr. George Shriver; and Mr. John Sexton of the Reuter Agency.

My study required extensive exploration in quite a number of archives and libraries in several countries. I am grateful to all the people who helped me in my research in Russia, the United States, the People's Republic of China, the United Kingdom, France, and Taiwan. Special appreciation is due to Dr. Alexander Chechevishnikov of Moscow State University and Dr. Konstantin Sheveliev of the Institute of Far Eastern Studies at the Russian Academy of Sciences; Professor Zhao Mingyi of Shandong University and Dr. Mi Zhenbo of Nankai University; Professor Emeritus Pierre Broué of Institute Léon Trotsky; Professor Emeritus Morris Slavin and his wife Sophie; Professor Woodford McClellan and his wife Irina; Mr. John Sexton and his wife Jane; Mrs. Dora Benton; Professor Gregor Benton; Professor William Pelz; Rev. Thomas Croak, C.M. of DePaul University; Professors

Ch'en San-ching, Ch'en Yung-fa and Dr. Yu Miin-ling of the Institute of Modern History, Academia Sinica, Taiwan; Mrs. Zeya Krasko and her husband Gennadii; and Mrs. Svetlana Sheinina and her husband Dmitrii.

I have profited from my personal contacts with those who witnessed and encountered the events which are being described in this book. I will always gratefully remember Mr. Wang Fanxi, Mrs. Nadezhda Adolfovna Joffe, Mrs. Tatyana Invarovna Smilga, Mr. Ivan Yakovlevich Vrachev. Professors Gregor Benton, Pierre Broué, Morris Slavin, William Pelz, and Woodford McClellan, as well as Mr. Wang Fanxi, Dr. Wang Danzhi (son of CCP activists Wang Ming and Meng Qingshu), Dr. Yuri Felshtinsky, Mrs. Rozaliya Ephraimovna Belenkaya (daughter of Russian repressed Trotsky- ist Ephraim Moiseevich Landau), and Mrs. Lin Yin (granddaughter of the Chinese Trotskyist Fan Wenhui), were particularly generous in lending and giving me unique materials from their private archives and libraries. I am also grateful to Mr. Nikolai Semenovich Kardashiev, son of the ECCI official Simon Karlovich Brike.

I also deeply appreciate the friendly attitude to my work expressed by fellows of the Russian Center for the Preservation and Study of the Records of Modern History and the Archives of the Russian Academy of Sciences. In particular, I would like to thank Drs. Kirill Anderson and Valery Shepeliev, as well as Svetlana Rozental, Larisa Rogovaya, Ludmila Kosheleva, Liudmila Karlova, and Yuri Tutochkin. I wish, further, to thank Director Richard Wendorf and the staff of the Houghton Library at Harvard University, and the staff of the Bureau of Investigation, Taipei, Taiwan for their generous assistance.

I must also mention my teachers of Chinese history and politics at the Institute of Asian and African Studies at Moscow State University and the Institute of Comparative Political Science at Russian Academy of Sciences to whom I will never be able to fully repay my debts, notably the late Professor Mikhail F. Yuriev and Professor Vilia G. Gelbras. A number of colleagues read sections of the manuscript and were charitable in making very helpful comments. Among them I am particularly grateful to Academician Boris Koval of the Russian Association of Political Science, Dr. Elena Belozerova of the Institute of Comparative Political Science at the Russian Academy of Sciences, Professor Lev Delyusin of the Institute of World Politics and Economy at the Russian Academy of Sciences, Professor Fridrikh Firsov, Professor Arlen Meliksetov of the Institute of African and Asian Studies at Moscow State University, Professor Moisei Persits, Professor Alexander Grigoriev of the Institute of Far Eastern Studies at the Russian Academy of Sciences, and Professor Georgii Cherniavsky.

The technical contribution of Professor Alexei Maslov of the Institute of Far Eastern Studies at the Russian Academy of Sciences and Mr. Daniel Nowak of DePaul University is also greatly appreciated.

Finally, I am grateful to my wife, Katya, my mother, Nina Stepanovna, and my daughter, Dasha, who provided me with enormous support throughout the entire process of my work.

Abbreviations

Agitprop	Agitatsiya i propaganda (Department of Agitation and Propaganda)
ARAN	Archives of the Russian Academy of Sciences
AUCP (B)	All-Union Communist Party (Bolsheviks)
AULCLY	All-Union Leninist Communist League of Youth
AUTUCC	All-Union Trade Unions Central Council
Bund	General Jewish Workers Union of Russia and Poland
Cadet	Constitutional Democrat
Cheka	Chrezvychainaya Komissiya (Extraodinary Commission, i.e., Political Police of the Bolshevik government, 1917–22)
CC	Central Committee
CCC	Central Control Commission
CCYL	Chinese Communist Youth League, successor of the Chinese Socialist Youth League from 1925.
CCP	Chinese Communist party
CEC	Central Executive Committee
Centrosoyuz	Central Cooperative
CER	Chinese Eastern Railway
Comintern	Communist International
Cominform	Communist Information Bureau
CP(B)U	Communist Party (Bolsheviks) of the Ukraine
CPI	Communist Party of India
CPSU	Communist Party of the Soviet Union
CSYL	Chinese Socialist Youth League
CYI	Communist Youth International
ECCI	Executive Committee of the Communist International
ECCYI	Executive Committee of the Communist Youth International
FER	Far Eastern Republic
GARF	Gosudarstvennyi Arkhiv Rossiiskoi Federatsii (State Archives of the Russian Federation)
GMD	Guomindang

Gosizdat	Gosudarstvennoye Izdatelstvo (State Publishing House)
ICC	International Control Commission
ISRNCP	Institute for Scientific Research on National and Colonial Problems
IWEIP	Institute of World Economy and International Politics
Inprekorr	*Internationalen Pressekorrespondenz* (*International Press Correspondence*)
IRP	Institute of Red Professors
Komsomol	Kommunisticheskii Soyuz Molodezhi (Communist Youth League)
KPD	Kommunistische Partei Deutschlands (German Communist Party)
KUTK	Kommunisticheskii Universitet Trudyashchikhsya Kitaya (Communist University of the Toilers of China)
KUTV	Kommunisticheskii Universitet Trudyashchikhsya Vostoka (Communist University of the Toilers of the East)
MSPI	Moscow State Pedagogical Institute
Narkomnats	Narodnyi Komissariat po delam Natsionalnostei (People's Commissariat for Nationalities)
NAZI	members of German National Socialist Labor Party
NEP	New Economic Policy
NKID	Narodnyi Komissariat Inostrannykh Del (People's Commissariat of Foreign Affairs)
NKVD	Narodnyi Komissariat Vnutrennikh Del (People's Commissariat of Internal Affairs, i.e., Political Police of the Bolshevik government, successor of Cheka and OGPU, 1934–46)
NRA	National Revolutionary Army
Octobrist	*October 17th Union* Member
OGPU	Ob'edinennoye Gosudarstvennoye Politicheskoye Upravleniye (United State Political Administration, i.e., Political Police of the Bolshevik government, successor of Cheka, 1922–34)
Partizdat	Partiinoye izdatel'stvo (Party Publishing House)
PCF	Parti Communiste Français (French Communist Party)
Politburo	Political Bureau
Profintern	Krasnyi Internatsional Professional'nykh Soyuzov (The Red International of Labor Unions)
PSS	*Polnoye Sobranie Sochinenii* (Complete Collected Works)
RCP(B)	Russian Communist Party (Bolsheviks)
Revvoensovet	Revolutsionnyi Voennyi Sovet (Revolutionary Military Council)
RKKA	Raboche-Krest'yanskaia Krasnaya Armiya (Red Army of Workers and Peasants)

RSDLP Russian Social Democratic Labor Party
RSDLP(B) Russian Social Democratic Labor Party (Bolsheviks)
RSFSR Russian Soviet Federated Socialist Republic
RTsKhIDNI Rossiiskii Tsentr Khraneniya i Izucheniya Dokumentov Noveishei Istorii (The Russian Center for Preservation and Study of the Records of Modern History)
SD Social Democrat
SDP Social Democratic Party
Sovnarkhoz Soviet Narodnogo Khozyaistva (People's Economic Council)
SR Socialist Revolutionary
TASS Telegrafnoye Agentstvo Sovetskogo Soyuza (Telegraph Agency of the Soviet Union)
UTK Universitet Trudyashchikhsya Kitaya (Sun Yat-sen University of the Toilers of China)
VSNKH Vserossiiskii (Vsesoyuznii) Sovet Narodnogo Khozyaistva (All-Russian [All-Union] Council of National Economy)
YCP Yugoslav Communist party

Introduction

Bolshevik policy in China before and during the Chinese revolution of 1925–27 has been the object of numerous scholarly enquiries. Historians have often been inspired to analyze the profound ideological impact that the Bolsheviks had on the Chinese Communist movement in its early years. The first Chinese Marxist nuclei originated with the direct assistance of Russian Communists; Chinese Communist Party (CCP) strategy and tactics in the 1920s were elaborated under Moscow's direct supervision. There has also been a great deal of interest in the role Soviet leaders played in events which culminated in the profound defeat inflicted on the CCP by the Guomindang (GMD, Nationalist Party), its former ally in the united front against foreign imperialism. To what degree was the Comintern, under first Lenin's and then Stalin's influence, responsible for this defeat? Could Trotsky have radically changed the situation in China had his ideas been accepted in time by the Comintern Executive (ECCI)? What considerations guided these three leaders of the All-Union Communist Party (Bolsheviks) [AUCP(B)] in formulating their China policy? How, precisely, did they differ in their assessments of the strategic and tactical tasks of the Communists in China?

Amidst the welter of discordant opinions, two approaches to these questions stand out in Western historiography. Most Western historians and commentators are inclined to believe that Lenin's united front policy, formulated at the Second Comintern congress in July 1920 and elaborated in 1921–22, before Lenin fell ill, created an opportunity for the Communist International to guarantee the CCP's hegemony over the national liberation movement and thus pave the way for a Communist dictatorship.

Stalin's views are seen in quite a different light. Most Western specialists argue that Stalin's tactics were characterized by a kind of totalist GMD-centrism, i.e., Stalin counted on a victory of the anti-imperialist revolution in China at any price, even at the expense of the CCP. Supporters of this view argue that at least from 1925 on Stalin's line was grounded in the notion that it was possible to build socialism in one country, namely, the Soviet Union. In other words, his was a policy of national communism. From this perspective, in the period under review the Politburo of the AUCP(B)CC, aiming above all to secure the state interests of the USSR in the Far East, bent its efforts toward activating the Chinese national revolutionary movement led by the Guomindang in order to deal the heaviest possible blow to British imperialism. At the time, the Soviet leadership perceived Great Britain as the main enemy.

Trotsky's position concerning China is assessed as being entirely internationalist. According to many historians, Trotsky, from the very beginning of the ECCI united front policy, persistently opposed it in favor of "permanent revolution" – thus adhering even more closely than Lenin to the Bolshevik tradition.

Presented in basic detail by Harold Isaacs,[1] these views were later fully developed by Isaac Deutscher.[2] These two authors are largely responsible for the popularity of the concept among specialists, but they did not originate it. It had already been expressed by several observers in the 1920s. In a June 27, 1927, declaration, the activists of one of the opposition factions of the Soviet Communist party, the Democratic Centralist group led by Vladimir M. Smirnov, branded Stalin's policy in China nationalist. They wrote that

> The Stalinist Central Committee is obviously trying to convert the Chinese Revolution into a Chinese war against imperialism rather than as a detachment of the world revolution . . . The CC views the Chinese Revolution simply as a means of inflicting a maximum blow against the enemies of the USSR. This is not the policy of the Comintern but of the People's Commissariat of Foreign Affairs.[3]

In April 1927 the Menshevik *Sotsialisticheskii vestnik* (Socialist Herald) noted,

> In principle the Bolsheviks also stood for the preservation of the 'united front' in the Chinese Revolution until the completion of the task of national liberation . . . But . . . in fact, the 'infantile leftism' of utopian adventurism was joined with the desire to 'use' the Chinese Revolution in the Soviet government's struggle against Britain.[4]

In October 1927 Louis Fischer, the Moscow correspondent of the American periodical *The Nation*, wrote that "the Stalin majority" of the Soviet Communist party "neglected the proper development of the Chinese revolution in order more quickly to spike the British."[5]

Without rejecting this position entirely, another group of Western historians more plausibly noted the absence of any well thought-out tactics in Lenin's, Stalin's or Trotsky's China policy. They maintained that Lenin's original plan concerning national revolutions in Asia was ambiguous and even failed to specify a time period for the anti-imperialist alliance. This made it possible for both Stalin and his critics to appeal to Lenin's authority in their mutual struggle. In the 1920s the Chinese question served the interests of the Soviet intra-party conflict, above all. The Stalinists shamelessly used it to expose Trotsky's "errors"; the latter did likewise in respect to Stalin's "misconceptions." This approach was represented most prominently by Conrad Brandt.[6] Earlier some considerations in this regard were advanced by Robert North,[7] who did not pursue them.

For all their seeming logic, however, both perspectives are open to question. Some key points of the first approach concerning the Stalin-Trotsky debate were disproved as early as 1939 by none other than Trotsky himself, in a conversation with the American socialist C. L. R. James (pseudonym Johnson). "Formalism" was Trotsky's reaction to James's contention that the Soviet bureaucracy was quite prepared to support a bourgeois-democratic revolution in China, but because it was a bureaucracy it could not support a proletarian revolution. He continued:

> What happened was that the bureaucracy acquired certain bureaucratic habits of thinking. It proposed to restrain the peasants today so as not to frighten the generals. It thought it would push the bourgeoisie to the left. It saw the Guomindang as a body of office-holders and thought it could put ... Communists into the offices and so change the direction of events ... Stalin and Co. genuinely believed that the Chinese revolution was a bourgeois-democratic revolution and sought to establish the dictatorship of the proletariat and the peasantry.[8]

The documentary materials likewise do not support some basic components of the second perspective. How could Lenin have been more specific in his original plan, which directly called on all Asian Communists to collaborate with national revolutionaries?[9] What time limits could he have agreed on? After all, he was a politician, not a prophet. Further, can one really explain Stalin's conviction in a September 26, 1926, private letter to Vyacheslav Molotov, his closest confederate, that "... Hankow [Hankou] will soon become the Chinese Moscow ..." as a lack of principle?[10] Finally, can one seriously charge Trotsky with shameless use of the Chinese question during the turbulent period after Chiang Kai-shek's coup in April 1927, when he was aware that the Opposition had no chance against the Stalin faction in the matter of China?[11]

It is hardly surprising that mainland Chinese historiography does not share the Western concepts of the Chinese revolution, but the reasons are not only scholarly in nature. In spite of the publication of a large number of

3

documents on Comintern-CCP relations, particularly since the Third Plenum of the Eleventh Central Committee of the CCP in December 1978, contemporary Chinese historians still maintain the traditional political interpretation of Bolshevik policy in their country. Prejudice accumulated over decades continues to influence them. They consider Lenin's and Stalin's policies the only correct tactics of the united front, which could definitely lead to the CCP establishment of a CCP dictatorship in China. According to this logic, the CCP failed due to an unfavorable balance of power in China and the sabotage of the Comintern course by some CCP "rightists." Although they have been paying increasing attention to Trotsky's views on China, they still analyze them through an official prism, with the aim above all of reinforcing anti-Trotskyism. There have been practically no serious disagreements among them on this matter,[12] although their "myths" are not confirmed even by the documents published in the People's Republic.

As for modern Russian historiography, it has been undergoing a profound evolution. It is developing and at the same time significantly revising some basic aspects of Soviet liberal Sinology, the foundations of which were laid in the 1960s and 1970s by a group of historians of whom the most notable are V. I. Glunin, L. P. Delyusin, M. A. Persits, A. B. Reznikov, and M. F. Yuriev.[13] Unlike their Chinese colleagues, the Soviet historians of the 1960s and 1970s were anti-Stalinists who never mentioned the dictator's name in a positive context; most simply ignored him. At the same time they viewed both Lenin's and the post-Lenin Comintern's China tactics as the only credible ones. They refused, however, to consider these tactics as directly aimed at establishing a CCP dictatorship. On the contrary, they placed the highest value on the "moderation" of Lenin and the ECCI, emphasizing Lenin's belief in genuine national revolutions in the East and contrasting his views with those of the Comintern ultra-leftists. These historians characterized the national revolutions themselves as quite "moderate." As for Trotsky's ideas on China, this subject had lain almost completely outside the field of Soviet research. Soviet historiography contains only a few pages devoted to this theme, and all reflect an anti-Trotskyist prejudice.[14]

The collapse of the Communist system in the USSR in the early 1990s deeply shook the positive assessment of the Lenin-Comintern China policy. More critical and sometimes openly anti-Communist approaches have appeared, notably from a group of historians at the Institute of Far Eastern Studies of the Russian Academy of Sciences led by A. M. Grigoriev. Having refined the anti-Stalinist orientation of their predecessors,[15] they now see an all-embracing "utopian" character in the Comintern platform. Lenin's and Stalin's policies are both considered "shady radical adventures," Trotsky's as even more "ultra-leftist."[16] At the same time, they maintain that Stalin's and Trotsky's positions had been irrepressibly drawn together in their "adventurism." For example, they insist that in July 1927 the Oppositionist and Stalinist platforms differed only on the question of soviets. This group of scholars now regards only a few minor ECCI members as "moderates." At the same time, the group obviously shares to some extent Brandt's concept of the Comintern policy in China, stressing the ambiguity and even "speculativeness" of Lenin's platform and explaining the Stalin-Trotsky debate as the "logic" of the intra-party conflict.[17]

This concept likewise raises questions. If Lenin's policy was utopian, i.e., if it could not make a CCP victory possible, how did it happen that the CCP, applying in the 1940s basically the same policy that Lenin put forward in 1920, ultimately won? If Trotsky was ultra-leftist, why did the Stalinist members of the Politburo commission on China and Japan consider his attitude toward the Chinese revolution "pessimistic"?[18] If in July 1927 there was only one issue of disagreement – on the soviets – between Stalin and Trotsky, why did the two polemicize on the CCP's presence in the "Left" GMD? Perhaps the claim about the absence of crucial differences between Stalin's and Trotsky's positions is simply deduced from the fact that Grigoriev's group believes that the documents on the Opposition's split with the Soviet Communist party majority "give nothing substantially new to our comprehension of the key Comintern direction in China."[19]

Meanwhile, the doors to the former secret Soviet archives and those of the International Communist movement are no longer closed, and many new documents are available. The opening of the archives has broadened the documentary base for a new study of Bolshevik policy in China on the eve of and during the revolution of 1925–27. The voluminous records and files preserved in these large depositories[20] enable us to take a fresh look at this question. Most of the documents have not yet been brought to public attention and are examined in this study for the first time. Only a portion, including materials of the Politburo of the Central Committee of the Soviet Communist party, has recently appeared in two collections published by a group of Russian archival workers and by Grigoriev's team in collaboration with Berlin Free University and the Russian Center for the Preservation and Study of Records of Modern History.[21]

The aim of the present work, therefore, is to incorporate these new documents into a scholarly study and on that basis to explore the essence of the Russian Bolsheviks' main concepts concerning the Chinese revolution, as elaborated in 1919–27. The work is also designed to determine the influence these concepts exerted on the Chinese Communist party through an analysis of the way various adherents of the Chinese Communist movement perceived them.

The range of primary sources used in the book can be grouped in the following categories:

First, previously unpublished archival material on the Comintern, the All-Union Communist Party (Bolshevik), and the CCP reflecting the theories and political practice of Leninism, Trotskyism, and Stalinism and of the Russian and Chinese Left Oppositions. This material includes more than one hundred previously unknown works of Lenin, Stalin, Trotsky, and a number of other activists of the international Communist movement collected by the author in various repositories: the Russian Center; the State Archives of the Russian Federation (hereafter State Archives); the Archives of the Russian Academy of Sciences (hereafter ARAN); the former Party Archives of Sverdlovsk Oblast (hereafter PASO); Trotsky Papers at the Houghton Library of Harvard University (hereafter Trotsky Papers); and the Archives of the Bureau of Investigation of the Ministry of Legislation on Taiwan (hereafter Bureau of Investigation); private archives of Meng Qingshu (the widow of a Chinese Communist Party activist Wang Ming); the archives of one of the organizers of the Trotskyist movement in China, Wang Fanxi; and the papers of the Russian Trotskyist Ephraim Moiseevich Landau.

Second, works on these questions by Lenin, Stalin, Trotsky, and other leaders of the Executive Committee of the Communist International and the CCP published in China, France, Germany, Holland, Hong Kong, Russia, the United States, and Taiwan.

Third, various periodicals including Comintern journals and bulletins; the party press of the Soviet Communist party and CCP; other Soviet, Chinese, and Oppositionist periodicals such as *Pod Znamenem Ilicha* (Under the Banner of Ilich), organ of the Communist University of the Toilers of the East; *Gongchan zazhi* (Communist Journal), organ of the Communist University of the Toilers of China; *Qianjin bao* (Forward), the newspaper of Chinese émigrés in Russia; and Trotsky's *Byulleten oppozitsii (bol'shevikov-lenintsev)* (The Bulletin of the Opposition [Bolshevik Leninists].)

Fourth, private interviews carried out by the author with the participants and eyewitnesses of the events treated in the book, along with their relatives. These include Wang Fanxi, Ivan Yakovlevich Vrachiev, Nadezhda Adolfovna Joffe, Tatyana Invarovna Smilga, Rozaliya Ephraimovna Belenkaya (Landau), Lin Ying, and Nikolai Semenovich Kardashiev (Brike).

Fifth, memoirs of various Chinese revolutionaries, including the autobiographies of activists of the Chinese Communist movement – Bao Huiseng, Chen Bilan, Guo Shaotang (A. G. Krymov), Jiang Zemin, Liu Renjing, Lu Yeshen, Ma Yuansheng, Peng Shuzhi, Pu Dezhi, Ren Zhuoxuan, Sheng Yueh, Sun Yefang, Tang Youzhang, Wang Fanxi, Wang Pingyi, Xiao Jingguang, Yang Zilie, Zhang Guotao, and Zheng Chaolin. Further, the memoirs of the Guomindang members Chiang Ching-kuo, Chiang Kai-shek, Deng Wenyi, Guan Suozhi, Wang Xuean, and Zhang

Xueyuan, and the Chinese Socialist Chiang Kanghu. Memoir literature also includes autobiographical writings of foreign participants or eye-witnesses to the Chinese revolutionary movement such as Aleksei Vasilievich Blagodatov, Aleksandr Ivanovich Cherepanov, Sergei Alekseevich Dalin, Louis Fischer, Nadezhda Adolfovna Joffe, Viacheslav Mikhailovich Molotov, Manabendra Nath Roy, Bertrand Russell, Vincent Sheean, Vera Vladimirovna Vishniakova-Akimova, Grigorii Naumovich Voitinsky, and Trotsky himself. This work is a result of an investigation which has been under way for a number of years. I hope it will contribute to a new understanding of the general history of Russian and Chinese Communism, free from political misinterpretations.

The study uses the Pinyin (*to put sounds together*) system of romanizing Chinese based on the speech of the northern (Beijing) dialect. A few exceptions are names of some historical figures (like Sun Yat-sen, Chiang Kai-shek, and Chiang Ching-kuo) which are better known in southern or idiosyncratic transliterations, as well as Taiwanese names.

Russian Communism and the Ideological Foundations of the Chinese Communist Movement

Chapter 1 _____

Communism in Russia as a Socio-cultural Phenomenon

By the end of the Russian revolution of 1905–07, Marxism, introduced into Russia in the 1860s, had given birth to three main trends of Russian Communism. These were expressed by Georgii Valentinovich Plekhanov, Vladimir Ilich Ulyanov (Lenin), and Leon Davidovich Bronshtein (Trotsky).

The Plekhanovists, who are better known as the Mensheviks (those who constitute the Minority)[1] placed the highest value on the Marxist thesis of the natural historical development of human society. According to this concept, a certain socio-economic system succeeds the preceding one not because of any subjective factors but because of the economic effectiveness of a new mode of production, which grows within the old system. The Mensheviks, therefore, followed Marxist classical thought, considering socialism a system in which the means of production are transformed into the property of the whole society (thus, their socialization) as a result of a broad development of productive forces. They believed that exploitation would be ended and the real sovereignty of the people established only as a result of the socialist revolution in a highly developed civil society. They viewed socialism as a post-capitalist stage of the natural evolution of human civilization, but not as an alternative to capitalism. Plekhanov and his associates Pavel B. Akselrod, Fyodor I. Dan, Vera I. Zasulich, Aleksandr S. Martynov, and others took into account that Russia was industrially backward and that the working class was relatively small and incapable of organizing production more effectively than the bourgeoisie. That is why they believed it their duty to assist the political revolution of the Russian bourgeoisie against tsarism and manorialism to speed up the development of capitalism and hence hasten the triumph of socialism. From the Mensheviks' point of view, a victory of the Russian bourgeois revolution was conceivable only under the leadership of the liberal bourgeoisie, to whom the revolution would have to yield power.

A bourgeois-democratic regime would make it possible for the Russian proletariat to wage the struggle for socialism with incomparably greater chances of success.

On the other hand, Leninism (or Bolshevism, i.e., the teaching of those who constitute the Majority) as it crystallized at the beginning of the twentieth century can be summarized as follows: In terms of its class position, the bourgeoisie of Russia is not capable of bringing its own revolution to completion, yet conditions are not yet ripe in Russia for a socialist revolution. Consequently, the revolutionary process must still first pass through the stage of bourgeois-democratic revolution, but the latter will take the form of a people's revolution under the hegemony of the proletariat. At the same time, a decisive victory of the revolution over tsarism will not lead to a dictatorship of the proletariat but to a revolutionary democratic dictatorship of the proletariat and the peasantry – that is, power shared jointly by these two classes. The dictatorship of the workers and peasants will pull the country out of its backwardness [*srednevekov'e*] in favor of a broad and rapid, European rather than Asian, development of capitalism; strengthen the proletariat in the cities and the countryside; and open possibilities for bringing the revolution to the socialist stage. The victory of the bourgeois-democratic revolution in Russia will generate a powerful impetus toward socialist revolution in the West, and this latter will not only safeguard Russia against the danger of restoration but also enable the Russian proletariat to seize power in a relatively short time.[2]

Trotsky, who created his own faction inside Russian Social Democracy, developed the following theses. Since the bourgeoisie of Russia is indeed incapable of leading the revolutionary movement, the complete victory of a democratic revolution in Russia is conceivable only in the form of the dictatorship of the proletariat, drawing on the peasantry for support. Only a workers' government supported by the peasantry is capable of dealing with the whole complex of problems facing the revolution. Neither a dictatorship of the bourgeoisie nor even a revolutionary democratic dictatorship of the proletariat and the peasantry is capable of accomplishing this. A dictatorship of the proletariat, which will inexorably accomplish not only socialist but also, in passing, democratic tasks, will at the same time give a powerful impetus to the international socialist revolution. The victory of the proletariat in the West will protect Russia against restoration of the bourgeoisie and ensure the triumph of socialism there.

Trotsky's central thesis, therefore, was the implementation of the world-wide permanent revolution ignited by the socialist overturn in Russia. He argued the notion not only of the possibility but also the inevitability of the victory of the socialist revolution in one country – and in a country that was backward in socio-economic and political terms, the weakest link in the world capitalist system. For the first time he presented a systematic exposition of this theory in his 1906 work *Results and Prospects*, though he had begun to develop these ideas earlier.[3] Here is what he wrote:

> In a country that is more backward economically the proletariat may come to power earlier than in an advanced capitalist country ... The notion that the dictatorship of the proletariat automatically depends on a country's technological forces and resources constitutes a prejudice of extremely oversimplified "economic" materialism. Such a view has nothing in common with Marxism. In our opinion, the Russian Revolution provides the kind of conditions under which power can (and with the victory of the Revolution must) come into the hands of the proletariat.[4]

At the same time Trotsky in no way denied the revolutionary role of the peasantry as an ally of the proletariat. This point should be stressed, given that his ideas in this respect were intensively falsified in Soviet historiography. In fact Trotsky overestimated the role of the peasantry at the time because, according to his concept (as set forth in *Results and Prospects*), it would seem that the peasantry in Russia was already willing in 1905–06 to support a proletarian dictatorship. Apparently, he also underestimated something quite different – the ability of certain strata of the peasantry to attain political independence. For this reason he considered it excessive for the proletariat to permit the peasantry, that is, the corresponding peasant parties, to exert influence on its government policies even temporarily, while the democratic tasks of the revolution were being dealt with. In doing so, however, he by no means ruled out – on the contrary, he considered it essential – the idea of allowing revolutionary representatives of non-proletarian social groups to become part of the workers' government. "A sound policy will compel the proletariat to involve influential leaders of the lower middle class [*meshchanstvo*], the intelligentsia, or the peasantry in the government," he wrote. "The whole question is who will give content to governmental policy? Who will rally a uniform majority in it?.. And when we talk about a workers' government, we are thereby answering that hegemony will belong to the working class."[5]

Therefore, of all main Russian Marxist tendencies that had formed by that time in the Russian Social Democratic Labor Party, it was Trotskyism that was the most extreme. However, Lenin's concept was quite radical as well. If we leave aside for a moment the intensive polemic taking place in the pre-February (1917) period between Lenin and Trotsky, we can see that the both doctrines indeed shared many features. Neither Lenin nor Trotsky believed in the revolutionary potential of the Russian bourgeoisie. This led them to the conclusion that from the very beginning the revolution in Russia would go beyond the limits of classic bourgeois democracy; how far beyond is another question. They also shared the idea that the revolutionary process in Russia would be supported by a series of socialist revolutions of the world proletariat. As Lenin wrote, "[T]he Russian revolution is strong enough to achieve victory by its own efforts, but it is not strong enough to retain the fruits of victory ... [T]he Russian revolution will need non-Russian *reserves*, will need outside assistance. Are there such reserves? Yes, there are: the socialist proletariat in the West."[6]

The implementation of Lenin's concept in practice would eliminate any discord between the Bolsheviks and Trotsky. Despite Lenin's assurance, it would actually lead to the same type of communist dictatorship expounded by Trotsky. The establishment of the democratic dictatorship of the working class and the peasantry was unlikely. First, because workers, the poor peasantry, paupers, and lumpens – the social base of the Russian revolutionary left wing – were not keen on any form of capitalism. On the contrary, they were led to the fight by sharply expressed anti-market feelings.[7] It is hard to imagine how they would encourage a "broad and rapid" development of capitalism after having fought the bourgeoisie for hegemony in the revolution. Second, it is doubtful that the proletariat, which according to Lenin would have already had to establish its hegemony in the revolution, would share power with the peasantry.

The vulnerability of Lenin's notion concerning the workers' and peasants' co-dictatorship was noticed by Trotsky himself in his polemics with the Bolsheviks:

> We could, of course, call this government a dictatorship of the proletariat and the peasantry, a dictatorship of the proletariat, the peasantry, and the intelligentsia, or, finally, a coalition government of the working class and the petite bourgeoisie. The question will still remain, however: who will possess hegemony in the government itself, and, through it, in the country?[8]

Of course, in practice hegemony would belong to the strongest and most active partner. It is clear that if the working class – actually the Bolsheviks – seized the leadership in the people's revolution during its process, it would never reject its own state dictatorship.

At the same time, we can see that Lenin's theory tactically could have a certain significance as a program that would attract potential allies, particularly peasant parties, to the Bolsheviks. As to Trotsky's concept, it was more solid and whole-heartedly committed to establishing communist dictatorship in Russia. The contradiction of Lenin's theory seems to be symbolized by its own name, "a revolutionary democratic dictatorship of the proletariat and the peasantry." (How can a dictatorship be democratic?)

The similarity of the initial positions of Trotsky and Lenin in some respects explains the fact that when the revolutionary tide in Russia placed the question of the actual struggle of the Bolshevik party for political power on the agenda in March – April 1917, Lenin altered his point of view and advocated a course toward socialist (i.e., permanent) revolution, during which the Bolsheviks "solved the problems of the bourgeois-democratic revolution in passing, as a 'by-product' of ... [the] main and genuinely *proletarian*-revolutionary, socialist activities."[9] Thus, at that time Lenin's position wholly coincided with Trotsky's.[10] To be fully convinced, one can compare Lenin's "Letters from Afar" – sent from Switzerland to the editors of *Pravda* in Petrograd – and his "April Theses" with Trotsky's articles published in late March – early April 1917 in the New York journals *Novy Mir* (New World) and *Die Zukunft* (Future).[11] The similarity of the conclusions drawn by the two revolutionaries is obvious.

Moreover, there is additional evidence that Lenin had come to accept the necessity of an immediate socialist revolution in Russia and had altered the nature of his theoretical discussions with Trotsky. In a letter written on November 16, 1927, shortly before his suicide, the prominent Bolshevik Adolf A. Joffe wrote to Trotsky, "I have told you not once that I heard with my own ears how Lenin admitted that in 1905 as well not he but you were right. One does not lie before one's death, and I repeat it to you again."[12]

He was clearly referring to the theory of permanent revolution. Joffe's remark cannot be considered irrefutable proof, but one cannot ignore it. Joffe was one of the most honest Bolsheviks, and it is unlikely that he would have lied on the eve of his suicide.

In any case, the February Revolution and the subsequent events eliminated the basic theoretical disagreements between Trotsky and Lenin. As a result, the Bolshevik coup d'état of October 1917 was actually conducted in accordance with a political theory put forward by Trotsky in 1906 and incorporated by Leninists into their own armory in 1917. (During the first years after the October Revolution, Trotsky's *Results and Prospects* was reprinted several times – including foreign-language editions – as a theoretical rationale of the October Revolution.) As to Bolshevism, it was enriched by its new – in fact, Trotskyist – ideological and theoretical component. It was further developed in post-February 1917 works by Lenin and other ideologists of Old Bolshevism, as well as in writings of Trotsky, who joined the Bolshevik party in July 1917. In the period immediately after the October Revolution Bolshevik propaganda put great emphasis on Trotsky's idea of permanent revolution in relation to foreign states, including the backward countries of the East. In March 1919 this idea formed the basis of the newly created Communist International.

All three doctrines – Menshevism, Bolshevism, and Trotskyism – continued to claim strict adherence to Marxism. But which was most in line with Marxist theory? Perhaps the most convincing answer was given by the Russian philosopher Berdyaev, who emphasised that Lenin – and this is even more applicable to Trotsky – "drew entirely original conclusions (in respect to Russia) from Marxism, conclusions which could scarcely be accepted by Marx and Engels."[13] In contrast, everything in Menshevik theory was formally in keeping with Marx's teaching. And that was precisely its "Achilles' heel". The Marxism of the Mensheviks was "the extreme expression of Russian Westernism", an "arm-chair interpretation of Marxism".[14] It did not fit Russia's social and political reality, traditions, or national culture, i.e., those conceptions which many believe character-istic of the Russian psyche – messianism, a totalitarian consciousness, lack of understanding of and hostility toward democracy, ascetic approach to culture, self-sacrifice, and a disposition to nihilism and cynicism.[15]

The Mensheviks believed that the impatience and revolutionary exaltation of Lenin and Trotsky was extremely harmful to the cause of real socialism. But both concepts – Leninism and Trotskyism – were in keeping with Russian reality. Russian Communism represented that part of the proletarian wing of the mass revolutionary movement which instinctively despised and repudiated the capitalist market. It refers first of all to the urban and rural proletariat classes, that in the very beginning of the twentieth century rose for the great anti-feudal, anti-imperialist, and anti-bourgeois revolution. Rural proletarians and poor peasants in particular spoke out in favor of the preservation of their traditional self-sufficient and self-regulated peasant communities (*obshchina*), based on collective farming and mutual assistance. Neither did Menshevism accurately reflect the economic and social reality of the world at the beginning of the twentieth century, which was characterized by sharp increases in revolutionary activity among the broad masses.

The accommodation of Marxism to Russia (or, in Berdyaev's language, "a Russification and orientalization of Marxism") led, therefore, precisely to the natural appearance and strengthening of Trotsky's and Lenin's ideological trends. In these circumstances the Mensheviks as well as other democrats had no serious chance of success. As Max Weber noted at the time of the Russian revolution of 1905–07, democracy in Russia was doomed. In his study of Russian society the German scholar paid particular attention to the role of the sacramental ideology of *obshchina* (he characterized it as so-called "archaic agrarian Communism") in the Russian mass revolutionary movement and pointed out the weakness of Russian liberalism.[16] It is noteworthy, that many of Weber's conclusions about the revolution in Russia, including his assertion of the political impotence of the Russian bourgeoisie, coincided with the key theses of the Bolsheviks and Trotsky. However, Weber was an independent observer, and the fact that his assessment in many respects resembled several of the main theses of the Russian radicals only testifies to their proper understanding of the situation in their own country.

Nonetheless, despite the radicalism of the Russian revolutionaries, Trotskyism, the most iconoclastic trend of Russian Communism in the pre-February 1917 period, did not enjoy great popularity. The majority of Russian Social Democrats continued to follow Lenin. This was mainly because Trotsky's world outlook combined various ideas borrowed from different socio-cultural sources. The theory of permanent revolution represented the core of Trotskyism, which was, however, certainly not limited to this point. Besides the problems of strategy and tactics of the future revolution in Russia as it pertained to the world revolutionary process in the new historical epoch, Trotsky paid considerable attention to questions concerning the organizational construction of the Social Democratic (later Communist) party. And in this field his fundamental positions differed on essence from Lenin's.

The first conflict between the two revolutionaries took place at the Second RSDLP Congress in July-August 1903. Judging by the minutes, the disagreement revolved only around organizational questions that were expressed in two fundamental points of the agenda – namely, section I of the Rules, and on the question of the election of central party organs. This is also evident from the *Diary of Proceedings of the Second RSDLP Congress*, which Lenin kept.[17]

The debates concerning section I of the Rules centered on two formulations, that of Lenin and that of Martov. Lenin proposed that anyone be considered a member of the RSDLP who, along with everything else, supported the party through "personal participation" in one of the party organizations. Martov insisted that "personal assistance" was sufficient. Hence, the polemics hinged on the concept of the "party" itself, the principles of its organizational structure. In effect, the focus of the disagreement was the question of the correlation of intra-party democracy and centralism. Lenin argued in favor of centralization and placed special emphasis on the necessity of safeguarding the firmness, steadfastness, and purity of the party.[18] Martov and those who thought like him – one of whom was Trotsky – argued in favor of a broad, flexible organization whose members need not bind themselves with rigid party discipline. They could not accept Lenin's point of view, underlined in his brochure *What is to Be Done?*:

> The only serious organizational principle for the active workers of our movement should be the strictest secrecy, the strictest selection of members, and the training of professional revolutionaries. Given these qualities, something even more than "democratism" would be guaranteed to us, namely, complete, comradely, mutual confidence among revolutionaries ... They [revolutionaries] have not the time to think about toy forms of democratism (democratism within a close and compact body of comrades in which complete, mutual confidence prevail), but they have a lively sense of their *responsibility*, knowing as they do from experience that an organization of real revolutionaries will stop at nothing to rid itself of an unworthy member.[19]

It was for this reason that Trotsky, both at the Congress and later, constantly reiterated the idea that any organizational subordination of the individual to the party would result in the degeneration of the latter into a narrow, radical-conspiratorial organization. Trotsky was most sharply critical of Lenin's organizational plans in his pamphlet *Our Political Tasks*, which came out a year after the Congress, in August 1904. Attempting to show the results of getting carried away by too much centralism, Trotsky painted the following picture:

> The party organization [that is, the party apparatus] "substitutes" itself for the party; the Central Committee replaces the party organization, and, finally, the "dictator" substitutes himself for the Central Committee.., committees set the "direction" and rescind it while "the people keep silent..," the "organization of professional revolutionaries" – or, more accurately, its top leaders – constitutes the center of Social Democratic consciousness, and under this center are the disciplined executors of technical functions.[20]

It is clear that Trotsky's views on this question in 1903 were much closer to Marx than were Lenin's. For instance, his views were in keeping with Engels's words in a letter to Marx:

> [W]e need neither popularity, nor the SUPPORT of any party in any country ... How can people like us, who shun official appointments like the plague, fit into a 'party'? And what have we, who spit on popularity ... to do with a 'party', i.e., a herd of jackasses who swear by us because they think we're of the same kidney as they? ...
>
> A revolution is a purely natural phenomenon which is subject to physical laws rather than to the rules that determine the development of society in ordinary times ... By the mere fact of keeping ourselves INDEPENDENT, being *in the nature of things* more revolutionary than the others, one is able at least for a time to maintain one's independence from this whirlpool ... Not only no official *government* appointments, no official *party* appointments, no seat on committees, etc., no responsibility for jackasses ... cannot deprive us.[21]

Nonetheless, the position of Marxism's founders – Marx did not oppose Engels' views on the problem – and the opinion of Trotsky and Martov obviously did not reflect the peculiarity of Russia. The creation of a disciplined, centralized organization was dictated to a large extent by the conditions of the opposition political activity in Russia at that time, which was oppressed by the tsarist autocracy. It is possible, nevertheless, to understand the position of the Martovites. After all, the participants in the revolutionary democratic movement still retained vivid images of

Robespierre, Tkachev, Nechaev, and other revolutionary extremists who had discredited the concepts "organizational centralism" and "revolutionary discipline." However, it was Lenin who proved to be more pragmatic, fitting his organizational schemes into the ethic of the Russian political opposition. That fact in many respects made it easier for him to create a strong mass party than it was for Trotsky.

Following the logic of the disagreement with respect to the Rules, Trotsky opposed Lenin on the election of the central party organs. That vote, as is well known, made Lenin the winner, while Trotsky wound up in the ranks of the minority.

Trotsky did not stay with the Menshevik faction very long. By 1904, his disputes with the Menshevik leaders over the possibility of the proletariat's hegemony in the revolution reached such a pitch that, in September, he announced he was quitting the faction. He did so also because shortly after the Second RSDLP Congress the Mensheviks actually accepted the Bolsheviks' views concerning the creation of a highly-centralized party organization. Of course, he did not join the Bolshevik faction either.

Trotsky continued to hold an independent position. While remaining formally outside the factions, until mid-1917 he devoted considerable effort to reconciling the Mensheviks and Bolsheviks. With that purpose in mind, in the summer of 1912 in Vienna he created the so-called "August bloc" within the framework of Russian Social Democracy, which in fact only brought Trotsky's associates together, as well as some of the Bundists, Mensheviks, and liquidators. Trotsky's point of view on the possibility of co-existence of various social democratic groups in one single party did not change even after the outbreak of the world war, despite the fact that he himself took definite internationalist positions, and, all through the war, spoke in favor of condemning imperialism under the slogan "proletarian revolution".

And even Trotsky's entering the Bolshevik party did not yet mean, despite outward appearances, that he had wholly accepted Lenin's party concept. Of course, by May 1917 he had already begun to make some revisions in his own organizational platform, having rejected reconciliation with those Mensheviks who held the position of the "defensists" (*oborontsy*). However, while joining the Bolsheviks, he seemed to be aware of what kind of organization he was entering. This can be seen from the recollections of Nadezhda Adolfovna Joffe, a daughter of Trotsky's close associate. In the beginning of summer of 1917 she overheard a discussion between her father and Trotsky in regard to the question of merging their small group, which called itself the "Interdistrict Organization of United Social Democrats", with Lenin's party.[22] According to Nadezhda Adolfovna, her father vigorously objected, but Trotsky insisted on the necessity of the unification. "Leon Davidovich! They are political bandits!"

said Adolf Joffe, who finally began to lose his nerve. "Yes, I know," answered Trotsky, "But now the Bolsheviks are the only real political force."[23] Only later, beginning in the fall of 1917, did Trotsky's views undergo a change. A close collaboration with Lenin, the preparation of the October coup d'état, and his leadership of the Red Army during the Civil War – all these factors overcame his previous reservations respecting the advocates of centralism. The extraordinary situation demanded unity, and Trotsky actively supported most of Lenin's measures concerning the restriction of intra-party democracy, including the famous resolution of the Tenth Party Congress "On Party Unity". Trotsky later attempted to explain that

> [Lenin's] own organizational policy [was] by no means a straight-line proposition. He frequently had to rebuff excessive centralism in the party and appeal to the lower levels against the top. In the long run, despite conditions of great difficulty, magnificent progress and upheaval, and whatever the waverings to one side or the other, the party maintained the necessary balance between elements of democracy and centralism. [24]

It is hard to suspect Trotsky of insincerity. Most likely he truly believed in what he was saying. But in a number of cases, even in that period, Trotsky opposed leaders of the Bolshevik party, including Lenin, when they revealed an appetite for centralism and intra-party sectarianism. His reaction in regard to Lenin's proposals of December 1921 concerning the party purge and conditions of admission into the party is particularly worth noting. The Eleventh Party conference was in session, and at its opening Lenin had supported the draft resolution that set strict limitations of the party admission; the draft even maintained the necessity of banning the entry of new members into the party for the next six months. Lenin expressed his considerations in his letter of December 19 to the Party Central Committee alternate member Pyotr Zalutsky, an author of the project, a Central Control Committee member Aaron Solts and all Politburo members.[25] In response Trotsky raised vigorous disagreements, believing that if the resolution were passed it would promote a catastrophic bureaucratization of the party apparatus. Here is what he wrote to Lenin on December 21:

> V.I.! I have very big hesitations concerning your prohibitive and restrictive proposals in regard to the admission into the party. Now we probably have 400,000 members, and it will remain almost like this for $1\frac{1}{2}$ years. While keeping the inevitable tendency to charge party members with any important and semi-important posts, we will get a closed party of administrators. For workers, who actually work at factories, we must make joining the party as easy as

possible, reducing a period of alternative membership up to $\frac{1}{2}$ year maximum.

It is better to clean a building from time to time, than to cork up all windows and cracks. A party of administrators means a party of those who enjoy privileges. Some people do it cautiously and "tactfully", others – less cautiously ... I surely underline only one side of the matter, but it is fraught with big complications.[26]

Lenin basically agreed with Trotsky's objections,[27] but in two years Trotsky once again began to feel, that "the balance between elements of democracy and centralism" in the party had appeared to be broken. In October 1923 he rebelled against the threat of bureaucratic degradation of the party-government apparatus. He argued in favor of expanding intra-party democracy and liquidating the system of the "apparatus terror" that was obviously taking shape. This was the subject of his letter to the members of the Central Committee and the Central Control Committee dated October 8, 1923, a number of articles in *Pravda*, a pamphlet entitled *The New Course*, a speech at the Thirteenth Party Congress in May 1924, and other articles and speeches. "That regime which basically took shape prior to the Twelfth Congress [that is, prior to April 1923] and which became finally fixed and shaped after the Congress," Trotsky wrote on October 8, 1923, "is much farther from workers' democracy than was the regime of the harshest periods of War Communism. The bureaucratization of the party apparatus has reached unprecedented heights ... There is no longer even a trace ... of any frank exchange of opinions on problems which are of genuine concern to the party ... It is necessary to put an end to secretarial bureaucratism."[28] It was the bureaucratization of the apparatus that Trotsky perceived to be one of the most important sources giving rise to another phenomenon within the party, one which threatened to undermine it from within – factionalism. "Mechanical centralism is inevitably being supplemented by factionalism, which is at the same time an evil caricature of party democracy and a menacing political danger", he stated in his letter "To Party Conferences" on December 8, 1923. Trotsky argued against factionalism and in favor of broad intra-party democracy, with consistent compliance with the principles of centralism, thus protecting every party member's right to make independent judgments and defend them.[29]

Trotsky's concept of the party, therefore, was in many respects more democratic than Lenin's. That is why it did not receive serious support in Russia, either before or after the October Revolution. It was psychologically alien to ordinary Russians, who did not have any idea about civil society and personal freedom, and viewed opposition activity in traditions of religious sectarianism.

Therefore, while incorporating into his theory of permanent revolution the social preferences of a huge part of the Russian population, Trotsky at the same time acted in the tradition of Western political culture in regard to the question of building the organization that was called to lead this same revolution. A major element of that culture was classical Marxism. In other words, while realistic enough regarding the aspirations of the Russian mass radical movement to seize political power, Trotsky was quite subjective when it came to propounding his theory of a "democratic" Communist party. This dichotomy in many respects prefigured his political achievements and defeats.

In contrast, the Bolshevism that was initially built on Lenin's anti-democratic perceptions in 1917 received its internal logical structure in large part from Trotsky's doctrine of permanent revolution. Not surprisingly, it very quickly became the dominant political ideology in backward Russia, and finally led the masses of the desperate poor to the great social upheaval.

Chapter 2 _____

The Theory of Permanent Revolution in China

The processes that took place in the Russian revolutionary movement in the beginning of the twentieth century were mirrored in the countries of the East, including China. This is hardly astonishing: the socio-cultural similarities of China and Russia were rather considerable. Like Russia, in China in the beginning of the century capitalism did not yet determine all spheres of public life. Of course, Russia was more advanced industrially, but in the economies of both countries all known economic structures were present. Individual territories and regions greatly differed from each other in their levels of social and economic development. This can be explained by the fact that within both states common markets, in essence, had not fully developed; the economic and social life of a significant part of the population (in China – its greater part, in Russia – a smaller one) had been isolated within stable local boundaries. The variety of social and economic structures had caused the co-existence of various historical types of social relations – pre-manorial, manorial, semi-manorial and capitalist. There was no civil society in either country.

In China, as well as in Russia and in all other states where the capitalist mode of production was in its early stages, a huge portion of the population found itself in opposition to the market system. No more than 10% of the Chinese population saw the production of commodities, if we use the expression of Karl Marx, as "the *nec plus ultra* of human freedom and individual independence."[30] Others treated the market with thinly veiled hostility.[31] In the regions where land taxes and rents were mostly taken in kind, the patriarchal peasant as a rule wholly underestimated the market; in areas where the payments were made in cash the attitude of a peasant to the market was more commonly one of great hatred. The commutation of taxes and rents made peasant payments higher: because seasonal prices fluctuated significantly, an ordinary Chinese lost money twice. In the fall he was obliged to sell a part of his produce at dumping prices in order to pay his obligations which were usually extremely onerous, and in the spring, when the prices normally rose, redeem the same part with large losses in order to avoid famine. A patriarchal peasant aspired to terminate or even cut off forever the commodity connections between a city and village, making the rural economy entirely self-sufficient. The Russian Sinologists V. I. Glunin and A. S. Mugruzin showed that a Chinese patriarchal peasant tried to reach the same goal when he demanded the lowering of his taxes and an end to exploitation.[32] The strong anti-market moods were also typical for Chinese paupers and lumpens, who made up approximately 9–11% of the population.[33]

The core of the social psychology of ordinary Chinese was the aspiration to restore a "fair" social order on the basis of customs rooted in the "ideal" patriarchal past. In other words, poor Chinese commoners dreamed of returning to a sacramental model of Oriental despotism, characterized by establishing a non-market society – the so-called state monopoly on all spheres of public life that strictly denied the rights of private ownership. The negative attitude to the latter is readily explained. Throughout Chinese history there had been a continuous struggle between large landholders, who aspired to fix their claims for unlimited possession of landed property, and the central authority, which personified the absolute power and monopoly of the state. This struggle had been taking place in the framework of the so-called "dynastic cycles" – intervals between the establishment of a monarchic dynasty and its fall. It took various, mostly political, forms. During the struggle the central authority was inevitably weakened, and the local landholders managed to consolidate their rights to the land. As a result, the norm of peasant exploitation sharply increased. On the one hand, landlords who started to consider themselves as complete owners of the land boosted rents; on the other hand, the government raised taxes, attempting to fulfill the treasury (feudal lords were tax-exempt.) It certainly displeased peasants, who had no recourse but to rise up in rebellion. As a rule, great peasant uprisings resulted in the fall of a weakening dynasty and in the emergence of a new one. The founder of a new dynasty always began his rule with the revival of an unlimited state monopoly on all kinds of economic activity. Life reentered the state-monopoly track, and new landholders resumed their struggle for private land property. The Manchu (Qing) dynasty that came to power in 1644 only brought formal changes to the existing social system: the court nominally acknowledged private landed property, but actually continued to restrict its development. This inevitably created a peculiar psychological situation in China. Certain social guidelines and mindsets were fixed in the minds of exploited people. Private ownership of the means of production, above all of the land, was perceived as something outrageous, something that destroyed sacramental social order, ruined the life of poor people, and hence deserved condemnation. Hatred of private ownership found expression in programs of practically all of China's peasants' revolts, and all aimed to turn society back to the past.

The penetration of capitalism that started in the 1840s exacerbated all of China's problems, coinciding with a time when Chinese society was entering a concluding phase of a periodic "dynastic cycle". The social status of a significant part of the population that had already worsened due to indigenous reasons soon became unbearable under the influence of Western and later of Japanese capitalism. The Chinese began to associate capitalism – indeed brought in from overseas – with alien imperialism. Capitalist penetration also complicated the matter because China had become a semi-colony of the imperialist powers, which had divided her into spheres of influence. That, of course, laid the foundations for the origin of an extremely contradictory Chinese indigenous capitalism. Having responded to the challenge of the epoch, the ruling elite – the Manchu government and local Chinese warlords – during the so-called "self-strengthening policy" (1861–94) launched the indigenous capitalization of China. They attempted to monopolize the process, ousting private businessmen and limiting the development of the market of free labor power. Such state-militarist capitalism of the power holders did not give much space for the generating of private business. The semi-colonial, humiliated status of the country along with China's dependent position in the global division of labor in the world market, also put great pressure on the Chinese national bourgeoisie. All this could only aggravate the anti-imperialist, nationalist mood in China, stirring up the determination of people who had lost or were losing their wealth, to "strive on the way of war" against imperialism and the Manchu government.

In the beginning of the twentieth century, after the successful 1911–12 revolution against the monarchy, the desperate straits of the national middle and small bourgeoisie, have-nots and semi-have-nots became even worse, due to disintegration of the country and continuous civil wars. The absence of political unity resulted in the destruction of the unified currency system, and negatively affected living standards. Anti-imperialist moods were, thus, strongly reinforced by anti-militarism. As in Russia, a powerful radical revolutionary movement unfolded in China. But unlike in Russia it was, in essence, directed above all against imperialism.

The social feelings of the masses were reflected in the painful ideological explorations of the Chinese intelligentsia, who sought a way out of the crisis, as China was being torn to pieces by imperialists and internal reaction. In their search for truth many educated people examined various western ideological theories; Marxism inevitably attracted their attention.

Marxism began to penetrate China at the very end of the nineteenth century. The name of Marx was mentioned in the Chinese press for the first time in February 1899, in the pages of the journal *Wanguo gongbao*

25

(World Survey), which published the first chapter of the English sociologist Benjamin Kidd's book entitled *The Social Evolution*. The name of Engels appeared in China three months later, in May 1899, in the same work by Kidd, issued as a separate brochure by Shanghai Publishing house *Guang xuehui* (Glory Society). There it was said that Engels, along with Marx, was one of those, who in Germany "was proselytizing the theory of how to feed the people."[34]

Early in 1903 a small fragment of Karl Marx and Frederich Engels's *Manifesto of the Communist Party* was published for the first time in Chinese – in the form of a citation in a work by a Japanese author Fukuda Shinzo titled *Modern Socialism*. The citations from *The Manifesto*, as well as Engels's *Socialism: Utopian and Scientific*, were made in a work by another Japanese writer, Kotoku Shusui, called *Socialist Heritage*, translated in September 1903 in Chinese by progressive journalists and appearing in the magazine *Zhejiang chao* (Zhejiang Tide).

At the end of June 1905 the second chapter of *The Manifesto* was for the first time summarized in compressed form by a Chinese author, Zhu Zhixin – one of Sun Yatsen's subordinates, in his article titled "Brief Biographies of German Social-revolutionaries." Zhu published this article in the second issue of a Sun Yatsen's journal *Minbao* (People) under the pseudonym Shi Shen. In the following two years three more exerpts from *The Manifesto* were printed in China – in *Minbao* and one in an anarchist journal *Tianyi bao* (Heavenly Justice), printed in Tokyo.

In January 1908 Chinese anarchists published in the same *Tianyi bao* (issue 15) the translation of Engels's *Preface to the 1888 English Edition of the Manifesto of the Communist Party*. It was the first work of the founders of Marxism to appear in Chinese in complete form. Shortly after this *Tianyi bao* (nos. 16–19) published the first chapter of *The Manifesto*. The same issues cited Engels's *The Origin of the Family, Private Property and the State*. In June–September 1912, a Shanghai journal *Xin shijie* (New World) finally published one of Engels's major works, *Socialism: Utopian and Scientific* (in Chinese translation *Utopian Socialism and Practical Socialism*.) It was translated by Shi Cuntong (under the pseudonym Shi Renrong), a man who later became a most prominent early Chinese Communist.[35]

The impressions of Marxism, however, remained inconsistent. Other than a tiny group of advanced intellectuals, no one else was acquainted with the new teachings. In the eyes of Chinese democrats, Marx's socialism at that time did not much differ from other socialist doctrines.[36] Here is what Mao Zedong said about it in April 1945:

[H]ere, in China apart from a small group of students who had studied abroad nobody had known [what Marxism was]. I also did not know that there was such a man as Marx in the world ... We ... did know nothing about the existence of any Imperialism or any

Marxism in the world ... Earlier there were people like Liang Qichao, Zhu Zhixin, who had mentioned Marxism. One also says that there had been somebody who in a journal translated Engels's *Socialism: Utopian and Scientific*. But generally speaking at that time I did not see [these editions], and if I did I just cast a glance, having paid no attention.[37]

It was not until after the October Revolution in Russia and the end of World War I that the spread of Marxist ideology accelerated. One reason for this was the disappointment of a significant part of Chinese intellectuals in Western democracy. At the 1919 Versailles peace conference, the leaders of the major powers did not respond to appeals for the restoration of the violated rights of China. Foreign imperialists continued to treat the Chinese republic as a semi-colonial country; the triumph of Anglo-American "democracy" over German "kaiserdom" changed nothing in regard to China. All war-time illusions concerning Anglo-American "liberalism" that were shared by thousands of Chinese patriots were ruined in a single moment. It provoked a crisis of bourgeois liberal thought in China, having radicalized politically many intellectuals.[38] During the anti-imperialist "May Fourth" movement of 1919 progressive members of Chinese society came to realize more keenly than ever the urgent necessity to find a way out of the domestic crisis. At that same moment industrial workers for the first time entered upon the stage of Chinese history. (About 100,000 industrial workers took part in the movement.) In the eyes of many revolutionaries the political awakening of their own working class looked like a vivid conformation of Marxist theory.[39] Thus, the necessity of a thorough study of Marxism was put on the agenda of the Chinese revolution by the "May Fourth" movement.[40]

However, the essential factors that determined the Chinese intellectuals' attitude towards Marxism were the victorious October Revolution, the anti-imperialist and anti-capitalist policy of the Soviet government, and the Bolsheviks' defeat of the imperialist intervention and internal counter-revolution in Soviet Russia. "Since the Russian revolution Marxism expressed itself as a force which could shake the world," wrote in 1919 Li Dazhao – one of the future organizers of the first Communist cells in China.[41] The success of the Russian Communists stimulated the desire to understand the ideology that the Bolsheviks used. It was the Russian experience that a patriotic segment of Chinese intellectuals turned to for answers to China's problems. Thus, Marxism actually began to spread and be perceived in China through the prism of Bolshevik interpretations. "The Chinese found Marxism as a result of its application by Russians," wrote Mao Zedong. "... To follow the Russian way — that was the conclusion."[42] From the whole rich spectrum of Marxist currents the advanced Chinese intellectuals, therefore, began to borrow only one – post-

February Leninism, which had at its core the Trotskyist concept of the permanent revolution. In the first years after the October Revolution this process was largely promoted by the direct theoretical and practical assistance given to the Chinese by Lenin's party, the Comintern, and the Soviet state.

It is not hard to see how the Bolshevik experience parallelled the kind of mentality that was typical for the radical part of the Chinese intelligentsia, who had absorbed the anti-capitalist social moods of the overwhelming majority of the poorest strata of the Chinese population. It also encouraged the Chinese revolutionaries' interest in the iconoclastic Russian type of Marxism. Trotsky was correct to say that

> Bolshevism's sense, power and significance ... [were determined by its appeal] not to the top of the working class, but to the crowd, to the bottom, to millions, to the most oppressed of oppressed ones. Not because of its theoretical content which is still far from being understood and comprehended, but given its liberative spirit, it became the favorite teaching in Oriental countries. That is why it happened ... We know that workers in China probably have not read any article of Lenin in their whole life, but they passionately gravitate to Bolshevism. That is because the impact of history is so powerful! They felt that it was the doctrine which addressed to parties, to those who were oppressed and pressed down, to millions, to ten hundred millions who otherwise had no rescue.[43]

Bolshevism was introduced to China soon after the February Revolution in Russia. On May 19, 1917, the Shanghai *Minguo ribao* (Republic Newspaper) published an article under the title *News About the Recent Internal Disorder in Russia*, which briefly characterized the situation in the Russian socialist movement. Among other parties, "a group led by Nikolai Lenin" which "without compromise acts against the war and calls for 'ultra-revolutionarism'" was named.[44] This was the first mention in China of Lenin's name.

On November 8, 1917, *Zhonghua xinbao* (China Newspaper) informed the Chinese public about the armed revolt in Petrograd. On November 10 *Minguo shibao* (Republic Paper of Facts) and *Shishi xinbao* (Facts Newspaper) conveyed the basic principles of Trotsky's and Lenin's statements at the Second All-Russia Congress of Soviets. (Incidentally in these puiblications the name of Trotsky appeared for the first time in Chinese.) The brief articles noted that Lenin had put forward three notions: to stop the world war immediately, to transfer land to peasants, and to overcome the economic crisis. In the subsequent days information about Lenin, Trotsky, Bolshevism and the October Revolution also appeared in other Chinese publications.

The first article acquainting the public with the theoretical views of Lenin was published in *Zhonghua xinbao* on December 28, 1917. Its author was Yang Paoan – a future participant in the Chinese Communist movement.

As to the first writings of the theoreticians of the Russian proletarian revolution, they began to appear in China in 1918, but in English translations. The earliest was apparently Trotsky's *War and the International*. In an English-language edition circulating in China it was entitled *The Bolsheviki* [Bolsheviks] *and World Peace*.[45] This work had a great impact on the outlook of Li Dazhao, a future leader of the "May Fourth" movement. It was Li who for the first time introduced some of Trotsky's key principles to a broad Chinese public, though in rather random form. He did so in his article *Victory of Bolshevism*, published in January 1919 in a Shanghai journal *Xin qingnian* (New Youth).[46]

Shortly thereafter, the English-language editions of Lenin's *The Immediate Tasks of the Soviet Government, State and Revolution, "Left-Wing" Communism – An Infantile Disorder* and Trotsky's *October Revolution* began circulating in China.[47] At the same time a collection of Bolshevik documents, entitled *The Proletarian Revolution* appeared. Compiled and published in 1918 in New York by one of the leaders of the American Communists, Lois Fraina, the collection included some articles and chapters from larger works by Lenin and Trotsky written between 1917 and the beginning of 1918. The appendices to the volume included a few short articles by Georgii V. Chicherin. A number of sections of the book were written by Fraina himself; he summarized basic principles of Bolshevik theory, larding the text with excerpts from Lenin's and Trotsky's writings.[48]

The first of Lenin's writings was published in Chinese on September 1, 1919, in the Beijing journal *Jiefang yu gaizao* (Liberation and Reconstruction). It was the article "Political Parties in Russia and the Tasks of the Proletariat," written in early April 1917. The translation was made from an English edition by a student at Fudan University at Shanghai, Jin Guobao. At about the same time the first Chinese translation of Trotsky's work came out in China. It was his *Manifesto of the Communist International to the Proletariat of the Entire World*, which Trotsky wrote for the First Congress of the Comintern. The Chinese title of the document was "Manifesto of a New Communist Party." The text appeared in consecutive issues of a Beijing newspaper *Chen bao* (Morning) on November 7–11, 1919 under the rubric *Revival of the World*. It was signed by a name of the translator, Yi. The Russian sinologist Konstantin Sheveliev discovered that this was the pseudonym of Luo Jialun – one of the most active participants of the "May Fourth" movement and a founder of a progressive society *Xinchao* (Renaissance). Of course, nothing was said about the real author of the document: as a rule, the Comintern did not reveal the identities of the authors of its documents.

Although the practically simultaneous publication of Lenin's post-February works and Trotsky's writings was most likely accidental, it was rather significant. At the time Trotsky was naturally perceived in China and everywhere else as the second-ranking person in the leadership of the Russian Communist movement, and one of the most prominent ideologists of the October Revolution. All major foreign initiatives of the Soviet government, including those related to China, and all Bolshevik victories during the Civil War, were associated with Trotsky's name. Thus the great interest in his works – alongside Lenin's – is not surprising. His popularity among leftist Chinese intellectuals was second only to Lenin's.

In the period between September 1919 and the beginning of 1922 in China there were published eleven more pieces by Lenin, all of which reflected his post-February political views. At approximately the same time (from November 1919 through the beginning of 1922) there were issued five more Chinese translations of Trotsky's works. Of all these publications the most important were Lenin's brochure *The Immediate Tasks of the Soviet Government*, published in December 1921 by the first clandestine publishing house of the CCP called *Renmin chubanshe* (People's Publishing house);[49] Trotsky's book *October Revolution*, printed in January 1922 by the same publisher; and Trotsky's *Manifesto of the Second Congress of the Communist International*, which came out in late August or early September 1921 in the sixth issue of the CCP journal *Gongchandang* (The Communist).

A more systematic distribution of Lenin's works began in the subsequent years, and between 1922 and 1927 more than thirty of his writings appeared in Chinese. Among these, however, just five were written before February 1917 including *Imperialism, the Highest Stage of Capitalism* and four small articles about China. Thus, the prevailing interest was in Lenin's works in which he shared Trotsky's concept of a permanent revolution. The active translation and publication of Lenin's heritage continued on an even broader scale in the 1930s and 1940s. By the time the People's Republic of China was proclaimed on October 1, 1949, practically all major works by Lenin were known in China.

It is difficult to estimate the extent of the Chinese translations of Trotsky's writings undertaken after the beginning of 1922. It is only known that in the publishing plans of *Renmin chubanshe* for 1922 there were two major Trotsky works – *War and the International* and *Terrorism and Communism*. However, it is hard to say whether they were printed or not. For the period from February 1922 through 1929 there can be documented in the available Chinese editions only one translation of Trotsky's writings, his speech celebrating the third anniversary of the Communist University of the Toilers of the East titled "Prospects and Problems in the East" (interpreter: Zheng Chaolin.)[50] Trotsky's works once again began to be translated in China after the formation of the Chinese Left Opposition, i.e., from 1928 on.

Besides Lenin's and Trotsky's writings, in the period after the October Revolution the works of other leading figures of the Bolshevik party including Bukharin, Preobrazhensky, Zinoviev, and Lunacharsky were also published in China. All of these incorporated the idea of the permanent revolution. In particular Bukharin's and Preobrazhensky's brochure *The ABC of Communism*, a popular summary of the Bolshevik party program adopted at the Eighth Party Congress was disseminated widely (in both English and Chinese editions) among the radical sections of Chinese youth.

By comparison, in the period between June 1919 and April 1927 there were published – in part or full – only ten of Marx's works in China, including *Critique of the Gotha Programme* (four editions), the preface to the first edition and a few chapters of *Capital*, and *Preface to the Critique of Political Economy*. In the same period four works by Engels were published, including *Socialism: Utopian and Scientific* (issued twice, in new translations), *The Origin of the Family, Private Property, and the State* (twice), the second and third chapters of the third part of *Anti-Dühring*, and *On Authority*. Joint papers by Marx and Engels – *The Manifesto* and *Addresses of the Central Committee to the Communist League* were also published. The first full edition of *The Manifesto* appeared in August 1920. The translation was made from Japanese by one of the first supporters of Communism in China, Chen Wangdao; this work also had been issued twice in condensed form.[51]

Of course, not all the translations were correct in details. An accurate perception of the Bolsheviks' thoughts was hindered by the fact that the conceptual instrument of contemporary social sciences used in the Chinese language was quite undeveloped at that time, primarily due to the backwardness of the social class structure of China. Such key sociological categories as "proletariat", "bourgeoisie", "class", and so forth had just begun to get their equivalences in Chinese, but the translations did not always transfer the meaning of the appropriate terms in exact form. Distortions were frequent as terms were adjusted to Chinese reality. For example, the term *bourgeoisie* was usually interpreted in China as *youchanjieji*, "a class (or strata) that possesses property." Such definition naturally is not clear; not only the bourgeoisie possesses property. The exact denotation of the word bourgeoisie – *zichanjieji*, i.e., "a class (or strata) that capitalizes property," came into the Chinese language later – in the mid-1920s.

Some expressions were borrowed from ancient Chinese and Japanese or were translated by anarchists and revolutionary democrats, who interpreted them through the prism of their own political convictions.[52] Many newly transcribed words simply became a set of characters that had no meaning: *suweiai* (Soviet), *buersaiweike* (Bolshevik), etc. Often in the translated literature of the 1920s, including works by Lenin and Trotsky, and in original writings of Chinese sociologists and politicians, a new word would be followed by its English translation in parentheses, to promote clarity.

The overall perception of the new doctrine was also affected by the paucity of translated literature: a few articles and three or four brochures by Lenin, Trotsky, Bukharin, Preobrazhensky, and Chicherin obviously could not create a whole picture of post-February Bolshevism. To a certain degree the shortage was fulfilled with the writings of some foreign popularizers of the October experiment, especially with John Reed's *Ten Days that Shook the World*, which was quite well known in China.[53] There also appeared a number of press publications about the new Russia and the Bolshevik party in China, as well as biographic sketches of the Bolshevik leaders, translated and written by Chinese writers.

A few biographies of Lenin and Trotsky had already appeared in Chinese in the first years after the October Revolution. Some printed materials also shaped the information about other leaders of Soviet Russia. The earliest biography of Lenin was published in March 1918 in the third issue of the magazine *Dongfang zazhi* (Orient). It was a translation of a work of a Japanese author entitled "On Lenin – the Leader of the Extremist Party of Russia." This article was earlier published in the Tokyo newspaper *Nitiniti simbun* (Day by Day). A photo of Lenin – the first image of him in the Chinese press – accompanied the article. On September 15, 1919 a large article by another Japanese, Masakiti Imai, "Lenin, Trotsky and the Realization of Their Principles" appeared in the second issue of *Jiefang yu gaizao*; a Chinese reader for the first time could obtain some biographic data on Trotsky.[54] It also included a brief Lenin biography – the biographic sketches were approximately equal in length – and set forth some basic ideas of Lenin's and Trotsky's teaching, mainly according to the Bolshevik party program. The author emphasized that the "ideal" to which the Bolsheviks aspired was the construction of a world republic as a result of the struggle of the international working class against the bourgeoisie and imperialists. "Therefore," he concluded, "the principles of the Russian group of the Bolsheviks can be called the principles of the true universal equality (*datongzhuyi*)."[55]

In August 1920 in Japan there was printed a book in Chinese titled *A Study of New Russia* written by a well-known journalist, Shao Piaoping, who published the Beijing progressive newspaper *Jing bao* (A Capital Newspaper). The 140–page book soon became popular in China. It presented the first relatively detailed history of the Russian Communist movement over the previous seventeen years. Two concluding chapters contained biographies of Lenin and Trotsky.[56] In the beginning of July 1921 the journal *Xin qingnian* published an article by Li Dazhao, titled "The Past and Present of the Russian Revolution." The article furnishes information about fourteen "central persons who had contributed to the construction of new Russia." Lenin was named first, and Trotsky second. Li Dazhao devoted relatively long sketches only to them and to Lunacharsky. All other leaders – including Stalin – were granted just a few lines.[57]

The interest of radical Chinese youth in the Bolshevik experiment was increased by lectures of the well-known philosophers and public activists John Dewey, who arrived in China in 1919 and remained more than two years, and especially by Bertrand Russell, who visited the country in the beginning of 1920. The latter came to China after having toured Soviet Russia. His notes on the journey to Russia were published in *Xin qingnian*,[58] and detailed reviews of these notes, translated from English language editions, were also printed in four subsequent issues of this journal as well as in a journal *Shuguang* (Dawn). Russell characterized the activity of the Russian Communists in rather objective terms,[59] and in his lectures and articles stressed the great international significance of the Bolshevik experience. He called for socialists of all countries to support Soviet Russia. At the same time he emphasized the incompatibility of the Bolsheviks' actions with the principles of democracy, pointing out that they had launched the reign of terror. As a whole, Russell's attitude to Russian Communism was rather critical.[60] Notwithstanding his critical stance, his writings attracted many of his students and readers to the study of Lenin's and Trotsky's theory. After all, Russell condemned the Bolsheviks for things that were actually admired by certain groups of Chinese youth. The latter keenly felt the weakness and humiliation of their country and considered the Bolsheviks' outrages as a manifestation of their unshakable might. "All of them [his students in China] were Bolsheviks," recalled Russell, "except one, who was the nephew of the Emperor. They were charming youths, ingenuous and intelligent at the same time, eager to know the world and to escape from the trammels of Chinese tradition ... There was no limit to the sacrifices that they were prepared to make for their country. The atmosphere was electric with the hope of a great awakening. After centuries of slumber, China was becoming aware of the modern world".[61] Thus, through various channels and in the face of certain difficulties, slowly but surely the general meaning of the major ideas of radical Russian Communism, including the most essential principles of the theory of permanent revolution, reached the public in distant China. And a section of the Chinese revolutionaries perceived it as a revelation. Li Dazhao, for example, was particularly impressed: "One can understand that Trotsky had considered the Russian revolution as a Bickford cord of the world revolution. The Russian revolution is only one of revolutions in the world. Incalculable popular revolutions will still rise one after another."[62]

Li Dazhao supported this concept enthusiastically. He was the first in China to accept the Bolsheviks' position:

Everywhere red banners fly, everywhere trade unions emerge. We have all reasons to say that these are the revolutions of the Russian model, the revolutions of the twentieth century . . . . The Russian revolution . . . foretells changes on the earth. Although Bolshevism has been created by Russians, it reflects the awakening of all humankind of the twentieth century.[63]

The desire to reproduce the Russian experience as soon as possible led Chinese supporters of Communism to accept the Bolshevik experiment without critical comprehension. Even those who had read Marxism's founders more or less seriously and thus were unable not to notice a certain difference between Bolshevism and Marx's and Engels's materialistic concept were inclined to see the Russian Communists' activity as real Marxism. In historical materialism they found some "flaws". It is hard not to agree with Sheveliev who, acquainted with Li Dazhao's heritage, concluded, "While continuing to share the existing attitude to Bolshevism which from the first he saw as 'a revolutionary Socialism' Li Dazhao sometimes talked about Marxism . . . with a certain degree of hesitation."[64]

Shi Cuntong even urged the adoption from the teachings of Marx and Engels only of ideas which "sounded" like the notion of Socialist revolution in backwards countries. In his article "Marx's Communism," published in August 1921, he wrote:

I believe Marxist theory on the whole is based on materials of industrially developed countries, so some things from his [Marx's] words can not be applied to the countries where industry is in an infantile condition . . . If in China one is to implement Marxism he perhaps will necessarily come into conflict with Marx's words. But it is absolutely unimportant because Marxism's sense is not a dead dogma . . . Marx's Communism can be implemented in China for sure.[65]

As to Marxism itself, activists of the embryonic Chinese Communist movement most easily comprehended the sharply revolutionary ideas of proletarian class struggle against capitalists, anti-capitalist social revolution, and dictatorship of the proletariat. And among Marx and Engels's works known to them, they were particularly fond of *The Communist Manifesto* – an openly polemical extremist brochure by the young Marx and Engels. Here is Li Dazhao's approach to Marxist theory:

Supporters of historical materialism are blamed as allegedly being determinist because they regard economic development as natural and inevitable. So Marx's opponents state that Socialist parties of Marxist direction which trust determinism propose nothing except to wait for a natural growing of social property. They do nothing else, and as a result they are allegedly standing before the great crisis. There is a certain flaw in the materialist comprehension of history. However, one must understood that it is impossible to implement Socialism without people, when in *The Manifesto of the Communist Party* Marx and Engels loudly called the world working class to unite and overthrow capitalism. This is the greatest deed of Marxism. It is immaterial whether one accepts or denies Marxism, this fact is obvious.[66]

It was mostly *The Manifesto* which supplied Chinese supporters of Communism with the conformation of the true Marxist characteristics of Bolshevik theory. This was revealed, for example, in lectures of Chen Duxiu, future leader of the CCP, titled "Critiques of Socialism," delivered at the Institute of Law in Guangzhou and published on July 1, 1921 in the Shanghai magazine *Xin qingnian*. While frequently citing *The Manifesto* and another of Marx's polemical works, *Critique of the Gotha Programme*, and making a comparison between ideas of these writings and political positions of Russian Communists and German Social Democrats, Chen Duxiu concluded, "Only in Russia was the gist of Marx's teaching revived and called Communism . . . Only the Russian Communist party according to its words and deeds is truly Marxist, and the German Social Democratic party not only forgot Marx's teaching, but absolutely and obviously opposes Marx, although it pretends to be Marxist."[67]

A member of the Shanghai Communist nucleus, Li Da, also expressed these ideas in the end of December 1920 in an article under the typical title "Marx's Revival":

> Marx's Socialism has already been implemented wholly in Russia . . . Lenin is not at all a creator, he can be called a practitioner. However, he also managed to reveal brilliantly the real gist of Marxism. And he managed to use it skillfully. There is Lenin's greatness in this, and his contemporaries should admire him. Marxism that had been perverted by Wilhelm Liebknecht, Bebel, Bernstein and Kautsky up to today has managed to revive its real character when illuminated by Lenin's light.[68]

Given all of those influences, it is clear that the first Communists of China should have settled concrete and strategic problems of the Chinese revolution in complete accordance with Lenin's and Trotsky's doctrine. This has been investigated in detail in the historiography. Here we shall analyze only a few illustrative points.

In the early 1920s all Chinese followers of the Bolsheviks shared the idea that the ultimate goal of their movement was the organization of their own October Revolution. According to this logic, the Chinese proletarian revolution would overthrow not only the rule of feudal and militaristic

35

forces, but would also put an end to the development of capitalist relations: it should be directed against both old and new exploiter classes, including the national bourgeoisie. At the same time the revolution was considered anti-imperialist, its aim was the overthrow of the domination of foreign capital. As a result of such a revolution there would be established the dictatorship of the proletariat in China. After a brief period of hesitation[69] revolutionaries such as Li Dazhao, Chen Duxiu, Li Da, Shi Cuntong, Yun Daiying, Cai Hesen, Li Ji and a number of other young Communists came to these conclusions.[70]

The "pure breath" of post-February Leninism – that is, of Trotsky's theory of the permanent revolution – is clearly sensible in documents of the First Congress of the Chinese Communist Party (July 23–31, 1921), that declared the following principles of the CCP program:

A. With the revolutionary army of the proletariat to overthrow the capitalistic classes, to reconstruct the nation from the labor class, until class distinctions are eliminated.

B. To adopt the dictatorship of the proletariat in order to complete the end of class struggle – abolishing the classes.

C. To overthrow the private ownership of capital, to confiscate all the productive means, such as machines, land, buildings, semi-manufactured products, etc., and to entrust them to social ownership.

D. To unite with the Third International.[71]

This course was also determining a political line accepted at the Congress: "Our party, with the adoption of the Soviet form, organizes the industrial and agricultural laborers and soldiers, preaches communism, and recognizes the social revolution as our chief policy; absolutely cuts off all relations with the yellow intellectual class, and other such parties."[72]

The last thesis sounded in "The First Program of the Chinese Communist Party" received further elaboration and development in "The First Decision about the Objectives of the CCP," which was also passed by the Congress:

Towards the existing political parties, an attitude of independence, aggression and exclusion should be adopted. In the political struggle, in opposition to militarism and bureaucracy and in demanding freedom of speech, press, and assemblage, when we must declare our attitude, our party should stand up in behalf of the proletariat, and should allow no relationship with other parties or groups.[73]

Members of the Communist party also held the equal isolationist position toward such a national revolutionary organization as the Guomindang headed by Sun Yat-sen. Given that, one should be very cautious when examining the well-known statement of one of the delegates of the First CCP Congress, Chen Tanqiu, who maintained that the Congress allegedly approved the following decision: "In general a critical attitude must be adopted towards the teaching of Sun Yat-sen, but his various practical and progressive actions should be supported, by adopting forms of non-Party collaboration."[74] The given point of view might have been sounded during discussions at the Congress, but according to the documents it was rejected by the majority of the delegates.

As we can see, the young supporters of Communism in China were even more radical than Lenin and Trotsky regarding some questions: the Bolsheviks' leaders, for example, never ruled out cooperation with other political groups. But the desire of the Chinese Communists to claim their own ideological and organizational autonomy seems to have been too powerful.

Having borrowed Bolshevik theory, the participants of the newly formed Communist movement in China focused most intently on its principles of internationalism. This is not hard to understand. Like their Russian idols, they also could more or less reasonably tie their hopes for the building of socialism in their country only to the victory of the world revolution. It was precisely their belief in the forthcoming world October that facilitated their disengagement from the realities of Chinese national and political conditions, namely, imperialist domination and militarist rule. This belief helped them to ignore the absence of the material premises in China, which, according to Marx, were essential for the transition to socialism, and generally speaking, allowed them to find the justification for their own radicalism.

"To solve the problem as to whether there are appropriate economic conditions for the building of socialism in modern China, one first of all has to answer another question: have the economic prerequisites for socialism ripened on a world scale?" declared Li Dazhao, who immediately explained that the latter factors were right at hand. But if so, he continued, it means that although "in China the contradiction between labor and capital has not become a serious problem yet, nevertheless it is useless and senseless to believe that one can preserve a capitalist regime here."[75]

The same ideas were being developed by Shi Cuntong. In his June 1921 article "How We Will Carry Out a Social Revolution" he wrote,

> The Russian Communist state has already opened a new era for the proletariat of the whole world. Now the proletariat of the whole world will start a powerful tide. The world proletariat will go ahead promptly in order to overthrow the bourgeoisie. It will combine its efforts with those of Russian comrades to build the Communist world. China is a part of the world, and the proletariat that lives in this part should perceive [these ideas] and pool its

resources and forces with the world proletariat. Together they will make the world social revolution and build the "World of a Human." But if we ourselves shall not rise, I am afraid that the "World of a Human" will not allow such paltry people to get in! Summing up, I shall say, although capitalism in China is not advanced, world capitalism has already been moving from growth into disintegration, and it is completely impossible to imagine that after the wreck of world capitalism that Chinese capitalism could still exist. Given the international tendency, China cannot fail in building Communism.[76]

Similar ideas were also expressed by other Chinese Communists.

All this testifies to the fact that by the time of the formation of the CCP the ideas of the October Revolution were rather well known to the most radical and advanced part of the Chinese intelligentsia. Russian Marxism had attracted the attention of the Chinese revolutionaries as the most dynamic political and ideological teaching. Therefore, Chinese Communists who called themselves Marxist found the theory which applied to China not in classical Marxism, but in the Bolshevik experience. The Chinese progressive intelligentsia most broadly adopted just one current from various Socialist trends – post-February 1917 Bolshevism. The core of this current was formed by Trotsky's concept of permanent revolution. Thus, the early socialist ideas which spread among Chinese intellectuals were Trotskyist in origin. As for Marx's world outlook, it did not make a deep impact on the political theory and practice of the CCP.

Trotsky's concept of permanent revolution had conquered the minds of supporters of the Communist movement in China, which constituted still a small, but extremely active group. The first members of the CCP – a tiny group of only fifty-sixty persons[77] – began their penetration into the working-class movement. In spite of incredible difficulties, in the beginning of the 1920s they tried to prepare the radical Chinese workers towards the organization of a Chinese October.

Life, however, soon forced their leaders to make significant corrections in their political line. First and foremost this was determined by the change in the appropriate tactical directives from the Communist International itself.

Part II

Lenin and the National Revolution in China

Chapter 3 ————————————————————

Lenin's Concept of the United Front

The spread of Bolshevik theory beyond the eastern fringes of Soviet Russia soon faced serious limitations. Other than tiny groups of left-wing radicals, no one seemed eager to convert to Bolshevism. Most intellectuals held nationalist views, and the masses found those easier to understand than the abstract ideas of internationalism. "Pure" Bolshevik tactics aimed at the preparation of permanent revolution were unlikely to be very effective in the East. The task of ideological penetration that the Russian Communists faced gave rise to the question of how to adapt their theory to the particular conditions in countries at once industrially more backward than Russia and in a state of colonial and semi-colonial dependence. Lenin was the first to understand this, and it was he who shaped a new perspective:

> The task is to arouse the working masses to revolutionary activity, to independent action and to organization, regardless of the level they have reached; to translate the true communist doctrine, which was intended for the Communists of the more advanced countries, into the language of every people.[1]

There ensued some revisions of the Bolsheviks' interpretation of the world socialist revolution. Soviet leaders began to consider it not as "solely, or chiefly, a struggle of the revolutionary proletarians of each country against their bourgeoisie", but rather "a struggle of all the imperialist-oppressed colonies and countries, of all dependent countries against international imperialism."[2] This approach underlay the effort to construct a new foundation for the Comintern's China policy. The core constituted a special theory of anti-colonial revolution, which the Communist International began to elaborate in the summer of 1920, on the eve of its Second Congress.

This theory rested on Lenin's ideas on national and colonial questions which had crystallized during World War I. It also embraced Lenin's pre-

February 1917 views on the possibility of a revolutionary democratic dictatorship of the proletariat and the peasantry in a backward country. The concept can be summarized as follows: The social emancipation of the working people of the industrially undeveloped colonies and semi-colonies of the East, in which the semi-patriarchal and patriarchal peasantry predominate, is inconceivable if foreign imperialist domination over these countries remains intact. Consequently, the revolutions in Eastern countries including China will not be socialist but rather nationalist in character. During the course of these revolutions, the indigenous Communists, who must address the national aspirations of the broad masses, should enter into temporary alliance with bourgeois liberation movements of the colonial and backward nations. In so doing, they will pursue, of course, their own tactical goals and will support bourgeois democracy only when it is genuinely national revolutionary, and when its exponents do not hinder the Communist work of educating and organizing the peasantry and the broad masses of the exploited in the most revolutionary, in fact, Communist spirit. If these conditions do not exist, if national revolutionaries oppose the Communist struggle against land-lords and all manifestations of feudalism, and if they put obstacles in the way of the Communist attempt to uphold the independence of the proletarian movement even if it is in its most embryonic form, then the Communists must combat the reformist bourgeoisie. In the alliance with revolutionary democracy the Communists must also have the right to strengthen their own organizations; the right to be brought together and trained to understand their special tasks, i.e., those of the struggle against the bourgeois democratic movements within their own nations.

According to this concept, the national revolutions in Eastern countries are considered part of the world proletarian revolution, in fact revolutions of a new type. Lenin specifically warned against a nationalistic, artificial contraposition of a national liberation movement to other currents of the world revolutionary process. The Communists who participated in these revolutionary movements must take a leading role, trying to make them as democratic as possible through conducting propaganda in favor of peasants' Soviets or Soviets of the exploited. And wherever conditions permit, they should immediately make attempts to set up these soviets: "It will readily be understood that peasants living in conditions of semi-feudal dependence can easily assimilate and give effect to the idea of Soviet organization . . ." Lenin emphasized. "The idea of Soviet organization is a simple one, and is applicable not only to proletarian but also to peasant feudal and semi-feudal relations."[3]

The concept claims that the victory of anti-colonial revolutions would be impossible without the closest alliance between the national revolu-tionary movements in colonies and semi-colonies, and Soviet republics of the advanced nations. This alliance creates prospects for the Eastern countries to pursue a "non-capitalist" direction, advancing to the Soviet system and – through various stages of development – to socialism, without having to pass through the capitalist stage. It is this direction, not bourgeois democracy, that is the goal of the proletariat – i.e., the proper Communist parties – in the national revolutionary movement. At the same time, Lenin does not entirely reject the bourgeois democratic prospects of the national revolution. Lenin only believed that the road to the capitalist stage of development of backward countries was not predictable.

This theory was set forth in the first instance in documents Lenin submitted to the Second Comintern Congress. These included "Preliminary Draft Theses on National and Colonial Questions", his speeches to the appropriate Congress Commission, his report on behalf of this commission at a plenary session of the Congress, and his remarks on the Draft "Supplementary Theses", prepared by the Indian Communist Manabendra Nath Roy, and some other works.[4]

During plenary sessions on July 26 and 28 the Congress simultaneously discussed both drafts – "Preliminary Draft Theses on National and Colonial Questions", edited by the Commission on national and colonial questions, and the "Supplementary Theses", which had been radically revised. On July 28 the first of these documents, now entitled "Theses on National and Colonial Questions," was almost unanimously approved.[5] The second one passed the next day.[6]

These documents were then incorporated into a single resolution. That this was the case can be seen from the manner of their official publication in the 1920s by the Executive Committee of the Comintern in Russian, German, English, and French, when they were always presented as a unified resolution consisting of two parts. The first, however, more precisely expresses Lenin's concept. As for the "Supplementary Theses", they appear contradictory: alongside the amendments introduced by Lenin and other Commission members – including the possibility of a "non-capitalist" development – these theses retain some points which as a whole reflect Roy's original views, albeit in garbled form.

Roy formulated his theory on the eve of the Second Congress and during the work of its Commission on national and colonial questions. It can be expressed as follows: In India, China, and various other colonial and semi-colonial countries where the prevailing social relations are capitalist, the masses of the exploited are not and cannot be affected by bourgeois nationalism, and the bourgeoisie does not play a revolutionary role. Thus it is necessary to refuse to assist bourgeois democratic movements in those countries. The Communist International must proclaim a course for the socialist revolution in the East which will also accomplish, in passing, national democratic tasks. Roy exaggerated the significance of the revolutionary process in the Eastern countries for the world revolution, asserting that the destiny of the West turned entirely on the progress of revolutionary movements in the East. He spoke in favor of rapidly forming Communist parties in colonies and semi-colonies and urged that they launch an immediate, uncompromising struggle for revolutionary hegemony.[7]

It is evident that Roy's views were close and in some respect identical to those of the first of the Chinese Communists. This stemmed from the similarity of social and psychological situations in Indian and Chinese societies in which the revolutionary views of the progressive intelligentsia were taking shape. The Asian intellectuals were searching for the shortest way to the ideals of justice which seemed to have been established by the October Revolution. Roy's political views represented post-February 1917 Bolshevism with Eastern characteristics.

As the Russian scholar Moisei A. Persits showed, Roy's "Supplementary Theses", even after Lenin's corrections, still largely proceeded from the assumption that capitalist relations predominated in some colonial and semi-colonial countries. Persits also demonstrated that these "Theses" retained some of Roy's basic ideas concerning the priority of the revolutionary movement in the East over the workers' struggle in the West. At the same time, according to Persits, the "Theses" maintain – if not so clearly as in the original version – that the Communists should not support the national bourgeoisie but rather actively and rapidly set up Communist parties in all Eastern countries and carry out the socialist revolution.[8] A careful examination of the "Theses" also shows that, besides these points, the document also contains the assertion that the national liberation is not a revolutionary event at all. The Sixth and Seventh Theses declare that the overthrow of foreign capital or its dominance will be only the first step "*towards* the revolution in colonies."[9]

Lenin compromised with Roy for tactical reasons, considering it necessary to make concessions to the sincere but unsophisticated Eastern revolutionaries. As Persits noted, Lenin accepted compromise in the belief that the exponents of ultra-left views would alter those views in the course of the ideological and practical revolutionary struggle.[10]

The accommodation of Lenin's theory of anti-colonial revolution to specific conditions in China found concrete expression in the organization of an anti-imperialist alliance between the CCP and the Guomindang. The form of the united front required individual Communists to enter this nationalist party where they were to cooperate closely with that party's leader, Sun Yat-sen, and its rank-and-file members in order to prepare and carry out the anti-imperialist revolution. According to these tactics, however, inside the Guomindang the CCP must retain absolute political independence. Adopting this decision, the Comintern took into account the weakness of the tiny Chinese Communist group as well as the opportunities presented by entering the Guomindang – the possibility of working legally in GMD-controlled territory in Southern China, use of the Guomindang channels of communication with the masses, and so on.

A policy of cooperation with Sun took shape shortly before the Second Comintern Congress, when Soviet Russia established contact with Sun Yat-sen and his Guangzhou government, although the first exchange of official greetings between Sun Yat-sen and the Soviets had taken place earlier, in 1918.[11] According to the Chinese historian Jiang Yihua, in April 1920 "the representative of the government of Soviet Russia Lubo [the Russian original of the surname is not identified] arrived in Zhangzhou (Fujian province) carrying a personal letter from Lenin, and met with Chen Jiongming, Commander-in-Chief of the Guangdong army."[12] Sun Yat-sen's close confidants Liao Zhongkai and Zhu Zhixin took part in the meeting. Zhu Zhixin prepared a draft reply to Lenin for Chen Jiongming. "Lubo" introduced his counterparts to the situation in Soviet Russia, offered some explanations of the Soviet government's foreign policy, warmly saluted the development of the Chinese revolutionary movement, and expressed the RSFSR's readiness to assist China in completing her national revolution. Liao Zhongkai and Zhu Zhixin reported to Sun Yat-sen about this meeting. Under their influence the biweekly *Mingxing* (Fujian Star) and the daily *Mingxing ribao* – both appearing in Fujian – began to devote more attention to the internal and foreign policy of the Bolshevik party and Soviet Russia.[13]

In the summer of 1920, in Shanghai Sun Yat-sen met a former general of the Tsarist army, A. S. Potapov, who was stranded in China by the October Revolution and was now preparing to return home. Obviously assuming that Potapov would be received by some leading members of the Bolshevik party, Sun Yat-sen asked him upon his arrival in Russia to pass along his regards to Lenin: "[He] refrained from any written statements to the Soviet government," Potapov wrote when he was already in Moscow, "due to the fears which were expressed by him and shortly confirmed by the search performed on me by representatives of the Entente powers."[14] Also in Shanghai, a little later in the same year, Sun Yat-sen through the mediation of Chen Duxiu met Grigorii N. Voitinsky, who was sent to China by the Vladivostok branch of the RCP(B) Far Eastern Bureau and the Comintern Executive Committee to establish systematic relations with Chinese progressive intellectuals. As Voitinsky later recalled, Sun Yat-sen was greatly interested in the question of how the national revolution in China could be joined with the struggle in faraway Russia. He expressed his desire to remain in contact with the RSFSR government.[15]

Voitinsky also held conversations with the editors of the Shanghai Guomindang journal *Xingqi pinglun* (Sunday Review) Dai Jitao, Shen Dingyi, and Li Hanjun, who reported the discussions to Liao Zhongkai and Zhu Zhixin. The latter in turn informed Sun Yat-sen. Ever more determined to establish close relations with Soviet Russia, Sun even engaged a Russian language tutor for Liao Zhongkai and Zhu Zhixin, hoping that in the near future they could go to the Soviet state to become acquainted with Bolshevik experience.[16]

On October 31, 1920, RSFSR People's Commissar of Foreign Affairs Georgii Chicherin sent a letter to Sun Yat-sen. Sun received it only on June 14, 1921, when he had already assumed the office of Extraordinary President of the Government of South China. Replying on August 28, 1921, he wrote,

> Meanwhile, I would like to enter into personal contact with you and my friends in Moscow. I am extremely interested in your work, and particularly in the organization of your soviets, your army, and educational system. I would like to know what you and your friends can tell me about these matters, and particularly about education. In the same way as Moscow has done, I would like to impress deeply the principle of the Chinese republic into the minds of the young generation, the workers of tomorrow.[17]

With the help of Li Dazhao and another Chinese Communist activist, Zhang Tailei, and of the GMD member Zhang Ji,[18] at the end of December 1921 Sun Yat-sen met the Comintern representative Hendrikus Sneevleit (alias Maring) in Guilin, Guangxi province.[19] During the conversations, for which Zhang Tailei acted as an interpreter, the two discussed the possibility of establishing an alliance between the Guomindang and Soviet Russia. Further, Maring proposed that the GMD leader direct the Guomindang toward supporting the popular masses, establish a school for training revolutionary military cadres, and transform the GMD into the strongest political party which would unite representatives of various strata of Chinese society. He also made a presentation about Soviet Russia before Sun Yat-sen's officer corps. Sun put Maring's proposals under consideration.

Maring also held long discussions with Liao Zhongkai in Guangzhou on the propaganda and organizational work of the Guomindang. He raised the question of the hostility of the British imperialists at Hong Kong toward the government of South China. Maring and Liao Zhongkai also discussed Chen Jiongming's unreliability, agreeing that this warlord would inevitably go over to the camp of Sun Yat-sen's foes.

His trip to South China, his conversations with Sun Yat-sen, other GMD leaders and Chen Jiongming, whom he met thrice early in 1922, and his acquaintance with the Guomindang's success in organizing labor, all strengthened Maring's determination to persuade the leaders of the CCP to give up "their exclusive attitude towards the KMT [GMD]." Moreover, it was Maring's idea that the Chinese Communists enter Sun Yat-sen's party in order to "develop activity *within* the KMT." Such a course, he believed, would make it easier for the CCP to get in touch with the workers and soldiers of South China, where the government was in the hands of Sun Yat-sen's supporters. Maring emphasized, that the CCP must not "give up its independence, on the contrary, the comrades must together decide which tactics they should follow within the KMT... The prospects for propaganda by the small groups [of the Communists], as long as they are not linked to the KMT, are dim."[20]

The Communist party leadership reacted negatively to his proposal, as did Party cells in Guangdong, Shanghai, Beijing, Changsha, and Hubei. The overwhelming majority of Chinese Communists still rejected any alliance with the Guomindang.[21] At the same time Maring's initiative received the support of Sun Yat-sen and some GMD activists who assured the Comintern representative that they would not create any obstacles to Communist propaganda inside their party. As for inter-party collaboration between the Guomindang and the CCP, Sun Yat-sen remained rather pessimistic.[22]

Maring brought his proposal to Moscow, where on July 11, 1922, he reported to the Executive Committee of the Communist International. His proposition about Communists entering the Guomindang on an individual base was approved by the Comintern after some delay. According to archival materials, it took a little more than two weeks for the Comintern Executive Committee to reach a final decision. In mid-July 1922, the ECCI in its letter to the CCP Central Executive Committee, had not yet made any recommendation in this regard. But the tone of the letter showed that the Comintern leaders were beginning to express interest in a closer alliance between the Communists and the GMD members:

In its political activity against foreign capitalist powers the party must act along with the revolutionary national movement ... In Guangdong there are favorable conditions for our work. First, the national movement is wider and most successfully developed there, and youth and worker organizations have great significance. Besides, the party can work legally there and use the opportunities in Guangdong province. We suggest you move the C[E]C to Canton [Guangzhou].[23]

In late July or early August 1922, the Comintern Executive at last adopted a special instruction. Written by Karl Radek, it was given to Maring to guide his and the CCP's further work.[24] With this document the Executive Committee of the Comintern first formulated the idea of the CCP's entry into the Guomindang. The decision stressed absolute independence of the Communist party inside the Guomindang and pointed out that intra-party cooperation with the GMD must last only until the CCP became a mass political party in its own right as a result of the deepening of the "gulf between the proletarian, bourgeois and petty-bourgeois elements" in the alliance.[25]

A further contribution to the concept of the Chinese revolution came from the Fourth Comintern Congress held in November-December 1922 in Moscow. This forum passed the "General Theses on the Eastern Question" which elaborated Lenin's anti-colonial tactics. International Communism had by that time accumulated a certain experience, and significant economic and political changes had taken place in the world. According to the "General Theses," changes have taken place in motive forces and leadership of the national-liberation movement in some Eastern countries. Although the movement still mainly has a nationalist character, the workers and peasants have begun to express their own political activity, and new, more radical people have appeared as national leaders. The leadership of the anti-imperialist struggle, therefore, is no longer solely in the hands of the revolutionary representatives of the feudal upper strata and the national bourgeoisie. These changes stimulate the intensification of the national revolution, whose objective tasks go beyond the limits of bourgeois democracy if only because a decisive victory is incompatible with world imperialism. The shift in the "social basis" of the movement, however, by no means testifies to a radical transformation in the social structure of the backward countries. Capitalism in colonial countries arises on feudal foundations and develops "in distorted and incomplete transitional forms" which give predominance to commercial capital. Industry is poorly developed; factory and plants are confined to a few regions and are incapable of absorbing surplus agricultural population. The industrial proletariat, even its most advanced elements, has been in a transitional stage between craft and artisan labor and the large capitalist factory. Although the levels of social and economic development of backward countries are different, the contrasts only reflect various stages of evolution from feudal or patriarchal-feudal relations to capitalism.

The "General Theses" claim that in the circumstances of a prolonged and protracted struggle with world imperialism, a prospect that confronts the national-liberation movement and demands the mobilization of all revolutionary elements, the Eastern Communists must not simply cooperate with national revolutionary forces, including the national bourgeoisie, but unite with them in an anti-imperialist front. They must, however, preserve their political independence, and not only fight for the complete national liberation of their countries but also organize the working and peasant masses for the struggle for their special class interests, exploiting all contradictions in the nationalist bourgeois-democratic camp. Moreover, the Communists of the East must prepare the indigenous industrial proletariat for its role as political leader of the national revolution. They must wholly realize that the hegemony of the working class can be achieved only as a result of the struggle against imperialist exploitation and their own ruling classes in proportion to the strengthening of the colonial proletariat socially and politically, and to the winning of influence over "the social strata nearest to them," above all the peasantry.

The final victory of the national revolution in the colonial periphery of imperialism directly depends on the extent to which such national movements win over the broad working masses to their cause and break with reactionary feudal elements, and give expression in their program to the social demands of these masses. The major condition for the triumph of the anti-colonial revolutions and the transition of the backward countries towards "non-capitalism" is the close alliance between the working masses of the East and the victorious proletariat of the advanced countries.[26]

The draft "General Theses on the Eastern Question", adopted by the Fourth Congress as a final resolution, was elaborated by the Comintern Executive Committee at the end of October 1922.[27] Several ECCI officials including Roy participated. At a meeting of some delegates on October 28, Roy reiterated his ultra-radical views,[28] and on November 22, he presented the basic theses of his concept at a plenary session of the Congress.[29] The starting point of his reasoning was his contention that the Second Comintern Congress had drawn up only general tactical principles of the Communist struggle for national liberation of colonies and semi-colonies. "During the Second Congress," he emphasized,

> only very few understood that a broad definition of 'colonial and semi-colonial countries' covered different peoples and different regions, which embrace inside their borders all kinds of social development, all kinds of political and industrial backwardness. We came to the conclusion that simply because they all lagged behind politically, economically and socially, they all could be unified into one group, into one general problem. But it was an erroneous view.[30]

Calling attention to some obvious changes in the social and political situation in the world since the Second Congress, Roy, however, went too far dividing the Eastern countries into "three categories." To the first category he consigned those countries that were in his opinion "developing close to a stage of the most advanced capitalism" (imperialism?); to the second, "the countries in which capitalist development [was] still at a rather low level, and in which feudalism still remaine[d] the backbone of society"; and to the third, those regions, where "the social system [was] based on patriarchal feudalism,"[31] i.e., where pre-feudal relations predominated.

In pursuit of his conclusions about the changing nature of the revolutionary process in some Eastern countries, Roy greatly overestimated the economic level of those backwards countries. His goal was to expedite revision of the Comintern tactics. At the Fourth Congress, however, he did not make these conclusions, contenting himself with the following declaration: "Since the social system of each of these countries is different, the nature of their revolutionary movements also differs. Thus, our program and tactics must likewise vary depending on the difference between the social systems of these countries."[32] He was obviously reluctant to undertake a more detailed elaboration that would contrast markedly with Lenin's approach. Moreover, in another passage, Roy formally acknowledged that the revolutionary process in Eastern countries still had a national character, and he kept accentuating the significance of the liberation movement in the East for the course of the world revolution.[33] At the same time he denied the revolutionary potential of the indigenous bourgeoisie, declaring that "the industrial development carried out by the bourgeoisie requires peace and order, which are maintained in most of the Eastern countries by imperialists."[34] According to his logic, the bourgeoisie – in particular that part which had "invested considerable capital in industry" – was already collaborating with the colonialists. That did not mean, however, that the national bourgeoisie would not be able to oppose imperialism in the future. As Roy maintained, "the temporary compromise between the native and imperialist bourgeoisie cannot last too long. It contains an embryo of a future conflict". But even during this conflict the bourgeoisie would not be far from a compromise with the imperialists because it does not conduct a "class war."

The report paid much attention to questions of forming Communist parties in Eastern countries. Roy kept insisting on accelerating this process in every country without taking into account the different levels of social and economic development. He even erroneously believed that in most Eastern countries there were by the end of 1922 functioning Communist groups. Though he called them "cells", he exaggerated their political maturity, considering them "political parties of the masses" in contrast to bourgeois democratic organizations.[35]

The Fourth Comintern Congress rejected Roy's theoretical system. Nevertheless, some particular points of his doctrine were accepted by many delegates. In the early 1920s Roy, an important ECCI functionary, was considered an authority on national and colonial questions. Other Comintern leaders, including Lenin, did not know much about the Afro-Asian countries.[36] Roy clearly understood this. At the Fourth Congress he said, "The particular difficulties of applying the program of the International to Eastern countries ... are caused by the fact ... (unfortunately, one must admit it) that until now our comrades in the Communist International have studied these [Eastern] questions too little."[37] One could conclude that there was only one person, in the Comintern, Roy, who devoted particular attention to the given problems, hence only his point of view could be considered irreproachable.

All this helps explain why an attentive reader can find a few points of Roy's concept in the final text of the "General Theses on the Eastern

Question." The document is quite contradictory.[38] For example, the "General Theses" obviously reflect one of Roy's assumptions, contending at the very beginning that the "[S]econd Comintern Congress drew up a general statement of principles on the national and colonial questions." The theses also follow Roy's exaggeration of the scope of the Communist movement in Eastern countries. The document repeatedly claims that by the end of 1922 the Communist or independent "proletarian class" parties had been organized "in practically all countries of the East." Further, it clearly contrasts nationalist organizations of the bourgeoisie with some "revolutionary parties" which are unambiguously identified as Communist groups. Moreover, the "General Theses" reflect Roy's original idea about the priority of the revolutionary movement in the Orient over the proletarian struggle in the West. Although the document emphasizes that "a colonial revolution can triumph and maintain its conquests only side by side with the proletarian revolution in the highly developed countries,"[39] it also declares that the "colonial revolutionary movements" have "*extreme* importance ... for the international proletarian revolution." French imperialism, for example, "bases *all* its calculations on the suppression of the proletarian revolutionary struggle in France and Europe by using its colonial workers as a reserve army of counter-revolution."[40]

It is clear that Roy's views also influenced one more essential document presented to the Fourth Congress, Radek's "Supplement to the General Theses on the Eastern Question." This document represented the Congress's special resolution on the tasks of the Chinese Communist Party. Contrary to Radek's directive to Maring,[41] it demonstrated scepticism toward the revolutionary potential of the Chinese national bourgeoisie and of the Guomindang. While saying nothing about the possibility of a close CCP-GMD alliance, it directed CCP members to "devote their main attention to the organization of the working masses, to the creation of trade unions and of a strong Communist mass party." At the same time the resolution stressed that the CCP should be cautious in giving its support to Sun Yat-sen, whose military blocs with unreliable warlords in China – for example, with a Japanese puppet Zhang Zuolin – was playing into the hands of Japanese imperialism. The resolution emphasized that "it is the task of the Chinese Communists to act as the front rank fighters for the national unity of China on a democratic base" and urged the CCP to "act as a force which unites democratic elements, whose growth ensures the unification of China not by a victory of arms of one of the particularist governments over the other, but by a revolutionary victory of the popular masses."[42]

The significance of these extreme leftist points should not be underestimated, for they reflected the mood of the Eastern Communist youth. Lenin's theses at the Second Comintern Congress, along with Radek's instruction to Maring and the CCP, Roy's "Supplementary

Theses," and the aforementioned documents of the Fourth Congress, all together laid the ideological foundation for Comintern policy in China. That policy was extremely contradictory from the beginning. After all, the original Bolshevik view of the revolutionary movement in the East, Trotskyist in essence, remained quite popular among many leading Communists, including a large number in Soviet Russia. Preparing for world revolution was intoxicating, and that made it possible simply to ignore objective reality: "Follow the Russian way" was a sacred exhortation. That is why the dissemination of Lenin's concept of anti-colonial revolution in China could not but collide sharply with those CCP members who acted as strict adherents of "pure" Trotskyism.

Chapter 4 _____

New Course of the CCP: From Permanent Revolution to the Tactics of Collaboration

The Chinese Communists were considering the question of their relationship with Sun Yat-sen as early as the First Party Congress in July 1921. According to one of the participants, Dong Biwu, the presence at the Congress of the ECCI representative Maring meant that the decisions of the Second Comintern Congress on national and colonial questions became known to all delegates.[43] A secretary of the Second Congress's Commission on national and colonial questions and a former activist of the Communist movement in the Dutch East Indies (Indonesia), Maring had substantial experience with national revolutionaries. At the First CCP Congress he informed the participants about his own activities on Java,[44] aimed at cooperation with Nationalists.

But as we have already seen,[45] the trend towards rapprochement with bourgeois national democracy was not fixed in the resolutions of the First Congress of the Chinese Communist party. It was difficult for the first adherents of Communism in China, most of whom did not yet thoroughly understand the general ideas of Marxism, to accept simultaneously the theory of the proletarian class struggle against the bourgeoisie and the concept of anti-imperialist collaboration.

In this connection, the participation of a Chinese delegation at the Comintern's Congress of Peoples of the Far East held January 21 – February 2, 1922 in Moscow[46] (a closing session took place in Petrograd), was of major importance for the Chinese Communists.[47] The Chinese contingent was one of the largest, with about four dozen delegates.[48] Among them there were at least twenty-eight CCP and CSYL members, and three Communist sympathizers. There were three GMD members, two anarchists, and several non-party activists. The delegation consisted of representatives of worker, peasant, student, women, teacher, and journalist organizations from Taiyuan, Hankou, Hangzhou, Tanshan, Shandong, Hunan, Anhui, Guangdong, and Zhejiang.[49] Some individuals who had participated in the First CCP Congress – Wang Jinmei, Deng Enming, Zhang Guotao, He Shuheng[50], Chen Gongbo – and other Communist leaders such as Gao Junyu, Deng Pei, and Yu Shude were members of the delegation.[51] A number of Chinese Socialist Youth League members who at the time were studying at Moscow's Communist University of the Toilers of the East, were also involved. Among them there were the future CCP activists Ren Bishi, Luo Yinong, Liu Shaoqi, Bu Shiqi, Xiao Jingguang, and Yu Xiusong.[52] A future general secretary of the CCP Central Committee, Qu Qiubai, who would join the Party in early February 1922, before the closing session of the Congress, acted as an interpreter. A former translator for Maring and now a secretary of the Chinese section of the Comintern Far Eastern secretariat, Zhang Tailei, was among those in charge of organizing the Congress, but he joined the delegation not earlier than the end of January.[53]

The Congress focused its attention on the Comintern's united front tactics in the national revolutionary movement. The leaders of the Comintern Executive Committee took advantage of the situation, trying to instill the idea of the united front into the minds of the delegates. They pointed out that

> Chinese, Korean, and Japanese communists, who for the time being are still a little group, [ought] not to stand apart, not to look down on those 'sinners' and 'publicans' who have not yet become communists, but to make their way into the deepest depths, among those millions of people who are struggling in China, among those people who for the moment are struggling for national independence and liberation.[54]

Lenin's private meeting with the CCP representatives Zhang Guotao and Deng Pei, and Guomindang member Zhang Qiubai exerted a particular impact on the Chinese delegates. Lenin especially raised the issue of cooperation between the Guomindang and the Communist party questioning Zhang Qiubai and Zhang Guotao in this regard.[55]

The Congress finally adopted a special Manifesto to the Peoples of the Far East. It urged the unification of all anti-imperialist revolutionary forces.[56]

On his return to China in March 1922, Zhang Guotao reported to the CCP Central Bureau on the results of the trip, stating in particular that

> [M]ost leaders in Moscow thought that the Chinese revolution was opposed to imperialism and to the domestic warlords and reactionary influences that were in collusion with it ... This Chinese revolution must unite the efforts of all the different groups of revolutionary forces in all China. In the final analysis there must be cooperation between the KMT [GMD] and the CCP. Lenin himself had emphatically brought out this point.[57]

Most of the Communist participants in the Congress reported to their various CCP organizations.[58] According to Zhang Guotao, the majority "praised . . . anti-imperialism."[59]

As a result, a certain shift toward an alliance with Sun Yat-sen and his followers took place in the consciousness of the CCP leaders. The intensification of the communist activity among the workers no doubt had the same effect. The Chinese Communists in practice began to be convinced that Sun Yat-sen's government's "not restricting the movement; its abolishing police regulations concerning 'public order and national security'; its abolishing the law by which workers were deprived of the right of strike, etc. can be considered as its support of the democracy."[60]

The evolution of the views of leading CCP activists on the united front issue was initially reflected in the decisions of the Chinese Socialist Youth League Congress held May 5–10, 1922, in Guangzhou. This Congress called on the Chinese proletariat and poor peasantry to support the revolutionary national liberation struggle against imperialism and warlordism.[61] The idea of a Communist-Nationalist union was accurately reflected in the first statement of the Chinese Communist party on the current situation (June 15, 1922.) Acknowledging that "of all the political parties in China only the GMD can be characterized as a relatively revolutionary and democratic party," the Communist leaders declared that "the CCP's method is to invite the GMD, other revolutionary democratic parties, and all revolutionary socialists groupings to participate in a joint conference and . . . establish a democratic united front to continue the fight against the warlords."[62]

These declarations, however, did not mean that the Chinese Communists were quick to perceive Lenin's anti-imperialist concept; they merely began to shift in that direction. They continued to interpret the idea of a CCP-GMD alliance in a sectarian manner. It was no accident that the Communist party statement referred not to an "anti-imperialist or national, or national-revolutionary front" but rather – for the first time – to a more radical-sounding "democratic united front" (minzhuzhuyide lianhe zhanxian.) Moreover, the statement as a whole was critical of the GMD, emphasizing such weaknesses as the absence of intra-party unity, the rapprochement with the imperialists, and periodic cooperation with Northern militarists.[63] Shortly after this statement, on June 30, Chen Duxiu wrote Voitinsky that "we hope that Sun Yat-sen's Guomindang will be able to realize the [necessity] of the reorganization [i.e. of the unification with the CCP and political radicalization] and will be able to temporarily go the same way as we do."[64] This was certainly an original interpretation of the united front policy. Conditions in China did not require the GMD members go together with Communists. They did call for a Communist-Nationalist alliance against the imperialists. Sun Yat-sen, who was at that time in Shanghai, became acquainted with the first CCP statement.[65]

55

The July 1922 Second CCP Congress set the party on a new course. It is significant that among twelve delegates to this forum, five had participated in the Congress of Peoples of the Far East: these were Wang Jinmei, Gao Junyu, Deng Enming, Zhang Guotao, and Zhang Tailei. The CCP Congress approved Zhang Guotao's report on this forum and wholly accepted its decisions.[66] It also passed a special secret resolution on the "democratic united front"[67] and a Manifesto which detailed the necessity of forming a bloc with the Guomindang and other national revolutionary organizations.[68] The Congress adopted the decision to strive for a joint conference of all revolutionary democratic forces of China, viewing the united front as a "temporary union" between the proletariat and poor peasants,[69] on the one hand, and the national bourgeoisie, on the other. The young Chinese bourgeois, the Manifesto admitted, "were able to unite their strength to resist foreign imperialism and the corrupted Peking [Beijing] government."[70] Elsewhere, however, the Manifesto held that the workers and poor peasants must unite with the petite bourgeoisie. There was no mention of the national bourgeoisie, most likely because the authors simply did not attach any particular social meaning to the term "petite bourgeoisie." For the CCP activists of the time the definitions "bourgeoisie" and "petite bourgeoisie" had the same social meaning; "petite bourgeoisie" bore only quantitative, restrictive significance. Sociological thought in China had not yet matured.[71]

The Congress passed over in silence Maring's proposal concerning the Communists' entry into the GMD and spoke out in favor of inter-party cooperation with the Guomindang. This form of the united front was supplemented by the so-called "Democratic Alliance" or an "Alliance of Movements for Republicanism,"[72] in which all trade union members and members of unions of peasants, merchants, teachers, students, women, lawyers, and journalists, as well as Parliamentary deputies who sympathized with Communism were supposed to be involved.[73] The Communists seemed to anticipate a broad "democratic alliance" which in practice would cover the CCP-GMD united front. After the Congress they began to set up organizations of the "democratic alliance" in various cities and provinces, first in Beijing, then in Hunan, Hubei, Shanghai, and Guangdong.[74] The GMD, however, did not support this initiative.

On August 12, 1922[75] Maring returned to China. According to Zhang Guotao, after arriving in Shanghai where the CCP Central Executive Committee was located, Maring informed the Communist leadership that "the Comintern endorsed the idea of having CCP members join the KMT [GMD] and considered it a new route to pursue in achieving a united front."[76] Some time later, in the second half of August, on Xihu Lake at Hangzhou, Zhejiang province, there took place a special enlarged meeting of the CCP CEC on the question of organizational forms of the united front with the GMD.[77] Apart from members of the Central Executive

Committee – Chen Duxiu, Zhang Guotao, Cai Hesen, Gao Junyu, and Li Dazhao[78] – Maring and Zhang Tailei also attended the meeting. According to Chen Duxiu's recollections, all the CEC members present opposed Maring's proposal. The Comintern representative attempted in vain to prove that the CCP entry into the GMD was in accord with Lenin's concept of anti-colonial revolution. In the beginning he was supported only by Zhang Tailei,[79] who had considerable experience in the Comintern, but was not a CCP CEC member. To crush the opposition, Maring invoked the authority of the Communist International, urging the participants to submit to its discipline.[80] Under such pressure the CCP leaders unanimously voted for the tactics of entering the GMD. Sun Yat-sen was satisfied with the decision.[81]

Immediately after the Xihu meeting Li Dazhao and the Communist activist Lin Boqu – who had connections among the GMD leadership – began negotiations with Sun Yat-sen. Li later wrote that he discussed with Sun Yat-sen the "question of revitalizing the GMD with the purpose of the revival of China." In other words, they talked about the reorganization of Sun Yat-sen's party in both political and organizational respects, and in particular the admission of Communists into the Guomindang: "I remember Mr. Sun and I once had an animated discussion concerning his plan of the state reconstruction," Li went on, "It had taken a few hours, and soon Mr. [Sun] himself spoke out in favor of the alliance. He recommended that I enter the GMD."[82] On August 25, 1922, Sun Yat-sen again met with Maring, who informed him that the Comintern leadership had advised the Chinese Communists to unite with the GMD.[83] He also told Sun about the Soviet offer of assistance and recommended that he step up GMD activity in developing the anti-imperialist movement of the working class and peasantry. These recommendations encountered resistance on the part of right-wing Guomindang members, but received the active support of Liao Zhongkai. Sun Yat-sen welcomed the readiness of Soviet Russia to render aid and spoke in favor of the Communists' entry into the GMD, which hence would be reorganized.[84]

At the same time Sun Yat-sen entered into correspondence with Adolf Joffe, who headed a RSFSR diplomatic mission which arrived in China in August 1922. The exchange helped Sun Yat-sen comprehend the basic difference between the foreign policy of Soviet Russia and that of the capitalist states, and it promoted cooperation between the GMD and the CCP.

In early September 1922, on the recommendation of Zhang Ji, Sun Yat-sen admitted the first Communists – Chen Duxiu, Li Dazhao, Cai Hesen, and Zhang Tailei – as members of his party.[85] From that time Communists participated actively in the reorganization of the GMD. In September-November, Liao Zhongkai, on behalf of Sun Yat-sen, conducted a series of discussions on possible Soviet military assistance with Joffe's military attaché.[86] In December Sun Yat-sen sent Zhang Ji to Beijing to negotiate with Joffe.[87]

All this work resulted in the publication on January 1, 1923 of Sun Yat-sen's Declaration on the Reorganization of the Guomindang. The next day a new Party program and charter were published; these documents contained Sun's famous "Three Principles of the People" in a new, more radical interpretation. Sun in particular stressed anti-imperialism, workers' rights, and democratic transformation of China.[88] Simultaneously, he invited the Communists Zhang Tailei, Tan Pingshan, Lin Boqu, and Chen Duxiu to work in the GMD central and local apparatus. He made every effort to build a mutually acceptable foundation for collaboration with the Soviets.

In January 1923 Sun Yat-sen himself held extended meetings with Joffe in Shanghai, and on the 26th the two signed the famous Sun Yat-sen – Joffe Declaration. In this document the Soviet envoy assured Sun that in the struggle for national unification and full independence, "China has the warmest sympathy of the Russian people and can count on the support of Russia." Both signatories agreed that at the time "the Communistic order or even the Soviet system cannot actually be introduced into China, because there do not exist here the conditions for the successful establishment of either Communism or Sovietism."[89] The rapprochement with Soviet Russia received further impetus when in February 1923 Sun resumed office as the head of the government in Guangzhou.

In the GMD as well as in the CCP there were then still many opponents of cooperation between the two parties. Such prominent Guomindang activists as Deng Zeru, Sun Ke (Sun Yat-sen's son from his first marriage), Feng Ziyou, Zou Lu, Ju Zheng rejected the idea of unification. There seems to have been even greater opposition in the CCP. It would be correct to say that the majority of the Chinese Communists, including such leaders as Chen Duxiu, Cai Hesen, Zhang Guotao, were at the time either skeptical or wholly negative. The Fourth CCP Congress (January 1925) would be obliged to conclude that, until the middle of 1923, "the Comintern proposal had not been implemented."[90] The burden of past hostility also played a role. As early as the summer of 1922, during the struggle between Sun Yat-sen and Chen Jiongming, the Communist party "found itself not on the side of Sun Yat-sen" but, in truth, also "did not openly support Chen Jiongming."[91] The CP Guangzhou organization, however, did support the insurgent general. In his June 1923 report to the Third CCP Congress, Chen Duxiu called the position of "Guangzhou comrades ... a serious mistake."[92] In this connection Cai Hesen's famous contention that "before the Third Congress only Chen Gongbo, Li Hanjun, Shen Xuanlu, Yang Mingzhai, and to some extent Guangzhou and Hubei comrades spoke out utterly against the entry into the Guomindang,"[93] sounds dubious. Most likely Cai, who himself was rather hostile to collaboration between the GMD and the CCP, considerably distorted the facts.

The decisions of the Fourth Comintern Congress naturally made an impact on the CCP. The Chinese delegation, led by Chen Duxiu, took an active part in its work, including that of its Commission on the Eastern question.[94] Soon after the delegation returned to China the Communists abandoned the slogan of a "democratic front." From the beginning of 1923, in all CCP documents and literature the term "anti-imperialist front" came into use, together with the expression "national revolutionary front."

The Fourth Comintern Congress's decisions were concretized, in regard to CCP tactics, in a January 12, 1923 ECCI resolution on the Chinese Communist party's relations with the Guomindang. Pointing out that Sun Yat-sen's organization was "the only serious national-revolutionary group in China," the ECCI emphasized that ". . . in present conditions it is expedient for members of the CCP to remain inside the Kuomintang [Guomindang]." The document also held that the Communists' stay in the GMD

> should not be at the cost of obliterating the specific political features of the CCP. The party must maintain its independent organization with a strictly centralized apparatus. The most important specific tasks of the CCP are to organize and educate the working masses, to build trade unions and thus establish a basis for a powerful mass communist party.

The resolution maintained that the CCP should try to persuade the Guomindang "to unite its forces with Soviet Russia for a common struggle against European, American, and Japanese imperialism."[95]

More significant, however, was practical experience. Exerting a profound impact on the CCP were the dramatically differing results of a January 1922 workers' strike in Hong Kong, led by the GMD, and a February 1923 strike on the Beijing-Hankou railway, headed by the CCP. The first, anti-imperialist and supported by the Guangdong population including the national bourgeoisie, succeeded; the second failed. The Communist-led workers, having raised social demands, did not receive any support. That indicated the importance of the united anti-imperialist front.

The Third Congress held in June 1923 in Guangzhou under the supervision of Maring, approved the tactic of individual entry into the Guomindang. The January resolution of the Comintern Executive Committee formed the basis for a secret "Resolution on the National Movement and the Question of the Guomindang" discussed at the Congress. This document emphasized the necessity of organizing "a powerful centralized party to act as the headquarters of the national revolutionary movement" and admitted that only the Guomindang could become such a party. As for the Communist party, the resolution declared that it could not be developed into a mass organization in the near future "because the working class [had] not become powerful ... Therefore, the ECCI passed a resolution that the CCP must cooperate with the Guomindang. The Communist party members must join the GMD. The CCP CEC also feels this need and decided to enforce the resolution. The resolution has also been adopted by this Congress."

The Communists were directed to extend the Guomindang organizations throughout the whole of China and to rally all revolutionary elements to the GMD. The document emphasized the principle of the CCP's independence in the united front and demanded that the Party strive to absorb the truly revolutionary elements from various workers' organizations and the left wing of the Guomindang.[96] It pointed out the necessity of preventing the GMD from concentrating all efforts on military operations at the expense of political propaganda among the masses. Further, it called for a struggle against the GMD tendency to compromise with imperialists and warlords and for speaking out against reformist trends in the labor movement. The basic points of this document were reflected in the Declaration of the Congress, which was published in a CEC central organ, *Xiangdao zhoukan* (Guide Weekly).[97]

After an expanded discussion the resolution was passed. A group of delegates led by Zhang Guotao and Cai Hesen openly and sharply opposed it,[98] and even most who voted in favor did so reluctantly. In July 1923 the CCP CEC drafted a second statement on the current situation, which was published on August 1 in the journal *Xianqu*.[99] The statement contained an appeal to the Guomindang to convene a National Assembly of representatives of chambers of commerce, workers, peasants, students and other professional organizations. The Assembly should form a new government which would become a real revolutionary force capable of developing a true constitution, unifying the country, and ridding China of warlords and imperialists.[100] In the circumstances this idea was not realistic and had no impact on the political struggle; it merely demonstrated the CCP leaders' maneuvers with respect to the united front. The National Assembly in practice would serve as a kind of united front between the GMD and the CCP, rendering the Communists' entry into the Guomindang superfluous. Sun Yat-sen did not accept this idea: "A written invitation to Sun Yat-sen to go to Shanghai to convene the National Assembly was to no avail," the CCP Central Bureau admitted in its report to the CEC plenum of November 24–25, 1923.[101]

The same report also made it clear that the Third CCP Congress's "Resolution on the National Movement and the Question of the Guomindang" did not receive substantial support from rank-and-file Party members. The Central Bureau found the following explanations: "1. Certain doubts [about the resolution] were spread among [our] comrades; 2. Heads of the GMD local departments did not demonstrate their own understanding; 3. Mutual suspicions and differences in political views between [our] comrades and GMD members were still strong; and 4. Our party had economic difficulties." For these reasons, the report goes on, it was impossible to implement the original plan of the CCP CEC to establish GMD organizations in all important centers of North and Central China in a short period. By that time the Communists had participated in the creation of only one GMD branch, in Beijing. In Tianjin, Harbin, and Hunan, efforts to form GMD branches were still under way; in Shandong and Sichuan, GMD branches had already been established by GMD members themselves. In Anhui GMD members had split into two factions, neither enjoying "public support." Therefore, Communists were to create a new GMD branch there.[102] Shortly after the plenum the CCP CEC informed the Comintern Executive Committee about all this.[103]

One can also judge the difficulty of the situation for the Chinese Communists from the well-known November 16, 1923 letter of Zhang Guotao to the Comintern officials Voitinsky and Isaac M. Musin concerning the Party leadership's disagreements with Maring.[104] This is also testified to by Mikhail M. Borodin, who replaced Maring as a Comintern representative in China, in his October-November 1923 initial letters to Moscow.[105] As the Fourth CCP Congress later emphasized, sectarian mistakes, typical for many Chinese Communists in the period after the Third Congress, "were to propose continuous propaganda about the proletarian revolutionary movement and the dictatorship of the proletariat [as an immediate goal], oppose joining the GMD, and even oppose participating in the nationalist revolution, regarding it as a compromise with the bourgeoisie and as changing our party's color to yellow."[106]

Characterizing such moods in his report to the Sixth Party Congress of June-July 1928, Qu Qiubai also would acknowledge that

> There seemed to be something like a left current in our ranks, which did not wish to enter the Guomindang, did not wish to make the national revolution together with the bourgeoisie. Then they, these comrades, agreed to compromise with the Comintern and considered it possible to enter the Guomindang, but not all of them did so. [They stated that] the industrial workers must not enter the Guomindang ... There also [was] another opinion, a compromise as well, that contended that in the North the workers must not enter the Guomindang, but in the South they must enter only in places where GMD organizations existed.[107]

The hesitation inside the CCP in regard to the question of the united front certainly affected Sun Yat-sen's policy and to some extent restrained Sun's own intentions to reorganize the Guomindang. Under these circumstances

Comintern and Soviet assistance to Sun in his anti-imperialist and anti-feudal struggle was of particular importance. It was the Soviets who – more than anybody else in China – were accelerating GMD-CCP cooperation.

In March 1923 the Bolshevik leadership and the Soviet government decided to render Sun Yat-sen all possible assistance. On May 1 Sun was informed of the decision.[108] On August 16 he sent an important delegation to the USSR composed of two GMD members – Chiang Kai-shek as head of the delegation and Wang Dengyun – and two Communists, Zhang Tailei and Shen Dingyi. This group arrived in Moscow on September 2 and during three months (through November 29) familiarized itself with the Soviet Communist party internal structure, the Soviets' work, visited some military detachments, and met several political leaders.[109] At the request of the delegation, in November 1923 the ECCI Presidium drafted for the GMD a special "Resolution on the Question of the National Movement in China and the Guomindang," which outlined a new, extreme leftist interpretation of the "Three Principles of the People." The Comintern offered the GMD a consistent program for the anti-imperialist democratic revolution, the key point of which was the call for a radical agrarian revolution and the nationalization of industry.[110] This document was adopted by the ECCI Presidium on November 28 and handed over to Chiang Kai-shek. Chiang carried it to Sun Yat-sen, who at least formally accepted most of the Comintern proposals except one concerning the agrarian question. The ECCI Presidium resolution was taken as the basis for the Second Section of the Manifesto that would be adopted by the First GMD Congress in January 1924.

At Sun's request, in the summer of 1923 the first group of Soviet military advisers came to Guangzhou. In early October a top Soviet Communist Mikhail Borodin arrived. He began to work in a dual capacity as both Comintern representative to the CCP CEC and "High Adviser to the Guomindang." Borodin would be followed by other Soviet political and military advisers.[111] Shortly before his arrival, Sun Yat-sen began corresponding with Lev Karakhan, who headed the Soviet embassy at Beijing.[112] The Soviet envoy tried to influence Sun to accelerate the reorganization of the GMD and the radicalization of the national revolution.

These efforts finally bore fruit.[113] In November 1923 Sun Yat-sen issued a "Manifesto on the Reorganization of the Guomindang" and a new draft program of the Party. On December 1 he delivered a major speech on reorganization at a GMD Conference in Guangzhou, defining the goal as the creation of a powerful mass Party that would rely not only on the military but on the civilian population. He noted in part,

> Now our good friend Borodin has come to us from Russia. The
> Russian revolution started six years later than ours. However, the

Russians managed to implement their ideas completely during one revolution. The position of the revolutionary government there becomes stronger day by day. Why did the Russians succeed, while we cannot gain victory? They won because the whole party supported by the military took part in the struggle. We should learn Russian methods, their organization, and their training of the Party members. Only then we can hope to achieve a victory.[114]

The developing GMD–Soviet relations and the arrival of the Soviet staff in Guangzhou to assist Sun Yat-sen could not but influence the CCP leadership. The November 1923 CCP CEC plenum resolutely condemned the "leftist distortion" of the united front policy and adopted a decision which directed the Communists to participate actively in reorganizing Sun Yat-sen's party. The plenum's "Resolution Concerning Implementation of the Plans for the Nationalist Movement" maintained that

In places where the GMD has a branch, such as Guangdong, Shanghai, Sichuan, and Shandong, our comrades, while remaining simultaneously in the CCP, [should] join it. In places where the GMD has no branch, such as Harbin, Fengtian [Shenyang], Beijing, Tianjin, Nanjing, Anhui, Hubei, Hunan, Zhejiang, Fujian, our comrades should help them to set up branches.[115]

The resolution stressed the need to "rectify the GMD's political tendencies." The authors of the document hoped to get the Guomindang to oppose imperialism and conduct anti-imperialist propaganda. The Communists should also establish or join various progressive organizations in the name of the GMD in order to strengthen their support of the Guomindang. The plenum made it incumbent upon the Communists to create their own secret organizations within the GMD and follow the CCP's directions under all circumstances. The Communists should struggle "to occupy a central position in the GMD" but not "force the issue" where this was not possible.[116]

On December 25, 1923, the CCP Central Executive Committee issued "Circular Number 13," signed by Chairman Chen Duxiu and a secretary, Luo Zhanglong. The Circular once again obliged all Communists to enter the Guomindang and make every effort to accelerate the process of its reorganization, trying their best to ensure the election to the forthcoming GMD Congress not only of Communists but also of "relatively progressive people." The CCP CEC emphasized the necessity of preparatory work so that at the Congress it would be possible "to correct old erroneous views of the Guomindang."[117] Special CEC envoys were sent to local Party organizations to promote the implementation of this document. Deng Zhongxia went to Beijing, Baoding, Tianjin, and Jinan, while Li Dazhao left for Hubei and Hunan. Lin Boqu set off for

Guangzhou, where he headed the Guangdong Publishing house *Geming pinglun* (Revolutionary Review) and participated in drafting the Manifesto of the First GMD Congress.[118]

The first Congress of the Guomindang was finally held in Guangzhou January 20–30, 1924.[119] By that time, in Guangzhou, Jiangxi, Hunan, and Hubei there were estimated to be more than 11,000 members of the GMD; data on other regions is not available. The Guangzhou organization was by far the largest, with 8,218 members. The Jiangxi provincial organization had about 2,000 odd members, while the Hunan and Hubei cells had only about 500 each. There were more than 300 GMD members in Hankou.[120] The CCP at that time could count only about 500 members.[121] Even if we assume that by the First GMD Congress, most Communists had already entered the GMD which was not the case, the CCP would still have resembled a small cell against the Guomindang background – not bigger than one local organization of the GMD, less than 5% of Sun's Party.

But the Communists were very active inside and outside the Congress hall. Of 198 delegates, only 165 actually attended the sessions. Among the latter were 23 CCP members – almost 14% of the total – including Chen Duxiu, Han Lifu, Li Dazhao, Lin Boqu, Mao Zedong, Qu Qiubai, Tan Pingshan, Shen Dingyi, Wang Jinmei, Yu Shude, and Zhang Guotao.[122] The most active were Li Dazhao, Tan Pingshan, and Mao Zedong. The Communists were represented in all Commissions of the Congress for which there are data.

As a whole, according to the composition of the Congress Presidium and commissions, the balance of power between the right-wing and left-wing GMD members including Communists was more or less equal. The question of Communist membership in the Guomindang was being resolved in a sharp struggle. At a banquet in honor of the delegates on the first day of the Congress, a right-winger, Mao Zuquan, insisted that, "If the Communists accept our program, they must leave their own party." During the January 28 debate on the report on the Party charter, the anti-Communists Fang Ruilin and Feng Ziyou demanded the insertion into the charter of a provision prohibiting members of other parties from remaining in the Guomindang. In response Li Dazhao, clearly dissembling, argued that,

> If the national revolution is to be accomplished, a unified and universal national revolutionary party is indispensable ... Looking around the country, we realize that ... only the KMT [GMD] can build up a great and universal national-revolutionary party able to shoulder the great mission of [the] liberation of the people, restoring the people's rights, and founding the people's livelihood. Thus, without hesitation we came to join the Party ... That we joined the Party is for the purpose of contributing something to the

Party as well as to contribute to the work of the national revolution and absolutely not for taking advantage of the name of the KMT to work for the Communist movement ... Not only I myself wished to join the Party, but hope that all Chinese people will join ... By joining the Party, we accept the Party platform; we do not force the Party to accept the platform of the CCP. If we examine the newly-adopted platform of the Party, it contains absolutely nothing of Communism ... [123]

At the same time Li Dazhao did not conceal the fact that in the united front the Communist party, as a section of the Comintern, acted independently. From his point of view it even gave some "advantages" to the GMD, as the CCP could serve as a link between Sun Yat-sen's party and the world revolutionary movement, i.e., the Comintern. A delegate from Tianjin challenged Li Dazhao,[124] but the right-wingers nevertheless found themselves in the minority. They were vigorously opposed by many delegates including such prominent figures as Liao Zhongkai and Wang Jingwei.[125] Liao Zhongkai, for example, declared that "The time has come to understand that only in cooperation with other revolutionary parties can we accomplish the revolution victoriously."[126]

Sun Yat-sen's position was of particular importance. Sun strongly affirmed the trend toward genuine reorganization of the GMD, aspiring to use Soviet assistance and speaking out in favor of the admission of the Communists into the Guomindang.[127] As a result, the overwhelming majority of the delegates voted to allow the Communists to enter their Party. Ten Communists were even elected to the GMD CEC, which was composed of 41 persons – 24 full and 17 alternate members. These Communists were Li Dazhao, Tan Pingshan, Yu Shude (full members), Lin Boqu, Mao Zedong, Han Linfu, Qu Qiubai, Zhang Guotao, Shen Dingyi, and Yu Fangzhou (alternate members.)

The inauguration of the united front based on intra-party collaboration was a major result of the First Congress of the Guomindang, which adopted a Manifesto in this regard. The Congress definitely had an impact on the CCP leadership, which soon finally began to display real interest in the Guomindang organizational work. On the one hand, the Communists obviously received a powerful charge of energy as a result of their progressive cooperation with Nationalists; on the other hand, Borodin, probably at his own initiative, assiduously guided them in that direction.[128] The CCP leaders, however, went too far. Their enthusiasm in February 1924 led them to adopt a special "Resolution on the National Movement" that recognized as a main task the expansion of the GMD organization by recruiting workers, peasants and representatives of the urban middle class. As for the CCP itself, the resolution contended that it should turn its position inside the GMD entirely into a clandestine one in order to prepare secretly for the seizure of power within that Party. The Comintern Executive Committee at the time reacted to this "deviation" negatively, considering it "right-wing." The Eastern Department made efforts to correct it, and on Comintern instructions Voitinsky explained to the Chinese Communist leaders that work inside the GMD was not end in itself but a means of strengthening the CCP and preparing it for the future struggle outside and against the GMD.[129] The May 1924 enlarged plenum of the CCP CEC, which was prepared and supervised by Voitinsky, repudiated the February resolution.[130]

The CCP leaders' enthusiasm was, therefore, short-lived, lasting only about three months. It had no serious effect on the Party as a whole, and official entry into the GMD did not radically change the anti-Guomindang mood of most Chinese Communists. The CCP was still very young, and the Communists were taking their first steps in the united front. A particularly difficult problem was the psychological reception of the "entrist" policy. Having been compelled by the Comintern Executive Committee to accept it, the Chinese Communists as a whole simply could not stomach the tactic. This becomes especially obvious from an analysis of Chinese translations of the basic Comintern documents which were to determine the tactical course of the CCP.

This has to do first of all with Chinese editions of the theses of the Second Comintern Congress on national and colonial questions. Perhaps the earliest was the one published by the Beijing Socialist Youth League on January 15, 1922 in the first issue of their journal *Xianqu*. Entitled "Principles of the Third International on National and Colonial Questions," it was signed with the initials G. S., used by Li Da.[131] In early April 1922 a new edition appeared in the fourth volume of "Library of a Communist" printed by the CCP's Publishing house *Renmin chubanshe*. The translator was Shen Zemin who used the pseudonym Cheng Zeren. Shen's translation was probably widely known among CCP members; Chinese students in Moscow used it extensively in their courses.[132] In 1928 the Communist University of the Toilers of the East reissued this translation – without crediting Shen Zemin – in the collected *Resolutions of the Second Comintern Congress*, edited by A. A. Shiik.[133] In December 1924 the Chinese Communist Jiang Guangci published his own translation.[134]

The only Chinese edition of the Fourth Congress' "General Theses" appeared on June 15, 1923, in *Xin qingnian,* signed by the translator, Yihong.[135]

An analysis of these translations shows first of all that the earliest (*Xianqu*, 1922, no. 1) was abbreviated, containing only the first five theses of the "Resolution on National and Colonial Questions." The "Supplementary Theses" were not published in *Xianqu* at all. We may suppose that the reduction was caused by certain limits of the journal's size; as at the end of the publication there is a reference to its incompleteness. However, the lack of continuation in subsequent issues leads one to assume that the appearance of the abridged text was not accidental. The table of contents of the first issue reprinted in the third does not indicate the incompleteness of the translation. This table was not reproduced in *Xianqu*'s further issues. The theses, pulled out of contexts resemble a separate integral document. The publication's preface claims that they demonstrate the course of the Comintern in the anti-colonial revolution. Nonetheless, the translated fragment, alongside the idea of rallying to Russia the advanced workers of all countries and all the national liberation movements of the oppressed nationalities, proclaims, first, the falsity of bourgeois-democratic phrases about the equality of all men and nations in a class society, and second, the necessity of the struggle of the working class and the toiling masses in the colonial and dependent countries led by their Communist parties against capitalism and for the proletarian dictatorship. At the same time the publication conveys no information about Lenin's major ideas on the necessity of cooperation between all anti-imperialist forces. As we know, Lenin developed this concept in the additional theses of his Second Comintern Congress's resolution which were not published in *Xianqu*. The translation even accentuates the anti-capitalist aspect of the introductory part of Lenin's document. It says nothing about Lenin's notion that the Comintern should lead the revolutionary struggle of the working masses in the colonies and semi-colonies not only against the bourgeoisie, but also against the feudal landowners. It only points to the workers' struggle against the bourgeoisie. This publication, appearing at the peak of the intra-party discussion about the possibility of a CCP-GMD alliance, could only strengthen the ideological position of the ultra-leftists.

Other Chinese editions seemed to serve the same purpose. A careful study comparing them with the originals and with other translations demonstrates that the Chinese documents were apparently not translated from the originals but rather from other foreign language translations. Some of those translations, for example those of Roy's "Supplementary Theses", are full of distortions which make Roy's leftist points even more striking. These distortions were wholly passed on in the Chinese texts, especially in Jiang Guangci's careful translation. This was of course not the fault of Chinese translators, who probably knew nothing of the originals. But, in any case the Chinese translations of the "Supplementary Theses" sound extremely leftist, almost openly calling for the immediate combating of the national bourgeoisie in the colonial and dependent countries.[136]

At the same time Jiang Guangci was not meticulous enough in translating Lenin's "Theses on National and Colonial Questions," into which he introduced some errors, all ultra-leftist in character. The Eleventh Thesis in his translation is particularly significant. It holds that "The Communist International must *sometimes* enter into a temporary

67

alliance with bourgeois democracy in the backwards countries."[137] The superfluous word does not seem to be accidental.

Shen Zemin's translation likewise cannot be accepted as wholly objective. It is clear that the translator everywhere purposely replaced a definition "national-revolutionary" by the more expansive "revolutionary." This metamorphosis opened the door to a perverted interpretation of the Eastern policy of the Comintern. After all, the Chinese – like many other Communists in the world – did consider as genuinely revolutionary only a purely Communist movement. Hence, the substitution could lead to an inaccurate interpretation of the Comintern documents. Moreover, Shen incorrectly rendered a few phrases. For instance, in his translation the Ninth Thesis of Roy's document asserts that workers' and peasants' Soviets in colonies and semi-colonies must be organized "as soon as possible."[138] There are also some erroneous points which amplify Roy's well-known assertion that the revolutionary movement in the East was of major significance for the world revolution.

Even if the Chinese translators committed all these distortions unconsciously they should have been more circumspect in dealing with Comintern documents. The Soviet Sinologist V. M. Alekseev's criticism of the same kind of translations of Lenin's writings done in the 1930s for a Chinese edition of *Lenin's Collected Works* applies to all the above-mentioned interpreters. Having found a number of errors in the edition, Alekseev wrote in his review that

> After all, it is not a question of ordinary ephemeral translation of literary texts . . . An interpreter here must understand that he has as his direct task to translate such texts which will be referred to as the original . . . As a matter of fact, there must be no room here for a lack of skill and ignorance, and for all anecdotes, amusing incidents, and absurdities which come out of them . . . [139]

Of course, not all Chinese translators of major Comintern documents made fundamental mistakes. Some, like the translator of the "General Theses," Yihong, did an excellent job. The Chinese text of the "General Theses" differs radically from all aforementioned Chinese editions of the documents of the Second Comintern Congress. Despite certain errors and deviations of non-principled character, and the incorrect interpretation of some social and political categories (a mixture of definitions "a working-class" and "laboring classes," "capitalists" and "capitals," "national" and "nationalist"), nevertheless, it is this text that as a whole accurately conveys the Comintern's contradictory tactics in backward countries to a Chinese reader. Such works were, however, quite rare.

The Chinese translations of the documents of the Second Comintern Congress were more typical. The fierce desire to leave no stone unturned in their rush to achieve as quickly as possible the same accomplishments in their own country as the Bolsheviks did in Russia, led the Chinese Communists first to an open, and then hidden opposition to Lenin's political course. The perception of the new Bolshevik theory proceeded slowly.

Nevertheless, by the middle of the 1920s the belief of most CCP leaders in an immediate Chinese October had receded into the background, even though it had by no means disappeared. A small percentage of the Chinese Communists would return to that view later, after the accumulated frustrating experiences of the united front during the revolution of 1925–27. At the same time, their revival of Trotskyism would not be a result of their negative attitude to Leninist tactics in China, but rather a reaction to Stalin's shift in the Comintern policy toward the Chinese revolutionary movement.

Part III

Stalin's Shift in the Comintern's China Policy

Chapter 5 _____

The Birth of Stalinism

As discussed earlier, the Bolsheviks placed their hopes of building socialism in backward Russia on the victory of a proletarian revolution in developed Western countries. It was this hope upon which all their calculations were constructed. They strictly believed that only the world revolution could ensure the socialist future of the Soviet State. As Lenin stated in March 1918 at the Seventh Emergency Congress of the RCP(B), "Regarded from the world-historical point of view, there would doubtlessly be no hope of the ultimate victory of our revolution if it were to remain alone, if there were no revolutionary movements in other countries."[1]

In the system of moral and ideological coordinates within which the Russian left-wing radicals operated, Soviet power in Russia was only a part of a huge whole, the world socialist revolution, the victory of which seemed at hand. The notion of the victory of socialism in one country did not exist. The Bolsheviks were above all internationalists. As Lenin declared, "When the Bolshevik party tackled the job alone, it did so in the firm conviction that the revolution was maturing in all countries and that in the end . . . the world socialist revolution would come – because it is coming; would mature – because it is maturing and will reach full maturity."[2]

The Bolsheviks, first of all, were of course inspired by revolutionary romanticism: they viewed the crisis of the capitalist system, exacerbated by the world war, as heralding its collapse. The core of their thoughts about the international character of the socialist revolution, however, was based on facts. After all, the development of European and American capitalism into imperialism had resulted in the formation of the world economic system. The capitalist common market directly and indirectly subjugated the world economy, and transformed it into a unified whole. In this connection the building of a socialist economy in any individual country – still more so in a backward one – in the absence of world revolution or at least of revolutions in the most developed imperialist countries, was doomed to defeat.

The Bolshevik party determined the direction of Soviet Russia's internal and foreign policy according to this concept. In anticipation of the world revolution, the Bolsheviks, in the period immediately following their seizure of power, tried to ignore the fact that Russia had lost the war against Germany. They glossed over the complete disintegration of the Tsarist army and the economic devastation, on the one hand, and the relative might of the German military, on the other. They were convinced that the imperialist war would in the very near future develop into a civil ("revolutionary") war on a world scale, a war in which world socialism had to carry the day. Lenin had developed this idea as early as 1915, arguing that such a war was both inevitable and desirable.[3] But immediately after the October coup d'état the Bolsheviks had no forces to export the revolution to wage "revolutionary" war against imperialism. That is why they first tried to urge on the world revolution, even making use of the peace negotiations with the Central Powers at Brest-Litovsk (November-December 1917[4] – March 1918), not to sign a peace treaty, but to achieve a quite different goal: to exert a stimulating influence on the international labor movement.[5] They could not then have acted differently.

The Bolsheviks' idea of inevitability of the world revolution, however, conflicted with the reality at Brest-Litovsk: Austro-German imperialism threatened to crush Soviet power. The Brest peace was the fruit of this conflict, the first harsh defeat of the Bolsheviks' course toward preparation of world revolution. The war against Poland in 1920 turned out to be a new ("huge, unprecedented"[6]) defeat. Although the Bolsheviks considered their Polish campaign as a long-awaited transition from a defensive war against imperialism, i.e., against the imperialist intervention, to an offensive one,[7] the Red Army could not break through into Europe to stir up the flame of the revolution. The plans for the world revolution were ruined once again. Nevertheless, even this did not shake the belief of Lenin, Trotsky, and their comrades-in-arms in the forthcoming world-wide conflagration. At the Ninth Party Conference in September 1920 Lenin emphasized,

> Our basic policy has remained the same. We use any opportunity to proceed from defense to offense ... We say that the revolution can be created only by the efforts of advanced workers of advanced countries. Any conscious Communist has no hesitation on this account ... In spite of the complete failure of the first attempt, in spite of our first defeat, we shall proceed from a defensive policy to an offensive one again and again until we finally crush everybody.[8]

The Riga peace negotiations between Russian and Polish representatives – October 1920 to March 1921 – only convinced the Bolsheviks that the world revolution had been delayed, and that it was now necessary to wait not for a few months but for a few years. These circumstances facilitated acceptance of the new economic policy (NEP), which aimed at stabilizing the economic and political situation in the country and strengthening the party's links with the peasantry. But even this was done in anticipation of the world revolution, with the purpose of preparing for future "revolutionary" offensives.[9]

Therefore, in spite of obvious failures, the Bolsheviks' general strategic course remained constant. The party's maneuvers were tactical, implementing temporary retreats on a twisting path toward world socialism.

Nevertheless, their hopes were in vain, and, correspondingly, another important thesis proved false: the possibility of a real *socialist* breakthrough at a weak link of imperialism. The Bolshevik seizure of power was supported and stimulated by an anti-capitalist revolution of the Russian poor, but it inevitably led to the formation of a bureaucratic state. The actual development of the world situation did not correspond to the theoretical plan of revolutionary romanticism. Imperialism did not become the last stage of capitalism, the prelude to the socialist proletarian revolution. It had remained on its feet and even underwent a dynamic new development. The working class of the Western world had shown no readiness for a socialist upheaval. The world revolution had failed. The defeat of the German proletariat in the fall of 1923 was most significant. Many Bolshevik leaders saw the German events as new confirmation that world revolution would be delayed for a long period of time.[10]

Under these circumstances the Bolsheviks faced enormous problems of economic reconstruction. At the same time, it became more difficult to protect the party against the incursion of elements that were incapable of doing creative work. During the Civil War of 1918–20 it was frequently necessary to accept into the party everyone who fought for Soviet rule. The situation became even more difficult after the war ended. Lenin commented uneasily on the real pressure exerted by those who were possessed by a gigantic "temptation to join the governing party."[11] In 1922, according to figures in the all-party census, 92.7 percent of the members of the RCP(B) were only semiliterate.[12] The situation was aggravated in that Russia had yet to shape a civil society; the overwhelming majority of the population consisted of a semipatriarchal peasantry devoid of any democratic traditions whatsoever; and a backward proletariat was unable to organize production, hence, incapable of implementing its own dictatorship. The working-class dictatorship turned out in practice to be that of the party-soviet *nomenklatura* (cadre). The bourgeoisie was swept away despite the fact that as class-organizer of production it had far from exhausted its progressive role, but the working class was unable to replace it. The vacuum that had emerged in the managerial system naturally came to be filled by a proletarian bureaucracy, that is, by party-soviet officials with a proletarian background. This group began to express more and more its own corporate interests and the social moods of the poor rural and urban masses, from which it came. The blind, semiliterate masses, accustomed to being submissive, found their dictator in the bureaucracy. The suppression of capitalist development of Russia thus turned out to lead the country to the construction of a society that would have become alternative, but not post-capitalist. As a matter of fact, this society could not be socialist. After all, a basic feature of a post-capitalist socialism with an advanced civil society (at least theoretically) should be a public ownership of means of production. However, Russia found herself to be thrown back into the epoch of an Asian mode of production or so-called Oriental Despotism:[13] a distinctive characteristic of this system, as an alternative to capitalism, was a state ownership of the means of production, or, to be precise, a state, non-market monopoly over all spheres of social and economic life – a sort of modern analogue of the ancient non-Western civilization. This monopoly eliminated the right of private property, and inevitably established special rights for bureaucracy, as only the extensive army of state officials could serve its interests. The party-soviet bureaucracy acquired its leader. That leader was Stalin. The newly created system began to develop itself unrestrictedly, removing those who stood in its way.

The new situation in the world and the USSR – a decline in the revolutionary activity of the proletariat in the advanced capitalist countries and the establishment of a bureaucratic regime in the Soviet Union – had resulted in a deep political and ideological crisis within the Bolshevik party. A group of leading Communists who had staked everything on the October victory, but as romantics had continued to expect subsequent developments to turn out differently, began to feel great concern in regard to external manifestations of the bureaucratic system such as the strengthening of intra-party centralism and the destruction of remnants of democracy, the growth and official legalization of privileges of the party-soviet apparatus, the uncontrollable concentration of power in the hands of the Secretariat and Organization Bureau of the RCP(B) Central Committee, etc. Among these leading figures were Lenin and Trotsky. But Lenin became the first victim of the bureaucracy in its rush to unrestricted power. Ailing, he was confined to house arrest; dead, he was turned into an icon. Anti-bureaucratic forces were led by Trotsky, and it was Trotsky who attracted a new attack by the bureaucracy.

The first step in the bureaucracy's fight against him was the secret formation of the bloc of the three other members of the Politburo – Zinoviev, Kamenev, and Stalin, none of whom could have competed individually with Trotsky either in terms of popularity or in terms of the level of theoretical expertise. Taking advantage of Lenin's illness, this triumvirate, striving to isolate Trotsky, essentially blocked any possibility of democratic decision making in the highest levels of the party. At the same time, a very cautious and camouflaged campaign to discredit him was launched in the Soviet Communist party and the Comintern. During the course of the August 1924 plenum of the Central Committee a group of like-minded leaders held a conference,[14] during which they formed a so-called executive organ – *semerka* (group of seven) consisting of Zinoviev, Kamenev, Stalin, Bukharin, Rykov, Tomsky, and Kuibyshev. Feliks E. Dzerzhinsky, Kalinin, Molotov, Uglanov, and Mikhail V. Frunze became candidates for membership in this illegal, openly factional organ. Essentially, the *semerka* usurped the prerogatives of the party's highest organ. It discussed in advance the same issues later submitted to meetings of the Politburo. As V. Nadtocheev writes, "All of this was done in order that when they came to a Politburo meeting they would be ready to rebuff Trotsky unanimously and speak from a unified position concerning the issues that were discussed."[15] In addition, public attacks against Trotsky were stepped up, and increasingly he was blamed for his past disagreements with Lenin of the pre-October period. In January 1925 Trotsky was removed from the posts of People's Commissar for Military and Naval Affairs and Chairman of the USSR Revolutionary Military Council.

On the other hand, in the party leadership there emerged serious disagreements concerning the prospects of the further "socialist" construction. The indefinite postponement of the world revolution more urgently shaped the issue: was it possible to build (achieve the victory of) socialism in the USSR under conditions of capitalist encirclement? The issue became particularly sharp in the middle of the 1920s, after Lenin's death.

Trotsky, Zinoviev, and Kamenev had similar approaches to its solution. It was preceded by the beginning of a struggle for power that ensued between Zinoviev, who acted along with Kamenev, on the one hand, and Stalin, on the other. All these factors resulted in the creation of the United Anti-Stalinist Opposition. At the April 1926 plenum of the AUCP(B) Central Committee and Central Control Commission, Trotsky and Zinoviev for the first time expressed identical positions as opposed to those of the Stalinist leadership. Three months later, on the eve of the July plenum of the Central Committee and Central Control Commission, the platforms of both oppositionist groups were merged. On July 11, Zinoviev and Trotsky signed a joint declaration sharply criticizing the position of the Central Committee and its official organ *Pravda* in regard to a number of questions of international policy and the internal situation in the party. They answered the question regarding the possibility of building socialism in the Soviet Union alone in the negative. Their point of view can be summarized as follows: Socialism is possible – provided there are guarantees against outside efforts to restore capitalist relations – only once the country in which the revolution has triumphed has attained the highest level of development of productive forces, i.e., when in general it has reached the level that has been approached by the advanced imperialist countries, for imperialism, the Bolsheviks had asserted, was the highest and final stage of capitalism, the prelude to the socialist revolution! As far as Soviet Russia is concerned, it faces the task of overcoming the gap that separates it from the most developed countries as soon as possible. In this connection, Trotsky, for instance, suggested using vigorously and effectively all opportunities made available to the USSR through the world market. He wrote, "We can speed up our own development in every possible way only if we skillfully use resources arising from the condition of world-wide division of labor."[16]

However, even had it overcome the gap, Russia would not be able to build socialism: without the victory of the proletariat in the main countries of Europe, Trotsky persistently pointed out that it was impossible to arrive at socialism – because, first of all, the world bourgeoisie will constantly strive to overthrow Soviet rule by armed force; second, the world economy "*in the highest echelons* ... controls each of its parts, even if this part stands under the proletarian dictatorship and is building a socialist economy."[17] The foregoing, of course, does not mean that Trotsky denied the necessity of "socialist" construction in the Soviet Union. "The question is not ... whether it is possible and necessary to build socialism in the USSR," he wrote:

> A question like this is tantamount to a question such as whether it is possible and necessary for the proletariat to struggle for power in a particular capitalist country ... Our work on the construction of socialism is just as much a component part of the world revolutionary struggle as the organization of a strike by coal miners in England or the creation of factory cells in Germany ... Every economic success we achieve signals the approach of the European revolution.[18]

Although he hypothetically considered the possibility of the long-term stabilization of capitalism, and even a new and more vigorous development of its productive forces under the same social structure, Trotsky categorically rejected this perspective, being convinced that such a situation conflicted with Marxism. In his work *Towards Socialism or Capitalism?* he argued:

> It is absolutely clear that if the impossible became possible, if world capitalism and first and foremost European capitalism found a new dynamic equilibrium ... for its productive forces, if capitalist production in the next few years and decades undertook a new powerful ascension, it would mean that we, a socialist state, although about to pass over from a freight train onto a passenger one have, however, to chase an express. To speak more simply, it would mean that we made a mistake in basic historical assessments. It would mean that capitalism did not exhaust its

"historical mission", and its expanding imperialist stage was not at all a stage of a capitalist decline, of its convulsions and decay, but rather a prerequisite for its new blooming ... However, there is emphatically not any sensible basis for this variant.[19]

Trotsky's attitude to the world revolution thus was tied closely to his attitude to the October coup d'état itself. According to his logic, not only the latter's fate but also the assessment of its appropriateness depended directly on the victorious revolts of the European working class.

Stalin and his subordinates responded to the challenge of their epoch in a different way. Given that the world situation did not ensure the successful completion of socialist construction in the USSR, they simply disengaged themselves from it. They directed the Soviet Union along the way of isolated economic, political, and cultural development. Their platform took its theoretical grounds from the concept of building socialism in a particular country, i.e., in the USSR.

The roots of the concept can be found as early as November 1922 in Bukharin's idea concerning a "growing into socialism." Bukharin developed and expanded this idea in February 1924.[20] However, the conceptual exposition belongs to Stalin, and it was Stalin who at the end of 1924 put forward a corresponding political course in his work *The October Revolution and the Tactics of the Russian Communists*.[21]

The sharp divergence of this theory from Marxist tradition compelled Stalin to resort to open falsification for its justification. As the basis of his "scientific" arguments he erroneously interpreted a number of Lenin's citations wrenched from their proper contexts. In his references to Lenin he was much more categorical than Bukharin, who in February 1924 also cited authority of the dead leader for the construction of his own concepts, but at the same time made a reservation: "V[ladimir] I[lich] did not formulate it precisely."[22] Stalin used just three citations from three of Lenin's works, "On the Slogan for a United States of Europe" (1915), a public presentation at a plenary session of the Moscow Soviet on November 20, 1922, and "On Co-operation" (January 1923). From the first Stalin borrowed the idea that the uneven economic and political development of capitalism created conditions under which "the victory of socialism [was] possible first in several or even in one capitalist country alone."[23] From the second one he used a passage which states that "socialism is no longer a matter of the distant future," borrowing Lenin's conviction in the transformation of "NEP Russia" into socialist Russia.[24] From the third work Stalin took the notion that the power of the state over large-scale means of production, the dictatorship of the proletariat, the alliance of the proletariat with the many millions of small peasants, the assured proletarian leadership of the peasantry, and co-operation were all that was necessary and sufficient for building a complete socialist society.[25]

79

It is true that these citations truly create the impression that Stalin only generalized Lenin's thought in formulating the slogan of the victory of socialism in the USSR. Lenin's writings, however, indeed had no relations to Stalin's theory. Until crippled by a stroke, Lenin had remained devoted to the idea of the dependence of socialism in a particular country on the prospects of the world revolution. It was this problem, for instance, to which the concluding pages of Lenin's last writing, "Better Fewer, But Better" were devoted.[26] As to his article "On the Slogan for a United States of Europe", as well as to his "Military Programme of the Proletarian Revolution" that was written a year later and was also used by Stalinists for the justification of their theory, it is obvious that with the words "the victory of socialism" (in one country) and "already victorious socialism"[27] Lenin assumed the victory of a socialist revolution. Here he was not original at all: the given notion, as argued earlier, for the first time in the history of the Russian Social Democracy, was expressed by Trotsky a few years before Lenin. As regards Lenin's speech at the plenum of the Moscow Soviet and his notes "On Co-operation", they were devoted to internal problems of the USSR. In these works Lenin consciously left aside the international theme, not because he considered it of secondary importance but because at the time he wanted to focus on questions of economic and cultural construction. In both cases he even gave appropriate explanations to which neither Bukharin nor Stalin ever referred! For example, at the Moscow Soviet he maintained, "As to foreign policy ... We pursued the line that we had adopted earlier, and I think I can say with a clear conscience that we pursued it quite consistently and with enormous success ... No changes are necessary in this respect ... We have not changed to other trains, or to other conveyances."[28]

It was internal policy that had changed, not foreign policy. A year and a half earlier the Bolsheviks had inaugurated the NEP. That is why Lenin devoted his entire speech to the economic problems of the country. He did not, however, repudiate the notion that the building of socialism in the USSR in the long run depended on a result of the world revolution. The same is clear in his notes on co-operation. The entire article is devoted to an analysis of internal tendencies of the socialist transformation of the Soviet Union. Lenin highlighted the issues of power, ownership, the alliance of the proletariat with the peasantry, and the role that co-operation should play in the socialist transition and "cultural revolution". And he added:

> I should say that emphasis is shifting to educational work, were it not for our international relations, were it not for the fact that we have to fight for our position on a world scale. If we leave that aside, however, and confine ourselves to internal economic relations [only then!], the emphasis in our work is certainly shifting to education.[29]

As far as Lenin's "On co-operation" is concerned, one cannot ignore Trotsky's explanations at the Fifteenth AUCP(B) Conference in November 1926:

> Vladimir Ilich ... lists state conditions, conditions of property, and organizational forms of cooperation. Only!.. But, comrades, after all, we also know another definition of socialism by Ilich, and it holds that socialism is soviet power plus electrification. So here, does the citation [from Lenin's "On Co-operation" concerning the possibility of building socialism] I have read cancel electrification or not? No, it does not. All other things that Ilich has said about building socialism [including the thesis of the dependence of building socialism upon results of the world revolution] ... are supplemented by this citation.[30]

Nevertheless, Stalin was not confused by all this. He needed Lenin's authority, and that is why, having put forward his own course, he declared: "It was Lenin, and no one else, who discovered the truth that the victory of socialism in one country is possible."[31]

The debate between Oppositionists and the majority of the AUCP(B) Central Committee focused on the essence of the Russian Revolution itself. And in this connection it directly related to the basic issue concerning the ratio between international and national aspects in the concept of Bolshevism. The internationalist doctrine of Trotsky and his comrades-in-arms rested on the idea that Soviet power in Russia does not represent an absolute value in comparison with the revolution throughout the world. Trotsky, Zinoviev, and Kamenev maintained an allegiance to the principles of proletarian internationalism formulated by Lenin. According to the leader of the Bolsheviks, these principles demanded: "[F]irst, that the interests of the proletarian struggle in any one country should be subordinated to the interests of that struggle on a world-wide scale, and, second, that a nation which is achieving victory over the bourgeoisie should be able and willing to make the greatest national sacrifices for the overthrow of international capital."[32]

On the contrary, Stalin's theory in its maturity claimed a priority of the Russian "socialist" state system over all other matters of the world Communist movement. In the beginning of August 1927 Stalin would openly declare that

> A *revolutionary* is one who is ready to protect, to defend the U.S.S.R. without reservation, without qualification, openly and honestly, without secret military conferences; for the U.S.S.R. is the first proletarian state, revolutionary state in the world, a state which is building socialism. An *internationalist* is one who is ready to defend the U.S.S.R. without reservation, without wavering,

unconditionally; for the U.S.S.R. is the base of the world revolutionary movement, and this revolutionary movement cannot be defended and promoted unless the U.S.S.R. is defended.[33]

Such statements led to replacing internationalism with "red" great-power hegemony. How this hegemonic course was carried out in the period following Stalin's total conquest of power in the party and the state – since the end of the 1920s – was described cynically by his closest confederate, Molotov: "My task as minister of foreign affairs was to expand the borders of our Fatherland. And it seems that Stalin and I coped with this task quite well."[34]

Of course, Stalin and those who shared his views by no means rejected the idea of the world revolution, and they never ceased plotting for and preparing proletarian takeovers in various countries. Nonetheless, in contrast to those Bolsheviks who remained loyal to the old positions, Stalin viewed these takeovers only as a means to strengthen the role of the USSR in global politics. As Robert Tucker concluded, Stalin's "creative Marxism" was "Russia-oriented."[35] Therefore, the Stalinists would really betray any foreign Communist party, if in their view such betrayal would serve the interests of the Soviet state.

Stalin's theory of self-sufficient, autocratic development that laid the foundation for a new trend in Russian Communism – Stalinism – was in its essence national-communist. It reflected first of all the social feelings of the party-soviet apparatus which preferred to work on consolidating its dominating and privileged position rather than deal with the abstract ideals of the world revolution. After all, the implementation of Stalin's theory would make it possible, in the words of Trotsky, "in advance to designate as socialism everything that takes place and will take place within the [Soviet] Union, regardless of what takes place outside its borders."[36] In other words, it made it possible to continue to manipulate the masses skillfully, carrying the people with the alluring idea of "close and quite achievable social happiness," thus subordinating them to the bureaucratic dictatorship. This policy in a long run would lead the country to catastrophe and the society to degradation, for the self-isolation from the world was equivalent to slow suicide. But the bureaucracy did not take this into account.

At the same time Stalin's concept also reemphasized elements of the traditional values of Russian political culture which had receded into the background during the "Storm und Drang" period of the social revolution. Berdyaev was correct when he spoke of the polarized Russian soul, of the typical Russian "Nature" in which "two elements are always in opposition – the primitive, natural paganism of boundless Russia, and an Orthodox asceticism received from Byzantium, a reaching out towards the other world."[37] It is such features of the Russian national psyche which make the

Russians related to Asian peoples, i.e., unconditional acceptance of the independence of the state from public opinion, its priority over society, the rule of society over an individual, of executive power over the legislative one, the lack of distinction between power and property rights, attraction to ceremonial rites, communal unity of *obshchina* (traditional mutual protection), humility and patience, belief in a kind father (Tsar), etc.

Hence, Stalinism represented a logical result of the process of the further accommodation of Marxist theory to the specific conditions of Russia, but that of a new epoch, when in the absence of the world revolution the Communist regime came naturally to see itself as a national government. As such it received complete support of the majority of a people tired of wars and revolutions, a people who recalled its centuries-old love of order. And just as the Mensheviks in their early polemic with the Bolsheviks and Trotskyists were doomed to defeat, so the oppositionists in the new period had to lose to the Stalinists. They challenged the system, having started to discuss the need to reform it precisely at the moment when it was feverishly engaged in strengthening itself. At that time it was impossible to stop the inexorable process of entrenchment of power by the party-state bureaucracy. The rival forces were obviously unequal. Besides, the system that was actually created by the October Revolution could not, in the absence of world revolution, reform itself.

Chapter 6

The Genesis of Stalin's China Policy

The emergence of Stalinism as the dominant political doctrine of the AUCP(B) certainly had an enormous impact on Soviet and Comintern tactics in regard to the international Communist movement, including the CCP. Moscow's foreign policy closely followed Stalin's party's general course.

But the formation of Stalinism took time, and Stalin did not become a Russian national Communist overnight. In the beginning his concept of socialism in one country, above all, justified a bureaucratic system of power. For a few years after the publication of *The October Revolution and the Tactics of the Russian Communists* Stalin's thought still was in a "period of evolution." The idea of national superiority came later. And it was the events of 1925–27 in China that played a profound role in this development.

Archival evidence make it clear that Stalin began to elaborate his own view of the Chinese Revolution no earlier than the spring of 1925, soon after his break with Zinoviev, then chairman of the Comintern. Grigorii Voitinsky, who headed the Far Eastern Section of the Eastern Department of the Comintern Executive Committee, was the person who exercised significant influence upon Stalin at this time. One can see this, for example, in a letter that Voitinsky wrote to the Soviet Ambassador to China Lev Karakhan on April 22, 1925. This letter said, in part,

> The other day, in the course of a lengthy conversation with Stalin, it became evident that he believes the Communists have dissolved themselves into the Guomindang, that they lack an independent organization, and that the Guomindang is 'mistreating' them. While expressing his regrets about the dependent position of the Communists, Comrade Stalin believed that in China such a situation was apparently historically inevitable for the time being.

He was extremely surprised when we explained to him that the Communist party has its own organization, one that is more cohesive than the Guomindang, that the Communists enjoy the right of criticism within the Guomindang, and that the work of the Guomindang itself in large measure is being carried out by our comrades. In defending his views concerning the position of Communists inside the Guomindang, Stalin cited newspaper reports and, in general, our information coming from China. One may truly suppose that for people who haven't been to China and are unfamiliar with the way things are there, Borodin's communiqués would create precisely such an impression.[38]

At the time, the problem of a split within the Guomindang became exacerbated, provoked by a struggle over Sun Yat-sen's legacy between competing factions (Sun Yat-sen had died on March 12, 1925.) Voitinsky considered this a propitious moment to raise with the leadership of the ECCI, the RCP(B), and the Chinese Communist party the question of increasing the latter's efforts to strengthen its ties with the Guomindang leftists with the objective of excluding the rightists from the party. (To the latter category, the Communists assigned those persons who, from their perspective, represented the interests of the large and medium bourgeoisie.) Thus, he aimed at the radical transformation of the class and political character of the Guomindang by means of an intra-party seizure of power by the leftists and the Communists. This was openly expressed in the Comintern and Soviet Communist press in March 1925, in *Kommunisticheskii Internatsional* (The Communist International) and *Bol'shevik* (The Bolshevik).[39]

In and of itself, Voitinsky's proposal was nothing new. As argued earlier, the Chinese Communist leaders had been the first to raise this issue in February 1924 only to be repudiated. At that time the Comintern Executive Committee and Voitinsky himself had not been ready to accept such a policy. Nevertheless, Voitinsky seemed to return to this proposition when the situation in the GMD sharpened. His notion corresponded with the idea of transforming the Guomindang into some sort of "workers' and peasants' (or people's) party" – likewise not new. It was during the Fifth Comintern Congress in June 1924 that the first public mention was made of the need to form "multi-class" leftist parties in a number of countries of the East.[40] On June 30 in his report on the national question Dmitrii Manuilsky, member of the ECCI and chairman of the Congress Commission on national and colonial questions, for the first time raised the problem of the creation in a number of Eastern countries of "workers' and peasants' parties" which would have "a comparatively radical program of the struggle against imperialism."[41] He was supported by Roy, who advanced the formula of a "people's party" as an organization of "exploited" classes.[42] At that time, however, nothing came of these conversations. The Congress did not discuss the issue. Nevertheless, on behalf of the Congress's Commission Simon K. Brike, head of Turkish section of the ECCI Eastern department, drew up the draft resolution on the "Colonial and Eastern Questions" in which the idea reappeared. After a two-week discussion in the Commission, the draft was sent to Stalin, but at the time he repudiated the idea, stating that "the creation of such hybrid parties in India and China would be harmful."[43] He agreed to consider the possibility of forming such parties only in "several very backward countries."[44] As to the bloc with the Guomindang, he still viewed it in the spirit of the Comintern policy that had been given concrete form by Karl Radek in late July 1922 in his instructions to Maring.

The situation changed in the spring of 1925. Stalin considered so likely the possibility that Communists and other leftists in the Guomindang might seize power, and also hoped that the same might happen in other bourgeois parties of the larger countries of the East, that he reexamined Manuilsky's and Roy's formula. He embraced the concept of a "workers' and peasants' (people's) party" as a maneuver that might facilitate the establishment of the Communist party's hegemony in the nationalist movement. This was the angle from which he analyzed the draft resolution of the Fifth Enlarged Plenum of the Comintern Executive Committee (March-April 1925) concerning work in India. (The plenum did not adopt any specific resolution concerning China.) In his remarks on this document, Stalin singled out the question of establishing Communist hegemony in the future Indian "people's party."[45]

Stalin's instructions were immediately put into effect by the Eastern Department of the Comintern Executive Committee which disseminated them throughout China without delay. In this connection, "The Communist Party of China," Voitinsky said rather transparently, "even though it is the party of the industrial proletariat, will not establish the hegemony of the proletariat directly as in purely capitalist countries nor even as it did in pre-revolutionary Russia, but rather via the national-revolutionary party. The maneuvering of the Chinese Communist party in this milieu, stirring up the waves of the anti-imperialist movement and simultaneously conducting a vigorous struggle against petite bourgeois wavering of this party in regards to the policy toward imperialists, are at present the main tasks of the Communists in this country."[46]

In May 1925 Stalin finally expressed himself openly on this issue. He dwelled on it in a speech to the Communist University of the Toilers of the East delivered at an anniversary gathering of students and teachers from this school on May 18, 1925. At this time, he defined the Guomindang as being already a real "workers' and peasants' party," and posed the question of establishing the CCP's hegemony within it as an immediate task:

In countries like Egypt and China ... the Communists can no longer set themselves the aim of forming a united national front against imperialism. In such countries the Communists must pass from the policy of a united national front to the policy of a revolutionary bloc of the workers and the petty bourgeoisie. In such countries that bloc can assume the form of a single party, a workers' and peasants' party, **after the model of the Kuomintang** [Guomindang], provided, however, that this distinctive party *actually* represents a bloc of two forces – the Communist Party and the party of the revolutionary bourgeoisie ... Such a dual party is necessary and expedient, provided it does not bind the Communist Party hand and foot,.. provided it facilitates the actual leadership of the revolutionary movement by the Communist Party. Such a dual party is unnecessary and inexpedient if it does not conform to all these conditions, for it can only lead to the communist elements becoming dissolved in the ranks of the bourgeoisie, to the Communist Party losing the proletarian army [emphasis added].[47]

In this speech as well as in his report delivered a few days earlier (on May 9) to the activists of the Moscow Party Organization on the work of the Fourteenth Party Conference which was held before, Stalin also publicly formulated his thoughts concerning the level of socioeconomic development in the East. His theses coincided with Roy's ideas: "Until now the situation has been that the East was usually spoken of as a homogeneous whole. It is now obvious to everybody that there is no longer a single, homogeneous East, that there are now capitalistically developed and developing colonies and backward and lagging colonies, and they cannot all be measured with the same yardstick."[48]

In the May 18 speech he elaborated this idea further:

We now have at least three categories of colonial and dependent countries. First, countries like Morocco, which have no proletariat or almost no proletariat, and are industrially quite undeveloped. Second, countries like China and Egypt, which are industrially little developed, and have a relatively small proletariat. Third, countries like India, which are capitalistically more or less developed and have a more or less numerous national proletariat.[49]

And in his May 9 speech he pointed to the "rapid rate" of development of capitalism in all colonial countries.[50]

This finally led him to the thesis about the changing character of the revolutionary process in some Eastern countries. He concluded that, by May 1925, the revolutionary movement in the "industrially developed and developing colonies" – i.e. India, China, and Egypt – already faced the need to resolve the same tasks that the Russian revolutionary movement faced on the eve of 1905.[51] He now believed that the revolutionary process in these countries had acquired more of a democratic than an anti-imperialist character. It was then generally accepted in the Comintern that in no circumstances could "representatives of the national bourgeoisie" implement a democratic program of revolution in the East; this was something only Communists could do. When one considers this formula, it is easy to see that Stalin's reasoning provided additional support for his idea that it was necessary to establish the hegemony of the CCP in the "workers' and peasants' Guomindang" as quickly as possible.

These statements did not surprise ECCI officials; Stalin's extreme leftist approach to the problems of the revolutionary movement in the East was well-known in the Comintern. Roy had indeed strongly influenced his analysis of the socioeconomic condition of the Eastern countries, the nature of their liberation movement, the level of class consciousness of the labor masses, and the prospects and pace of the transformation of their national revolutions into the democratic and the socialist ones. This became obvious in the summer of 1924, when Roy for the first time since Lenin's death resumed his attempts to revise the basic principles of Comintern anti-colonial theory. Asked to draft a Fifth Comintern Congress resolution on the "Colonial Question,"[52] he once again put forward the thesis that "The Communist International admits the necessity of mobilizing the colonial masses on the basis of class policy, on the basis of class interests with a view to conducting a ruthless struggle against imperialism and conciliatory policy of an indigenous bourgeoisie."[53]

Raskolnikov and Manuilsky actively polemicized with him. As a result his draft was rejected by the Fifth Comintern Congress Commission on national and colonial questions. Then Roy attempted to formulate his views as an amendment to the draft resolution outlined by Brike. Here is what he proposed:

> Taking into account the fact that a bourgeois national movement in practically all important colonial and semi-colonial countries (Egypt, India, Turkey, Persia, the Dutch East Indies, China, the Philippines) is not a revolutionary struggle against imperialism and that in many countries it has resulted in a compromise with imperialism, the formulation [of the Comintern course which had been outlined in accordance with the decisions of the Second and Fourth Comintern Congresses] ... should be changed. The bankruptcy of bourgeois nationalism, which has refused to struggle against imperialism and only desires to get an opportunity to exploit native laborers in the alliance with imperialism, transfers all weight of the struggle for the liberation onto the shoulders of workers and peasants.[54]

The Commission turned down this amendment and, as we know, sent Brike's draft to Stalin. The document was accompanied by a letter from Manuilsky in which the head of the Fifth Congress Commission informed Stalin about Roy's opposition. But Stalin remained dissatisfied with the draft not only because at the time he disliked the idea of "workers' and peasants' parties." He explained his point of view in his July 31, 1924 reply to Manuilsky:

> You speak about your disagreements with Roy, who is emphasizing the social aspect of the struggle in colonies. I do not know how these disagreements basically look like. But I must say that I also dislike some parts of the Congress resolution from the point of view of a social aspect [!] . . . I think the time has come to raise the question on the hegemony of the proletariat in the liberation struggle of such colonies as India, whose bourgeoisie is conciliatory (vis-a-vis the imperialism of England), and the victory over which (that is over a conciliatory bourgeoisie) is the basic condition of the liberation from imperialism . . . It is necessary to crush a conciliatory national bourgeoisie . . . It is necessary to concentrate all blows on a conciliatory national bourgeoisie and to put forward the slogan of hegemony of the proletariat as a basic condition of liberation from imperialism.[55]

At the time, however, Stalin advised Manuilsky not to revise the draft but to postpone the question until the next Comintern Congress. Nonetheless, he himself suddenly went back to the issue nine months later.

Accepting Stalin's views as their guide, the Eastern Department of the ECCI again responded without delay. The Department's report to the Sixth Enlarged Plenum of the Comintern Executive Committee in February-March 1926 emphasized that, "In the period covered by this report, the work of the Eastern Department was based on the concepts Comrade Stalin outlined in his speech at the anniversary celebration of KUTV [the Communist University of the Toilers of the East]."[56]

The influence of the corresponding Stalin directives was also evident in the work of the Sixth Plenum, which in contrast with the Fifth Plenum adopted a special "Resolution on the Chinese Question." The resolution declared:

> The political actions of the proletariat[57] have provided a powerful impetus to the further development and strengthening of all revolutionary democratic organizations in the country, in the first instance the **people's revolutionary party, the Guomindang**, and the revolutionary government in Canton [Guangzhou] . . . The tactical problems of the Chinese national revolutionary movement closely resemble the problems faced by the Russian proletariat during the 1905 Revolution.[58]

The rapid upsurge of the anti-imperialist movement in China at this time helped to crystallize Stalin's views. The movement was characterized by the intensification of workers' struggles, an increase in the activities of the CCP and of Soviet advisors in the Guomindang and its army, and also the obvious and apparently long-term increase of interest on the part of the Guomindang leaders in the development of relations with the USSR and even with the Communist International. The latter manifested itself in a flurry of "leftist," pro-Communist rhetoric at the Guomindang's Second Congress in January 1926. This was also evident in the speech by Hu Hanmin, one of the leaders of the Guomindang, on the first day of the Sixth Plenum of the ECCI. He actually said the following, "There is only one world revolution, and the Chinese Revolution is a part of it. On basic questions the teachings of our great leader Sun Yat-sen concur with Marxism and Leninism ... The Guomindang's slogan is 'For the popular masses!' This means that the workers and peasants must take political power into their own hands."[59]

In February 1926, soon after the Second Congress of the Guomindang, the GMD Central Executive Committee even directed an official request to the Presidium of the Comintern, asking that the GMD be admitted into the Comintern. In a letter transmitted by Hu Hanmin, the GMD Central Executive Committee emphasized that, the "Guomindang is striving to fulfill the task that the revolutionary movement in China has faced for thirty years, namely, the transition from a national revolution to a socialist one."[60]

This was indeed startling. In February 1926, leaders of the Central Committee of the AUCP(B) and the Comintern Executive Committee seriously considered the aforementioned request by the Guomindang CEC. A majority of the Politburo even voted to admit the GMD as a sympathizer party.[61] However, caution then gained the upper hand. Acting on a proposal of the Presidium of the ECCI, and following consultation between Voitinsky and Stalin and Zinoviev, an evasive letter was drafted to the GMD CEC.[62]

Events did not move, however, in the direction that the leaders of the Comintern were urgently pushing them. The implementation of the Comintern resolutions, which were directed at communizing the Guomindang, turned on the almost transparent attempt of Soviet advisors and Chinese Communists to seize control of the apparatus of the GMD Central Executive Committee and the Nationalist government. This naturally led to Chiang Kai-shek's anti-communist "coup" in Guangzhou on March 20, 1926, just five days after the conclusion of the ECCI Sixth Plenum. The connection between the "coup" and the "offensive line and seizure of power" that the Comintern Executive Committee conducted toward the Guomindang was acknowledged indirectly, i.e. without directly accusing the Comintern Executive Committee. This was done by a

Politburo Commission of Inspection, visiting Guangzhou in February–March 1926 to carry out inspections, which stumbled into the epicenter of events[63] as well as by Moisei Rafes, the Secretary of the Far Eastern Bureau of the ECCI, who was in the city in late July and August.[64]

There could be no mistake that the "coup" was directed against both the Chinese as well as the Soviet Communists (that is, Soviet military and political advisers), and their attempts to strengthen their influence in the Guomindang. The "coup" signaled the establishment of a virtually open military dictatorship of Guomindang "centrists" on the territory controlled by the GMD's Nationalist government. Furthermore, the "coup" significantly weakened not only the position of the Communists, but also the Guomindang leftists who were grouped around Wang Jingwei, the chairman of the Nationalist government. Wang left the country, and several Communists found themselves temporarily under arrest. The League of Chinese Military Youth that they headed was dispersed, and peasant unions in the villages which were mass organizations that had constituted one of the most important fields of the Guomindang and CCP activity since the summer of 1924 were disarmed. The most serious development from the CCP's perspective was that soon after the "coup", in May 1926, at the Second Plenum of the GMD Central Executive Committee, the Chiang Kai-shek faction put forward a series of demands aimed at significantly limiting the political and organizational autonomy of the CCP inside the Guomindang.[65]

What was Stalin's immediate reaction to these events? Historians usually point out that the General Secretary of the AUCP(B) Central Committee forced the Chinese Communists to make concessions to Chiang Kai-shek in order to preserve the united front.[66] This is true. But exactly how and when did he do this, and what motivated him to do so?

The documents make it evident that in the first days after the "coup", the Bolshevik leadership was certainly gripped by confusion. Awareness of defeat could not come at once and the dearth of information also made itself felt.[67] At first, Stalin and his supporters simply tried to play for time, counting on a rapid upsurge of the mass worker-peasant movement in Guangdong which might make it possible to neutralize the putschists. This is evident, for example, from the fact that at the very beginning of April, in a discussion of general problems of Soviet-Chinese-Japanese relations – the draft resolution had been prepared by a commission headed by Trotsky – it was Stalin who proposed including the two following paragraphs in the text:

> In the near term the Guangzhou government must concentrate all its efforts on the internal strengthening of the republic by carrying out appropriate agrarian, financial, administrative, and political reforms, by drawing the broad masses into the political life of the

South China republic, and by strengthening its internal defense capacity.

In the present period, the Guangzhou government must put aside any ideas about conducting offensive military expeditions and, in general, of taking any actions that might push the imperialists onto the path of military intervention.[68]

Needless to say, what was meant by "offensive military expeditions" was the Northern Expedition. In speaking out against this, Stalin was obviously motivated by the entirely logical fear that under the pretext of wartime conditions, the advance of Guomindang armies to the North would inevitably limit the possibility of radicalizing the Guangzhou regime. The Politburo agreed with his point of view.[69]

Not a single Soviet leader, in the period immediately following the "coup", proposed that the Communists leave the Guomindang. At a session of the Politburo discussing reports from Guangzhou that some Chinese Communists were contemplating anti-Chiang Kai-shek actions, even Trotsky proposed a resolution condemning such "insurrectionary" intentions. [70] It was not until some time later, in the second half of April 1926, that Trotsky proposed to the Politburo that the CCP withdraw from the Guomindang.[71] Approximately at the same time Voitinsky temporarily hesitated with regard to this question. In a letter to Chen Duxiu of April 24, he proposed "terminating efforts to form a joint alliance with the Guomindang."[72] Shortly thereafter, the April 29 meeting of the Politburo discussed a report from China saying that the forthcoming May plenum of the GMD Central Executive Committee would address head-on the question of the CCP's future in the Guomindang. At this meeting, Voitinsky proposed that "in case of dire necessity" the best-known Communists should leave the Guomindang of their own accord. He also expressed the view that "in the extreme case" consideration should be given to the possibility of wholly "demarcating the boundaries between the Communists and members of the Guomindang in conducting future work on the basis of collaboration between two independent parties." Zinoviev supported him.[73]

Stalin, however, could not accept these proposals, which demolished his entire tactical plan. After all, from his perspective, a few weeks earlier, the Communists were on the eve of seizing power in the "workers' and peasants' Guomindang." According to Stalin's logic, one could not simply surrender the positions that had been "conquered"; this would be tantamount to unjustified capitulation to the Guomindang "rightists."

On April 29, 1926, a secret Politburo resolution on the problems of the united front in China was adopted. A CCP split with the Guomindang was considered out of the question; Stalin, however, agreed to return to the matter later if it turned out the trend inside the Guomindang "for organizational demarcation with the Communists was strong . . ." For the time being, the policy of active CCP intervention in the internal affairs of the Guomindang with the aim of ousting rightists from the party was confirmed. The only innovation was the decision to slow down the tempo of the Communist offensive inside the GMD in order to regroup forces. Stalin considered it necessary to make only "internal organizational concessions to the *Guomindang leftists* in the sense of a shuffling of personnel . . ."[74] The focus was only on "leftists." The Politburo considered Chiang Kai-shek's action as a conflict between the Communists and their objective allies (none of the Soviet leaders viewed Chiang Kai-shek at the time as a "rightist.") The resolution was adopted unanimously. Zinoviev also voted for it; Trotsky did not attend the meeting.

In May 1926, the Politburo expressed opposition to the Northern Expedition as it had done before. "In view of the complicated . . . circumstances," it reluctantly approved the dispatch of only a small expeditionary corps of the National Revolutionary Army of China "to defend Hunan province as the approach to Guangdong, with the proviso that the troops not disperse themselves beyond the borders of this province." At the same time, it ordered the Comintern Executive Committee and the Soviet government to "increase its assistance in all ways, in terms of finances and personnel, to the Communist party, advising it, incidentally, to step up its work inside the Guomindang, and pursue a line of isolating the Guomindang rightists."[75]

Chiang Kai-shek's rather skillful maneuvering, among other reasons, helps to explain why the Politburo considered concessions to Chiang Kai-shek necessary measures to facilitate the regrouping of forces in the leftist camp. A short while after the "coup", Chiang placed limits on the activity not only of Communists, but also of "rightists," some of whom were relieved of their posts. At the end of May, one of the most ardent advocates of excluding the CCP from the GMD, the Guangzhou Chief of Police, Wu Tiecheng, was even arrested. Borodin, Moscow's chief informant on Chinese affairs, viewed this as a concrete manifestation of the "power-lessness" of the rightist faction. He interpreted the resolution adopted by the Second Guomindang Plenum limiting the activity of the CCP as merely a tactical step intended to "remove misunderstandings" between the Communist party and "honest Guomindang members." He even believed that, "the resolution adopted by the [GMD] CEC Plenum on the Communists dealt a sharper blow to the rightists than to the Communists."[76]

The Politburo's tactics could not be successful, however, in the concrete conditions unfolding in China. The Northern Expedition became a reality against Stalin's will. Because it had incorporated some of the militarists into its own ranks, the officer corps of the National Revolutionary Army became increasingly conservative; the influence of the rightists thus grew. Commander-in-Chief Chiang Kai-shek increasingly shifted toward their position. In the summer of 1926, even the AUCP(B) CC Politburo ceased to consider him as a "leftist" and began to view him as a "centrist". Inasmuch as the balance of forces in the GMD was not in its favor, the CCP was powerless to effect a purge of "anticommunists" from within the ranks of the Guomindang. It was in these circumstances that Stalin was forced to abandon his tactic of cautious offensive and the regrouping of forces and shift to a temporary retreat. He decided to make concessions to the "rightists," although neither he nor his supporters had abandoned their hopes for the communization of the Guomindang. As Aleksandr Martynov, one of Stalin's collaborators later characterized the tactics of retreat, "We retreat so that we may leap forward better."[77]

Judging from the archival materials, Moscow's decision that the Communists should make concessions to the "rightists," was made no earlier than the end of October, 1926. On October 26, on the proposal of Stalin's collaborator, Kliment Voroshilov, USSR People's Commissar for Military and Naval Affairs, the Politburo adopted the directive to the Far Eastern Bureau of the ECCI in Shanghai forbidding the development of a campaign against the Chinese bourgeoisie and the feudal intelligentsia, i.e. those elements whom the Comintern traditionally considered as "rightists." The directive emphasized that:

> As long as the danger from the imperialists and the North exists, and the prospect of conflict with them is unavoidable, the Guomindang must protect all of its potential allies and fellow-travelers. We agree that the agrarian problem must be put onto the agenda as a practical matter, and that victory is impossible without the peasants. However, the near-term development of civil war in the villages at a time when war with imperialism and its agents is at its height would weaken the fighting capacity of the Guomindang.[78]

The directive was addressed to the Far Eastern Bureau in response to its telegraphic report of October 22. The latter was composed by Voitinsky[79] who sought the leadership's permission for the Chinese Communists to unleash a mass movement in the rear of the NRA.[80]

Commenting on the Politburo's October directive, shortly after the defeat of the Communist movement in China, Stalin characterized it as an unfortunate misunderstanding. "It was an isolated, episodic telegram, totally uncharacteristic of the line of the Comintern, of the line of our leadership," he explained at the July-August 1927 Joint Plenum of the Central Committee and Central Control Commission of the AUCP(B).[81] Voroshilov also considered it an isolated, spur-of-the-moment occurrence.[82] However, Stalin's and the Politburo's refusal to support Voitinsky's proposals was indeed evidence of their new political course in China.

Judging by Rafes's declaration, which was made at the end of November 1926, shortly after his return to Moscow from China, this was exactly how the Far Eastern Bureau interpreted the telegram. This, moreover, was the only political directive of a general nature that this organ had received during the five months of its operation in China (June-October 1926).[83]

The ideas formulated in the aforementioned directive were affirmed and elaborated in the speeches of Stalin's comrades-in-arms, Nikolai Bukharin and Fyodor Raskolnikov, who were leaders of the Comintern, at the Fifteenth Conference of the AUCP(B) which ran from October 26 to November 3, 1926. Their speeches offered a different characterization of the social composition of the Guomindang than that given at the Sixth Plenum of the ECCI. Reverting to the assessments that had prevailed in the Comintern until mid-May 1925, Stalin's supporters characterized the Guomindang on this occasion as a party that united in its ranks not only workers, peasants, and the "urban democrats," but also the medium commercial-industrial bourgeoisie. Moreover, they no longer called for transforming the GMD into a "worker-peasant" organization at a rapid tempo, but for the most part stressed the need to make every effort to preserve and strengthen the united front in China. They underscored the need for the CCP to avoid any sort of actions whatsoever that might lead to splits or even cracks within the united front.[84]

The retreat did not continue for long, however. The aggravation of the situation inside the Guomindang where the struggle for power among various leaders intensified in late 1926, compelled Stalin once again to make adjustments in his China policy. The Seventh Enlarged Plenum of the ECCI (November-December 1926) signaled the beginning of a new, albeit this time rather cautious, Comintern shift in the direction of seizing power in the Guomindang.

On the eve of the plenum, disagreements arose within the leadership of the AUCP(B) concerning the immediate tasks of the revolutionary movement in China and, correspondingly, over the line of the CCP. Two extreme points of view were represented. First was Raskolnikov's, vigorously supported by Bubnov, and Manuilsky. Second was Pavel Mif's, the pro-rector of the Sun Yat-sen University of the Toilers of China whose views were also shared by a number of Soviet and Comintern representatives in China.

Raskolnikov proceeded to develop a variant of the notion that the CCP should continue to retreat before Chiang Kai-shek, the "centrists" and the "rightists," believing that the pursuit of agrarian revolution in China was "inappropriate" while the national liberation movement was developing. He also was extremely cautious with respect to the revolution's future prospects, hypothesizing that it might "take one of two paths." First, it might go the way of Turkey, i.e. degenerate into a military dictatorship of the large industrial bourgeoisie, with Chiang Kai-shek becoming a Kemal

Pasha. Second, it might lead to the creation of a "petite bourgeois government *supported by* the working class and peasantry, under the protection of the Soviet Union."[85]

Mif stood much more to "the left," emphasizing the need to "develop the proletarian tendencies of the Chinese revolution." He categorically rejected a "Turkish" or "Kemalist" path of development for China, affirming only one prospect. "In China [we] will have the power of the revolutionary petite bourgeoisie *with the organizational role* of the proletariat. We will have a full worker-peasant government."[86] In his draft theses Mif even included the demands to "organize peasant soviets without delay" and "evict all gentry,[87] notables, and landlords who held the instruments of power and exploited the Chinese peasantry."[88]

Finally, on November 30, 1926, speaking at the session of the Chinese Preparatory Commission of the ECCI, Stalin intervened in the dispute between Raskolnikov and Mif. His speech was rather conciliatory. On the one hand, he supported Raskolnikov, putting special emphasis on the nationalist character of the unfolding Chinese revolution and didn't say a word about the "tendency toward compromise" of the Chinese national bourgeoisie. On the contrary, once again, as he had prior to 1925, he saw this class as a real, albeit "weak" member of the united front. Moreover, he censured "some comrades" who believed that "there would have to be a repetition among the Chinese of exactly the same thing that took place here in Russia in 1905."[89] He also expressed disagreement with Mif on the question of establishing peasant Soviets:

> Mif is running too far ahead. One cannot build Soviets in the countryside and avoid the industrial centers of China. But the establishment of Soviets in the industrial centers of China is not at present on the order of the day. Moreover, it must be borne in mind that Soviets cannot be considered out of connection with the surrounding situation. Soviets – in this case peasant Soviets – could only be organized if China were at the peak period of a peasant movement.., on the calculation that industrial centres of China had already burst the dam and had entered the phase of establishing the power of the Soviets. Can it be said that the Chinese peasantry and the Chinese revolution in general have already entered this phase? No, it cannot.[90]

On the other hand, Stalin demonstrated that he had not abandoned his hope for the establishment of CCP hegemony in China at what he deemed an appropriate time. His speech makes it clear that the ideal which took shape in his brain in the preceding period was merely temporarily pushed forward into the future. He again grounded his thought in the notion that sooner or later the national bourgeoisie would pass over to the side of reaction, and that the role of the leader of the revolution would inevitably pass into the hands of the Chinese proletariat and its party. Under their leadership a revolutionary democratic dictatorship of the proletariat and peasantry would be established in China, which would resemble a democratic dictatorship of the proletariat and the peasantry such as the Bolsheviks had foreseen for Russia in 1905, "with the difference, however, that it will be first and foremost an anti-imperialist government."[91] The reference to the anti-imperialist character of the future "worker-peasant" power in China first and foremost lacked any substantive meaning, however. Stalin frankly emphasized that this would be a government "transitional to a non-capitalist or, more exactly, a socialist development of China."[92]

The General Secretary also opposed excessive caution with respect to the revolution in the Chinese countryside, albeit only in general terms. He simply emphasized that one should not be afraid of the involvement of the peasantry in the revolution. "The more quickly and thoroughly the Chinese peasantry is drawn into the revolution," he pointed out, "the stronger and more powerful the anti-imperialist front in China will be."[93] Stalin refrained, however, from stipulating any concrete steps that might attract the peasants to the CCP and the Guomindang, noting only that "What the perspectives should be in this regard, and how far it is possible and necessary to go, depends on the course of the revolution."[94]

The Seventh Plenum naturally agreed with Stalin's point of view. A new draft composed by M. N. Roy, a member of the Chinese Preparatory Commission, formed the basis of the final text of the resolution concerning the situation in China. Roy's draft was supplemented by Raskolnikov, Bubnov, and Stalin.[95] It was passed by the Plenum on December 16, 1926. The document as a whole characterized the social composition of the Guomindang differently from that of the Sixth Plenum of the ECCI. It had defined the Guomindang as a bloc of four social groups – the proletariat, the peasantry, the urban petite bourgeoisie, and parts of the national bourgeoisie – rather than as a "workers' and peasants' party."[96] The Seventh Plenum of the ECCI also defined the prospects for the development of the Guomindang differently, observing that even when "the basic motive force becomes a more revolutionary bloc – a bloc of the proletariat, the peasantry, and the urban petite bourgeoisie," this will not mean the elimination of the entire bourgeoisie from the arena of the national liberation struggle.[97] In this connection, the Plenum cautiously approached the formulation of demands which, from its perspective, the CCP and the Guomindang ought to put forward as their agrarian program in the districts under the control of the Nationalist government. The resolution presented Raskolnikov's proposals, namely, no agrarian revolution, but rather rent and tax reduction, confiscation of land from counterrevolutionaries, and so forth.[98]

At the same time, the resolution expressed the idea that as the Chinese revolutionary movement developed, the CCP would succeed in converting the Guomindang into a "genuine people's party," establish its own hegemony within it, and then form a revolutionary, anti-imperialist government which would conceive of itself as a "democratic dictatorship of the proletariat, the peasantry, and other exploited classes." Moreover, the document indicated that in pursuing its policy in the countryside, the CCP should not be afraid of the possibility of exacerbating the class conflict. On the contrary, it was obligated to accord the question of agrarian revolution "a prominent place in the program of the national liberation movement," without worrying that such a formulation would weaken the united anti-imperialist front.[99]

These new tactics were also reflected at this time in Stalin's directive on China sent to Borodin on December 17, 1926. On the one hand, it still stipulated the need to direct the urban struggle only "against the big bourgeoisie and, most of all, against the imperialists, so that to the maximum extent possible the petite and medium bourgeoisie would remain within the framework of the united front against a common foe ..." On the other hand, it also emphasized that, "the general policy of retreat in the cities and the curtailment of the workers' struggle to improve their position is incorrect ... Decrees against the freedom to strike, against workers' meetings and so forth are absolutely impermissible."[100]

This was still a far cry, however, from a real offensive. In practice, the tactics of flirting with the rightists was continued for a while longer. In the beginning of 1927, it even led to the establishment of official relations between the Communist International and the Guomindang. It was made in response to another request from the Guomindang Central Executive Committee and this time from Chiang Kai-shek himself. The request was delivered via Shao Lizi, a well-known Guomindang figure, who visited Moscow in September 1926. The Presidium of the ECCI, with the blessing of the Politburo, passed a resolution concerning the mutual exchange of representatives between the Comintern and the Guomindang. According to it, the representative of the Guomindang Central Executive Committee, which Shao Lizi himself became, was made a member of the Presidium of the ECCI with a consultative vote.[101]

Thus by the spring of 1927 Stalin's attitude to the Chinese revolution had been shaped in most details. It was in sharp contrast with Lenin's theory of anti-colonial revolution.

Part IV

Trotsky's Views on China in Flux

Chapter 7 _____

Trotsky and the Formation of the United Front in China

As a member of the Political Bureau of the Bolshevik party Central Committee through October 1926 and of the Party Central Committee until October 1927, Trotsky was intimately involved in top-level discussion on Soviet foreign policy. What was his attitude toward the Politburo-ECCI tactics of the united front in China? How did he react to Lenin's shift, in regard to Eastern countries, away from the concept of permanent revolution to the idea of national collaboration?

The available documents indicate that Trotsky at first could not wholly accept Lenin's views concerning the anti-imperialist united front. This is evident, for instance, from his report to the June 1921 Third Comintern Congress, entitled "On the World Economic Crisis and the New Tasks of the Communist International."[1] In this report he insisted that an indigenous bourgeoisie's

> struggle against foreign imperialist domination cannot . . . be either consistent or energetic in as much as the native bourgeoisie itself is intimately bound up with foreign capital and represents to a large measure an agency of foreign capital. Only the rise of a native proletariat strong enough numerically and capable of struggle can provide a real axis for the revolution. In comparison to the country's entire population, the size of the Indian proletariat is, of course, numerically small, but those who have grasped the meaning of the revolution's development in Russia will never fail to take into account that the proletariat's revolutionary role in the Oriental countries will far exceed its actual numerical strength. This applies not only to purely colonial countries like India or semi-colonial countries like China, but also to Japan, where capitalist oppression blends with a feudal-caste, bureaucratic absolutism.[2]

As can be seen, Trotsky' view came directly into conflict with Lenin's "Theses", but he was quite in agreement with Roy's "Supplementary Theses", favoring the preparation of an immediate Socialist revolution of the Russian type in the Eastern countries.

How long did he continue his opposition to the united front? Did he oppose the ECCI's decision to push the Chinese Communists into the Guomindang?

Many historians have taken the answer to these questions as self-evident. After all, Trotsky himself, in a well-known letter to Max Shachtman dated December 10, 1930, said that he had opposed joining the Guomindang "from the very beginning."[3] Therefore, he had never changed his negative attitude to Lenin's tactics. However, the issue is not as simple as Trotsky's claim implies. One problem is that there are several inconsistencies in Trotsky's well-known later accounts (written and published while he was in defeat and exile) of his position on this question – inconsistencies that no one up to now seems to have noticed. They begin with the above-mentioned letter to Shachtman, in which, while claiming always to have opposed joining the Guomindang (a policy decided in 1922), Trotsky at the same time dates the start of his opposition to 1923. On January 8, 1931, a month or so after writing this letter, in his reply to a message from the Chinese Left Opposition,[4] Trotsky again explained his position on the question of entering the Guomindang. He said,

> The entrance of the Communist Party into the Kuomintang [Guomindang] was a mistake from the very beginning. I believe that this must be stated openly – in one or another document – especially since in this instance the Russian opposition to a large extent shares the guilt. Our group (the 1923 Opposition) was from the first, with the exception of Radek and a few of his closest friends, *against* the entry of the Communist Party into the Kuomintang and against the admission of the Kuomintang into the Comintern. The Zinovievists held the opposite position. With his vote, Radek put them in a majority in the Opposition center ... As a result, the United Opposition [of Trotskyists and Zinovievists] took an equivocal position on this question, which was reflected in a whole series of documents, even in the Opposition platform.[5]

We are entitled to ask "from the very beginning" of what? From the beginning of the offending tactic, in 1922? From the beginning of the first Trotskyist Opposition, in October 1923? Or from the beginning of the anti-Stalin bloc, in April 1926? If from 1922 or 1923, why then did Trotsky say that he was prepared to "share the guilt"? Between 1922 and 1926 Trotsky was under no factional restrictions, so if he had wanted to oppose the Comintern's policy in China, there was nothing to stop him from doing so.

However, by insisting that he "shares the guilt", he would seem to be implying that even before 1926 he had at the very least tacitly tolerated the tactic. Whatever the case, his real position on the united front before 1926 is by no means clear from this document.

Finally, in his book *The Stalin School of Falsification*, completed in the autumn of 1931, Trotsky twice pointed out that Stalin's policy in China had been wrong from 1924,[6] implying that his opposition to the policy had begun in that year.

The second problem is that some of Trotsky's public statements from the period between 1922 and August 1926 contradict all the accounts from the exile period that we have just quoted. They suggest that Trotsky fully supported the basic principles of the united front as expressed by Lenin and then developed by Radek in his instruction to Maring. In other words, at least sometime in 1922 he changed his opposition to Lenin's tactics, and wholly accepted the ECCI policy in the East, including China. Perhaps this change occurred in the fall of this year and was perhaps connected with his participation in the organization of the Fourth Comintern Congress that gave so much attention to the Eastern world.

For example, on December 28, 1922, shortly after the Fourth Congress, in accordance with ideas adopted by the Communist International, Trotsky told a session of the Communist Faction of the Tenth Soviet Congress,

> It goes without saying, that colonies – Asia, Africa (I am talking about them as a whole), despite the fact that like Europe they represent greatest divisions, if we take them separately and isolated, they are not ready at all for the proletarian revolution. In the colonies, we see a growing national revolutionary movement. There, Communists make up nothing more than small cells grounded in the peasantry ... The development and influence of the ideas of socialism and communism, the liberation of the toiling masses of the colonies, the weakening of the influence of the nationalist parties can be guaranteed not only and not so much because of the role of the indigenous Communist cells but because of the role of the revolutionary struggle of the proletariat of the metropolis for the liberation of the colonies.[7]

Continuing to admit the national character of the revolutionary movement in the East, he wrote in March 1923 in his "Thoughts About the Party",

> In the West we are dealing with the struggle of the proletariat for power, but in the East we "only" deal with the emancipation of mostly peasant nations from a foreign yoke. Surely, if we discourse abstractly, these two movements belong to different epochs of social development, but, after all, they are connected together

historically. They are directed against the same enemy – imperialism, from two different sides.[8]

Trotsky repeated the same ideas in his report to the Seventh Conference of the CP(B) of the Ukraine on April 5, 1923, having especially attracted the attention of the audience to the fact that the Comintern leaders, including himself, had viewed the world revolution "as the struggle of the proletariat for power in the West and the struggle of colonial and semi-colonial peoples of the East for their national liberation."[9] At the same time he found it necessary to consider settling national revolutionary problems especially "tactfully", having pointed out that "if . . . the misunderstanding between the proletariat and peasantry as a whole is very dangerous, it is a hundred times more dangerous when the peasantry does not belong to the same nationality that [is] a dominating nationality."[10]

Trotsky expressed his ideas about the anti-colonial revolution most systematically in a speech delivered on April 21, 1924, on the occasion of the third anniversary of the founding of the Communist University of the Toilers of the East. He said,

> There is no doubt that if the Chinese Guomindang Party succeeded in uniting China under the national-democratic regime, capitalist development of China would move ahead in leaps and bounds. All this is paving the way for the mobilization of the innumerable proletarian masses that will wrench themselves free from their prehistoric semibarbarian existence into the factory furnaces of industry . . . The national movement in the East is a progressive factor of history. The struggle for the liberation of China, Sun Yat-sen ideology, is a democratic struggle and a progressive ideology, but it is bourgeois. We stand for the Communists supporting the Guomindang in China, pushing it forward.[11]

Trotsky also followed Lenin's emphasis in adjusting Bolshevik theory and politics to the concrete situation faced by Eastern countries, holding that "the temporary exploitation of Marxism in the interests of bourgeois-progressive politics is possible and inevitable in the countries where capitalism is only just developing." In this connection, he urged the Comintern to "translate not only the ideas of Marxism and Leninism into the languages of China, India, Turkey, and Korea," but also to "translate into the language of Marxism the sufferings, passions, demands, and needs of the labor masses of the East."[12]

These views were reflected as well in a number of other of Trotsky's works which were devoted to the Eastern countries including China and Japan.[13] Were these statements diplomatic gestures toward other Party and Comintern leaders? Apparently not. An even greater objection to Trotsky's later version of events can be found in intra-Party correspondence sent by

Trotsky to other members of the Soviet leadership in the first half of the 1920s and in unofficial documents circulated by him among his followers in the second half of the 1920s.

One document relevant to this study is a letter, dated January 20, 1923, from Trotsky to Adolf Joffe, at the time a Soviet representative in China, written in reply to a letter of thirty-odd pages in which Joffe complained of the Politburo's lack of confidence in him and accused it of chaining him hand and foot in his China work.[14] Joffe was at that time busy drafting an aformentioned declaration together with Sun Yat-sen. He was then among the strongest supporters of the entry of the CCP into the Guomindang. In his reply, Trotsky rejected Joffe's complaint and said,

> You wrongly assess the Politburo's policy on the Chinese question. The Politburo has adopted your general theses. In particular, there has been emphasis on the need – in spite of each and every change in the composition of the government in China – to continue systematic work in order to support the democratic Organization of Sun Yat-sen and to combine with it [i.e., that Organization] the work of the Chinese Communists ... So in these basic questions there has been no question of distrusting you.[15]

Another relevant document is a note that Trotsky wrote on November 2, 1923, to Chicherin, then People's Commissar of Foreign Affairs, and to Stalin in which he said, "From letters of Karakhan [then in China], it is clear that Chinese affairs are proceeding very badly ... There is no party and no serious propaganda. By the way, taking account of the amorphousness of Chinese political life, a somewhat organized and centralized Guomindang Party would have a decisive meaning."[16]

As for unofficial documents from the second half of the 1920s, one particularly striking piece of evidence regarding Trotsky's view of the united front is contained in his private letter to Radek of June 26, 1926. In it he wrote: "The organizational cohabitation of the Guomindang and the Communist party was correct and progressive for a certain epoch."[17]

Another important document is Trotsky's note "The Chinese Communist Party and the Guomindang", written on September 27, 1926, but not published at the time. In it Trotsky said: "The participation of the CCP in the Kuomintang [Guomindang] was perfectly correct in the period when the CCP was a propaganda society that was only preparing itself for future *independent* political activity but which, at the same time, sought to take part in the ongoing national liberation struggles."[18]

Many years later Trotsky wrote practically the same thing to Harold Isaacs.[19] In a letter dated November 1, 1937, Trotsky explained to Isaacs the background to the Comintern's decision to press the CCP to enter the Guomindang, and his understanding of the significance of this policy in the initial period:

He [Maring] was on an official mission and based his activity ... on the mandate of Zinoviev, Radek, and Bukharin, possibly with the consent of Stalin .... [T]he whole episode falls in 1922 if I remember well. Lenin was sick. I was totally isolated from the work of the Comintern and saw Maring for the first time later on his trip back from China ...

[T]he entering in itself in 1922 was not a crime, possibly not even a mistake, especially in the south, under the assumption that the Kuomintang [Guomindang] at this time had a number of workers and the young Communist party was weak and composed almost entirely of intellectuals ... In this case the entry would have been an episodic step to independency [sic], analogous to a certain degree to your entering the Socialist Party. The question is what was their purpose in entering and what was their subsequent policy?[20]

These archival materials reveal the truth about Trotsky's position on the united front "from the very beginning": he not only failed to oppose the CCP's entering the Guomindang, but actively favored it. This notion is supported by the fact that no one working in the various Trotsky archives anywhere in the world has up to now ever discovered the slightest evidence that Trotsky denounced the entryist tactic in China in the first half of the 1920s.

Even later, in the period of 1924–25, when in the ECCI there was shaped a concept of a "workers' and peasants' (multi-class) party", Trotsky's attitude to the policy of entrism did not change. Here is how Trotsky himself explained this fact in a letter to Isaacs, dated November 29, 1937:

You mention for the first time the attitude of the Left Opposition in the Chinese question. For your own knowledge it is necessary to say the following: During '24 and '25 the Chinese question was handled through the channels of the Comintern by personal agreement between Stalin and Zinoviev. The Polit-Bureau was never consulted. The policy of Borodin was never even mentioned in the Polit-Bureau. It was the prerogative of the Comintern, in reality of Stalin-Zinoviev. Only episodically could I intervene in the matter; for example, when I voted in the Polit-Bureau against the admission of the Kuomintang [Guomindang] into the Comintern as a sympathizing party. Only in '26 after the split between Zinoviev and Stalin did the secrets become by and by revealed. But Zinoviev himself was bound by his previous policy and a series of internal discussions in the Left Opposition proceeded [sic] our first open statements. This explains the great delay in the public fight on the Chinese question.[21]

These words are confirmed by an analysis of Trotsky's episodic statements on China which were made in the period followed the Fifth Comintern Congress.[22] One can judge from them, that at the time Trotsky just contented himself with general phrases concerning the significance of a national liberation movement in China and the necessity of the alliance between the proletariat of advanced countries and the Chinese democrats.[23] That was also typical for his open speeches of the winter-spring 1926. It is difficult not to agree with Deutscher, who pointed out that at the time Trotsky appeared to have given to China "far less attention and far less weight than he gave British and even Polish Communist policies."[24] While being removed from participation in the determination of Comintern policy in China, he almost constantly tolerated the ECCI course. His opposition to the Politburo decision to admit the Guomindang to the Comintern that took place in February 1926 remained an isolated episode. At the same time his non-interference into the ECCI business in China also seems to have been favorable to the Comintern. Although Trotsky remained uninitiated in all details of ECCI China policy, he could follow events in this country and did so with great interest and sympathy for the national revolutionary movement. At the time he made no criticism at all of the Comintern doctrine of "multi-class" parties.

Nor did he change his position in January-March 1926 when he finally found himself actively involved in Chinese problems. His attention was not, however, centered on the Communist movement in China. Trotsky was drawn into the Chinese Eastern Railway (CER) problems after they had became acute. The railway, which crosses North Manchuria, was constructed by Russian industrialists on the basis of an unequal 1896 treaty concluded by the Tsarist and Chinese governments. According to agreements signed on May 31, 1924, by the USSR and China and on September 20 the same year by the Soviet representatives and Zhang Zuolin (an actual ruler of Manchuria), on October 3, 1924 the railway was passed over to joint Sino-Soviet control. In the beginning of 1926 the Zhang Zuolin regime in Manchuria organized a series of armed provocations in the Chinese Eastern Railway area which turned into violent acts against Soviet railway workers. The situation was given careful consideration by the Bolshevik Politburo. A number of steps were undertaken to settle the conflict peacefully and it was Trotsky among the Politburo members who played a major role in this process. Most of his propositions became part of the final decision of the Politburo. They combined a vigorous pressure on Zhang Zuolin via the Soviet Commissariat of Foreign Affairs with the punishment of those Soviet officials at the Chinese Eastern Railway who had demonstrated great-power bias towards the Chinese.[25] The Politburo decision in this regard was passed on March 18, 1926.[26] The Politburo, however, did not accept one of Trotsky's proposals – concerning the necessity of making a public declaration on the "constant readiness" of the USSR to "hand the railway over to the People's government of China."[27]

Having temporarily decreased the tension in the Chinese Eastern Railway area, the Politburo nevertheless recognized that it was still an issue. On the same day, March 18, 1926, it passed a resolution concerning the organization of a special commission that would work out a long-term program of Soviet foreign policy in the Far East, mainly toward China and Japan.[28] Chicherin, Voroshilov, and Dzerzhinsky were confirmed as its members,[29] and Trotsky was appointed chairman.

The work of the commission comprised two stages. By March 22 a rough draft on Soviet policy toward Japan and Manchuria had been prepared, and by March 24, theses concerning relations with China. The main author of both documents was Trotsky.[30] The commission brought them together and on March 24 passed the final draft resolution sent by Trotsky to the Politburo the next day.[31] The basic contents of the resolution titled "Problems of Our Policy with Respect to China and Japan" defined the major priorities of Soviet diplomacy in the Far East. Two key points were emphasized: first, to orient Soviet foregn policy toward ensuring the most favorable conditions possible for the development of the revolutionary movement in China; second, to stimulate diplomatic activity directed at strengthening peaceful and mutually advantageous relations among the USSR and Japan, Manchuria, and China. The authors in particular emphasized the need to promote a situation in China that would stimulate the peasantry's involvement in the revolution, and secure the leadership of "proletarian organizations" over the revolutionary movement. As regards those steps which should be undertaken by Soviet diplomacy in order to improve relations with Manchuria and Japan, practically all of them concerned problems of the Chinese Eastern Railway; the commission, in essence, repeated Trotsky's offers, which had been already approved by the Politburo on March 18. Besides, the resolution contained some recommendations of a tactical character addressed to the Guomindang and the CCP – to improve their relations with Japan, to play on political contradictions between Japan and England, and to establish a *modus vivendi* with France.

On March 25, 1926 the Politburo ratified basic propositions of the commission with respect to USSR foreign policy toward Manchuria and Japan,[32] and on April 1, the draft resolution, slightly corrected and supplemented by some amendments, was passed as a whole.[33] Besides the already mentioned Stalin amendment in regard to concentrating the GMD government efforts on internal strengthening of the Guangdong base and putting aside any plans about the Northern expedition, the most serious additions were the offer to the Guomindang Central Executive Committee to strengthen the work in the National Revolutionary army as much as possible and the decision to develop a vigorous political campaign in

China, England, and elsewhere against the expulsion from China of the USSR's ambassador Karakhan.[34] The demand to expel the latter had been put forward by Chinese conservatives.

The meetings of the Politburo at the end of March and on April 1 disclosed some disagreements between Trotsky and the majority of the Politburo with respect to China. Unlike other Politburo members Trotsky seems not to have considered the Northern military expedition of the Guomindang army harmful to the Chinese revolution, at least not on March 18 while preparing for the meeting of the Politburo that was to have been held later that day. Instead, he was thinking over "a strategic and political plan (the moving of the Guomindang north.)"[35] As to the Karakhan question, he believed it possible to make certain concessions, suggesting some sort of chess castling: to send Karakhan as the USSR representative to Japan where he would replace Victor L. Kopp who, in his turn, would be transferred to Beijing.[36]

The thesis about strengthening work in the army did not engender any polemics. Having brought the authorized corrections into the text of the resolution, on April 3, 1926 Trotsky sent the final document to the Politburo.[37]

The disagreements with the majority of the Bolshevik leadership still were not principled in character. Trotsky did not yet feel that Stalin's China policy had been shifting far from Lenin's initial course. Only when he realized that the gulf between bourgeoisie and proletariat in China was rapidly widening, but that the AUCP(B) CC Politburo did not want to direct the Chinese Communists to distance themselves from the Guomindang, did he began to reexamine Comintern tactics in China. It was his proposal in the second half of April 1926 to withdraw from the GMD after Chiang Kai-shek's "coup" that provoked disagreement.

Chapter 8 _____

The Rise of the Russian Left Opposition and the Chinese Question: In Search of a United Platform

Trotsky at first failed to find his bearings after the March 20 "coup", most likely, because of the dearth of information. It appears that the possible decisions in respect to the CCP that were to be made by the forthcoming May Plenum of the GMD Central Executive Committee broke the ice. At the moment Trotsky acted impulsively; it is obvious that he was not prepared to seriously defend his proposal that the CCP make a break with the Guomindang, as he still had little knowledge of China.

From all indications, it appears that Trotsky presented his corresponding April opinion in oral form. In the open conflict that ensued, the Stalinists frequently referred to his proposal, but never once presented documentary evidence of what had been said, although at times the situation seemed to call for such proof.

The proposal by Trotsky, as well as the later one by Zinoviev, revealed for the first time crucial differences among Politburo members on the most important questions of the Chinese revolutions. "Our first disagreements with the leading core of the present Politburo in regard to the Chinese question already refer to the beginning of 1926," Zinoviev and Trotsky wrote later at the end of May 1927.[38] (Voitinsky's similar notions were not of great importance to members of the Politburo. Voitinsky himself was a minor person in a great gamble between Stalin and Trotsky. Besides, he actually belonged to the Stalinist majority. In subsequent years nobody except Zinoviev mentioned his propositions.) Here is how Bukharin, at the July (1926) joint Plenum of the Central Committee and Central Control Committee recalled what happened, "It was proposed to us, first by Comrade Trotsky, and then by Comrade Zinoviev, that the Communist Party must *break with the Guomindang*, must withdraw from the Guomindang and on this question there exists a specific resolution by the Politburo."[39]

Stalin informed the Plenum essentially along the same lines, adding only a few details to Bukharin's account. "It was about two months ago," he said,

> when Zinoviev came to the Politburo with a number of directives for the Chinese Communists, demanding that we allow *the Chinese Communist Party to withdraw from the Guomindang*. Even earlier, Comrade Trotsky came to the Politburo with this same proposal, but the Politburo rejected it. Comrade Zinoviev actually repeated Comrade Trotsky's proposal. The Politburo rejected this a second time, stating that the policy of withdrawal of the Chinese Communist Party from the Guomindang, given the present international situation, would be a policy of liquidating the Chinese revolutionary movement, a policy of surrendering the Guomindang to the mercies of the Right Guomindang members ... [40]

The Politburo resolution referred to by Bukharin and Stalin was adopted at the session of April 29, 1926. Regarding Trotsky's and Zinoviev's proposals, it stated in part, "The question of a break between the Guomindang and the [Chinese] Communist Party is recognized as having prime political importance. Such a break is to be regarded as absolutely inadmissible. It is recognized as essential to pursue a line of maintaining the Communist Party as part of the Guomindang."[41]

Although Trotsky was the first who raised the question, it was Zinoviev who provoked the greatest ire among Stalin and his supporters. After all, being chairman of the Comintern Executive, Zinoviev bore the whole responsibility for the policy that had been carried out by the AUCP(B) CC Politburo in China and led to the Chiang Kai-shek "coup" of March 20. An analysis of his declarations regarding China made from 1924 to the beginning of 1926 confirms this. His characterization of the Guomindang as a "workers' and peasants' (multi-class) party", and his assessment of the role and tasks of the CCP, were entirely in keeping with those of Stalin. Zinoviev's theses "Immediate Problems of the International Communist Movement" prepared for the Sixth ECCI enlarged Plenum are particularly revealing. He stated in part,

> The labor movement has made a number of important gains in China: the organization of trade unions which hold a class point of view, the growth of influence of the people's revolutionary party, Guomindang, that has ties with the Communists, the strengthening of the revolutionary government in Canton [Guangzhou] – the first example of the revolutionary democratic government in the East that relies on the broad masses of toilers in cities and countryside and conducts a steady struggle against imperialism.[42]

It the beginning of February 1926 Zinoviev was one of the most active adherents of the idea of admitting the GMD into the Comintern. This, for example, is demonstrated by the surviving record of his talks with Hu Hanmin, who visited him on February 8, 1926. Here is what Zinoviev held at the time: "Now, I think, it is necessary for me to put forward one important question for my discussion with you, Comrade Hu. It concerns whether the Guomindang should unite with the Third International, and whether these relations should be not only by name, but also in essence."[43]

Certainly, Hu Hanmin warmly supported Zinoviev; it was during this meeting when he handed over to the chairman of the ECCI an official letter from the GMD Central Executive Committee that contained the request for admitting the Guomindang into the Comintern.[44] And it was Zinoviev who requested Hu Hanmin to address the Sixth ECCI Plenum.

Having cooperated with Stalin vigorously in everything that concerned the CCP's forward policy in the Guomindang, from the beginning of 1925 Zinoviev had begun to distance himself, however, from the General Secretary in all other matters. As mentioned earlier, in the beginning of April 1926 for the first time he and Trotsky expressed identical positions opposing those of the Stalinist leadership in regard to a number of questions of international policy – China was not mentioned – and the internal situation in the party. That might explain why at the April 29 meeting of the Politburo Zinoviev actually supported Trotsky's preceding proposal concerning the possibility of the CCP's withdrawal from the Guomindang. Of course, formally he supported Voitinsky's notion, not Trotsky's, but he must have been aware of how his statement would have been interpreted by the Stalinists, who were upset over his new alliance with their principal enemy.

Stalin sought revenge by inflicting a painful blow. He decided to discuss the statements of the Oppositionists at the next, July 1926 Joint Plenum of the AUCP(B) Central Committee and Central Control Comission. On June 15, 1926 he confided to Molotov and Bukharin his intention to "give the Plenum the Politburo's report on the Special File[s][45] issues and, when discussing it in the Plenum, mention all the squabbles in the Politburo, so that the Plenum can have its say."[46] And along with Bukharin he did so in spite of the fact that neither Trotsky nor Zinoviev insisted on their proposals concerning the CCP and the Guomindang. Having received no support in the Politburo, Zinoviev, for example, not only voted for the Stalinist resolution at the April 29 meeting of the Politburo, but also did not get back to the matter even during the Politburo hearings of the Bubnov Commission report about its work in China – the hearings took place on May 20, 1926. The report dealt directly with Chiang Kai-shek's "coup".[47]

Bukharin was particularly critical. While speaking on China he dredged up practically all the past disagreements and differences demonstrated by his opponents since the beginning of 1926. He not only mentioned the proposal to withdraw from the Guomindang, but also the Karakhan question. Among other charges he accused Trotsky of having proposed to "surrender" the Chinese Eastern Railway to China. Bukharin interpreted Trotsky's proposal to make an official statement about the readiness of the USSR to pass the Chinese Eastern Railway over to the People's government of China as a betrayal. Later, in May 1927, at the Eighth ECCI Plenum, Trotsky addressed Bukharin's attack:

> [W]hat he says is a lie. The only thing I proposed at that time – after the words of comrade Rudzutak who said this railroad becomes an instrument of imperialism now and then (for which Bukharin attacked Rudzutak) – was a declaration from our side in which we repeat in an open and solemn manner, that which we had already said once in the Peking [Beijing] decisions:[48] The moment the Chinese people has created its own democratic unified government, we will freely and gladly deliver the railroad to them in the most favorable conditions. The Po[l]itburo said: No, at this time such a declaration will be interpreted as a sign of weakness, we will make this declaration a month from now. Although not in agreement with this, I raised no protest against it. It was a fleeting discussion which was only later, transformed in a wretched manner, in an untruthful way, then, coined over into a rounded-off formula, launched in the party organization, in the nuclei, with warped insinuations in the press – in a word, just as it has become the custom and practice with us in recent times.[49]

The Plenum's word was final. The resolution adopted by an overwhelming majority of votes with only eleven voting against, stated:

> The Plenum of the CC ... declares the proposals of the Opposition (Trotsky, Zinoviev) to be plainly opportunist and capitulationist ... The CC considers that such a position would make sense only in the event of the complete elimination of the national-revolutionary movement in China, i.e., a complete and solid capitalist stabilization on this most important sector of the colonial front of the class struggle. Without by any means excluding a wide-ranging freedom to maneuver, the CC considers that under the existing conditions there are absolutely no grounds for the above-mentioned proposals of the Opposition and that, taken as a whole, they constitute the expression of an inadmissible defeatism.[50]

In their speeches at the Plenum, neither Zinoviev nor Trotsky tried to explain their position on China. Apparently they hoped to do this in a statement dealing specifically with the differences on the Chinese question. Zinoviev wrote the statement,[51] but was not allowed to attach it to the minutes of the Plenum.

In August 1926 Trotsky returned to the problems of the revolutionary movement in China (although this time he did so on a strictly private basis, not bringing up the question for open discussion in the party). Nor was he the initiator of the discussion on this occasion. The debate was renewed by one of his most active supporters in the struggle against the Stalinist majority of the Bolshevik party, Karl Radek, who since 1924 had engaged in a systematic study of China[52] and who since the autumn of 1925 had headed the Sun Yat-sen University of the Toilers of China, a special educational institution established in Moscow for the theoretical training of both Guomindang members and the Communist cadre of the Chinese revolution.

Until the summer of 1926 Radek had wholeheartedly supported the line of the ECCI on China, and as one of the Comintern's "China specialists" had played an important role in promoting the ECCI line. Despite his participation in the Trotskyist Opposition and his sharp polemics against the Stalinists on questions of bureaucratization of the party, economic policy, and "socialism in one country," on everything relating to China Radek essentially shared Stalin's and Zinoviev's point of view.[53] Sometimes he was even more explicit on China's problems than the leaders of the Bolshevik party and the Comintern. For instance, having picked up the thesis about the "worker-peasant Guomindang" when it was openly, but casually proclaimed by Stalin, Radek made it an absolute formula and in August 1925 conceived an idea that the Guangzhou government was "the first worker-peasant government" of China.[54] However, he temporarily doubted the necessity of the entry policy at the beginning of 1926, but nothing came out of his doubts. He discussed his ideas with "some comrades, who led ... [the Comintern] work in China" – these must have been Zinoviev and Voitinsky. They turned them down, and Radek submitted to their judgment.[55] Shortly after this he confirmed his thesis about "the worker-peasant nature" of the GMD government.[56] Being confused about the real outcome of Chiang Kai-shek's "coup", in a March 26, 1926 *Pravda* article Radek contended that nothing serious had happened in the South of China.[57] At a crucial Politburo meeting of April 29, in a discussion of the resolution on the problems of the united front in China, he wholly supported Stalin and opposed Voitinsky's and Zinoviev's proposals concerning the withdrawal from the Guomindang. (Nothing is known about his attitude to Trotsky's corresponding notion.) He expressed the idea that "at the moment of the rightists' offensive ... one should not overstrain horses when water threatened to sweep away a wagon."[58]

The further development of the situation in Guangdong, however, in which the Chinese Communists suffered a partial loss of political independence inside the Guomindang, forced Radek once again to begin to question the correctness of the Central Committee's China policy. On June 22, 1926, he completed some rather sharply polemical material on this question and acquainted his Oppositionist comrades with it. It was titled "On Fundamentals of the Communist Policy in China." In this document he pointed out the "incessant frictions" that had arisen between the CCP and the GMD. He then explained that both organizations had begun to transform into mass parties. Under these circumstances, he went on, the policy of entrism was not already ensuring the revolution, but rather weakening it. "There are two ways out of this situation," Radek maintained:

> Either the Communists' repudiated their independent policy and accepted complete subjugation to the Guomindang ... or they had to pass from the present forms of cooperation to a bloc with the Guomindang as a bloc of two independent parties ...
>
> Now we have reached the moment when it is necessary to put forward the question concerning the modification of forms of relations between the Guomindang and the Communist party ... The Guomindang and the Communist party should have independent local and central organizations.[59]

Radek's position attracted Trotsky's attention, and on June 26, 1926, Trotsky sent Radek a note in which he set forth several propositions in regard to questions Radek had raised. First, he asked Radek to think through how to disprove the argument of Stalin's majority which justified the necessity of the united "democratic-communist party" in China by the fact that the bourgeois and laborers of this country were fighting a common enemy – foreign imperialism. Second, he suggested that Radek investigate in detail how powerful the Chinese labor movement was at the time. Concluding the letter, he wrote that, "The organizational cohabitation of the Guomindang and the Communist party ... has approached the end. In the present epoch this cohabitation more and more becomes a brake."[60]

As he continued to reflect on the problems of the Communist movement in China, Trotsky addressed another letter to Radek, on August 30, 1926, emphasizing the following point in particular:

> The fact of the matter is that the existence of national and even colonial oppression does not at all necessitate the entry of the Communist Party into a national-revolutionary party. The question depends above all on the differentiation of class forces and how this is bound up with foreign oppression. Politically the question presents itself thus: is the Communist Party destined for an extended period of time to play the role of a propaganda circle recruiting isolated co-thinkers (inside a revolutionary democratic party), or can the Communist Party in the coming period assume the leadership of the workers' movement? In China there is no doubt that the conditions are of the second order.[61]

The tone of the letter testifies to the enormous amount of inner mental work that Trotsky was forced to do before finally reaching the conclusions he came to. He was still guided mainly by intuition. He had no deep or systematic knowledge of China, and that fact prevented him from presenting to the Politburo, the Central Committee, and the ECCI his doubts about the correctness of the Stalinist line in China. This circumstance to a large degree explains why for several months after speaking out in April he did not again take up, on an official level, the question of the revolutionary movement in China.[62] In the same letter developing his proposition of June 26, he asked Radek to help provide information about the CCP, the Guomindang, and China in general, and he frankly admitted that the ideas he had arrived at "must be proved, perhaps if only in a very general way."[63] The following explanation is significant:

> This question deserves attention and elaboration ... It is extremely important to organize the basic factual data on the development of the Kuomintang [Guomindang] and the Communist Party (the areas where they spread; the growth of the strike movement, the conflicts within the Kuomintang; etc.).
>
> It is important, in my opinion, to compare the situation in China with the situation in India. Why is it that the Indian Communist Party is not joining a national-revolutionary organization? How are things going in the Dutch Indies?[64]

By all indications, the same questions disturbed Radek. On August 31, 1926, he wrote a letter to the Politburo in which, after expressing his concern regarding the events in China, he raised a question dealing with the political assessment of Chiang Kai-shek's dictatorship which was established after the March 20 "coup". The question was raised with the aim of keeping his activity as rector of Sun Yat-sen University consistent with the political line of the Soviet Communist Party.[65] He received no reply, which of course is not surprising.

Trotsky hoped that the questions troubling him and Radek would be clarified before the Fifteenth Party Conference in October – November, 1926, where he expected these questions would be raised.[66] As early as September 1926, having acquainted himself with relevant literature including informational reports from the ECCI Far Eastern Bureau, he felt he had "an absolutely indisputable answer to the problem of further relations between the Communist Party and the Kuomintang [Guomindang]."[67] He made it in two draft notes, one of which, titled "The Chinese Communist Party and the Guomindang" obviously was not intended for publication, and the other, "On the Fifteenth Party Conference," seems to have been a preliminary text of his planned speech at the forthcoming Party forum. Trotsky's view was as follows: with the development of the revolutionary movement in China, the moment had already arrived when the Chinese Communist Party could no longer remain a "propaganda group" inside the Guomindang, but must immediately withdraw from it in order to carry out its own, independent political line. The aim, however, would not be to withdraw the proletariat from the national-revolutionary struggle, but to win hegemony within the national liberation movement. To confirm his opinion Trotsky referred to "facts and documents from the political life of China" which at the time seemed to testify to the rapid growth of a mass movement in the country – a fact that was not denied by the Stalinists.[68] He held: "The revolutionary struggle in China has, since 1925, entered a new phase, which is characterized above all by the active intervention of broad layers of the proletariat, by strikes and the formation of trade unions. The peasants are unquestionably being drawn into motion to an increasing degree."[69]

Contrary to Stalin and his confidants, Trotsky now saw in the Chinese events signs of a leftward movement of the working masses and a simultaneous rightward movement of the Chinese bourgeoisie. It was the combination of these two factors that impelled him to the logical conclusion that the Guomindang was being torn apart by the "centrifugal tendencies of the class struggle." Here is what he wrote:

[T]he solution to the problem of relations between the Communist Party and the Kuomintang [Guomindang] differs at different periods of the revolutionary movement. The main criterion for us is not the constant fact of national oppression but the changing course of the class struggle, both within Chinese society and along the line of encounter between the classes and parties of China and imperialism.

And further:

To think that the petty bourgeoisie can be won over by clever maneuvers of good advice within the Kuomintang is hopeless utopianism. The Communist Party will be more able to exert direct and indirect influence upon the petty bourgeoisie of town and country the stronger the party is itself, that is, the more it has won over the Chinese working class. But that is possible only on the basis of an independent class party and class policy.[70]

In the given instance, Trotsky quite plainly based himself on the early documents of the ECCI favoring entry of the CCP into the Guomindang, which stated that the length of the CCP's stay within the Guomindang would depend on the balance of power between proletarian, bourgeois, and petite bourgeois elements in the alliance. Given the specific conditions in China at the time, Trotsky repeatedly stressed the point that the independence of the Communist Party did not exclude, but presupposed the continued existence for a long time of a bloc between the CCP and the Guomindang – on the basis of two separate parties.[71]

In these documents Trotsky launched a sharp criticism not only of Stalin's Politburo but also of the CCP Central Executive Committee that at its July 1926 plenary session confirmed the entrist policy. Of course, the main accusations were aimed against Stalin's group in the AUCP(B). Trotsky understood that "[t]he policy of remaining in the Kuomintang [Guomindang] in spite of the whole trend of developments was directed from Moscow."[72] And the position of Moscow he defined as "completely opportunistic" and "tailist" (that is of following behind the Guomindang), which is "cruelly reminiscent of the old Menshevik cuisine."[73]

Vigorously calling for the complete independence of the CCP in the united front with the Guomindang, Trotsky at the same time took into account the possibility that "the struggle of the Communist party for influence on the proletariat and for the latter's hegemony in the national revolutionary movement in the coming years can ... fail ..."[74] However, in Trotsky's opinion, even under such circumstances the withdrawal from the GMD was necessary. Given the deepening of class differentiation in society, he stated that the CCP's further presence in a bourgeois organization would undermine the need for a Chinese Communist party and could result in the CCP's unpreparedness for a new "right-wing" shift in the Guomindang policy; thus, without its own social base the Communist party would find itself under the threat of a profound defeat.

The subsequent development of events in China supplied Trotsky with additional information that seem to have confirmed his warning. Toward the end of 1926, troops of the Guomindang National Revolutionary Army, conducting the Northern Expedition, which had begun in July of that year, and whose aim was to smash the feudal-militarist forces and unify China, had made considerable progress. They had reached the Yangzi River valley, after thoroughly routing the forces of the Hunan and Hubei warlords. It was quite obvious that in the near future the victory of the Guomindang over feudal reaction would be achieved. In this situation, Trotsky was more and more concerned about the fate of the CCP: if it continued to stay in the Guomindang, with its political and organizational independence restricted, things could end in disaster for the CCP. After smashing the warlords, the Guomindang army could easily turn and deliver a blow against its temporary ally, the CCP, since after the success of the Northern Expedition, the Guomindang would no longer need a united front with the Communists.

The situation was becoming increasingly tense. Nevertheless, Trotsky decided not to risk speaking out on these questions at the Fifteenth Party Conference or at the Seventh ECCI Plenum, for it was in this very period that his allies in the opposition, Zinoviev and Radek, once again reversed their attitude toward the CCP remaining inside the Guomindang. Feeling bound by the policy they had pursued in the ECCI (up until April 1926), they returned to their former positions. For all practical purposes, Trotsky was isolated.

Radek's shift was especially abrupt. As late as September 28, 1926, after preliminary consultation with Trotsky and Zinoviev[75] he had sent a second letter to the Politburo in which he once again raised a number of questions concerning relations between the CCP and the Guomindang. They were:

1. [A question of] the establishment of the Chiang Kai-shek's military dictatorship after March 20 and our attitude towards it. The difficulty of this question is that Chiang Kai-shek now is the official leader of the Guomindang formally supported by Borodin. Any statements against Chiang Kai-shek here will have sharp political significance.
2. A question of the balance of the work of the Guomindang in the poor peasant milieu.
3. A question of the Guomindang members' demand that the Communists do not criticize Sunyatsenism [i.e., Sun Yat-sen's teaching].
4. A question of whether the Guomindang should work among the proletariat.
5. A question of how we can support the left Guomindang members.
6. A question of the semi-Menshevik tone of the last manifesto of the Chinese Communist party Plenum,[76] which states that we only carry on a minimum of class struggle and that, if it is possible to call the Communist party's policy Bolshevik, it implies not Communist Bolshevism, but Bolshevism in the interests of the whole people.

Radek concluded the letter by requesting "an official directive."[77]

Again he received no direct reply. Then, as early as October, on the eve of the Fifteenth Party Conference, Radek suddenly shifted his position. He was preparing the first collection of essays by Soviet and foreign authors on problems of the Chinese revolution at Sun Yat-sen University at that time.[78] (It was published in early 1927.) In this collection Radek included an older article of his, "Questions of the Chinese Revolution," written in August 1925, which contained his earlier recommendations for the CCP's entrism, along with his assessment of the GMD regime as the first "worker-peasant government" in China.[79] This demonstrated Radek's evident desire to revive the tactic that the leadership of the ECCI had imposed on the CCP from 1924 to early 1926, before Chiang Kai-shek's ultimatum. As already noted, the intent of this tactic was for the Communists to systematically accumulate positions of power within the Guomindang, and that in essence was what provoked Chiang Kai-shek's "coup d'état." This move obviously demonstrated Radek's wily attempt to find a compromise with the Politburo.

Nonetheless, on October 27, 1926, at the Fifteenth Party Conference, Raskolnikov caustically criticized Radek for his thesis that the GMD regime was the first "worker-peasant government" in China.[80] His challenge must have been carefully planned and represented a particular reaction to Radek's letters to the Politburo. Generally speaking it was not correct, as Radek was never the author of the concept of a "worker-peasant Guomindang."

Soon after this, Radek changed the formula of the "worker-peasant government." Its definition remained only in the reprint of his article "Questions of the Chinese Revolution" published in the corresponding collection of articles – at the end of October 1926 the book may have already been in press, so Radek could not have made any correction in it. At the same time he seems to have buried himself head and shoulders in scholarly and educational work during the last few months of 1926: he was especially busy developing a study course on the history of the Chinese revolutionary movement for Sun Yat-sen University, and he continued this work into 1927. Radek succeeded however, in preparing only seventeen lectures, covering the prehistory of this movement. These lectures were organized into three sections. The first dealt with a comparison of the basic laws of development in China and the West during ancient and medieval times. The second dealt with the particular features of China's economic and political evolution during the nineteenth century under the influence of foreign capitalism. The third gave a description of social and class relations in China at the end of the nineteenth century and the beginning of the twentieth century. At the very end of 1926 and beginning of 1927, these lectures were published in a small edition (of 250–300 copies) by using of the method of "steklografiya" at the print shop of the university.[81]

The outline presented in these lectures was fairly original. According to Radek, who relied not only on his own research but also on that of his colleague at the university, Mikhail Zhakov, who had specialized in the philosophical legacy of Mencius,[82] feudal relations in China had dominated it only until the third century B.C. After that, in his view, a struggle for dominance by commercial capital had begun, ending with the latter's victory in the thirteenth and fourteenth centuries. This was followed by a weakening of commercial capital, connected with the disintegration of the Mongol empire and the corresponding loss of an enormous foreign market for Chinese goods. (This was the reason, in Radek's opinion, for China's subsequent lagging behind the West.) A new strengthening of indigenous commercial capital had begun, in Radek's view, in the 1840s under the influence of foreign capital. Basing himself on this hypothesis, Radek concluded by formulating the thesis that, although modern capitalism had taken over only the coastal regions of China, the age of feudalism in China had largely become a thing of the past. Radek characterized the exploiting class in the Chinese countryside of his day (the large landowners and owners of medium-sized land holdings), not as feudal (or semi-feudal) but as capitalist.

This conception appeared not only in these lectures. Radek had presented his views, though, to be sure, without the concluding argument as to the capitalist nature of the social system in China in the nineteenth and twentieth centuries, in "Disputed Question of Chinese History," his report to the Society of Historians-Marxists at the Communist Academy on November 26, 1926.[83] That report provoked a lively, but on the whole, amicable, scholarly discussion.[84]

Radek's hypothesis was not purely abstract and scholarly in nature. Its author had far-reaching political goals in mind.[85] He was trying to demonstrate that the theory of social development worked out by Marx and Engels based on their study of European civilization was entirely applicable to Chinese history as well. This conclusion made it easier for him to overlay upon backward China the pattern of social relations characteristic of the more advanced countries. Furthermore, this enabled him to apply rather freely to China certain tactical prescriptions from the arsenal of the Bolsheviks. Such tactical prescriptions included those which, from his point of view, were aimed at helping the CCP to gain hegemony within the national-revolutionary movement, and then further to consolidate this hegemony. Among these tactics were strengthening the alliance of the proletariat, the peasantry and the urban petite bourgeoisie; "placing the revolution on 'workers and peasants basis'"; and isolating the national bourgeoisie, so that subsequently a revolutionary democratic dictatorship of the proletariat and peasantry could be established and the bourgeois revolution be switched over onto the socialist track. At the same time Radek continued to insist on the necessity for the hegemony of the CCP to be realized through the Guomindang. In January 1927 he briefly and cautiously presented his point of view in an article published in *Pravda*.[86] The article however, did not yet indicate that Radek was counterpoising the position to Stalin's: it gave the impression that the author was merely developing and making more specific the positions taken by the Seventh ECCI Plenum.

Radek's views were expressed more distinctly and in greater detail in an essay published in the March issue of the Soviet literary-political magazine *Novy Mir* (New World.)[87] It was here that for the first time in the Soviet press concern was expressed over the fact that in the areas under Guomindang control, the local administration and a number of Guomindang army commanders were suppressing the workers' and peasants' movement. "Workers have been patient too long," he noted in this connection, "... but this patience can be exhausted." The hint was clear: his article repeatedly stressed the idea that the Guomindang government ought to orient itself toward the mass movement of the workers and peasants, since, as Radek put it, the Guomindang's fate depended on its attitude toward that mass movement. For the time being, however, Radek did not polemicize against the Stalinists.

He expressed himself more definitely in a memorandum of March 3, not intended for publication. In it he wrote: "All the actions of the Guomindang – or more exactly, of its right wing and a section of the military – are aimed against the interests of the masses and in defense of the interests of the capitalists and large landowners . . ." In this connection, he considered it necessary for the Chinese Communists, while remaining in the Guomindang for the time being, to "come up out of the underground," i.e., to carry out a massive campaign of open criticism against any measures of the Guomindang government aimed against the interests of the workers and peasants and, consequently, as Radek saw it, against the interests of the national revolution. He now assessed the class nature of the Guangzhou government as bourgeois.[88]

As for Zinoviev, he agreed with Radek's view on relations between the Guomindang and the CCP, though he did not share Radek's conception that remnants of feudalism "were absent" in China.[89]

Under these circumstances Trotsky decided against trying to develop a full-scale, open polemic inside the Politburo. Instead, he retreated once again. In the fall of 1926, for instance, he was preparing Volume 14, Part Two, of his *Sochineniya* (Collected Works) for publication, and in a footnote to one of his essays dealing with problems of the Chinese revolution he in effect expressed agreement with the Comintern line as defined by the ECCI Seventh Plenum. This footnote is also in keeping with Radek's and Zinoviev's views:

> Now, in the period of the exclusive successes of the heroic Canton [Guangzhou] army, the political contradictions inside the Guomindang, including those concerning the Guomindang and the [Communist] party naturally recede into the background. Certainly, it would be a crime to take any organizational step [i.e., CCP withdrawal], which could weaken these successes. However, the policy of the Chinese Communist party should not superficially depend on the successes. It has to be aimed at deepening them socially and strengthening them ... Only under these circumstances there will be created a serious guarantee against any changes of a military situation and against the counterrevolution successes on the whole. To achieve progress in this way, the Chinese Communist party should not allow itself to bind its freedom of action in leading strike struggle, agrarian revolts of the peasants and so forth. Only complete freedom in these questions can and should be a basis for its bloc with the Guomindang, on the basis of as close as possible a union with its left wing.[90]

Of course, it did not mean that Trotsky accepted Radek's and Zinoviev's position. He considered their way of posing the problems of the Chinese revolution inadequate and in private correspondence with them vigorously tried to convince his comrades-in-arms of their "mistakes." On March 4, 1927, for instance, in response to Radek's memorandum of March 3 he wrote a long and irritated letter, in which he declared in part:

> [W]e are dreadfully late [putting forward the question of withdrawal]. We have turned the Chinese Communist Party into a variety of Menshevism, and worse yet, not into the best variety; i.e., not into the Menshevism of 1905, when it temporarily united with Bolshevism, but into the Menshevism of 1917, when it joined hands with the right SR movement and supported the Cadets.

Trotsky admitted that he was not familiar with some parts of Chinese reality, but as before, passionately defended his position that the CCP needed to get out of the Guomindang.[91] Thus, the Opposition entered the spring of 1927 without having achieved unity in its views on the Chinese revolution. The process of working out a unified opposition platform was still under way, and an open, intensive struggle with Stalinists on the Comintern's China policy was yet to come.

Part V _____

Trotsky vs. Stalin: The China Factor in 1927

Chapter 9 _____

The Stalinists and the Opposition at the Apex of the Chinese Revolution

By early March 1927 troops of the National Revolutionary Army had brought significant areas of central and eastern China under their control. A Guomindang government led by so-called "Left" Guomindang members had moved from Guangdong to the central Chinese city of Wuhan, a conglomerate composed of three towns, of Hankou, Wuchang, and Hanyang. Comintern agents informed Moscow of the upsurge of a mass worker-peasant movement in the Yangzi River valley. On February 19, 1927, the workers of Shanghai launched a political struggle, and three days later their general strike grew into an armed uprising. Although it was suspended on February 24, it appeared that the general situation in the country had become sharply radicalized. Under these circumstances, Stalin now attempted to resume an aggressive policy within the GMD. In February, the Politburo adopted urgent measures to assist the return to China of Wang Jingwei, the leader of the Guomindang "leftists," who was then living in France. With Wang Jingwei's return (via Moscow[1] of course, where Comintern officials were ready to discuss Chinese affairs with him), the Soviet leadership quite logically placed its hopes on the strengthening of the Guomindang's leftist faction.

On March 3, 1927, the Politburo categorically resolved to make changes in the Chinese Communist party's policy and work methods. Acting on the proposal of its Chinese Commission, the Politburo ordered the CCP "come what may" to launch a workers' and peasants' movement, and draw the workers into the Communist party, and the working and peasant masses into the Guomindang. The Politburo asserted that it was necessary to:

> Energetically create a peasant, petite bourgeois, and worker base under the left Guomindang ... to aim at ousting Guomindang rightists, to discredit them politically, and systematically strip them

of their leading posts ... pursue a policy of seizing the most important positions in the army .... strengthen the work of Guomindang and Communist cells in the army... look toward the arming of workers and peasants, and convert the local peasant committees into actual organs of power with self-defense capacity.

The CCP was charged with the responsibility of operating under its own slogans "everywhere and always." The resolution emphasized that, "A policy of voluntary semi-legality is impermissible. The Communist party must not act as a brake on the mass movement ... Otherwise, the revolution will be gravely threatened."[2]

The new course, however, did not influence the Politburo's view of the agrarian question in China.[3] Not without reason, Stalin and his lieutenants feared that a radical revolution in the Chinese countryside would destroy the intra-party bloc of the Communist party and the Guomindang. Meanwhile, the return of Wang Jingwei in early March 1927 inevitably led to a split in the Guomindang. Determined to take power, the leaders of the "left" faction, notably Wang Jingwei, sought in every way to diminish Chiang Kai-shek's authority. The Third Guomindang CEC Plenum that was held on March 10–17, 1927 in Wuhan, passed a number of resolutions aimed at limiting the power of Chiang Kai-shek within the Guomindang. The Plenum decided on the make-up of a new Nationalist government, with two posts – the Ministry of Labor and the Ministry of Agriculture – being offered to the Communists Su Zhaozheng and Tan Pingshan, CCP Central Committee member. Chiang Kai-shek was obliged to announce that he accepted these decisions. All this intensified the polarization of the Guomindang. At the same time, Comintern informers were reporting to Moscow that the mass movement of the workers and peasants was on the rise. On March 21, a new uprising erupted in Shanghai, and this time it ended successfully with the overthrow of the local warlord, Sun Chuanfang. On the evening of March 22, NRA troops entered Shanghai, which had already been liberated by workers' militia units. Nanjing was taken the next day.

Soon, however, disturbing news began to arrive from China. On March 24, two days after the entry of NRA troops into Shanghai, and the following day after their seizure of Nanjing, the imperialists openly intervened in the war in China. British and American warships shelled Nanjing. Chiang Kai-shek, the Commander-in-Chief of the National Revolutionary Army, obviously intended to repeat the events of March 20, 1926, but this time with a much harsher outcome.[4] Clashes between his soldiers and armed contingents of workers and peasants multiplied. In a number of places, Chiang Kai-shek's supporters smashed trade union organizations.

Under this circumstances, Stalin, who was afraid of provoking Chiang Kai-shek, retreated again. At the end of March 1927, the Politburo decided to make concessions to Chiang Kai-shek. Directives were sent to China ordering the CCP Central Executive Commission "to make every effort to avoid clashes with the National Army in Shanghai and with its leaders."[5]

The Politburo's tactical zigzags were not reported in the Soviet media; Stalin's maneuvers were undertaken in top secret. The Party press concentrated on the unfolding Northern expedition and the victories of the national revolution. *Pravda* and other newspapers played a special role in Stalin's gamble, skillfully covering the "arm-chair" schemes of the ruling bureaucracy. It is quite understandable because the seizure of power in the GMD through a well-prepared "quiet" Communist coup d'état that had actually become Stalin's true obsession, could be successful only if it were conspiratorial.

Knowing nothing of Stalin's gambits, underestimating his true leftist intentions, and increasingly worried about the tense situation in China, in the spring of 1927, the United Opposition at last decided to challenge the Stalinists on the China question in a debate. Their main concern can be expressed in the question, What can be done to protect the Chinese Communists in the event of an armed attack by the Guomindang generals? With spread of NRA control over the industrialized eastern part of China the National revolution was approaching final victory. In the opinion of the Oppositionists, the question of an inevitable "betrayal" by Chiang Kai-shek was being posed more and more sharply. Most Oppositionists saw the only protection in immediately stirring up, broadening and radicalizing the Chinese workers' and peasants' movement, infusing the revolution with a mass social upheaval. Their recommendations proceeded along the lines of the Russian revolutionary experience.

Again Radek was first to act. During the first three weeks of March 1927 he presented several reports on the Chinese revolution and the life and work of Guomindang founder Sun Yat-sen at the N. K. Krupskaya Academy of Communist Education,[6] Sun Yat-sen University,[7] and the Communist Academy. (The second anniversary of Sun's death occurred on March 12).

Radek's speeches resonated widely, especially that entitled "Motive Forces of the Chinese Revolution" delivered on March 13 at the Communist Academy.[8] Together with the disputes on the report given by Raskolnikov on the same date, March 13, and a speech by general secretary of the Profintern, Solomon A. Lozovsky, given on March 17, it provoked long and lively debates. No fewer than seventeen people took part, among them supporters of the official line, including Rafes, Martynov, Shumyatsky, and Zhou Dawen,[9] but also Oppositionists: Sergei A. Dalin, M. Alsky, Semion V. Gingor, Mikhail P. Zhakov, Abram G. Prigozhin, and Abram Ya. Guralsky. On March 27, Radek summed up the discussion.

At these meetings Radek and other Oppositionists attempted to alert the audience to the critical situation in China, which in their view was characterized by the strengthening of an anti-proletarian and anti-peasantry tendency in the revolutionary movement. They first urged public disclosure of the truth about power relations in China and within the Guomindang, and sounded the alarm concerning a likely victory of the bourgeoisie. The sedative and diplomatic tone of *Pravda* and other Soviet media was the main factor that caused their discontent. Even if they assumed that the Soviet press was trying to camouflage the Politburo's real policy – there is no evidence, however, that they did – they vigorously insisted on carrying on class propaganda. As Radek summed up,

> Chiang Kai-shek ... allows [his troops] to shoot workers ... The shootings are being conducted under the Guomindang banner but at the same time the Communists do not speak out before the broad masses as an independent Communist party ... The time has come to strengthen the independent Communist party, to make it speak out openly before the masses. It is absolutely out of the question ... If we ignore the shootings ... Chinese generals will believe that we do not want to put pressure on them and they will have our help even when executing workers. In his theses to the Second Comintern Congress Lenin ... states: "We shall support a national-bourgeois movement only when it will not hinder our organization of workers and peasants".[10] But when one smashes peasants' organizations, when one shoots workers, does it hinder our organization of workers and peasants? It seems to me that it does a little. That is why I think that it is necessary to have comrades who supervise our press know it. Otherwise, one can get an impression that we pay no heed to such things as executing workers and smashing peasants' organizations.[11]

The reference to Lenin was very significant. The Oppositionists sounded the alarm that the CCP would lose its class character having been pushed by the Comintern to unprincipled maneuvering inside the GMD. They made reference to the proper radical ideas formulated in the ECCI Seventh Plenum resolution on China and called for them to be implemented immediately. At the same time they did not yet accompany their motions with the suggestion to withdraw from the Guomindang. Their tasks were still quite limited. "My presentation first of all had only one goal: to make all of us start talking about class contradictions in the Chinese revolution," Radek maintained.[12]

Of course, the Stalinists could not accept these proposals. They did not want to show their cards to the Oppositionists or anybody else. At the same time Radek's demands made them angry. That is why they simply avoided a serious discussion, instead accusing Radek and his supporters of expressing "panic moods", holding a "liquidationist" position, "slander-ing" the Chinese Communist party, and "playing into the Chinese reaction's hands." "He [Radek] began to shout when there are neither reasons nor objective conditions for [this]," Rafes summarized, promoting the Guomindang as one of "the driving belts that link the Communist party with the layers which are related and close to it." Rafes also falsely accused Radek of secretly desiring a CCP withdrawal from the GMD, and maintained, "We can say that one who wants the Communists' withdrawal from the Guomindang is an enemy of the Chinese revolutionary movement, and one who himself favors withdrawal is a fool."[13] Such were the arguments!

The Stalinists' indignation with Radek was amplified by the fact that both before and after his presentation at the Communist academy – on March 11 and 15 – he managed to publish in *Izvestiya* an extensive article which developed key points of his perspective on the Chinese question. Radek made the first public mention of the March 20, 1926 events in Guangzhou, wrote on the growing class contradictions between the Chinese bourgeoisie,[14] on the one hand, and workers', peasants' and urban petite bourgeoisie, on the other. He demanded "a decisive turn of the Guomindang against the big bourgeoisie" and declared that "one will be able to strengthen a bloc between workers and petite bourgeoisie that will guarantee the transition of the revolution up to a new, not yet proletarian phase, but the phase of a democratic dictatorship of the proletariat, peasantry and urban petite bourgeoisie, when there will be an anticapitalist front in countryside and city." The article also contained a poorly hidden challenge against the Comintern's official course. Radek warned that, "An open imperialist offensive against China may compel the proletariat to put its hand on the economic strongholds in China earlier than, ... the leaders of the Chinese revolution expect according to their international tactical calculations."[15] His comrade-in-arms, Dalin, also managed to express publicly a certain anxiety concerning the GMD right-wing "offensive tendency" against the working class and towards a break with the Communist party." He did it in *Pravda* on March 12.[16]

Rumors began circulating in Moscow about disagreements in the ruling party on the China question,[17] and the Stalinists felt obliged to take counter-measures. Their first reaction was to publish a TASS report from Hankou (Wuhan) in *Pravda* on March 15 with the characteristic title "The Situation in the Guomindang – A Refutation of False Rumors." Citing the Guomindang National Agency, the TASS article spoke of the absence of any "internal disputes" in that party. The same issue also reproduced excerpts from Chiang Kai-shek's declaration made after the Third Guomindang Central Executive Committee Plenum in which the Commander-in-Chief of the National Revolutionary Army swore loyalty to the ideals of the Chinese revolution and to intra-party discipline. Thus, three days after the publication of Dalin's article, *Pravda* refuted itself.

On March 16 there appeared in the same newspaper an editorial rather harshly condemning "certain 'specialists' on the China question" (i.e., Radek) who had fallen for the "imperialist theory of the degeneration of the Chinese revolution." It pointed out that these kind of people were "accomplices" of the "rightists" and "liquidators." The author of the editorial – probably Bukharin – did not hesitate to attribute again to the Oppositionists the demand that the CCP withdraw from the Guomindang. In turn, *Pravda* declared that the "right-wing" circles of the Guomindang, Nationalist government, and the army as well as those who were close to them, including Chiang Kai-shek, were obliged to submit to pressure from the workers and peasants.[18] On March 22, Radek, however, published a new article in *Izvestiya*, in which he cautiously answered some of the charges made in *Pravda*. He also predicted that "the taking of Shanghai will intensify the struggle between classes." But in a few days, on March 29, 1927, Stalin himself, in a speech to the Fifth All-Union Conference of the Communist Youth League (Komsomol), once again spoke of the consolidation of forces within the Guomindang and the new shift to the left of the revolutionary movement in China.[19]

The situation in Shanghai, which had been taken over by a workers' uprising before being occupied by the National Revolutionary Army, also gave the greatest cause for concern to Trotsky. In a private memorandum of March 22, 1927, apparently intended for discussion in Opposition circles, he expressed the strongest apprehension that the inclusion of Shanghai in territory controlled by the Guomindang government could have disastrous consequences for the CCP, which continued to remain inside the Guomindang:

> There can be no doubt that the Nationalist government in China, upon seizing huge territories and finding itself face to face with gigantic and extremely difficult problems, upon experiencing the need for foreign capital and clashing daily with the workers, will make a sharp turn to the right, toward America to a certain extent and Britain. At this moment the working class finds itself without leadership ... We find ourselves in the position of a hen who hatched a duckling ... [20]

That is why Trotsky again insisted on complete organizational independence for the Communist party. For the second time since April 1926 he called for posing this question before the Politburo. Still he believed that the CCP could continue to assist the National army and the GMD government and he did not yet oppose CCP members' participation in the Guomindang cabinet of ministers.

He presented the same concerns in a March 29, 1927 letter addressed to the Oppositionist M. Alsky (Victor Moritsevich Shtein) in regard to Alsky's pamphlet *Canton Victorious*. The immediate occasion for the letter was Trotsky's disagreement with Alsky's thesis that, after the Shanghai events, "two camps bitterly hostile to one another" had come into being: the imperialists, militarists, and compradors, on the one hand, and the workers, artisans, petty bourgeoisie, students, intelligentsia, and certain groups from the middle and big bourgeoisie with nationalist orientation, on the other.[21] Trotsky assessed the situation in the light of the existence in China of three camps: the reactionaries, the liberal bourgeoisie, and the proletariat, pointing out that all the camps are fighting "for hegemony over the lower strata of the petty bourgeoisie and peasantry." In his view, the illusion of two camps was created by the Communist party's entry into the Guomindang that was quite dangerous because it was making the bourgeoisie's "betrayal" of the National revolution course easier. In this letter Trotsky spoke in favor of putting forward in China without delay, a call for the formation of Soviets of workers', peasants', artisans', and soldiers' deputies.[22]

Trotsky raised the question of Soviets in China at almost the same time as Zinoviev, who was the first to put this in writing on March 25, 1927 while working on his "Theses on the Chinese Revolution," addressed to participants in the forthcoming April Plenum of the Party Central Committee.[23] Zinoviev's assessment of the situation that had developed in China and inside the Guomindang was much the same as Trotsky's. In his preliminary draft theses completed at that time he wrote in part,

> Objectively, the economic policy of the Guomindang until now = frequently *social reaction*. Chiang Kai-shek ... is worse than Kerensky because his *real power* is stronger. The disarming of the workers and peasants, suppression of peasants' movements, the dispersion of workers' meetings by Chiang Kai-shek's cadets, dismissal of the leftists, and arrests [are facts]. One cannot keep all this in secret. These questions cannot be arranged in a "diplomatic" way (Stalin). These questions are of a class character.

That is why he came to the conclusion that it was necessary to form Soviets – "*a center* of a revolutionary movement of the workers' and peasants' masses." He expounded some main points of the program ("first platform") of the Chinese Soviets as follows:

1. Nationalization of the land;
2. Nationalization of the railroads;
3. Eight-hour day for workers (and a number of [other] freedoms);
4. Genuine agrarian revolution (not mere reform) with all its consequences;
5. Confiscation of the *Chinese* shops and factories (large and medium);

6. Prospectively, the confiscation of the *foreign* shops and factories (the concessions) – *the buying out* can be permitted "in principle" (in order to make it softer at the beginning);
7. Creation of a regular and genuine Red army;
8. Arming of workers;
9. Cancellation of state debts;
10. Social equality (emancipation of women etc.)[24]

Zinoviev recognized the urgency of the formation of Soviets in China (both he and Trotsky then regarded them as "organs of a democratic dictatorship of the proletariat and the peasantry"), but this did not lead him to revise his views on the CCP's presence in the Guomindang. Even after Chiang's troops had entered Shanghai he and Radek continued to express disagreement with Trotsky on this question.

Once again Trotsky was obliged to compromise. On March 31, 1927, he sent a brief note to the Politburo in which he placed all the emphasis on the need for the immediate formation of Soviets in China, deliberately avoiding the question of relations between the CCP and the Guomindang.[25] His note expressed the official point of view of the United Opposition.

Trotsky's missive of March 31 resulted only in an intensification of the debate. The Party leaders were, of course, not about to agree to a proposal made by Trotsky. But neither were they able to ignore it, especially since, a few days after sending his note, Trotsky submitted to *Pravda*, on April 3, 1927, a lengthy article criticizing the views of the Stalinist Politburo.[26] Immediately after submitting this article, Trotsky apparently intended to write a critique of several items by Stalin's confederate Martynov in *Pravda*. He was unable to complete his critique, however; only some draft materials for the critique remain in the archives.[27]

On April 4 Bukharin, then head of the Comintern Executive, and on the following day Stalin, explained their positions at a closed meeting of Moscow Party organization activists in the Hall of Columns at the House of Soviets.[28] The main report was made by Bukharin, who acknowledged "the beginning" of a sharp class struggle in China, manifested in the Guomindang rightists offensive against the CCP, and the workers' and peasants' movement. He even noted instances of shooting of workers by Guomindang soldiers. Nevertheless, the core of his report was directed toward justifying the policy of retreat. "One does not need to suppose that this is a comprehensive campaign against the workers and peasants," he reassured his audience ". . . We will not attempt to disguise the ugliness of the rightists. They must be unmasked. But we must make use of the features of the organizational structure."[29] He characterized the Guomindang as some sort of "middle organization between a party and Soviets" and declared the ECCI's aspiration to "transform the Guomindang as much as possible into an elective organization, to move it to the left." He also severely criticized Radek for his "underestimation of feudalism in China." In Bukharin's view, it was the struggle against "feudal remnants" that – along with the resistance to imperialism – constituted the true nature of the Chinese revolution. The existence of these "feudal remnants", he maintained, encouraged the revolutionary potential of the Chinese bourgeoisie.[30]

Stalin gave an even more soothing speech.[31] He rejected the Opposition's accusation that Comintern and Soviet leaders had hushed up instances of suppression of the Chinese worker-peasant movement by Chiang Kai-shek's forces. "We do not want to conceal this, " he stated, "but we do not want to exaggerate it in our press." Overall, according to Stalin, the situation inside the GMD was quite favorable to the Communists, as together with the "leftists," they constituted "the majority" in the Guomindang, in this "sort of revolutionary parliament." The "rightists" listened to them, and Chiang Kai-shek was directing his army against the imperialists. "The peasant needs an old worn-out jade as long as she is necessary," Stalin summed up; "So it is with us. When the Right is of no more use to us, we will drive it away. At present, we need the Right." In general, things were going well, and the Comintern was in control of the situation. Such was Stalin's conclusion. The "rightists" were demoralizing the militarists, and were giving money to the revolution. Only in a united front with them could the Communists and the "leftists" withstand the combined forces of the imperialists.[32]

Radek defended the Opposition's point of view at the April 5 meeting, warning again that there were signs that Chiang Kai-shek would inflict bloody reprisals on the Chinese Communists.[33] The very next day he was removed from his post as rector of Sun Yat-sen University of the Toilers of China.

Several days later, Stalin's confederate Martynov, systematically set forth the tactic of retreat.[34] The essence of Martynov's explanation was as follows. In China, he wrote, what is taking place is an anti-imperialist bourgeois revolution, the leading force of which at the present stage is "a bloc of four classes" – the industrial bourgeoisie, the proletariat, the peasantry, and the urban petite bourgeoisie – whose organizational expression is the Guomindang. The proletariat is striving to achieve hegemony in this bloc and in the revolution in general, and to transform the Guomindang "into an instrument of the revolutionary dictatorship of three classes, " i.e., a bloc comprising the same social forces minus the bourgeoisie. However, the proletariat must not be in a hurry. The bourgeoisie will drop away of its own accord as a result of the strengthening of the proletariat. Forcing the pace of events may only strengthen the position of the big bourgeoisie inside the GMD and lead to the isolation of the working class. The article criticized Radek, the only Oppositionist

135

mentioned by name. But in attacking him Martynov was of course speaking against the entire platform of the Opposition on the Chinese question.

It is not hard to see how sharply this concept contrasts with the tradition of radical Russian Marxism, both Trotskyist and Leninist, which was based on the idea that activization of the natural historical process was essential. This very contrast did seem to bring the concept Martynov presented close to the theory of the Mensheviks. Before the October Revolution Martynov had been a theoretician of the Menshevik group, and that obviously made him vulnerable to criticism by the Opposition. Immediately after the appearance of this article, his opponents began an all-out campaign against "Martynovism" and "Menshevism" in the China policy of the Soviet party and the Comintern. On April 12 Trotsky wrote an especially extensive commentary on Martynov's article.[35] Zinoviev also subjected Martynov's arguments to a thoroughgoing critical analysis, which he sent to *Pravda*.[36]

The sharpening of debate coincided with the Shanghai coup d'état of April 12, which confirmed the Oppositionists' warnings. Assured of the support of the imperialist powers, Chiang Kai-shek unleashed a "white terror" in Shanghai and other parts of eastern China. Despite their foreboding, many of Trotsky's supporters were deeply shocked when it happened, as were most members of the Bolshevik party. The emotional pain felt by many Russian Communists at that time was accurately reflected in a letter to the Party Central Committee and Central Control Commission from the Oppositionists Varsenika D. Kasparova and Grigorii L. Shklovsky:

> We also cannot hide from the central organs of the party our anxiety concerning the Chinese events. They cause doubts concerning the correctness of the party and Comintern leadership in China. These doubts are shared by very many comrades who belong to the majority.
>
> Relying on the confident and reassuring tone of *Pravda*, many of us considered the predictions of the Opposition on the impending and inevitable betrayal of the Chinese revolution by Chiang Kai-shek to be unfounded and alarmist. For this reason Chiang Kai-shek's coup d'état and the treason of the national bourgeoisie have deeply shaken the party to its very foundations and have caused uncountable doubts and questions.[37]

Some of the Oppositionists began to forecast a victory over the Stalinists. Instead, they soon found themselves in much harder straits. The defeat in China made Stalin and his confidants angrier, and it worsened the psychological climate in the Bolshevik party. Here is what Trotsky wrote about this new situation several years later:

Our comrades expressed optimism because our analysis was so clear that everyone would see it and we would be sure to win the party. I answered that the strangulation of the Chinese revolution is a thousand times more important for the masses than our predictions. Our predictions can win some few intellectuals who take an interest in such things, but not the masses.

Chiang Kai-shek's coup d'état would have provoked a moral depression and disenchantment in the party, and they could only strengthen Stalin's fraction that maintained the course for building socialism in one country.[38]

The Opposition decided to give battle at the regularly scheduled Plenum of the Central Committee of the AUCP(B) on April 13–16, 1927. Zinoviev authored main Opposition documents presented at this forum. On April 13 he sent the Politburo his "Theses on the Chinese Revolution,"[39] and the next day he submitted a draft resolution concerning the situation in China, consistent with the "Theses," for consideration by the Central Committee members. Of these materials, the second, written immediately after news reached Moscow of Chiang Kai-shek's coup,[40] was the most important.[41] As for the "Theses," Zinoviev had written them in late March – early April, and on the morning of April 14 he was able to add only a brief postscript, which he forwarded to the Politburo.

Both documents called for the formation of Chinese Soviets as organs of a democratic dictatorship of the proletariat and peasantry. This concept was developed at greater length in the "Theses," where it received a detailed theoretical foundation, buttressed by extensive references to Lenin's writings. The draft resolution of the Plenum was on the contrary brief and effective. It contained an analysis of the concrete situation in China and outlined measures to deal with it. Besides the call for propaganda and the formation of the Soviets ("where possible"), among the most urgent measurers were the following: carrying out an agrarian revolution; arming the workers; purging right-wing GMD members; and broadly assisting the Wuhan government, which opposed Chiang Kai-shek. Zinoviev again vigorously insisted on the necessity for the Chinese Communists to preserve their complete organizational and political independence, but he continued to call on the CCP to remain in the Guomindang – however, now in the "Left" GMD. In Zinoviev's view, the Communists in the "Left" GMD should take active steps to win important party positions and subject the "left"-wing Guomindang members to the CCP's influence. Contrary to Trotsky, at this time (spring of 1927) he continued to advocate the same offensive policy toward the Guomindang that the Comintern Executive Committee had proposed on several occasions during and after Zinoviev's term as chairman. Unlike Stalin, Zinoviev was extremely persistent in pursuing these offensive tactics. That is why he advocated the idea of Chinese Soviets.

Stalin, however, had no intention of continuing the polemic with the Oppositionists; Chiang Kai-shek's coup had radically changed the situation. Now Stalin's main concern was to save his reputation. He did not want to admit his errors as this would have strengthened the Opposition. He was not ready to engage in an open debate, especially as Zinoviev's draft resolution called on the Comintern to admit its "huge mistakes" in China and mentioned Stalin by name as one responsible for the defeat. In this connection, Stalin's initial reaction was to torpedo any sort of discussion whatsoever about the causes of the failure. Notwithstanding the insistent demands of Trotsky and Zinoviev, the April Plenum of the Central Committee that met after the coup devoted no more than three or four hours to the Chinese problem. In essence, it limited itself to hearing the report of the chairman of the Council of People's Commissars, Aleksei I. Rykov, on the latest events in China and the decisions of the Politburo relating to them.[42] On Molotov's proposal, no stenographic record was made of the corresponding session on the evening of April 14. The members of the Central Committee, with the exception of supporters of the Opposition, endorsed the Politburo's policy "on the international question."[43] Zinoviev's "Theses" were not distributed, and his draft resolution was summarily rejected by majority vote with hardly any discussion.

A genuine examination of the situation in China did take place, apparently, outside the Plenum – at lengthy private sessions that Stalin held with his supporters – that at least is what the Oppositionists gathered.[44] As for public reaction in the first days after Chiang's coup, it was rather general: at first the Stalinists did nothing more than denounce Chiang as a traitor who had sold out to the imperialists. They blamed the Shanghai tragedy on world imperialism.[45] But a more probing analysis soon materialized. *Kommunisticheskii Internatsional* printed an editorial which advanced the notion that as early as the Seventh Plenum in December 1926, the ECCI had "foreseen" the events in Shanghai.[46] The author had in mind the general thesis contained in the appropriate resolution adopted by the Seventh Plenum concerning the inevitable withdrawal from the revolutionary camp of "the bulk of the big capitalist bourgeoisie." He naturally expressed satisfaction with the perspicacity of the Comintern, the more so as, in his words, the "treachery" of the big bourgeoisie bore witness to the fact that the Chinese revolution had entered a higher stage.[47]

All this was of course highly unsatisfactory to the Opposition. In a special declaration on April 16, the last day of the Plenum, Trotsky again attempted to draw the attention of the Party leadership to the question of Soviets in China. "The Plenum did not address itself to this fundamental question," he pointed out. "However . . . it cannot be postponed any longer because the entire fate of the Chinese revolution is bound up with the question of the formation of soviets."[48] Trotsky urged that measures be taken in China in response to Chiang's coup that would lead to the formation of a genuinely revolutionary government, one truly dependent for its existence on the workers, urban petite bourgeois, peasants, and soldiers. "This organization is the soviet," he concluded.[49]

The Opposition's arguments during the Plenum received surprising confirmation in factual material and conclusions contained in a letter by four staff members of the ECCI Far Eastern Bureau, supporters of the Stalinist majority – T. G. Mandalyan, N. M. Nasonov, N. A. Fokin, and A. Ye. Albrekht. Sent from Shanghai on March 17, the letter reached Moscow in mid-April. The authors of the letter, written three weeks before the coup, complained that the Comintern representatives in China – Voitinsky and Borodin – were preventing development of an active Communist policy in that country and were not giving the CCP a chance to arouse the masses and bring them into action. Expressing profound alarm over this, the four – completely independent of the Opposition – insisted that the Chinese revolution needed to be deepened.[50] This letter was neither circulated among those attending the Central Committee Plenum nor brought to the attention of members of the Comintern Executive Committee, but it quickly became known to both Trotsky and Zinoviev, who used it countless times as proof of their own argument.

On April 20, Trotsky prepared a new document, calling again for the formation of Soviets in China.[51] In a special letter sent on April 22 to the Central Committee and to a Party branch at the Institute of Red Professors,[52] he spelled out his position on the need to call for Soviets in that country.[53]

On April 20, Zinoviev and Trotsky also submitted a proposal to the Politburo and the Central Control Commission Presidium calling for a new, closed plenary session of the Central Committee to be held within two or three days – with members of the CCC Presidium included – for a discussion of the international situation. "The significance of the Chinese defeat cannot be hushed up," they declared. "And the fact that the danger for us [the USSR and the Soviet Communist party] is growing cannot be hushed up."[54]

The reply came, in effect, on the following day, when *Pravda* published Stalin's article entitled "Questions of the Chinese Revolution," which in essence constituted the platform of the AUCP(B) majority. It was couched in the form of some "Theses for Propagandists," supposedly approved by the Party Central Committee. In fact, these "Theses" had been authorized for publication by a narrow group consisting of Stalin, Bukharin and Molotov, whom the Politburo had empowered to do this.[55] Stalin attempted to provide a theoretical explanation for what had happened in

China and to outline the main directions for the future. The general content of his "Theses" was in keeping with Martynov's article of April 10: the basic point was that in the Chinese revolutionary movement it was necessary to follow the principle of "natural transformation." Taking account of the changed situation, however, Stalin offered some new points. He divided the Chinese revolution into two stages, defining the first as continuing until Chiang Kai-shek's April 1927 coup. Stalin characterized this stage as "the revolution of a united *all-national* front," in which national bourgeoisie and proletariat tried to use each other for their own purposes. According to this logic, the Shanghai events marked the "desertion of the national bourgeoisie from the revolution" and the beginning of a second stage, in which "a *swing* has begun away from the revolution of an *all-national* united front and toward a revolution of the vast masses of the *workers* and *peasants*, towards an *agrarian* revolution." In this situation, Stalin stressed, one must work toward the concentration of all power in the country into the hands of "the revolutionary Guomindang" in its capacity as a bloc between the "leftists" and the Communists, transforming it in fact into an organ of the revolutionary democratic dictatorship of the proletariat and the peasantry. As the principal "antidote" to counter-revolution, Stalin proclaimed "the arming of the workers and peasants." At the same time, he reminded his readers that the Chinese revolution, as before, remained national in character, and that it was unfolding in specific conditions that differed from those in Russia. One of the most important differences, in his views, was the existence of a united anti-revolutionary front of the imperialists.

In this connection, Stalin briefly dwelt upon the mistakes of the Opposition, observing that "Radek and company" – he did not refer to Trotsky or Zinoviev by name – did not understand that the revolution in China, a backward, semi-colonial country, could not proceed at the same pace as the October revolution in Russia, and that they were bringing up the slogan of Soviets at an unfavorable moment. What he meant was that in China the formation of Soviets would be aimed against the authority of "the revolutionary Guomindang." Of course, he could not accept this slogan. All of his calculations concerned the ultimate communization of this party itself. In conclusion, Stalin accused the Opposition of advocating the withdrawal of the Chinese Communist party from the Guomindang.[56]

This work testifies that the General Secretary of the Central Committee of the AUCP(B) had again begun to reexamine the tactic of the CCP's retreat inside the Guomindang. The objective conditions for this, according to his logic, were created by the action of the "rightists" in "cutting their ties" with the revolution. He still refused, however, to compromise with the Oppositionists. Stalin wanted to radicalize the revolution cautiously, "wisely" combining "offensive" maneuvering within the Guomindang with the development of the mass movement.

A few days later, he elaborated upon the basic points of his "Questions of the Chinese Revolution" in a new release, the May 7 declaration written in the Politburo's name in reply to Zinoviev's "Theses on the Chinese Revolution," which had been addressed to the Politburo on April 13. Stalin's document, which was stamped "Absolutely Secret," and which, along with Zinoviev's "Theses", was distributed only to the members of the Central Committee, took direct aim at the views of the United Opposition. It was never published, but Stalin repeated a number of the inferences drawn therein in his public speeches of that period.[57] In addition to his previous accusations he declared that the Oppositionists borrowed some premises from the ECCI Seventh Plenum resolution on China: as argued earlier, this resolution was quite contradictory. Having borrowed these premises, Stalin held, they drew out of them "liquidationist" conclusions. At the same time Stalin also presented several specific charges against the Oppositionists that had been circulating widely.

The Declaration was particularly notable in stating that it was inappropriate to organize Soviets in China. On this occasion Stalin characterized the slogan of Soviets not only as a call for an uprising against "the revolutionary Kuomintang [Guomindang]", but also as an expression of the Oppositionists' unrealistic desire to establish a proletarian dictatorship in China. From Stalin's arguments it appeared that one could speak of Soviets as organs of the democratic dictatorship of the proletariat and peasantry only when applied to the most backwards countries of the East, such as Persia, Afghanistan, and others. But, he argued, this slogan was in no way applicable to China. Stalin placed special emphasis on the point that if Soviets were formed in China, they would take the form of councils of workers' deputies, not be simply peasants' or toilers' Soviets. But workers' Soviets, he held, could only be organs of the proletarian dictatorship, and on this point he recommended that Zinoviev recall a resolution of the Second Comintern Congress entitled "When and Under What Conditions Councils of Workers' Deputies Can Be Formed." The point being that this could only be done when the stage of socialist revolution had been reached.[58]

Stalin's writings did not, of course, remain unanswered. Trotsky took up Stalin's "Theses for Propagandists" in an article entitled "The Chinese Revolution and the Theses of Comrade Stalin." The main portion of Trotsky's article was completed on May 7, 1927; in ten days Trotsky wrote two "Postscripts" to his paper: one was entitled "Comrade Chen Duxiu's Speech on the Tasks of the Chinese Communist Party" (a reference to Chen Duxiu's report at the Fifth Congress of the CCP in April 1927); the other postscript was called "The Necessary Final Accord." The article was intended for publication in the party theoretical journal *Bol'shevik*, but along with other writings by Oppositionists it was banned.

It was here that Trotsky presented his current views on the Chinese revolution in the most systematic form. The main argument Trotsky developed in this article was the following: the tactics of the Communist party in China in the course of the national, anti-imperialist revolution, for all its particular nuances, should have essentially corresponded to the political course followed by the Russian Social Democratic Labor Party (Bolshevik) in the period of the anti-monarchic revolution of 1905. Trotsky was speaking only of the tactical line of conduct pursued by the Chinese Communists; his conception of the national character of the revolutionary process in China remained unchanged. "The Bolshevik way," he pointed out, consisted "of an unconditional political and organization demarcation from the bourgeoisie, of a relentless exposure of the bourgeoisie from the very first steps of the revolution, of destruction of all petty-bourgeois illusions about a united front with the bourgeoisie, of tireless struggle with the bourgeoisie for the leadership of the masses, of the merciless expulsion from the Communist Party of all those elements who sow vain hopes in the bourgeoisie or idealize them."[59]

While making this argument, Trotsky also took into account the specifics of China's semi-colonial status. He did not oppose blocs between the Communist party and bourgeois organizations. Furthermore, in this article, in keeping with the line of the United Opposition, he justified the entry of the CCP into the Guomindang. What he did not agree with, as has been said before, was the loss of the Communist party's independence within the united front due to Stalin's policy of frequent retreats. He continued:

> If, in spite of a workers' mass movement, in spite of the powerful rise of the trade unions, in spite of the revolutionary agrarian movement on the land, the Communist Party should remain as before an integral appendage to a bourgeois party, and what is more, should it enter the national government created by this bourgeois party, it would be better to say frankly: the time has not yet come for a Communist Party in China.[60]

Much of the article was devoted to criticizing Stalin's position on Soviets for China. Chiang Kai-shek's coup, Trotsky wrote, made the workers lose confidence in the GMD high command. After all, the pogrom in Shanghai was organized by those whom the workers had considered their leaders. That is why, in Trotsky's opinion, it was necessary to create some sort of a new revolutionary center that would grow out of the ranks of the workers themselves and inspire confidence in the deceived masses; "[t]he Wuhan authorities are not enough for this: workers', peasants', and soldiers' soviets are needed for this, soviets of the toilers." This was especially so, he added, because the "Left" Guomindang in the countryside had no real authority. In this connection the slogan of Soviets would be a call for the creation of new organs of state power right through the "transitional regime" of a dual government. The Soviets' attitude toward Wuhan,

Trotsky noted, would correspond to the attitude of the "revolutionary" GMD itself to the Soviets because the latter "will tolerate over them only such a government as bases itself upon the armed workers and peasants." Trotsky openly laughed at Stalin who believed it was possible to carry out the "arming of workers and peasants" without creating of Soviets. He observed ironically that, if we believe that the "Left" GMD would finally realize the Stalinist dream of a "workers' and peasants' party," there should be no conflict between the Soviets and Wuhan: "Why then will the creation of workers' and peasants' soviets mean a war against the authority of the workers' and peasants' Kuomintang [Guomindang]?"[61]

Trotsky refuted Stalin's other points as well and countered his sallies against the Opposition, accusing him in turn of having a mechanistic understanding of the nature of imperialist oppression. He argued that Stalin did not take into account the interconnection between the internal class struggle and the oppression of foreign imperialism, and he denounced Stalin for attributing to the Opposition the "senseless contention" that China allegedly was on the verge of ("stands before") a socialist dictatorship of the proletariat. He charged Stalin with citing "feudal domination" in China to justify a line of unscrupulous compromise with a hostile class, and accused him of misunderstanding the question of tempo, the pace of development of the Chinese revolution, and of sacrificing the interests of the workers and peasants in an attempt to save face in a bad situation. Finally, he warned that the "left" leaders of the Guomindang "secretly cherish the thought of a compromise with the right" and that only by the formation of Soviets could one push the revolutionary elements of Wuhan "to the left and force the counter revolutionaries to retire . . . Only the deepening of the revolution can save it."[62]

In early May, Radek produced a long essay, intended for publication as a pamphlet, called "The Chinese Big Bourgeoisie's 'Betrayal' of the National Movement."[63] Differing a little from Trotsky's writings, it presented a systematic analysis of the main factors that, in Radek's view, had led to Chiang's coup. Both Trotsky and Zinoviev paid close attention to this document. Trotsky made a number of critical if general observations. His only serious criticism concerned what he saw as excessive praise for the Comintern's China policy between 1920 and the first half of 1926. That, however, was a key point in Radek's analysis: as one of the architects of the ECCI's Eastern policy in the early 1920s, Radek attempted to show the crucial difference between his own policy (and Zinoviev's) and that of Stalin. Radek devoted a special chapter of his essay to justifying the Comintern's early tactics. On this occasion, Trotsky wrote,

> In my opinion, the chapter 'The Comintern Warned, the Chinese Communist Party Knew the Danger' insufficiently characterizes what has been going on. The Comintern indeed warned about

nothing, and the Communist party did not know the danger. Otherwise, how to explain what has happened?.. In my opinion, this chapter needs to be reconstructed or entirely excluded.[64]

Zinoviev did not agree with Trotsky's criticism and even borrowed some of Radek's ideas. He had begun at that time to rework his "Theses on the Chinese Revolution" into an article that he called "Lessons of the Chinese Revolution" and in it he included – without attribution – extensive excerpts from Radek's chapter "The Comintern Warned, the Chinese Communist Party Knew the Danger" – the chapter that Trotsky particularly criticized.[65] This study was never completed, however.[66]

On May 17 Zinoviev wrote "An Obligatory Reply" to the May 7 Politburo criticism of his "Theses". It contained practically the same ideas as Trotsky's critique of Stalin's "Questions of the Chinese Revolution" and added a few new points to meet Stalin's new challenges to the Opposition. Zinoviev paid considerable attention to refuting the General Secretary's thesis that Soviets of workers' deputies could only be organs of the proletarian dictatorship. "In order to 'prove' this thesis," Zinoviev declared, "it was necessary ... to forget the entire history of our revolution of 1905, and ... to pervert Lenin's doctrine of Soviets." After all, he argued, in 1905 the Russian workers' Soviets were organs of a democratic government of the proletariat, peasantry and urban poor. They could become organs of the dictatorship of the proletariat only in the process of transformation of the bourgeois revolution into a socialist one. Regarding Stalin's invitation to recall the resolution of the Second Comintern Congress, Zinoviev demonstrated undisguised scorn: "The resolution in question was written by me." He then explained that it spoke about workers' Soviets in those countries where a bourgeois revolution had been completed.

Zinoviev also did not accept Stalin's accusation that the Opposition borrowed certain planks from the resolution of the ECCI Seventh Plenum on China. "We indeed shared some general statements of the ECCI Seventh Enlarged Plenum ... But we consider the entire resolution of the ECCI Seventh Plenum a mistake that has been denied by facts and consequently needs to be revised," he pointed out. He also offered a detailed criticism of Stalin for his concept of the two stages of the Chinese revolution, declaring it inappropriate to contrast a national liberation movement with an agrarian revolution.[67]

The main Oppositionists – Trotsky, Zinoviev, and Radek – continued to expound their views. On May 17, Radek again publicly criticized the Comintern's China policy, speaking at the Institute of World Economy and International Politics during the debate on a report by the Stalinist Lev Geller on the workers' movement in China.[68] At the same time, Zinoviev made an extensive critique of the Chinese Communist party for its subservience to Comintern policy,[69] using the occasion provided by the publication at the end of April 1927 of a report to the Seventh Plenum of the Comintern Executive by CCP Politburo member Tan Pingshan who, in April, was already serving as a minister of the Wuhan Nationalist government.[70] On May 10, Trotsky composed an article titled "The Sure Road" in which he called anew for "giving the agrarian movement and the workers' soviets [in China] a clear program of practical action."[71] On May 16 Trotsky, and the following day, Zinoviev, sought to explain their position to Nadezhda Krupskaya, Lenin's widow, who was also a Central Control Commission member.[72]

At the beginning of May, the Stalinists introduced a number of organizational measures. On May 11, 1927, the Politburo passed a resolution establishing a special commission of Stalin, Molotov, and Stanislav V. Kosior to decide whether to print "the articles by Comrades Zinoviev and Trotsky on the Chinese question."[73] The very next day the Politburo accepted the commission's recommendation that publication would be "inexpedient."[74] Five days later Trotsky addressed a protest to the Politburo and the CCC Presidium.[75]

Earlier, on May 9, the Politburo had approved a text submitted by Bukharin as the reply from the Central Committee and the Central Control Commission Presidium to the April 20 letter from Zinoviev and Trotsky. The latter called for a special session of the Central Committee to discuss "the international question," but the reply leveled several harsh political accusations at them: "undermining the Soviet Union from behind the lines", seeking to "liquidate" the Chinese revolution, "fighting against the party." The highest bodies of the Soviet party refused to accept Zinoviev's and Trotsky's request.[76]

On May 12, making use of the fact that Zinoviev, at a meeting to celebrate *Pravda*'s fifteenth anniversary (May 9), had publicly criticized the newspaper for publishing Martynov's articles and a work by Aleksandr A. Svechin,[77] the Politburo initiated a furious anti-Zinoviev campaign.[78] The party press and some Communist cells accused Zinoviev, one of the leading Oppositionists, of "violating the party's discipline" for criticizing a party newspaper in the presence of non-party activists.[79] The aim of the campaign, apparently, was to discredit Zinoviev on the eve of the Eighth Plenum of the Comintern Executive Committee in order to prepare public opinion for denying him admission to the Plenum. The Stalinists had been longing to take this measure and formally, of course, they had the right to do so, for on November 22, 1926, he had been removed from his post as chairman of the Comintern Executive Committee, and no longer worked for the ECCI. But certain moral obligations still existed. After all, Zinoviev had been ECCI chairman since the founding of the Comintern in 1919.

Widening their struggle with the Opposition, Stalin's leadership at the same time was taking secret steps to bring the CCP policy into line with the general course set down in Stalin's writings in late April and early May.

These works – "Questions of the Chinese Revolution" and the May 7 Politburo declaration – defined the direction of the Politburo's and Comintern's China policy for the period from Chiang Kai-shek's coup to the end of June 1927. If until mid-April 1927 the Soviet leadership was preoccupied with the question of how to "clean out" the "rightists" from the Guomindang while maintaining a united front with the "leftists" and the "centrists," now Moscow staked its hopes on radicalizing the GMD "left" itself. This time, however, the Chinese Communists had to make sure not to force their partners out of their very own Guomindang; instead, they had to "push" the Wang Jingwei types persistently to organize a real social revolution by explaining to them that if they "do not learn to be revolutionary Jacobins they will perish so far as the people and the revolution are concerned."[80] On May 13 the ECCI sent to the Central Committee of the CCP an instruction of the Bolshevik Politburo containing a directive to push the "Left" GMD to launch an agrarian revolution in all provinces and form "eight or ten divisions" of revolutionary peasants and workers as a "Wuhan guard."[81]

The Politburo course was supported in its entirety by the Eighth ECCI Plenum (May 18–30, 1927). At this time the Politburo raised the question of the intra-party debate with the Opposition over China. It addressed a letter to the Comintern Executive on May 19 (with copies to members of the Party Central Committee and the Central Control Commission Presidium), which brought the Comintern Executive up to date on the disagreements between the majority and the Opposition, and advanced a number of major accusations against Zinoviev and Trotsky. It did not hesitate to grossly falsify their views, alleging that the two were talking about the "destruction" of the Chinese revolution, moving in the direction of "surrendering revolutionary positions in China," and "refusing to transform the proletariat in China into the leader of the bourgeois-democratic revolution in order to please the liquidators."[82]

The Oppositionists also prepared to do battle at the Plenum. This preparation seems to have been going on in intensive intra-fractional debates. On May 10, 1927, in his private correspondence, Trotsky proposed that the CCP withdraw from the "Left" Guomindang,[83] but his point of view was once again rejected by other leaders of the United Opposition. The basic oppositionist documents on the Chinese question circulated among ECCI members at the Plenum included those which presented Zinoviev's views. These were his "Lessons of the Chinese Revolution: Regarding Comrade A. Martynov's Article", "Once More on Lessons of the Chinese Revolution: A Shocking Document", and "An Obligatory Reply", Zinoviev's and Trotsky's letter to the Politburo and the CCC Presidium of April 20, 1927. Also circulated were the record of Zinoviev's speech at a meeting to celebrate *Pravda*'s fifteenth anniversary and his letter to *Pravda*'s editorial board concerning the Politburo campaign against him.[84] Trotsky's articles "The Chinese Revolution and the Theses of Comrade Stalin", and "The Sure Road", and the letter of four members of the Far Eastern Bureau to the Russian delegation of the ECCI were also distributed. In addition, Zinoviev and Trotsky wrote a "chronological note" especially for the Plenum, entitled "Facts and Documents That Must Be Available for Checking by Every Member of the AUCP(B) and by the Entire Comintern", in which they described the history of the Oppositionists' struggle against Stalin's Party majority on the Chinese question since April 1926.[85]

During the Plenum, on May 25, a large group of Oppositionists submitted to the Central Committee a detailed declaration containing their principal disagreements with the Stalinist line on major issues of current politics, including China. This document, known as the "Declaration of the Eighty-three", was actually signed by eighty-four persons. Among them were Trotsky, Zinoviev, Radek, and a number of other old members of the Soviet Communist party and the Comintern.[86] The ECCI Plenum participants were given this declaration.

At the Plenum itself Trotsky bore the brunt of the majority's attack. Two members of the Comintern Executive Committee, Sergei M. Gessen and Vujo Vujović, did what they could to support him. Vujović also took part in the debate on the Chinese question at the Plenum. Another member of the ECCI, Albert Treint, gave support to Trotsky's position, though with some reservations. Zinoviev, of course, was not permitted to attend the Plenum. He nevertheless followed the proceedings closely, and continued to analyze the Chinese revolution. Shortly after the Plenum he began to work on a long article, "The Revolution in China and Stalin as an 'Expert' on Revolution," which he intended as a thorough analysis of Stalin's speech at the Plenum on the Chinese revolution. The article was never completed.[87]

Trotsky attempted to draw the attention of the leaders of the international Communist movement assembled at the Plenum to the ever more urgent necessity of assuring the full independence of the CCP within the framework of the united front. He urged that a call for the formation of Soviets be proclaimed in China, warned of inevitable "treachery" by the "Left" leaders of the Guomindang, and demanded that the policies of the Stalinist leadership be changed immediately.[88] Taking the floor eight times, he spoke on China thrice, and presented several written statements to the Plenum Secretariat. His main propositions were finally summed up in his alternative draft resolution:

> In the first place, peasants and workers should place no faith in the leaders of the left Kuomintang [Guomindang] but they should instead build their Soviets jointly with the soldiers. In the second place, the Soviets should arm the workers and the advanced

peasants. In the third place, the Communist Party must assure its complete independence, create a daily press,[89] and assume the leadership in creating the Soviets. Fourth, the land must be immediately taken away from the landlords. Fifth, the reactionary bureaucracy must be immediately dismissed. Sixth, perfidious generals and other counterrevolutionarists must be summarily dealt with. And finally, the general course must be toward the establishment of a revolutionary dictatorship through the Soviets of workers' and peasants' deputies.[90]

But it was all to no avail. The overwhelming majority of Plenum participants did not want to hear what he had to say. The resolutions adopted by the Plenum – "Tasks of the Comintern in the Struggle Against War and the War Danger" and "Problems of the Chinese Revolution" – officially approved the Stalinist position on the situation in China. They once again directed the CCP to transform the "Left" GMD into a pro-Communist "workers' and peasants' party" which would lead an agrarian revolution in the Chinese countryside, arm workers and peasants, and turn the Wuhan government into an organ of a revolutionary-democratic dictatorship of the proletariat and peasantry.[91]

These decisions were concretized in a number of instructions from the Politburo to the Central Committee of the CCP and Comintern representatives in China, dated May 30, June 3, 6, 9, 18, and 20.[92] On June 23 the Politburo even sent a telegram to Wang Jingwei in an attempt to convince him that "the Guomindang must definitely support the agrarian revolution and the peasantry."[93] On June 27, the leaders of the GMD were sent another telegram calling on them to organize "workers and peasants" into military units faithful to the revolution.[94] In this connection, the Soviets actively provided loans to the Wuhan government.

In response to a motion by the delegations of the Communist parties of Germany, England, France, Italy, Czechoslovakia, and the United States, on the last day of the Plenum, the majority of the assembled delegates passed a special "Resolution on the Activity of Comrades Trotsky and Vujović at the Plenary Session of the ECCI." It accused the Oppositionists of "beginning a bitter fight against the Comintern . . . and the Soviet Union" and authorized the ECCI Presidium along with the International Control Commission to "formally expel Comrades Trotsky and Vujović from the ECCI" in case of their continuing resistance. The resolution also contained a proposal addressed to the Bolshevik party Central Committee requesting it to take decisive measures to "rid the Bolshevik party" of the "factional work of Comrades Trotsky and Zinoviev."[95]

Shortly after the Eighth ECCI Plenum the two leaders of the Opposition were summoned before a subcommission of the Central Control Commission assigned to "hear their case." Zinoviev and Trotsky

I. Lenin and Trotsky, November 7, 1919 (Russian Center, 393/1/171/1).

2. Lenin and Stalin. August 30, 1922 (Russian Center, 393/1/324/1).

3. Stalin, Rykov, Zinoviev, Bukharin. 1924 (Russian Center, 82/2/1629/3).

4. Radek
(Russian Center, 490/2/282).

5. Raskolnikov
(Russian Center, 421/1/430/1).

6. Voitinsky
(Russian Center, 495/65a/2474/2).

7. Roy
(Russian Center, 490/2/105a).

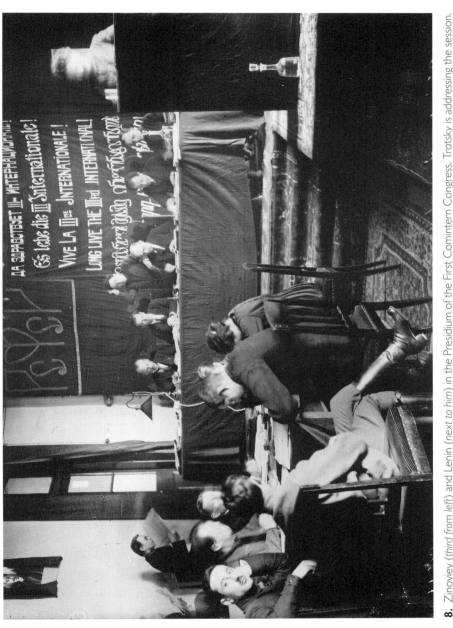

8. Zinoviev (*third from left*) and Lenin (*next to him*) in the Presidium of the First Comintern Congress. Trotsky is addressing the session. Early March 1919 (Russian Center, 393/I/105/I).

9. Founders of the Comintern. Sitting in the second row from right: Lenin (*fifth*) and Bukharin (*third*). Standing: Trotsky (*center*) and Zinoviev (*eleventh from right*). Early March 1919 (Russian Center; 393/1/106/1).

10. Lenin speaking on the international situation and fundamental tasks of the Communist International at the Second Comintern Congress. Next to him is Radek. July 19, 1920 (Russian Center, 393/1/244/1).

11. Lenin, Bukharin, and Zinoviev at the Second Comintern Congress. Summer 1920 (Russian Center, 489/2/120).

12. A group of delegates to the Second Comintern Congress. From left: Karakhan (*second*), Radek (*third*), Bukharin (*fifth*), Lenin (*eighth*), the writer Maxim Gorky (*ninth*), Zinoviev (*twelfth*), Roy (*fourteenth*), Lenin's sister, Maria Ulyanova (*sixteenth*). Summer 1920 (Russian Center, 393/1/252/1).

13. Maring
(Russian Center, 495/244/176/8).

14. Borodin, late July 1923
(Russian Center, 495/261/1969/0).

15. Dalin
(Russian Center, 495/65a/384/28).

16. Martynov
(Russian Center, 495/65a/10403/5).

17. Vujovič
(Russian Center, 495/277/1797/48a).

18. Mif
(Russian Center, 495/65a/1325/52).

19. Sun Yat-sen and his
wife Song Qingling
(Russian Center, Collection of
Comintern photographs, 2).

20. Chen Duxiu. November 1922
(Russian Center, 491/2/93).

21. Li Dazhao.

22. Qu Qiubai
(Russian Center, Collection of
Comintern photographs, 2).

23. Chen Shaoyu (Wang Ming)
(Russian Center, Collection of
Comintern photographs, 1).

24. 'Pregnant Europe'. A cartoon by an unknown Bolshevik (Russian Center, 326/2/19/19).

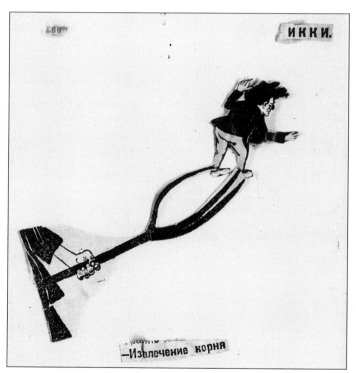

25. 'Extraction of the root'. Radek's collage on Zinoviev's expulsion from the Comintern Executive. Late 1926 (Russian Center, 326/2/19/14).

26. Trotsky's doodlings on the Chinese issue, June 1927 (Russian Center; 325/1/359/2).

Shanghai, 3rd Nov., 1924.

Dear Comrade Kahrahan:

Money from the Red Aid for Chinese comrades imprisoned in North China, we ask you to give directly to the secretary of the Peking organization.

We have already started the anti- imperialist work according to your instruction, but we have not received the necessary fund which you promised to pay. Our budget for changhai is $ 600. Please let us know as soon as possible.

With communist greetings,

T. S. Chen

Secretary of F%C% of C%C%P%

27. Letter from Chen Duxiu to Karakhan, November 3, 1924 (The author's private archive).

Dear Com. Karakhan,   April 1º 1926

Before Mr. Malone left I decided with Com. Roseen that Mrs. Brohme would succeed him to send out telegrams and she must be paid. It is she who sends out telegrams at present instead of Malone. And She wants to know how much money will be granted for sending telegrams and for her as salary per month. Please at once tell me all about it as she wishes to have the answer to-night.

With comrade greetings yours

T. C. Li

28. Letter from Li Dazhao to Karakhan, April 10, 1926 (The author's private archive).

were accused of attacking the Bolshevik line of the Communist International and the Soviet Communist party's Central Committee. On June 13 Zinoviev presented his case; Trotsky followed him on June 14. Both refused to admit their "faults" and vigorously continued to defend their views.[96] Unable to counter the arguments, the subcommission limited itself to vague condemnation of the Opposition leaders.

This kind of "investigation" was of course totally unsatisfactory to Stalin. He flew into a rage when he read the stenographic record of the subcommission's sessions. "The impression given is one of utter confusion on the part of the Central Control Commission," he wrote to Molotov.

> Zinoviev and Trotsky, not the Commission members, did the interrogating and the accusing ... I resolutely protest against the fact that the commission to charge Trotsky and Zinoviev has turned into a forum for charges against the Central Committee and the Comintern, with an emphasis on the 'case' against Stalin ... Will Trotsky and Zinoviev really be handed this 'transcript' to distribute! That's all we need.[97]

Under pressure from Stalin, the investigation of Trotsky's and Zinoviev's "factional activity" was transferred to the CCC Presidium, which at a special session on June 24, 1927,[98] threatened the two main Opposition leaders with expulsion from the Party Central Committee.

Meanwhile, from China there continued to come ever more alarming news. In mid-June it became known that Feng Yuxiang, whom the Comintern considered one of the most reliable "Left" Guomindang military leaders, was actively preparing to follow the road taken by Chiang Kai-shek. Under these conditions Trotsky renewed his attempts to persuade his fellow combatants in the united anti-Stalinist alliance – above all Zinoviev and Radek – to accept his longstanding proposal for an immediate end to the CCP's entrist policy. On June 20, 1927, he showed them a statement he had drafted for the ECCI Presidium in which this was the central idea.[99]

This time even Zinoviev was forced to agree. The Opposition leaders decided to submit a joint letter to the Politburo, the CCC Presidium, and the Comintern Executive. All that troubled them now was the need to explain why they had not previously called openly for the withdrawal of the CCP from the GMD: they did not of course wish to reveal to their opponents the existence of internal disagreements. Discussions within their faction took several days; Trotsky and Zinoviev had different assessments of the past course of the Opposition. Zinoviev thought the Opposition had been "right all along the line".[100] Trotsky proposed that past errors be acknowledged.[101] Radek agreed with Trotsky.[102] For the time being the disputed question remained unsettled. The Oppositionists seem to have agreed not to raise it in the meantime, and the letter to the Party and

Comintern leading organs was compiled in the form of short slogans wholly reflecting the Oppositionists' current mood. It contained demands for the immediate transition from intra-party cooperation with the Guomindang to an inter-party alliance with the GMD "masses", Communists' withdrawal from the Nationalist government, raising the slogan of Soviets, carrying out an agrarian revolution, and struggling for the establishment of a revolutionary and democratic dictatorship of the proletariat and peasantry under the proletarian (i.e., Communist) leadership.[103] It was signed by Zinoviev, Trotsky, Radek, and Grigorii Ye. Yevdokimov and sent on June 25.

Not until the beginning of July did the Opposition leaders finally reach a compromise on their assessments of the past. Zinoviev's explanations were finally accepted, and the main theses were elaborated in a long article sent to *Pravda* on July 2, 1927.[104] Needless ro say, the authors had little chance of being published in that newspaper. Two days after the letter was sent, Zinoviev, Trotsky, and Yevdokimov filed charges against the editors of *Pravda*, asking that they be tried by a party court – the Central Control Commission – for their distortion of events in China.[105] On July 7 Vujovič, Zinoviev, and Trotsky addressed a new letter to the Presidium of the Comintern Executive proposing the immediate convocation of a session in order to correct "the mistaken line" of the Communist International in China.[106]

These actions only further angered the Stalinists. Their ire was intensified by the fact that at the end of June and the beginning of July Stalin himself began to realize that the Comintern's policy in China was about to collapse; his private letters to Molotov and Bukharin indicate this rather clearly. In a letter of June 27 he admitted that: "I am afraid that Wuhan [a reference to the "left" Guomindang government there] will lose its nerve and come under Nanking [Nanjing, i.e., Chiang Kai-shek]."[107]

Events were swiftly overtaking Stalin as the Nationalist government in Wuhan was literally falling apart before his eyes. One after another, the generals who had recently sworn allegiance to the Guomindang "left" renounced Wuhan. A most difficult situation was also created as a result of withdrawal by the industrialists and merchants from the cities under its control. Unable to salvage the situation, the government leaders themselves began to adopt increasingly open anti-worker and anti-peasant policies. Relations between the Guomindang "leftists" and the Communists became increasingly strained.

All this contributed to mounting dissatisfaction with the Wuhan government on the part of Stalin and the Party Politburo. In the meantime, Stalin considered possible concessions to Wang Jingwei along government and Comintern lines, such as removing Borodin "if Wuhan wants", and sending new subsidies "just in order to have a guarantee that Wuhan does not surrender to the tender mercies of Nanjing."[108] Paralleling this anxiety, however, was his growing dissatisfaction with the obvious unwillingness of the

Wuhan government to radicalize itself. In the end, Stalin decisively rejected the idea of concessions. The Soviet leadership began to lean toward the idea of mobilizing the CCP to seize power inside the GMD "left."

A specific instance of this was Bukharin's June 30, 1927 article in *Pravda* which was written immediately after General Feng Yuxiang switched to Chiang Kai-shek's side.[109] (Stalin, having familiarized himself with Bukharin's article, believed that it "turned out well.")[110] The article called for the purging of "bourgeois riff-raff and renegades of every sort" from the Guomindang "left", and the organization of a "real Jacobin 'left,'" i.e. a sort of Wuhan 'revolutionary committee.'" It devoted particular attention to the need for a "most decisive" struggle against traitors. The entire article pointed the reader toward the conclusion that soon the leaders of the "left" Guomindang would also turn out to be "betrayers." At the same time, no mention was made of Soviets, and the CCP was ordered not to withdraw from the Guomindang under any circumstances. After uniting with the "Guomindang lower ranks," the CCP should aim at transforming it into a "mighty worker-peasant ... party, an organ of the democratic, plebeian revolution." Attempting to shield the Comintern Executive Committee from the consequences of the inevitable failure of its political line in China, Bukharin leveled a series of charges against the leaders of the Chinese Communist party, albeit still in a general form, and without directly mentioning the CCP. The most important of these was their "failure to implement" the "correct" directives of the Comintern, and also "inhibiting" the agrarian revolution and the arming of workers.

Soon afterwards, on July 8, the Executive Committee of the Comintern sent a directive, approved in advance by the Politburo, to the Central Committee of the CCP, demanding that Communists withdraw from membership in the GMD's Nationalist government since "the main armed forces of Wuhan ... have become the instrument of counter-revolutionaries." The ECCI, however, did not link the resignation of ministers who were members of the CCP with the withdrawal of the CCP from the Guomindang.[111] On the very same day, Stalin commented on this directive in a letter to Molotov, "We used the Wuhan leadership as much as possible. Now it's time to discard them. An attempt should be made to take over the periphery of the Guomindang and help it oppose its current bosses."[112]

But this last directive, too, was powerless to alter the situation in China. Just like the leaders of the Wuhan government, the Guomindang "leftists" on the periphery were in no hurry to become "revolutionary Jacobins." On the contrary, everyone adhered more openly to an anti-Communist position. The defeat of the Chinese Communist party, and of Stalin's policy in China, became a reality. In essence, Stalin had doomed himself as well as the CCP, to defeat.

Chapter 10 _____

The Fall of the Opposition and the Evolution of Stalin's and Trotsky's Views on China

As an anti-Communist reign of terror took hold virtually throughout China, Stalin's paramount concern became saving his own reputation. Even in private letters to his closest collaborators he did not admit mistakes. In a note to Molotov of July 11, 1927, he wrote, "Our policy [in China] was and remains the only correct policy. Never have I been so deeply and firmly convinced of the correctness of our policy . . . in China,.. as I am now."[113] Two weeks later, on July 28, he published an article in *Pravda*, the overall aim of which was to explicit justify the Comintern's China policy.[114]

Stalin decided that the chief blame was to be placed on the CCP Central Committee. In a July 9 letter addressed to Molotov and Bukharin, whom he permitted "to give it to the other Politburo members to read," Stalin put forward a whole "package" of complaints directed against the Chinese Communist leaders, harshly and crudely accusing the CCP Central Committee of being "completely unadapted" for the new, agrarian, phase of the revolution. "There is not a single Marxist mind in the Central Committee [of the CCP] capable of understanding the underpinning (the social underpinning) of the events now occurring," declared Stalin, commenting further that since this was the kind of CCP Central Committee that had taken shape, there was only one thing required of it: to carry out the ECCI's directives; but it did not, "because it did not understand them, because it did not want to fulfill them and has *hoodwinked the Comintern,* or because it wasn't able to fulfill them."

An infuriated Stalin specifically proposed the following:

> It's time to really busy ourselves with the organization of a system of party advisors attached to the CCP Central Committee, the Central Committee departments, regional organizations in each province, the departments of these regional organizations, the

party youth organization, the peasant department of the Central Committee, the military department of the Central Committee, the central organ [newspaper], the federation of trade unions of China ... The structure has to be set up so that all these party advisors work together as a whole, directed *by the chief advisor to the Central Committee* (the Comintern representative). The 'nannies' are necessary at this stage because of the weakness, shapelessness and political amorphousness, and lack of qualification of the current Central Committee. The Central Committee will learn from the party advisors. The party advisors will compensate for the enormous shortcomings of the CCP Central Committee and its top regional officials. They will serve (for the time being) as the nails holding the existing conglomerate together as a party.[115]

It was, however, senseless to wax indignant about the failure of the Chinese Communists to implement the Comintern's directives. The Stalinist policy could not but lead to the cruelest rout of the Communist movement in China. This proposal was never implemented, but it revealed Stalin's general approach toward "fraternal relations" with another Communist party – i.e., control of it from top to bottom through his agents. Stalin also placed a large share of the "blame" on the Comintern's representatives in China – the chief ones in 1927 had been Borodin and Roy – demanding that the Comintern "purge" them from that country.

His criticism was reflected in an essay by Mandalyan published in *Pravda* on July 16, 1927, entitled "Why the Chinese Communist Party Leadership Went Bankrupt." Zinoviev examined this "shameful article" in his unfinished paper, "Events in China."[116]

On July 15, 1927 the Guomindang "left" leaders unleashed a reign of "white terror" in Wuhan. This definitive evidence of the failure of Stalin's tactics naturally exacerbated the question of relations with the Opposition from whom Stalin could no longer tolerate criticism. In early July, for example, he toyed with the idea of sending Trotsky to Japan (apparently as ambassador),[117] but he soon abandoned the idea: his China policy had been thoroughly discredited, and that, together with the deepening differences over internal problems in the USSR and the Soviet party, ruled out a peaceful outcome of the conflict with the Trotsky-Zinoviev minority. The next joint Plenum of the Party's Central Committee and Central Control Commission was therefore bound to be a landmark in the struggle between the Stalinists and the Opposition.

The Plenum took place from July 29 to August 9, 1927, with the China question one of the central issues debated, although viewed in the framework of the overall international situation of the USSR. Chicherin and Bukharin delivered the main reports on this topic defending the Politburo's position.[118] The views of the Opposition on the Chinese revolution were represented only by Zinoviev, Kamenev, and Trotsky.[119] The Chinese issue was closely related to one formulated as "On the recent statements of the Opposition and Comrades Trotsky's and Zinoviev's violation of the party discipline." Ordzhonikidze presented a report on this issue.

The Plenum added nothing constructive to the problem of interpreting the experience and lessons of the Chinese revolution. The positions of each side had been systematically spelled out earlier; serious discussion and theoretical analysis were drowned in a flood of mutual recriminations. The leaders of the Opposition, persistently citing the "Menshevism" of the AUCP(B) and ECCI leaders, accused them of betraying the revolution in China and creating conditions that made it possible for the imperialists to unleash a new war against the USSR.[120] In turn, the Stalinists accused the Oppositionists of adventurism, double-dealing, and anti-party behavior. Both sides blamed each other for "breaking" with Leninism with regard to the tactics of the anti-colonial revolution. The outcome of the discussion was predetermined. By a majority vote the Plenum issued a strict reprimand against Trotsky and Zinoviev and warned them against further factional activity.[121] The Opposition found itself in profound crisis.

The new situation in China, however, made it incumbent upon the leaders of the Comintern and the Opposition to decide on a new tactical line for the Chinese Communist movement. This, of course, was impossible without at least a preliminary assessment of what stage the Chinese revolution was then passing through.

On the eve of the Wuhan coup d'état in early July 1927, the Stalinists began to take the first steps in the direction indicated. It was precisely at this time that Stalin, in a private letter to Molotov and Bukharin, raised the question of the "possibility of an interval" between the bourgeois revolution in China which had been coming to the end, and "a *future*" bourgeois revolution, "analogous to the interval that we had between 1905 and 1917 (February)."[122] He elaborated this thought in another letter to Molotov, saying that such an interval could not be "**rule**[d] **out**", nor could a new upsurge "in the *next* period" be excluded.[123] The role of organizer of this new phase of the bourgeois-democratic movement he assigned to the CCP, which for the time being would operate under the flag of the "left" Guomindang.[124]

These letters in essence presented Stalin's overall concept of the new stage of the Chinese revolutionary movement, which he characterized as still bourgeois in nature, although he acknowledged the temporarily defeat of the revolution, i.e., of the CCP. At the same time he anticipated a new stirring of the mass movement in the near future under the leadership of the CCP working through a left "workers' and peasants' party." These ideas corresponded to a notion Stalin had often expressed before, namely, the "impossibility" of the so-called Kemalist path for China. By this he meant the development of China along capitalist lines as a result of a victorious bourgeois revolution.[125]

Bukharin had developed these views on the eve of the Joint (July-August 1927) Plenum of the Central Committee and Central Control Commission in his draft theses of the Politburo on the international situation. The document says in part,

> The present period of the Chinese revolution is characterized by profound defeat and the simultaneous radical regrouping of forces. A bloc of workers, peasants, and urban poor is organizing against classes of owners and imperialism. In *this* sense, the revolution is rising to the highest phase of its development, the phase of the direct struggle for a dictatorship of the working class and peasantry... The national bourgeoisie ... cannot accomplish *internal* tasks of the revolution for it does not only support the peasants, but also acts actively against them. Thus, it is more inclined toward a bloc with feudal elements and does not even solve the elementary problems of the bourgeois democratic revolution ... Therefore, the most probable outcome is that the short-term prospect of the temporary defeat of the revolution will be replaced by a new upsurge.[126]

Following Stalin, Bukharin did not indicate whether Chinese Soviets should now be formed. Most likely the Party leadership at the time had some disagreements on this question; and Stalin and Bukharin themselves were wavering. This can be deduced from the fact that right at the time when the Politburo was discussing Bukharin's draft, *Pravda* published an editorial calling for Soviets in China.[127] During the Plenum, however, this call was subjected to criticism on the grounds that conditions in China still "compelled" the Communist party to "use ... the 'Left' Guomindang", which could not accept the slogan of Soviets. Bukharin, Manuilsky, Molotov, and Rykov all defended this point of view,[128] which the majority of the Plenum approved.

Only in September 1927, soon after the nearly formed Chinese Communist army units began to engage in guerrilla actions against the Guomindang and warlord troops, were changes in the CCP's strategy initiated. A September 30 *Pravda* editorial argued that the Chinese revolutionary movement, which remained anti-imperialist and bourgeois-democratic in nature, had finally entered the initial phase of a new upsurge. But at the same time, the editorial said: "[I]t had become definitely clear" that the CCP was the only political organization capable of leading the masses. The "Left" Guomindang could not cope with this task. From now on, *Pravda* held, the struggle in China would be conducted under the leadership of the Chinese Communist party and it would aim at establishing a truly anti-imperialist and revolutionary-democratic dictatorship of the proletariat and peasantry in the form of Soviets of workers', peasants', soldiers', and artisans' deputies. The editorial welcomed the formation of a "revolutionary army of Chinese workers and peasants" and expressed confidence that "given correct leadership, and with a bold course directed toward developing the agrarian revolution," this army would "accomplish a *great* historical task."[129]

The leaders of the Soviet Union and Comintern, thus effectively adopted large parts of the program that the United Opposition had proposed earlier. But they did not do so until late September 1927.

Meanwhile, within the Opposition itself a thorough theoretical discussion was taking place concerning divergent assessments of the stage through which the Chinese revolution was currently passing and, consequently, of how the tactics of the CCP should be determined. In mid-September 1927, as he continued to reflect painfully on the difficulties facing the revolutionary movement in China, Trotsky drafted some theses and sent them to Zinoviev. Again he analyzed the Comintern's China policy, but now presented some new proposals that, in his view, corresponded to the needs of the moment.[130] His central point was to call for a struggle to establish the dictatorship of the proletariat in China instead of continuing with the *"historically overdue"* slogan of a "democratic dictatorship of the proletariat and peasantry." In other words, after the defeat of the CCP Trotsky moved away from Lenin's position concerning China as expressed in the Comintern theory of anti-colonial revolutions adopted at the Second Congress in July-August 1920. In essence, this was the first time since he had accepted Lenin's concept in 1922, that Trotsky returned to his own formula of permanent revolution in regard to an Asian country, the one that had guided the work of the Comintern on the countries of "the East" before the Second Congress.

Trotsky had not arrived at this idea suddenly. As he later acknowledged, he began to suspect that there would be no democratic dictatorship of the proletariat and peasantry in China from the time the Wuhan government was first formed, i.e., from January 1927. In a spring 1928 letter to Evgenii A. Preobrazhensky he recalled that

> I based myself precisely upon the analysis of the most fundamental social facts, and not upon the manner in which they were refracted politically, which, as is well known, often assumes peculiar forms, since, in this sphere, factors of a secondary order enter in, including national tradition. I became convinced that the basic social facts have already cleared the road for themselves through all the peculiarities of political superstructures . . ."[131]

It was about this time that he also started to apply variants of his old concept to China. One can conceive how his thinking proceeded from some of his brief notes which survive in the archives. At the end of June 1927 he wrote the following:

Lenin's teaching about the revolutionary significance of the struggle of backward and oppressed peoples for their national liberation does not give a general or automatic solution to political questions for all oppressed nations. Ways and methods of a national struggle depend upon the class structure of an oppressed nation, and, first of all, upon the role and significance of the proletariat in it. According to a general rule, the role of the bourgeois revolutionary elements, more precisely, of the petite bourgeois revolutionary elements will be increased in inverse proportion to the number and independence of the proletariat. On the contrary, the presence of the quickly growing proletariat beforehand determines the counterrevolutionary role of the bourgeoisie.

In this sense, it is necessary to distinguish strictly two extreme types, between which there are intermediate ones, i.e., ... patriarchal colonies which do not have their own industry, ... and those colonies of which the most complete sample is China, which contains inside her borders all phases of economic development ... and where the newest capitalist relations are obviously growing quickly.[132]

This reasoning was apparently in step with Roy's ideas and as such did not differ from Stalin's social views. However, unlike Stalin, but in line with Roy, Trotsky drew the following political conclusion: "Many things in China will become clearer to us, if we use correctly the experience of Russia and, first of all, remind ourselves how and why the course of the class struggle in backwards Russia passed the power over into the hands of the proletariat earlier than in advanced capitalist countries."[133] This thesis resembled his statement at the 1921 Third Comintern Congress.

Until mid-autumn 1927, however, Trotsky continued to doubt Lenin's views on the establishment in China of a revolutionary democratic dictatorship of the proletariat and peasantry. He gained confidence in the necessity of immediate changing Lenin's classic theory only after the defeat of the Chinese Communist movement. Trotsky formulated a new course in his mid-September 1927 theses:

Right now the business at hand for the proletariat is to win over to "revolutionary democracy" the poor lower classes of the city and countryside and lead them forward for the conquest of power, of the land, of national independence, and better living conditions for the toiling masses. In other words, the business at hand is the *dictatorship of the proletariat*.[134]

He explained the reasons for raising this slogan, however, only by noting the peculiarities of the current situation in China. Trotsky implied that the

157

unfolding of the "white terror" in Wuhan came about as a result of the transition into the camp of counterrevolution not only of the big and middle bourgeois, but also of the "upper petty bourgeoisie" and "intelligentsia" in the city and the countryside. He did not shape any general theoretical reasoning. He seemed to believe that the United Opposition would accept his proposals and send the suggested theses to the Politburo or the Comintern Executive Committee. He pointed out that

> The call for a democratic dictatorship of the proletariat and peasantry, if it had been advanced, let us say, at the beginning of the Northern Expedition, in connection with the call for soviets and the arming of the workers and peasants, would have played a tremendous role in the development of the Chinese revolution, would have completely assured a different course for it.

However, he added, the Leninist slogan that was "not applied at the right time," could not be mechanically carried over into the new situation, for "after the experience with the Kuomintang [Guomindang] in general and with the left Kuomintang in particular, a *historically overdue slogan will become a weapon of the forces working against the revolution.*"[135] Nor did Trotsky link the call for a struggle for the proletarian dictatorship in China with the question of whether the bourgeois revolution had won: he could not answer the question precisely.

A few days after sending a copy of his draft theses to Zinoviev, Trotsky elaborated his thoughts in a special article entitled "Old Mistakes at a New Stage",[136] also addressed to Zinoviev. He intended to send it to the *Bol'shevik* editorial board or to the Politburo.[137]

Trotsky's point of view found little support within the United Opposition. Neither Zinoviev nor Radek nor many others could renounce what they regarded as the Leninist approach. Once again Trotsky felt obliged to make concessions to his colleagues in order to maintain the anti-Stalinist bloc. He did not raise the slogan of dictatorship of the proletariat in China again until after his bloc with Zinoviev had fallen apart. The slogan did not form part of Oppositionist material circulated in the fall of 1927 and in particular it was not included in the September "Declaration of the Thirteen: The Draft Platform of the Bolshevik Leninists (Opposition) for the Fifteenth AUCP(B) Congress." That document contained the following thesis of Zinoviev: "Lenin's teaching that the bourgeois-democratic revolution can be carried through to the end only by an alliance of the working class and the peasantry – under the leadership of the former – against the *bourgeoisie*, is not only applicable to China and similar colonial and semi-colonial countries; it in fact points to the only road to victory in those countries."[138] This passage was taken from Zinoviev's article "Our International Situation and the Danger of War," written at the end of July 1927, that as a whole does not deal with China.

At the same time the Oppositionists continued to criticize the mistakes of the Stalinists in China, intensifying their struggle against Stalin on questions concerning the internal political development of the USSR and the situation in the Bolshevik party. Their wrathful declarations, however, were still addressed to that selfsame apparatus which was becoming increasingly bureaucratized. The conduct of Trotsky and his comrades only embittered the Stalinists, who in the fall of 1927 intensified their repression of the Opposition. On September 24 the ECCI Political Secretariat decided to discuss the issue of the "continuation of a factional activity" by the ECCI members Trotsky and Vujovič at a joint session of the ECCI Presidium and the International Control Commission.[139] On September 27 that session unanimously expelled Trotsky and Vujovič from the Comintern Executive Committee.[140] A month later, at the October 1927 Joint Plenum of the Central Committee and Central Control Commission, Trotsky and Zinoviev were expelled from the Central Committee and a resolution was passed to submit the evidence of their "splitting activity" for consideration by the Fifteenth Party Congress.[141]

The Stalinists did not even stop short at organizing deliberate provocations. One of the most blatant provocations and, as is apparent from archival documents, one that was planned and prepared in advance, was a series of street clashes, inspired by Stalin's associates, during the celebration march dedicated to the tenth anniversary of the October Revolution.[142]

All the blame for the events of November 7, 1927, was pinned on the leaders of the Opposition. A week later, and just two weeks before the Fifteenth Party Congress, Trotsky and Zinoviev were expelled from the party by a decision of the Central Committee and Central Control Commission.

Immediately after that a crack appeared in the Trotskyist-Zinovievist bloc as Zinoviev and Kamenev began to lean toward the idea of capitulating to Stalin. The final break-up of the bloc occurred at the Fifteenth Party Congress (December 2–19, 1927). On December 10, shortly after the Congress had unanimously approved a resolution based on a report from the Party's Central Committee stating that membership in the Opposition faction or advocacy of its views was incompatible with party membership, a group of Zinoviev's supporters (Kamenev, Bakaev, Avdeev, and Yevdokimov) and a group of Trotskyists (Muralov, Rakovsky, Radek), independently submitted statements to Ordzhonikidze, chairman of the Congress's special commission on the question of the Opposition's activities. The statements revealed two differing attitudes toward the resolution the Congress had just adopted. The Zinovievists declared unconditional submission. The Trotskyists stated their disagreement with the point in the resolution banning advocacy of oppositionist views.[143] The Congress, however, was not interested in such nuances. It confirmed the earlier decision to expel Trotsky and Zinoviev, and on December 18 it passed a further resolution expelling other active members of the Opposition. This led to the the final episode in the history of the United Opposition.[144] On December 19, a group of 23 Zinoviev supporters submitted a statement to the Presiding Committee of the Fifteenth Party Congress: they were "disarming ideologically and organizationally."[145]

The United Opposition in the Bolshevik party had ceased to exist and its struggle against the Stalinist majority on the subject of the Chinese revolution ended in defeat. The Trotskyist group, early in 1928 deported to remote areas in the USSR, continued for a while to discuss the Chinese question. First exiled to Central Asia and then early in 1929 forcibly deported to Turkey, Trotsky was one of the most active participants in the discussion. He never stopped examining the Chinese revolution. His efforts produced some new and original ideas in this area, but they were not accepted by the overwhelming majority of the Russian Opposition, nor, after the defeat of the United Opposition, did his views have any impact inside the Soviet Communist party. Only a small group of his closest supporters, among them the Chinese Oppositionists, shared his new approach.

Part VI

The Stalin-Trotsky Split on China and the Chinese Communists

Chapter 11 _____

Chinese Revolutionaries: From Moscow Students to Dissidents

Until the end of 1926, the disputes in the ECCI between Trotsky and Stalin were largely unknown to the individual sections of the Communist International. Not only the rank and file but also the leaders of these parties were ignorant of Trotsky's, Zinoviev's or Radek's positions on the fundamental issues of the inner-party regime, economic construction in the USSR, and the direction of world developments, including the Chinese revolution. This was the result of Stalin's attempt to fence off the world Communist movement from the influence of his principal rival. In this, however, he was only partially successful. Despite his best efforts, both the foreign staff of the ECCI and other foreign Communists who were, for various reasons, living in the USSR were drawn into the struggle within the Bolshevik party. Above all, this meant those who had come to study in the various universities and "cadre schools" set up to train militants of the world Communist movement. And if the CCP as a whole, knowing nothing about Trotsky's position, mechanically followed Stalin as leader of the International Communist movement, it was precisely within the circles of Chinese students in Moscow that the Left Opposition in the Chinese Communist Party was born.

The Bolsheviks began establishing international schools in Soviet Russia shortly after the October Revolution, offering aid to foreign revolutionary movements in developing a system for training cadres. Aid was given on an especially large scale to the Chinese movements and many Chinese came to study in Russia, having to a greater or lesser degree thrown in their lot with the Communists.

Since it was practically impossible for Chinese revolutionaries to make the journey to Russia in the early years following October, the Bolsheviks concentrated their efforts politically on educating those Chinese workers who, for one reason or another, already found themselves on Soviet territory. In organizing courses for them, the Bolsheviks believed that these Chinese revolutionaries, having witnessed and participated in fierce battles in Russia, "would act as a link between the existing movement [in Soviet Russia] and that soon to be born in China."[1] And indeed some of this first wave of Chinese, having studied at the school of the class struggle so to speak, subsequently played prominent roles in the Chinese Nationalist and Communist movements, for example, Yang Mingzhai and Liu Changsheng.

With the end of the Civil War in most parts of Russia by 1920, however, and with national liberation movements springing up the East, the task of organizing systematic education for revolutionaries of the East assumed a more urgent character. Young freedom-fighters would travel spontaneously to Russia seeking help and there was a need to set up a central school which could teach them Marxism-Leninism and revolutionary strategy and provide them with some military training which they could later put to use in their own countries. A proposal to found such an institution was put to the Second Congress of the Comintern on June 26, 1920 by Maring, who declared that,

> The Third International should make it possible for students from the Far East to live here for a year or so, to study courses in Communism, so that they properly understand what is taking place here and can breathe life into the theses [of the Congress], create Soviet organizations, and carry out Communist work in the colonies ... Moscow and Petrograd are the new Meccas of the East. We here in Russia must make it possible for Eastern revolutionaries to get a theoretical education, so that the Far East becomes a living part of the Communist International.[2]

On February 10, 1921, the RCP(B) Central Comniittee decided to set up the University of the Toilers of the East.[3] A resolution concerning this was adopted by the Central Executive Committee of the Soviet Union on April 21, 1921.[4] The institution soon became known as the Communist University of the Toilers of the East (in Russian abbreviation – KUTV.) In 1923, it was renamed the J. V. Stalin Communist University of the Toilers of the East. Its initial aim was declared to be the political education of representatives of the working masses of the Soviet Far East – "... treaty lands, autonomous republics, autonomous areas, workers communes, and national minorities."[5] But from the outset, it was given the additional task of educating Eastern revolutionaries from beyond the borders of the USSR, including, of course, from China.[6]

With the foundation of KUTV in Moscow, the education of Chinese revolutionaries in the Soviet Union entered a new phase. Between 1921 and 1925, and again in the 1930s, all Chinese students were educated alongside those from other nationalities. But from 1925 to 1930, there was a university devoted exclusively to educating Chinese revolutionaries. It was founded in response to the outbreak of the national anti-imperialist revolution in China, and from 1925 to 1928 it was known as the Sun Yat-sen University of the Toilers of China (in Russian abbreviation – UTK.) On September 17, 1928, after the defeat of the CCP and the institution of a fierce "white terror" in China, the university was renamed the Communist University of the Toilers of China (in Russian abbreviation – KUTK.)[7] Just before this, Chinese students at KUTV had been transferred there. The aim of KUTK expressed in its journal *Gongchan zazhi* (Communist Journal) was to give a Marxist education to "the leaders of the mass Communist movement in China, the Bolshevik leaders of the Chinese revolution."[8] Toward autumn of 1930 it was closed down. Following this, the International Lenin School became the focus for the education of Chinese revolutionary youth. A special Chinese department was established within the school known as department "C." Members of the Chinese Socialist (Communist) Youth League were also educated at the Central Komsomol School. In 1934, a Chinese section was again opened at KUTV but it lasted only two years. On March 25, 1936, the overseas department of KUTV (known at this time as the cadre department) was transferred to the Institute for Scientific Research on National and Colonial Problems (ISRNCP), which then became responsible for the education of students from abroad. The Chinese students at KUTV (143 persons) were transferred to the new institute, making up about 80 percent of its intake. In September 1938, however, the institute was dissolved by a decision of the ECCI Secretariat.

Apart from KUTV, UTK/KUTK, the International Lenin School, the Institute for Scientific Research on National and Colonial Problems, and the Central Komsomol School, there were other institutions where Chinese revolutionaries studied during the 1920s and 1930s. In December 1921, a decision of the Agitprop Department of the Russian Communist Party's Central Committee led to the opening of a department of KUTV in Irkutsk devoted to the education of Far Eastern peoples including Chinese.[9] In June 1922, a decision of the party's Far East Bureau established a political education department of the military-political school of the people's revolutionary army of the Far Eastern Republic.[10] This was intended to educate Chinese partisans from Manchuria among whom Communist influence was practically nonexistent. A Chinese Lenin school functioned in Vladivostok in the mid-1920s.[11] In 1932, a series of courses entitled "The Workers' Movement" were organized on the initiative of A. Lozovsky, the general secretary of the Red International of Labor Unions (Profintern). They were intended to prepare Chinese graduates of Soviet universities for their return home. Lozovsky and others taught the young revolutionaries the art of leading strike movements among the workers, building trade unions, etc.[12] Chinese were given technical industrial training in various Soviet firms. There were many other specialist courses available to Chinese Communist cadres.[13]

The Bolsheviks gave great assistance to the Chinese Communists in the field of military training. Special departments for Chinese students were set up at the Frunze Military Academy, the Tolmachev Military Political Academy, the Aeronautical Military-Theoretical School, the Artillery School, the Moscow Infantry School, and in military schools in Kiev and other provincial centers. From September 1927 until June 1928, KUTV ran special military-political courses.[14] Chinese commanders were also sent on the *Vystrel* (Shot) courses organized for Red Guard commanders. In an official message to the military academies, Voroshilov directed that they should aim to train officers capable of commanding "large-scale military units in China."[15] The Soviets routinely organized military training for Chinese Communists coming to Moscow on Comintern or other business.[16]

The process of selecting Chinese students for study in Russia and the composition of the student groups varied with the political situation in China and, of course, with the particular profile of the institute in question. For example, military schools differed from Communist universities. It also depended on the importance attached to the institution by the GMD or CCP leadership.

The selection of students for specifically Communist institutions lay entirely with the ECCI and the central committees of the Russian and Chinese Communist parties. For the general political schools and, during the period of the CCP-GMD united front (1924–27), for military academies, the selections were made jointly by the central executive committees of the USSR and the GMD, with the participation of the CCP Central Committee. After the breakup of the united front, responsibility for choosing students for military schools fell to the Chinese delegation at the ECCI. Naturally, a great deal of the practical work of selection was carried out in China itself, by Soviet and Comintern workers. In 1920, the ECCI representative Voitinsky, together with his assistants M. F. Kuznetsova and Yang Mingzhai, organized the so-called School of Foreign Languages in Shanghai.[17] This was actually intended for socialist-minded youth who wanted to study in Moscow. The secretary of the Shanghai Union of Socialist Youth, Yu Xiusong, also played an active part in setting up the school in which he served as the technical director. Several groups of ten to twenty students passed through the school where, for the most part, they studied the Russian language, which was taught by Yang Mingzhai. Once a week a member of the Shanghai Communist circle, the first Chinese translator of the *Manifesto of the Communist Party*, Chen Wangdao gave a lecture on Marxism.[18] It is likely that other members of the Shanghai Communist organization gave lectures, though given the low level of development of Chinese Marxist thought at the time, it is unlikely that the students came away with any clear picture of Socialism. In the spring of 1921, apparently in April or May, the first fourteen graduates of the school were sent to Soviet Russia, on the recommendation of the Shanghai Communist circle and Yang Mingzhai. Among them were some who later became prominent figures in the CCP – Liu Shaoqi, Ren Bishi, Peng Shuzhi, Luo Yinong, and Xiao Jingguang.[19] According to Bao Huiseng, one of the first supporters of Communism in China, a special commission for education was set up in Shanghai in early 1921 by himself, Yang Mingzhai, and probably Dong Biwu.[20] Its function was to choose worthy representatives of Chinese socialist youth to be sent to study in Moscow.[21]

The first large intake of Chinese students, including Liu Shaoqi and Xiao Jingguang, were enrolled at KUTV on August 1, 1921.[22] A total of twenty-six Chinese were issued student cards on that day, having arrived in Moscow on the recommendation of various Communist circles. Prior to this, only two Chinese had enrolled at the school, arriving on July 9 and 23 respectively.[23] By the second half of 1921 there were thirty-five or thirty-six Chinese students at KUTV; by 1924, fifty-one; and in mid-April 1925 there were 112.[24]

As revolutionaries and conspirators, the majority (and after December 1922, all) were given pseudonyms by which they were known in all official documents. Peng Shuzhi was known as Ivan Petrov, Ren Bishi as Brinsky, Luo Yinong as Bukharov, and Liu Bojian, who later rose to prominence in the CCP, as Sherstinsky.[25] The students represented a significant percentage of CCP and Socialist Youth members. In April 1924, about 9 percent of the CCP membership were in Russia.[26] The majority came from non-proletarian backgrounds. In China, as in other countries, the intelligentsia predominated in the early stages of the Communist movement.[27]

Following the formation of the national united front by the CCP and GMD, the basis on which students were selected for study in the USSR changed. After the foundation of the Sun Yat-sen University of the Toilers of China (October 7, 1925), a central selection committee was set up in Guangzhou on the proposal of Borodin. A number of prominent leaders of the Nationalist party and government took part, including Tan Yankai, Gu Yingfen, and Wang Jingwei. Borodin acted as adviser. Selection boards sat in several large cities, including Shanghai, Beijing, and Tianjin. In Shanghai, Yang Mingzhai and Zhou Dawen were in charge.[28] All the students had to sit arduous three-part examinations. Finally, a contingent of 310 students was selected, including 180 from Guangzhou, 100 from Shanghai, Beijing, and Tianjin, and 10 each from the military schools in Hunan and Yunnan, and the Whampoa Academy. An extra 30 were added to the group without having to sit the exams, on account of their close family relations with important GMD officials.

Although the rules of the new university laid down that the number of CCP and GMD students should be roughly equal,[29] both parties did their best to obstruct members of the other party from getting to Moscow. For example, 90 percent of those chosen in Guangzhou, where the right was strong, were GMD members. On the other hand, the majority of students from Shanghai, Beijing, and Tianjin were members of either the CCP or its youth wing.[30] Taking the group as a whole, the number of Communists was greater. Among those who had arrived in Moscow by December 1925, 188 (68 percent) were Communists.[31]

The whole process of getting the group to Moscow took several months.[32] The first group of 119 people received their student cards on November 23, 1925,[33] while others had to wait for a passage from Guangzhou where they were taught Russian by Soviet advisers to the GMD.[34]

Chinese emigres could also be selected for study in Moscow and this was left in the hands of the particular party they were attached to. Some, of course, simply turned up in Russia on their own initiative. The first group to arrive, from France, were members of the CCP or its youth organization and enrolled at KUTV in April 1923. Among them were Wang Ruofei, Gao Feng, Xiong Xiong, Zheng Chaolin, Chen Qiaonian, Chen Yannian, and Zhao Shiyan, all of whom were active members of the CCP's European Department which had been set up in 1922 in Paris.[35] In mid-November of the same year, another group of twenty arrived at KUTV from France. Among them was Yin Kuan, one of the future leaders of the Trotskyist movement in China.[36] In October 1924, another group from France enrolled at KUTV, including Nie Rongzhen who was later to play a prominent role in the CCP.[37] In January 1926, ten Chinese, mainly GMD members, arrived from Germany to enroll at UTK, followed in autumn of the same year by ten CCP members from Belgium and France.[38] Chinese students also arrived from the Philippines and the United States and a number enrolled who had previously been resident in Soviet Russia.

At the end of the first academic year at UTK, the selection process had to be repeated and the Organization Bureau of the Soviet Communist Party Central Committee appointed Dalin, one of the staff at the university, to take charge.[39] Thanks to his efforts, the links between UTK and China were maintained throughout the revolutionary period of 1926–27. During these years groups from central and south China continued to arrive in Moscow, mainly enrolling at UTK, but also at KUTV and various military academies. In August 1926 and at the start of 1927 commanders and political commissars from the Nationalist Army of Feng Yuxiang arrived at Sun Yat-sen University and in the winter of 1926 a large party arrived from north China.[40] By July 1927, around the time of Wang Jingwei's coup in Wuhan, there were 562 students at the university.[41] Their social backgrounds reflected the makeup of the national united front in China, in that they included members of the bourgeoisie and landowning class as well as workers and peasants.

On September 13, 1927, the GMD Central Executive Committee formally broke relations with Sun Yat-sen University of the Toilers of

China, deciding to "send no more students to this university."[42] But even before this, the GMD had forbidden its members to remain at UTK and on August 5, 239 students quit the university and returned to China.[43] With the withdrawal of the GMD, the selection of students was left in the hands of the Communists. UTK was reorganized into a Communist institution and in March 1928 its rector, Pavel A. Mif, presented a document to the Chinese commission of the Soviet Communist Party's Central Committee Politburo recommending a maximum of 20 percent non-Communist members of the student body. He also proposed that no less than half of the students should be industrial workers. As regards emigres, only those with a solid record in the CCP or its youth wing should be accepted and, above all, no one who had spent more than five years abroad should be considered.[44] At the beginning of August 1927 there were 320 students at UTK.[45] Some of them returned to China, having finished their courses. Others were kept on as translators, instructors, or researchers and still others went on to study in military academies around the Soviet Union.

In autumn 1927 a group of prominent CCP members arrived at the university. Some of them, including Wu Yuzhang and Lin Boqu, had held high posts in the GMD in Wuhan until the July coup d'etat. At the beginning of 1928 a large group of working class and peasant youth, veterans of the Nanchang uprising and the "autumn harvest" uprisings of 1927, arrived in Moscow. They were accompanied by many trade unionists and activists from the women's movement. Most of these people were members of the CCP or its youth wing. A number of delegates to the CCP's Sixth Congress, which was held near Moscow, in August 1928, were sent to study at UTK at the conclusion of the Congress. Among them was the fifty-two-year-old founder-member of the CCP, He Shuheng. At this time, the university, now renamed KUTK, numbered around 600 students, including 137 who had been transferred from the Chinese Department of KUTV.[46]

As a whole, looking at the period of the 1920s and 1930s, it is evident that a significant proportion of the Chinese revolutionary movement, both the CCP and the GMD, received a political education in the USSR. A whole network of higher educational establishments was created for this purpose. About 1,600 Chinese studied at UTK/ KUTK[47] and no less than 500 at KUTV. A large number of officers both from the Chinese Communist Red Army and the GMD-controlled National Revolutionary Army studied at Soviet military schools. From various sources we can conclude that of the 118 top leaders of the CCP who studied abroad, 80 (70 percent) studied in Russia.[48] (We are talking here of the period from the 1920s to the 1940s.) More than half of these (47) became members or alternate members of the Central Committee and 15 became members of the Politburo. Apart from those we have already referred to, there were such prominent figures as Wang Jiaxiang (studied at UTK/KUTK), Guan Xiangying (studied at KUTV), Deng Xiaoping (KUTV, later UTK), Li Fuchun (KUTV), Xiang Jingyu, Cai Chang (KUTV), Zuo Quan, Zhang Wentian (UTK/KUTK), Zhu De (KUTV), Qin Bangxian (UTK/KUTK), Chen Boda (alias Chen Shangyu, UTK/KUTK), Chen Changhao (UTK/KUTK), Chen Shaoyu (alias Wang Ming, UTK/KUTK), Yang Shangkun (UTK/KUTK), and others. Four of the five members of the executive committee of the united Trotskyist organization founded in May 1931 in China had studied in Moscow. These were Chen Yimou (UTK), Zheng Chaolin (KUTV), Wang Wenyuan (alias Wang Fanxi, KUTV, later KUTK), and Song Fengchun (UTK/KUTK).

The majority of these people came to study in the Soviet Union at a comparatively early age, on average about twenty to twenty-one years. As a rule, they had little practical experience of revolutionary work and their understanding of Bolshevik theory was still more limited. Liu Shaoqi, for example, before arriving in Soviet Russia, "understood only that Socialism was a good thing. I had heard of Marx and Lenin, about the October Revolution and the Bolshevik party. However, at that time I did not have a clear idea of Socialism and how it could be brought about."[49] The theoretical level of the majority of young Chinese left-wing democrats at the time of their arrival in the USSR can be gauged by the admission of Sheng Yueh that he and the overwhelming majority of his colleagues before arriving to study in the USSR "had only a weak acquaintance with traditional Chinese philosophy and knew virtually nothing of Western, bourgeois philosophy."[50] Judging from reports on the newly arrived students held in the archives of KUTV and UTK/KUTK, at best they could be expected to have read *The Manifesto of the Communist Party* or Bukharin and Preobrazhensky's *The ABC of Communism*.[51] Of course, a student might write down that he had read such and such a work without really understanding its contents. According to Wang Fanxi, he and his comrades "in fact did not understand what Communism really was" even after reading the few Marxist books available in China in the mid-1920s. They desperately sought reading material and, still more, teachers who could educate them.[52]

The task facing the authorities of the Soviet international schools, therefore, was to devise a special teaching program suitable for students of whom the majority carried with them the baggage of patriarchal and national traditions, had a very feeble grounding in Marxism, and did not even have a grasp of the basic social, political, and economic concepts of the modern world. Of course, the levels of education of the students varied widely. Workers and peasants who had not even attended elementary school would study at KUTV and UTK/KUTK alongside graduates of Chinese universities such as Beijng University, the Beijing National University of Law and Political Science, the Sun Yat-sen University of

Guangzhou, and Shanghai University, or foreign universities like Göteborg, the Lyon Franco-Chinese Institute,[53] and the University of Labor at Charleroi,[54] Belgium. However, even the most educated had little knowledge of Marxist theory.

The students at both KUTV and UTK/KUTK were divided into study groups according to their level of education. In the Chinese section at KUTV, at first known as department "A," later as department "C", they were split into seven groups with about half a dozen students in each. By contrast, the eleven groups at UTK each had between thirty and forty members.[55] The makeup of the groups was determined by party allegiance and age as well as educational attainment. An example of such a group which existed in 1926–27 at UTK was the so-called Theoretical Class consisting of leading CCP and GMD members. The secretary of its party cell was Deng Xiaoping.[56] In 1928, a Special Class was set up for CCP members over thirty years of age. There were fifteen members, including Dong Biwu,[57] Ye Jianying, Lin Boqu, Xu Teli, Wu Yuzhang, Fang Weixia, He Shuheng, and Zhao Ruzhi.[58]

The universities had special access departments, similar to those run for workers, which ran foundation courses for those students with little formal education. On the other hand, there were also advanced study groups, whose members were proficient in Russian and worked as lecturers and translators. These advanced students were also expected to prepare course summaries and translate any necessary special material into Chinese. The student-translators could be attached to a particular study group or to the faculty as a whole. At KUTV in 1921 there were two student-translators, Li Zongwu (alias Li Zhongwu) and Qu Qiubai. The latter worked as an assistant in the social studies department.[59] By September 1927 there were twenty Chinese graduates of UTK in the general lecturers group at the university. All had received the permission of the CCP Central Committee to remain in Moscow. Among them were Wang Jiaxiang, Dong Yixiang, Bu Shiqi, Huang Li, Shen Zemin, Zhang Wentian, Chen Shaoyu, Chen Yuandao, and Lu Yuan, the last a leader of the Chinese Left Opposition.[60]

The revolutionary movement needed highly trained cadres and the course of study was extremely arduous. At KUTV initially, the course lasted seven months. In 1922 it was extended to three years and in 1927, to four. The length of time students spent on military training also increased, to between six and nine months at KUTV and two years at UTK. It was planned to run a three-year military course at KUTK.[61] The best teachers in Moscow were attracted to work at KUTV and UTK/KUTK. These included the distinguished Sinologists M. G. Andreev, G. N. Voitinsky, M. Volin (alias S. N. Belenky), A. A. Ivanov (A. Ivin), E. S. Iolk, V. S. Kolokolov, V. N. Kuchumov (who from mid-1927 to May 1928 was pro-rector of UTK), L. I. Madyar (sometime director of the economics faculty at UTK), I. M. Oshanin, and E. D. Polivanov (director of the native languages department at KUTV). As already noted, Radek also lectured at UTK, where he was rector from 1925 until April 6, 1927. Shumatsky was rector of KUTV from 1926 to 1929 and taught a course on the history of revolutionary movements in the East. Many other historians, economists, philosophers, and graduates of the Institute of Red Professors and the J. M. Sverdlov Communist University taught at KUTV and UTK/KUTK. In 1922–23 at KUTV, there was a teaching body of 165 lecturers; in 1925–26 there were 146.[62] In 1926–27 there were 62 teachers at UTK and in 1930 there were 70.[63]

Many leaders of the AUCP(B), the Comintern, and the Profintern, including Stalin, Trotsky, Bukharin, Krupskaya, Lozovsky, Manuilsky, Pieck, and Katayama, attended as visiting lecturers. The students were also able to meet with leaders of the CCP delegation to the ECCI such as Zhou Enlai, Deng Zhongxia, Zhang Guotao, and Qu Qiubai.

The course work was extremely intensive. At KUTV in 1923 students had to study the Russian language, political economy, historical materialism, history of class struggle, history of the working class movement, history of the Russian Communist Party, as well as a number of natural sciences.[64] The first-year students at UTK studied the Russian language, the history of the development of social forms,[65] history of the Chinese revolutionary movement, history of the revolutionary movement in the West, general Western history, history of the Soviet Communist Party, economic geography, political economy, party-building, military affairs, and one other subject which went under the name "Gazette."[66] In the general lecture group at UTK, only four subjects were studied – political economy, general history of the West, historical materialism, and the theory and practice of proletarian revolution.[67] In the foundation (access) courses, they studied the Russian language, history, geography, arithmetic, and social science.[68]

The most intensive and effective were the Russian language courses. The principal aim was to permit the students to read social and political texts and to carry on discussions on these themes, which naturally were of most relevance to young revolutionaries. Social science courses were influenced, of course, by ideological and political developments within the Russian Communist Party and the Comintern. Before 1924 and Trotsky's defeat following his first clash with the Stalinist bureaucracy, students were taught according to the Leninist-Trotskyist theory of world development. But as Stalin's role in the Bolshevik party grew in importance and the struggle against Trotsky and later, the joint Left Opposition, intensified, the spirit of the ideology taught in these schools underwent a fundamental change. This process was under way from the time of the very foundation of UTK, despite the fact that Oppositionists held many leading positions in the university and the rector, Karl Radek, was one of Trotsky's closest collaborators. According to the prevailing norms of party discipline, Radek and his colleagues were obliged to publicly defend the party line as defined by Congresses, plenums, and other leading bodies controlled by the Stalinists. They had certain room for maneuver and attempted to outline their own views in their lectures and seminars,[69] but only within definite limits, bearing in mind that they were under constant surveillance by Stalin's supporters on the staff at UTK, headed in 1925–27 by the pro-rector Mif. At the end of 1926 the Chinese students themselves were drawn into the inner-party struggle by order of the AUCP (B) CC[70] and many of them subsequently saw it as their duty in the fight against the Opposition to inform on their teachers to the university party committee.[71]

Of course, the changes in the study programs took place gradually and many general points of theory continued to be taught in the spirit of the ideas of Lenin and Trotsky though, to be sure, without references to the latter's contributions to their development. The changes that took place related especially to the areas of revolutionary tactics and the construction of socialism in the USSR. There were also special topics in the program dedicated to criticizing Trotsky's theoretical and practical "mistakes" in relation to both the Russian and the international workers' movement.[72] The "Stalinization" of the university also found expression in the introduction of a special course in Leninism (at KUTV in 1924 and at UTK in 1926) based on Stalin's books *The Foundations of Leninism* and *Problems of Leninism*. At UTK this course was taken by second-year students and was clearly viewed very seriously by the university authorities. The chief lecturer was Pavel Mif himself and rated by the number of hours spent on it (104 per semester), it was ranked third, after party-building (146 hours) and political economy (106 hours).[73] In addition, there were seminars on Leninism organized in a lecture group.[74]

An ongoing problem in the teaching process was the lack of suitable material in Asian languages and above all in Chinese. KUTV only really started to grapple with the question of "Easternizing" social and economic studies at the end of 1927.[75] Eastern topics formed only 35 percent of the general history course in 1935, in previous years it had been as low as 10 percent.[76] The situation was no better at UTK, where the authorities only began to address the question of "Sinicization" of the study program in March 1928. Even such an issue had to be approached "in stages." This is partly explicable by the undeveloped state of Marxist scholarship on Eastern affairs at this time, but the result was that students learned more Western history than Chinese, which instilled in the majority of them a tendency toward dogmatism.

There was, in truth, very little modern political, economic, and philosophical literature available in Chinese at this time, which obviously exacerbated the problem of organizing effective tuition for the Chinese revolutionaries. As a result, the schools turned to preparing their own textbooks and other literature. In 1921, the first rector of KUTV, Broido, directed that lecture materials should be translated into Chinese.[77] UTK/ KUTK followed suit. The resulting translations of lectures and course summaries were diffused by various means, being duplicated, printed on wall newspapers, or simply circulated in manuscript. In 1925, a group of students wrote and published a special handbook/guide to translating lecture materials on political economy. It became the practice to publish extracts from the translated lectures in the Moscow-based Chinese-language daily newspaper *Qianjin bao* (Forward) which had a print run from 3,000 to 6,000.[78]

The ongoing task of translating the works of Marx, Engels, and Lenin and the documents of the Comintern and the Bolshevik party continued alongside the above work. At the outset, students prepared short summaries and expositions of Lenin's views, passing on later to the systematic translation of his writings.[79] These were printed and published either by the typographical departments of KUTV and UTK/ KUTK, or by the "Chinese Worker" publishing house which was, in reality, a department of Gosizdat, the state publisher. Many works were published during the 1920s, including those by Marx and Engels, Lenin, Plekhanov, Kautsky, and Luxembourg. Handbooks of quotations from Lenin were also issued, for example, *Lenin on the Soviets* and *Lenin on the Revolution in the East*. A collection of articles by Lenin and Stalin on the national and colonial question was also published. The aforementioned collected *Resolutions of the Second Comintern Congress* (editor Shiik) and other programmatic documents of the Comintern and the party were published. The collection *China and Chinese Youth* is of interest because of its editor, Ho Chi Minh. Various works by Stalin and a number of works by Bukharin were published, including some on China.

At this time some works by Oppositionists were still being published, such as "On the Anniversary of the Death of Sun Yat-sen" by Trotsky, *The History of the Revolutionary Movement in China* by Radek, and "Sun Yat-sen, 1866–1925," also by Radek. A *Textbook of European History* was produced by A. G. Prigozhin and S. V. Gingor, and a book, *Lectures on the History of Development of Social Forms* by A. P. Zhakov, who were all teachers at UTK.

To acquaint Chinese students with the basic documents of the Comintern, the Soviet Communist Party, and the CCP, and to educate them about international affairs and the problems of economic construction in the USSR – in other words, to indoctrinate them with a Stalinist outlook – UTK produced a Chinese-language magazine called *Guoji pinglun* (International Review). Its contents were broadly similar to those of the Comintern organ *Inprecor*. Later, KUTK published the weekly *Meizhou yaolan* (Weekly Cradle) and *Gongchan zazhi* which featured works by Chinese Communist leaders and articles about life at KUTK.

KUTV and UTK/KUTK did not simply have a teaching role, they also carried out a considerable amount of research work, undertaken by both staff and students. In 1922–23, a social science research bureau, actually a department of the All-Union Research Association for Oriental Studies, was established at KUTV. In spring 1924, a bureau of Oriental studies and colonial politics was established under the sponsorship of KUTV, and set itself the task of assembling a library of Orientalist material, intended to be used mainly for teaching. By 1926, despite the book famine, they had collected 5,000 volumes. The bureau obtained all the latest Orientalist publications, including Western ones, and had subscriptions to 123 periodicals (82 magazines and 41 newspapers).[80] Chinese students were allowed to use the library under supervision of bureau staff members. In 1926, the bureau helped publish an economic atlas of China, detailing its exploitation by the imperialist powers.

As regards research work at UTK, shortly after the foundation of the university, a China research bureau was established. Its stated aims were to compile a dictionary of modern terminology and to digest two new major works on Chinese history (one of which was to be one of the books written by the well-known Chinese reformer Liang Qichao) as well as producing press reviews, and so on.[81] In February 1926, the Agitation and Propaganda Department of the AUCP(B) CC decided to set up a scientific research institute on China, based at the university.[82] Due to subsequent delays, it was not until January 1, 1928, that the China research bureau was finally launched as the Scientific Research Institute for Chinese Studies.[83] A significant proportion of the Chinese students took part in the work of the bureau and at any time could receive individual tuition from staff members who included M. Volin (first director of the institute), Dalin (in 1927, director of the China research bureau), Mif (who succeeded M.Volin as director), M. G. Andreev, M. M. Kazanin, G. S. Kara-Mursa, and G. B. Ehrenburg. Qu Qiubai was one of the "active members" of the institute and Wang Ruofei, Deng Zhongxia, and Zhang Guotao from time to time also took part in its work.[84]

Soviet specialists from the Scientific Research Institute for Chinese Studies and UTK/KUTK worked together on the complex problem of Chinese writing reform.[85] A group of university staff, headed by Oshanin and assisted by students, undertook the standardization of modern social, economic, and political terminology in the Chinese language.[86] One of the institute's most prominent workers, Kolokolov, oversaw the publication of a Chinese-Russian dictionary, which, though published in 1927, is still considered one of the best of its kind in the field.

The primary aim of the education process, of course, was to develop and improve the party-political work of the Chinese students, to solidify their conviction of the correctness of the political choice they had made, and their devotion to the Communist party, that is, in the first place, to its leaders. Until the summer of 1926, this side of things was controlled by the Moscow Committee of the CCP and the Chinese Socialist (from 1925 on Communist) Youth League, whose leaders, like many adherents of Communism in China, held radical views about party organization and the training of party militants. The period in which the leaders of these committees held sway became known as the "Rafaelovshchina" after the pseudonym of Ren Zhuoxuan, Moscow secretary of the CCP in 1925–26. It was also referred to as the Moscow Regionovshchina.[87] As the prominent Chinese economist Sun Yefang recalled in 1941: "Ren Zhuoxuan thought that theoretical work was for party leaders only."[88] A pamphlet written by the Rafaelites, "A Concrete Policy for the Work of Training the Chinese Communist Branch and the Chinese Socialist Youth Corps [League] in Moscow,"[89] defended what was in effect a ban on Chinese students spending time on theoretical work. Chinese students taking their first steps toward a study of socialism were not allowed to study the Russian language. Concerning the inner-party regime, the pamphlet had this to say: "We should destroy family, local, and national concepts ... Destroy unity based on sentiment – sentimental unity is petty bourgeois unity – we will build our unity on Party interests ... We must employ in our work for the Party the same kind of interest we have in love and literature – love and literature are the foundations of romanticism."[90] This declaration is strikingly similar to that of Bakunin and Nechaev in *The Revolutionary Catechism*,

> The revolutionary is a dedicated man. He has neither personal interests, nor affairs, nor feelings, nor attachments, nor property, not even a name ... All feelings of affection, all the softening feelings of kinship, friendship, love, and gratitude must be stifled in him by a unique and cold passion for the revolutionary cause ... The nature of the true revolutionary excludes all romanticism, all sensitivity, enthusiasm, and passion.[91]

After the rout of the Rafaelovshchina in spring of 1926,[92] the leadership of party work among the Chinese students passed into the hands of Soviet Communists. Party work from this time on mainly took the form of open meetings and discussion groups on current political issues in which practically all the students took part. The discussions, which were guided by the party leadership, encompassed international affairs, problems of building socialism in the USSR, and Comintern and Soviet Communist Party resolutions, as well as issues facing their own universities. The practice of criticism and self-criticism was encouraged within the universities and each student was obliged to maintain an individual diary, a "Register of Group Work," which contained records of their academic progress and, in addition, critical comments on themselves and other students.[93] It is not difficult to imagine what this developed into in practice. The diaries have been preserved in the archives and are full of denunciations of fellow students. As Stalin's supporters strengthened their grip on UTK/KUTK and KUTV, the practice of informing on one's fellow was elevated to the status of party policy and became particularly prevalent.

In sum, we can say that the ideological training given to Chinese students in the USSR had a contradictory character. On the one hand, it enabled them to make the transition from intuitive patriotism and revolutionary feeling to conscious anti-imperialism, and for many it awakened an interest in theory which was never extinguished. On the other hand, during their long stay in the USSR, they were heavily influenced by Soviet Communists who did everything in their power to mold them in their own image. And it was precisely at that time, when Chinese students were being educated in large numbers in the Soviet Union, that Russian radical Marxism began to undergo a profound evolution. The Stalinists who now controlled the international schools set about indoctrinating their wards with great zeal. In doing so, however, they came up against very real opposition, especially from those Chinese students who, despite the dramatic circumstances, never lost their capacity for independent thought, although, it must be said, their differences remained entirely within the framework of Communist doctrine.

Strange as it may seen, documentary evidence supports the view that the formation of the Chinese Left Opposition was triggered by the activities of Soviet Stalinists who, as noted earlier, insisted on drawing Chinese students at international schools into their struggle against the Trotskyist-Zinovievist minority in the Soviet Communist Party. Until then, there were no supporters of the Opposition among the Chinese at UTK or KUTV for the simple reason that they knew nothing about the debate within the Soviet party. This is how Meng Qingshu (alias Meng Jingshu, UTK, 1927–29) recalls the start of the anti-Trotskyist campaign at UTK,

> Previously at Sun Yat-sen University there had been no open struggle against the Trotskyists as it had until then been an affair internal to the Soviet Communist Party. But in 1926, Sun Yat-sen University booked a hall at KUTV for a meeting to celebrate the fifteenth anniversary of October 10 [the outbreak of the Xinhai revolution.] When Radek began to speak from the platform, Berman, a teacher from KUTV, and others began to shout slogans, "Down with Radek," "Down with Trotsky," "We're on the side of Leninism," "Long live the Central Committee," etc.
>
> The following day Radek called a meeting of the rectorate at UTK. The participants were Radek himself, the pro-rector Mif, director of studies Agor, party secretary Ignatov, and student union president Golubev [Chen Shaoyu, Wang Ming.] Radek tried

to get the meeting to send a letter to KUTV protesting the "obstruction" of the UTK memorial meeting and the "insult" to its rector. But Mif, Agor, and Ignatov voted against. When Radek asked for Golubev's opinion Ignatov intervened, saying, "As a party member, you should be with us." [Chen] Shaoyu replied that he had not yet looked into the matter and therefore would not vote – Ignatov was pleased with this response and after the meeting described to Shaoyu the struggle against the Trotskyists in great detail. He explained that previously it had been the policy not to bring this matter out into the open at UTK but that the Central Committee had decided to spread the struggle to the university in the near future. A few days later, an enlarged meeting of the party committee was convened to discuss the struggle against Trotskyism at UTK.

At that time all the students knew about Trotsky and the Trotskyists was what was contained in the history course on the Soviet Communist Party [Meng has in mind Trotsky's line in the pre-February period, his evaluation of October, etc.] We knew nothing of their activities in 1924–26. Therefore, after the party committee meeting, a general meeting of all Communists and young Communists at the university was called. Party secretary Ignatov addressed the gathering, delivering a lecture on Trotskyism. In this way the intense struggle against Trotskyism at the university began.[94]

The Stalinists employed the same methods as in their campaign among the broader party masses. The international schools were plunged into a constant round of meetings and worked up into an atmosphere of hysteria. Teachers who held oppositional views were subjected to public humiliation. Most worked at UTK where Radek was rector. Apart from him, there were about ten Oppositionists on the staff, including (on the evidence of the archives) Gingor, Dalin, Dorofeev, A. P. and M. P. Zhakovs, Mazunin, Polyakov, Prigozhin, and Bella Epshtein.[95] The majority were social scientists and worked in the departments of History of the Development of Social Forms, History of the Chinese Revolutionary Movement, and General History of the West. The most prominent was M. P. Zhakov, leader of the Opposition in the Khamovnicheskii district of Moscow where UTK was situated.[96] At KUTV, Trotsky's supporters included the military studies teacher Dreitser and the researcher Zurabov.[97]

Judging from the recollections of Meng Qingshu, the Stalinists clearly expected the Chinese students to play the role of extras in the struggle against the Opposition. The students were expected to criticize Trotsky and his followers merely on the say-so of his irreconcilable enemies. Reading Opposition material was forbidden and the students were constantly reminded of the necessity to observe strict discipline and to bind themselves to the leadership. In these circumstances, naturally enough, a large proportion of the students decided to toe the Comintern line. But others fell prey to doubts and wavering and felt an increasing desire to examine for themselves the Opposition's documents and get to the root of the questions raised by Trotsky, Zinoviev, and Radek. Naturally they turned to their teachers in the first instance, and to the party committee and the China research bureau. But the supporters of Stalin and Bukharin who dominated these organizations were unlikely to be helpful. They refused to let the students have Opposition documents. In fact, they themselves quite often did not possess and, in some cases, had never seen such documents. If a student gave any hint of disagreement with the Comintern line, the teacher was quite likely to accuse him of being under the influence of the Trotskyists.[98] The most persistently curious students began to make approaches to the Oppositionists among the teaching staff. Until April 1927, however, it has to be said that their interest in Trotskyist ideas remained purely academic.

The situation was changed radically by Chiang Kai-shek's coup of April 12, 1927. This shook the young Chinese Communists like an earthquake. Naturally, events in their homeland were close to their hearts and the shock was intensified by the fact that right up to the moment of the "betrayal" by the leadership of the National Revolutionary Army, none of them, like the majority of the Soviet party, were prepared for it. The doubts which had been welling up in the critically-thinking section of the Chinese student body, developed into outright rejection of the Stalino-Bukharinist line on China. "I first began to waver ideologically at KUTK[99] in April or May 1927 – at the time of the report on China by Cde. [Comrade] Martynov of the ECCI and on the occasion of Chiang Kai-shek's betrayal," Qi Shugong (also known as Ji Shugong and Ji Bugong), one of the first Chinese Oppositionists, later revealed under interogation.

> I thought that Comrade Martynov was wrong to oppose the arming of the workers and peasants at the time of the Hong Kong strike in 1925–26.[100] This view was shared by two other students in the fourth group ... Elizarov and Yuriev ... Since the Trotskyist Prigozhin had spoken out against Martynov at a meeting, we, that is, I, Nekrasov, Elizarov, and Yuriev, approached Prigozhin for clarification ... We also approached other Trotskyists, Zhakov and Gingorn [Gingor]. All were teachers at KUTK. Prigozhin began to supply us with Trotskyist documents and literature, clandestine leaflets, and so on, which we read, and in this way our Trotskyist ideology was formed.[101]

The two UTK students referred to, Elizarov and Yuriev, were, respectively, Chiang Ching-kuo (the son of Chiang Kai-shek) and a certain Xu Yunzuo.

All three students were members of the Komsomol at the time and many documents attest to the depth of their feelings about the tragedy which had befallen the Communist movement in China. As summer and autumn approached, a number of other students came round to the Opposition, including Wang Wenhui, Wang Zhihao, Wen Yue, Li Guangya, Lin Aimin, Lu Yuan (alias Shen Shi, Yi Bai, Lu Yiyuan), Liu Renshou, Liang Ganqiao, Xu Zheng'an, Xiao Changbin (alias Zhi Qi), Feng Qiang, Huang Ju, Zhu Huaide, Chen Qi, and Yang Huabo. Strangely enough, the Opposition also attracted a GMD member, Deng Yisheng. Oppositional sentiments were also expressed, though not so actively as in the case of the above-named students, by Gao Heng (alias Guan Yu), Ge Chonge, Song Fengchun, Feng Yuxiang's son Feng Hongguo, Zeng Hongyi, and also, apparently, by Bei Yunfeng and Dong Rucheng (alias Dong Zicheng or Dong Jianping).[102] Ou Jiuxian, Tu Qingqi (alias Du Weizhi), Chen Yuandao, and Dong Yixiang could be classed as waverers. Meng Qingshu also recalls that one of the "openly Trotskyist" students at UTK went under the name of Roy (according to UTK documents, a student called Guo Shouhua went under this name.) As regards students from other colleges, the most prominent was the veteran CCP member Liu Renjing (who studied at the International Lenin School.) Another, Wang Pingyi, who studied at KUTV and UTK, worked with the anti-Stalinist Oppositionists within the Soviet Communist Party and later became one of the leaders of the Trotskyist movement in China itself.[103] According to some sources, Guo Miaogen, a student on the military-political courses at KUTV, expressed sympathy with the views of the Opposition. Other who showed some sympathy to the Opposition were Luo Han (KUTV, UTK),[104] and the KUTV student Duan Ziliang.[105]

Published histories of Chinese Trotskyism and memoirs of those who took part in these events invariably list among the original supporters of Trotsky in Moscow those who subsequently became leaders of the Trotskyist movement in China itself, people such as Ou Fang, Zhang De (alias Zhang Wei), Shi Tang, Chen Yimou, and Li Xuelei.[106] These names, however, appear in none of the contemporary documents that I have been able to locate in the archives of the Moscow international schools, including personal notes made by the students themselves. It is most probable that the above names were pseudonyms, adopted by activists from UTK only on their return to active political work in China. The biographies of a number of UTK militants such as Wang Zhihao, Li Guangya, Lin Aimin, Feng Qiang, Zhu Huaide, and Yang Huabo fit more or less with what we know of the aforementioned Trotskyist leaders.

As is evident, the first Chinese supporters of the Opposition were few in number; in August 1927 at UTK, for example, including sympathizers and waverers, they numbered just over thirty or 10 percent of the student body.[107] Of these, around fifteen were more or less known as such at UTK.

At least that was the figure mentioned at a meeting by M. I. Shchukar, a teacher at UTK, who said, "I personally knew of fifteen."[108] The most active Oppositionists appear to have been Feng Qiang, Zhu Huaide, Liang Ganqiao, and Lu Yuan. The last mentioned, judging from his personal file and educational record, was one of the most sophisticated Marxists among the students. Before his arrival in Moscow with the first group of students on November 23, 1925, he had studied Marxist and Bolshevik literature for three years at Shanghai University, an institution set up in October 1922 by the CCP.[109] It was him that Sheng Yueh had in mind when he recalled a certain Trotskyist at UTK by the name of Lu Yen (Lu Yan)[110] who was "the most well-versed in theory amongst the Trotskyists of Sun Yat-sen University."[111] Another five of the Oppositionists had studied at Chinese universities before arriving in the USSR, namely, Feng Qiang and Song Fengchun at Beijing University; Wang Zhihao at Beijing Pedagogical University; Ge Chonge at a university in Tianjin; and Chen Qi, who completed part of a university course.[112]

Several Oppositionists held leading posts in the UTK Komsomol which bears witness to their having enjoyed a certain authority among their fellow students. Zhu Huaide, for example, was secretary of the second-year Komsomol committee until November 1927.[113] Huang Ju and Chen Qi also held Komsomol posts.[114]

What sort of oppositional work did these young Chinese followers of Trotsky engage in? To begin with, they busied themselves with translating and diffusing documents: the Appeal of the United Opposition, open letters from Trotsky and Zinoviev addressed to the Politburo and the ECCI, and their articles on the Chinese revolution. In this first period, they were not so concerned to make propaganda among their fellow students as to influence the leadership of the CCP. The literature they translated was dispatched to its Central Committee."[115] They restricted themselves to ideological struggle and made no attempt to set up their own organization either inside or outside the party. "It was simply a group of like-minded individuals," recalled Qi Shugong.[116]

Naturally they combined their propaganda work with some agitation among the students, using wall newspapers and posters – Chiang Ching-kuo was particularly active in this regard[117] – intervening at party and Komsomol meetings and speaking in class to defend the platform of the Opposition insofar as they were permitted to do so. They began to intensively canvass individual support, using the Chinese question as the main issue, since this was the terrain on which they were most confident and the question which troubled ordinary students the most. But they also raised other questions, such as the growing bureaucratization of the party-state apparatus in the USSR, and they spoke of the necessity to struggle for reform of the party and against "Stalin's White Guard regime." They called for a change in the Stalinist-Bukharinist line in the countryside toward the peasantry and in the cities toward the working class. They also raised other international issues.[118]

Judging from the documents that have survived, they did not develop political or theoretical positions of their own, but simply popularized the conceptions of the Trotskyist-Zinovievist Opposition. We can judge the intensity of their work from the denunciations which from time to time found their way to the UTK party committee – the work of ever vigilant student-Stalinists. "Our Oppositionists not only carry on their work among us but also among the GMD," reads one of these:

> Last week Comrades Ogarev [Lu Yuan] and Lastochkin [Liang Ganqiao] tried to win over Qiu [?], De [?], and Ying (?) on the train to Moscow. Comrade Ogarev said: "Comrade Radek is right on the Chinese question and the Comintern has made tactical mistakes." The students were sympathetic to his point of view and Lastochkin told them if they had any concrete questions, he could pass them on to Radek. At a meeting of the CCP fraction of the university GMD committee, Comrade Platonov [Li Yueting] stated that Ogarev recently tried to win him over and said "if you want to read Opposition documents, I can let you have some."[119]

In another statement made to a party investigatory committee, it is related how "in a discussion with A. Zhakov in a seminar, all supported his opponent Pogorelov [Qin Bangxian], except for Leonidov [Lin Aimin]. Comrade Leonidov declared that the CCP had done nothing to prevent Chiang Kai-shek's treachery, and the mistakes of the CCP had allowed Chiang to disarm the Shanghai workers'."[120]

The author of another such document alleged that,

> Polevoi [Deng Yisheng] carried out oppositional agitation and propaganda among the masses at the Hotel Passade. He said that the Chinese comrades do not understand the question of the Chinese revolution; that Russia is a dictatorship under Stalin and the dictatorship of the proletariat no longer exists [this took place in November 1927]. He said the present line of the Chinese revolution demanded a different policy and when the other comrades confronted him, he himself admitted that he was an Oppositionist.[121]

In all their activities, the young Chinese internationalists could rely on the support of Russian adherents of the Trotsky-Zinoviev bloc, primarily their own instructors at UTK who, right up to the start of the arrests and exiling of Opposition supporters, regularly invited them to meetings and arranged for them to meet the leaders of the movement. Qi Shugong recalls how Prigozhin took him, Chiang Ching-kuo, and Xu Yunzuo to the apartment of Vujović (apparently Vujo Vujović), while Zhakov managed to arrange for him to meet with Trotsky himself at the State Concessions Committee building. He recalls that they discussed the prospects for the Chinese revolution,[122] but unfortunately no detailed record of the meeting survives.

Working together with supporters of the Opposition among their teachers, the most determined proponents of the Chinese Left Opposition made preparations for the celebrations to mark the tenth anniversary of the October Revolution. On the morning of November 7, they took part in a parallel, unofficial Trotskyist demonstration in Red Square. Ten or eleven students took part – Wang Zhihao, Deng Yisheng, Li Guangya, Lin Aimin, Lu Yuan, Liang Ganqiao, Xu Zheng'an, Feng Qiang, Zhu Huaide, Yang Huabo, and according to some reports Xiao Changbin.[123] It is difficult to re-create in detail the confused events of that day. The documents that have survived in the archives ("Minutes of the Sun Yat-sen University party committee, November 9, 1927, no. 9"; "Extracts from the minutes of the Khamovnicheskii presidium RKK [District Control Commission], November 22, 1927, no. 46"; and "Minutes of the University Directorate, November 10, 1927, no. 4") are rather contradictory in character. Nevertheless, it is possible to get a general impression of the fundamental facts. The affair seems to have taken place as follows. A day or two before the demonstration the students named above, assisted by the UTK teacher Bella Epshtein, constructed a red banner with the slogan "Long live the leaders of the world revolution, Zinoviev, Radek, Preobrazhensky!"[124] There were probably other placards prepared in advance and taken by the Oppositionists to Red Square. As they came alongside the mausoleum, the students, to the astonishment of the other marchers, unfurled their banner and began to shout slogans in support of the leaders of the Opposition. Their demonstration lasted only a few minutes as supporters of the Stalinist majority in the party marching with the university contingent moved swiftly to "restore order." The Oppositionists were forced to retreat and they returned home. However, none were arrested at this time.[125]

This public demonstration by Chinese Oppositionists, despite its brief duration, made a deep impression on many of those present in Red Square that morning. Attention was drawn to the fact that among the Chinese, whose revolutionary movement was followed with avid interest not only in the Soviet Union but the world over, there were also opponents of Stalin, prepared to openly declare their solidarity with the United Left Opposition within the Soviet party. Louis Fischer, present that day in Red Square as correspondent for *The Nation*, wrote many years later about the group of Chinese Oppositionists demonstrating in front of Lenin's mausoleum.[126] Another American, Vincent Sheean, who arrived in Red Square after the break-up of the Trotskyist demonstration, wrote of the rumors which swept Moscow following the events. He could not bring himself to believe what seemed to him one of the most fantastic of these rumors, that "a woman member of the Chinese Communist delegation carrying red flags inscribed with orthodox slogans, suddenly stepped forward in front of Stalin and the other members of the Central Committee and unfurled a banner emblazoned with the slogan 'Long Live Trotsky'."[127]

The following day the party committee at UTK called two meetings in rapid succession. At the first, it decided it was "necessary" to remove Zhu Huaide from his post as second-year Komsomol secretary "in view of his political unsoundness"; the committee simultaneously decided "it was necessary to relieve of their duties" other Oppositionists who had been members of course committees. Who exactly was not stated.[128] At the second meeting, the "anti-party activity of a group of comrades during the demonstration" was examined. Judging from the minutes, the first meeting passed off fairly calmly. Zhu Huaide was not present and the committee members, being of like mind, found no reason to disagree among themselves. The second meeting, however, was stormy. Feng Qiang and Liang Ganqiao were invited to attend as representatives[129] – the minutes refer to them as "ringleaders" – of the Oppositionists who took part in the counter-demonstration. Accusations were hurled at them, describing their actions as "anti-Soviet" and charging them with using "fascist" methods against "those comrades who were attempting to restore order within the contingent." They were also variously accused of maintaining links with "right"-wing GMD members, of factionalism, and of attempting to "wreck" the party.[130] Naturally these accusations provoked an indignant response. We can judge the temperature of the meeting from the following extracts from the minutes:

Comrade Miller:[131] I don't know all the Oppositionists ... only the leaders; Varsky [Feng Qiang], Lastochkin [Liang Ganqiao], Ogarev [Lu Yuan] ... On the demonstration I was walking among the Oppositionists when Comrade Volk approached us and linked arms with Lastochkin and myself. As we were passing Lenin's mausoleum, the Oppositionists unfurled their flags and Lastochkin tried to join them but Comrade Volk would not let him go. The Oppositionists began to shout "Down with the fascist Central Committee," "Long live the Opposition," and "Long live Trotskyism." I began to shout "Long live the Leninist Central Committee." Ogarev was carrying a flag and began to attack Comrade Volk with the flagpole. Then Okunev [Zhu Huaide], Latyshev [Xu Zheng'an], and Polevoi [Deng Yisheng] got together and tried to throw Comrade Volk out of the demonstration. (At this point Lastochkin is shouting incessantly.)

Comrade Sedyakin: If Comrade Lastochkin cannot conduct himself as befits a party member, then the party committee will be obliged to ask him to withdraw from the meeting.

Comrade Brandler:[132] In his statement Comrade Varsky says that Comrade Pogulyayev searched him at gunpoint. This is a lie; he does not possess a revolver. (Lastochkin shouts.)

Comrade Sedyakin: I am putting to the vote a motion I have received to exclude Comrade Lastochkin from the meeting. (The motion was carried unanimously and Lastochkin, with a cry of indignation, left the meeting.)

Comrade Golubev:[133] We should note that this fight was not a fight between comrades. Why did this clash take place precisely on the tenth anniversary of October in the presence of all the international delegations ... ?

Comrade Proletariev:[134] We allowed five minutes at the party committee meeting for an explanation, but the Opposition comrades want to talk for longer and accuse the party of silencing them. On the day of the demonstration Ogarev came up to Doronin[135] and declared, "You are celebrating the tenth anniversary of October. It's a great celebration but it's not our celebration." The CCP sent you here to study Leninism and the history of the Russian revolution, nothing was said about studying Trotskyism. We've no use for Trotskyism in China.

Comrade Varsky: This is all lies! I cannot explain in five minutes ...

Comrade Mif: We need to talk about the circumstances the university finds itself in. Oppositional sentiment is growing within the university, not decreasing. The reason for this lies in the defeat of the Chinese revolution. Our students come increasingly from petite bourgeois backgrounds and oppositional sentiments come naturally to them. All are recent recruits to the party – for example, Comrade Mikhailov[136] who joined in 1926[137] – Komsomolists as well ... perhaps these latter joined the Komsomol under orders from reactionary organizations. They welcomed the defeat of the Chinese revolution ... gambled on it ... We are not going to educate them here just so they can take Trotskyist ideas back to China instead of Leninism ...

Comrade Mikhailov: I am being lumped together with the Oppositionists and I object to this since it's wrong to compare real Oppositionists with waverers.

Comrade Varsky: The "facts" referred to in the resolution are simply not believable; for example, on links with the right wing of the GMD, there are no such links. The October Revolution was not just a Russian but an international revolution and we must salute all the leaders of this revolution. No one shouted the slogan "Down with the fascist Central Committee." The party of Lenin is united and the Central Committee of the party is united. The CCP has made mistakes as has the Soviet Communist Party. We need to correct these mistakes. Members of the party should not shut their eyes.[138]

After a "discussion" of this nature and without even hearing out the point of view of the Oppositionists (the five minutes allowed to Feng Qiang was clearly insufficient), the committee decided unanimously to expel from the party Bella Epshtein, Liang Ganqiao, Feng Qiang, Wang Zhihao, and Zhu Huaide and to propose to the Komsomol that they expel Lu Yuan, Li Guangya, Yang Huabo, Lin Aimin, and Zhu Huaide.[139]

No decision was taken regarding Xiao Changbin; the fact that he denied holding Oppositional views at the meeting gained him the support of committee members Berman and Li Benyi. For some inexplicable reason, no one paid any attention to the question of Xu Zheng'an. As regards Deng Yisheng, since he was not a member of the Communist party, the committee had no direct power to impose sanctions on him. It solved this problem by taking a decision to purge the university of so-called "right Guomindang elements,"[140] starting with those who had links with the Opposition. The bureau also took the opportunity to warn all remaining Oppositionists that any attempt on their part to renew factional activities would be suppressed in the most resolute manner. It was decided that it was necessary to hold discussions at party general meetings and study circles on the struggle against Trotskyism and, in addition, to "look into the question" of organizing under the auspices of the bureau of Leninism special consultations on a long-term basis for all those interested in these problems.

The resolution of the party committee received the assent of the party membership that same day, or at the latest at the next general meeting of the party at UTK. Altogether, 137 people voted on the resolution to expel the Oppositionists with only 6 voting against. These 6 were among those being expelled.[141] At some point on November 9 or 10, at a meeting of the Komsomol committee at UTK and at a subsequent general meeting of the Komsomol, the five Oppositionists named by the party committee were expelled from the youth organization.

On November 10, the university directorate met and decided to send Feng Qiang, Liang Ganqiao, Zhu Huaide, Wang Zhihao, Li Guangya, Yang Huabo, Lu Yuan, and Lin Aimin, as well as Deng Yisheng back to China.[142] On November 16, *Pravda* published an article on the "smashing" of the Trotskyist Opposition at UTK.[143] It had been written by one of the lecturers at the university, possibly by Mif himself. (The article was signed Aleksandr, Mif's real name being Mikhail Aleksandrovich

Fortus.) On November 22, the decision to expel Feng Qiang, Wang Zhihao, and Liang Ganqiao from the party came up for review in front of the presidium of the Khamovnicheskii district control commission of the Soviet Communist Party. (The question of Zhu Huaide was set aside because of his non-appearance before the presidium; whether it was reviewed at a later date we do not know.) Strange as it may seem, the presidium did not agree with the decision of the UTK party organization and, having examined the evidence, decided to change the sentences on Feng Qiang, Wang Zhihao, and Liang Ganqiao from expulsion to a severe reprimand and a warning.[144]

This, however, in no way affected the decision of the university directorate to send the students home. And on the very same day as the presidium hearing (November 22), Feng Qiang, Wang Zhihao, Liang Ganqiao, Yang Huabo, Lin Aimin, Zhu Huaide, Lu Yuan, and Li Guangya received their travel documents for China. For some unknown reason, it took until December 25 to assemble Deng Yisheng's documents.[145]

A few days before their departure for China, three or four of the students, including Liang Ganqiao, met with Trotsky in the offices of the State Concessions Committee. As Liang Ganqiao recounted to Wang Fanxi, the main question discussed was the future of the Opposition in China. Seeking to gain Trotsky's approval, Liang said, "Don't worry. As soon as we get back to China we will immediately set up a mass party of at least half a million members." But Trotsky smiled and replied, "The revolution has just suffered a defeat. Today we must take things one step at a time. And if each of you," and here he pointed at each of the assembled Chinese, "gathers around himself five or six workers and educates them, this in itself will be a big achievement." (According to Wang Fanxi, he remembers Liang Ganqiao's account of this meeting extremely clearly.)[146]

On the evening of November 23, the first group of expelled students left UTK. They were bid farewell by Bella Epshtein who, as described in an informer's statement delivered to the university party committee the following day, ran toward them when they were already sitting in the car and shouted, "You have suffered because of your struggle. That is the true path to victory. Our ideas will rise again and we will meet again soon under different circumstances."[147]

But they were not to meet again. The students were sent to Vladivostok, from where, having overcome the many difficulties and obstacles placed in their way by the Soviet bureaucratic machine,[148] they finally left for China in February or March of 1928. Epshtein herself suffered a tragic fate. Like the majority of oppositionist teachers, she perished in the Stalinist mincing machine. In the Spring of 1938, she was shot along with dozens of other prisoners at Vorkuta consetration camp.[149]

With the departure to China of the most active of Trotsky's supporters, the first phase of the history of the Chinese Left Opposition in the USSR, that of open struggle against Stalinism, came to a close. A new period of intense underground work would now begin.

Chapter 12 ⸺⸺⸺⸺⸺⸺⸺⸺

The Tragedy of the Chinese Trotskyists in Soviet Russia

Those Chinese internationalists who were left behind in the Soviet Union faced the future with different problems from those who had been expelled. Chiang Ching-kuo was apparently the first to quit the Opposition. According to Qi Shugong, "the thought of active Trotskyist activity simply terrified him."[150] Chen Yuandao and Dong Yixiang,[151] "recovered" from their Trotskyist leanings and after finishing their courses at UTK, stayed on as translators. They broke off all relations with the remaining oppositionists, "sympathizers," and "waverers." However, a few students did keep faith with the Opposition. From the few scraps of evidence available, it appears that they included Wang Wenhui, Wen Yue, Guo Miaogen, Ge Chonge, Duan Ziliang, Luo Han, the brothers Liu Renjing and Liu Renshou, Song Fengchun, Xu Zheng'an, Xu Yunzuo, Tu Qingqi, Feng Hongguo, Huang Ju, Qi Shugong, and Chen Qi.[152] Xiao Changbin was evidently still a "waverer," despite his retraction at a party committee meeting on November 9,[153] as was Gao Heng.

Up until this time, the majority of the Chinese Oppositionists had been students at UTK and at the end of 1927 there were still eleven of them there. There were another three, apart from Luo Han, at KUTV or on military courses run by KUTV, who could be classed as sympathizers; these were the translators Gao Heng, Xu Yunzuo, and Qi Shugong, who had been transferred from UTK in August.[154] Guo Miaogen was at this time on a temporary placement at UTK.[155] Liu Renjing was a student at the International Lenin School, while his brother Liu Renshou was transferred in mid-autumn to the Moscow Military Engineering School.[156]

It appears that a large number of these people had been forgiven for their past transgressions. No administrative or party disciplinary measures were taken against Wang Wenhui, Gao Heng, Guo Miaogen, Ge Chonge, Luo Han, the Liu brothers, Song Fengchun, Tu Qingqi, Huang Ju, Qi Shugong, Xu Zheng'an, Xu Yunzuo, or Xiao Changbin. Possibly the university authorities did not have sufficient evidence to prove their membership of the Opposition.

A different fate awaited those the university Stalinists had decided to make an example of. Following the Fifteenth Congress of the Soviet Communist Party, which drew up a balance sheet of the anti-Trotskyist campaign, the UTK administrators and party leaders decided to expel from the university Wen Yue, Chen Qi, and Feng Hongguo, but following this did everything in their power to prevent them from leaving for China. In the case of Feng Hongguo, Pavel Mif petitioned the Central Committee, the United State Political Administration (OGPU, Soviet secret police), the Commissariat for Military and Naval Affairs, and the Fourth (intelligence) Directorate of the Red Army headquarters staff, requesting that, as the son of Feng Yuxiang, one of the leaders of the anti-Communist coup in China and, in addition, a "politically unstable" element and an Oppositionist, he should be detained on the territory of the USSR. Mif argued that Feng, his sister Feng Funeng (the wife of Chiang Ching-kuo), and another relative of one of the Chinese anti-Communist generals should effectively be held as hostages.[157] But he failed to convince the authorities of the expediency of this course of action. The UTK leadership was forced to back down and on May 25, 1928 Feng Yuxiang's children were allowed to return to China.[158]

Despite suffering a setback in the case of Feng Hongguo, whose fate had been decided by more influential people who used the student as a pawn in a game of high politics, the rector of UTK continued to pursue Wen Yue and Chen Qi with great enthusiasm and not a little subtlety. He received support from the Chinese delegation to the ECCI which, on its own initiative, proposed that they not be allowed to return to China.[159] A former KUTV student, Wang Fanxi, many years later recalled the impression these two men made on him during a visit to UTK:

> They stayed on at the university awaiting their punishment, isolated from all others. No one dared speak to them and they, for their part, communicated with no one. From morning to evening, the two of them sat in the library reading weighty Russian tomes. The "loyal elements" (students from the Chen Shaoyu group) were completely unaware of their existence, while the majority, who belonged to neither camp, looked on them with awe and amazement as if they were museum exhibits bearing the label "Trotskyists."[160]

On more than one occasion, Wen Yue and Chen Qi petitioned the rector to be allowed to return home. But in vain; what was expected of them was repentance and an unequivocal, irreversible renunciation of Trotskyism. But they continued to stand by the Opposition, as is evidenced in their statements. "Although we have only been studying Marxism-Leninism for a short time," they wrote (in Russian) to Mif, "we are convinced we have already acquired the revolutionary light and spirit of Marxism-Leninism . . . We support the Opposition precisely because the views of the Opposition are not just theoretically correct and follow the line of true Marxism-Leninism, but also because the facts have borne out and continue to demonstrate the correctness of the Opposition's views."[161] Having been expelled from the university, Wen Yue and Chen Qi existed in a kind of limbo, unable to return home, but also unable to continue their studies. Finally, in the summer of 1928, they were exiled to Azerbaijan, near the border with Iran. They attempted to leave the USSR illegally, and were captured and put in prison in Baku.[162] Chen Qi was freed and returned to Moscow but was then exiled to the Far East.[163] What happened to them subsequently is unknown. It is possible that they were killed.

In 1928, Xu Yunzuo was also expelled from the university and the Komsomol for his opposition activities. Like Wen Yue and Chen Qi, he was refused permission to return to China. He worked at the Centrosoyuz (Central Cooperative)[164] in Moscow until 1930, when he was exiled to Siberia. In 1932 or 1933, he and another Chinese Trotskyist, Yao Binghui, who had been expelled from UTK in 1930, escaped to China. It is not known what became of him following this.[165]

Until they were exiled to Azerbaijan, Wen Yue and Chen Qi continued their oppositional work together with those other students who remained true to their ideals, although by now only underground activity was possible. In practice, this consisted of establishing clandestine links with the Russian Bolshevik-internationalists, collecting and translating Trotskyist literature, and individual recruitment of new supporters into their circle. Toward the end of 1927, Qi Shugong met with Radek in private – about a month before the latter was exiled from Moscow. Radek "ordered" him to "hold fast" to the line of the Opposition. At least this was the interpretation put on his words by Qi Shugong. "He told me," Qi recounted later, "don't be afraid to set up a faction. This does not mean a second party . . . it doesn't amount to a split." And Radek gave this example, "Suppose a house has a leaky roof; it's impossible to live in, so we would build a cabin next to it to live in while we repaired it. When the house was repaired, we would move back in. This is quite a different thing from demolishing the house."[166]

But organizing a faction required a basic minimum of forces and everything depended on how quickly the numbers of Chinese Trotskyists could be increased. So Wen Yue and Chen Qi did not simply sit in the library avoiding the glances of the curious but threw themselves, together with their colleagues, into the task of recruitment. From among the older students, they won over Yu Lantian, alias Kuk, who enrolled at UTK on December 20, 1926 but had remained uninvolved during the period of open struggle against the Stalinists. But the university authorities soon found out about his links with Wen and Chen and in the summer of 1928, like Wen and Chen, he was expelled from UTK.[167] His subsequent fate is not known. Some time after the November incident in Red Square, Guo Miaogen, who was temporarily on a placement at UTK from his military-political course at KUTV, managed to win over one of his colleagues from the KUTV course, Chen Dingjiao, who was also temporarily at UTK. A report to the secretary of the special party group (the foreign department) describes how when they returned to KUTV they began to "carry out propaganda for Trotskyism and to talk about the mistakes of Comrade Stalin." The report describes the support they received from their comrades at UTK in their work. "Last Saturday, a group of Oppositionists arrived from Sun Yat-sen University to carry out propaganda against Leninist ideas and theory, confusing the minds of those worker and peasant comrades who have not yet fully grasped Leninist principles. The Opposition propaganda caused these students to become disillusioned with the prospects of the Chinese revolution. These activities are extremely dangerous. A number of comrades on the military-political course have already begun to waver."[168] The author of the report asked the party secretary to "take decisive measures" to prevent any further oppositional activities by Guo Miaogen and Chen Dingjiao. What the reaction of the party secretary was we do not know. Most probably he shelved the affair and, having taken the precaution of obtaining confessions from Guo and Chen, was content to leave the threat of party sanctions hanging over them. Guo and Chen continued their studies in the military-political course and at the end of 1928, they were transferred with other students to UTK. Guo was even invited to carry on his studies at the International Lenin School. There are no more references to them in archival material relating to the Chinese student Oppositionists.

The Trotskyists paid particular attention to work among the newest intakes of students, who had real, practical experience of revolutionary struggle and who had tasted the bitterness of defeat. Naturally the political orientation of the new arrivals was also a matter of great concern to the Stalinists. In November 1927 the party leadership at UTK began to gather around itself groups of students who had distinguished themselves in the anti-Trotskyist campaign. These students would be placed in shared rooms with the new students so that they could carry on all-day discussions with them.[169] But this approach was not always effective. Those who arrived from the end of 1927 onwards had all to some degree or other put their lives on the line in the cause of the revolution and felt able to draw their own conclusions as to the causes of the bitter defeat they had suffered. Their experience of armed struggle had reinforced their Communist maximalism and for the most part they were hot-blooded and fearless. And they were as hostile to any manifestation of injustice in the USSR as they were in China. Many of these militants, even before their arrival in the

USSR, had been groping empirically toward the same conclusions on the Chinese question as Trotsky and his co-thinkers. The following report, written by a member of the UTK party bureau and dated November 19, 1927, is extremely revealing: "On the question of the Opposition, they absolutely do not have things sorted out. They claim to be standing aloof because they don't yet understand the situation sufficiently well." But, the report continues, "en route they argued a great deal about the nature of the revolution in China. The question was even put to the vote, which decided that the Chinese revolution was not a nationalist revolution."[170] No less revealing is the following statement from Wang Fanxi, who arrived in Moscow in October 1927:

> I began to have doubts even earlier [that is, while in China]. For a start, it had always seemed absurd to me that in the north [from 1925 to 1927 Wang was a member of the Peking party organization] we put all out energy into building up the GMD organization. (I didn't know what the situation was in the south.) Secondly, I could not understand why we placed so much faith in GMD generals and politicians and when they betrayed us we transferred our trust to other liars. Thirdly, I could not help asking the question – Why was it necessary to hand over the guns of the Wuhan workers to Tang Shengzhi,[171] and why did we suppress the so-called "extremist" activities of the Wuhan peasants?[172]

Such sentiments naturally rendered the newly arrived students susceptible to the propaganda of the Trotskyists.

A factor influencing their political outlook was their confrontation with the realities of Soviet life. This was everywhere and in every way at odds with the illusions they had nurtured in China about a just society and a workers' and peasants' state. What shocked them most was the widespread social inequality they encountered. "Stalin has a fat belly, while the workers starve." This, if we can take the word of an informer,[173] was the opinion of the Soviet fatherland held by Hu Chonggu, who started the military-political course at KUTV in September 1927.[174] A striking picture of rural life was painted in a letter received from a comrade on holiday in the south. (Chinese students were allowed trips to the Crimea for rest and recuperation). "Although ten years have passed [since the October Revolution], looking from the train I saw peasants living in holes in the ground, without clothes – that's the reality of Soviet power."[175] The bureaucratic nature of the regime at KUTV and Sun Yat-sen University, which reflected the wider situation in the Soviet Communist Party and the Soviet state, caused an equal, if not greater, degree of dissatisfaction. Judging from the recollections of Wang Fanxi, this factor was to a large extent responsible for the sympathy the students showed toward Trotsky and the Opposition."[176]

We can sum up the situation by saying that by mid-1928, the number of Chinese Trotskyists was steadily increasing. They recruited approximately thirty new members in that year.[177] The following people, in particular, were won over to a consciously Trotskyist position: An Fu (enrolled at UTK November 1927), Bian Fulin (also enrolled at UTK November 1927), Li Ping (UTK/KUTV), Liu Yin (joined KUTV September 1927), Fan Wenhui (alias Fan Jinbiao, enrolled at UTK mid-December 1927), Ji Waifang (KUTV), Ji Dacai (September 1927–March 1928, KUTV, then UTK), Zhao Ji (KUTV, later KUTK), Zhu Qingdan (UTK, later at military school), and Wang Fanxi (KUTV, later KUTK, real name Wang Wenyuan). These individuals soon became the main organizers of the Chinese Trotskyist underground as around this time a number of the old Oppositionists – Ge Chonge, Luo Han, Duan Ziliang, Song Fengchun, Xu Zheng'an, Xiao Changbin, and Tu Qingqi – were among a number of groups returning to China.[178]

Around this time or shortly afterwards, the following persons also threw in their lot with the Opposition: Lai Yantang, Li Cailian, Lu Mengyi, Pu Dezhi (alias Pu Qingquan), Xie Ying, Wu Jiyan (alias Wu Jixian, nephew of Chen Duxiu), and Zeng Meng. All these later played prominent roles in the Trotskyist movement in China itself.[179]

The growth of the ranks of the Opposition and the necessity of avoiding its collapse in the new circumstances led to the formation of a strongly centralized, conspiratorial organization. The center of the organization was KUTK, which held the greatest concentration of Oppositionists. Wang Fanxi describes how the organization was established:

> One Sunday at the end of September or the beginning of October [1928], about ten of us Chinese students bought some food and took a tram to the end of the line. Then we walked through the outskirts of Moscow to a wood and sat down to a picnic. People lay on the ground, ate, and sang songs. And as a result of this meeting of "activists," three persons were chosen to lead [the organization]. These were Fan Jinbiao [Fan Wenhui], An Fu, and myself. I can no longer remember all who were present at the meeting ... I remember best of all Ji Dacai ... and the former textile worker Bian Fulin made a deep impression on me.[180]

There are documents in the archives relating to this "picnic." The most significant, "Testimony of a Student," judging from the knowledge it displays of the internal life of the Trotskyist organization, was clearly written by one of its leading members. Sifting various pieces of evidence (transcripts of interrogations, lists of the events those interrogated were alleged to have taken part in) and comparing these with the testimony of other KUTV Oppositionists, we can come to only one conclusion, namely, that the author of this report was Li Ping. On February 8, 1930 he stated:

"The first meeting took place around October in a wood near the October camp. There were eight or nine persons present – Forel, Nakhodkin, Lektorov, Vitin, Kletkin, Fu Feirang, Wang Wenyuan, Vershinin, and Dorodny. We discussed how to carry on our work at Sunovka [Sun Yat-sen University], and in the military schools. A three-person committee was elected, consisting of Lektorov, Vitin, and Dorodny."[181] The first thing to notice is that Li Ping names Wang Fanxi twice, once under his pseudonym (Kletkin) and once under his real name (Wang Wenyuan), an obvious mistake. He also refers to one Fu Feirang who is not referred to in any of the records of KUTK. It is possible that he was a student at one of the military schools but it is more likely that Li Ping had in mind Fu Xueli, who was one of the most active members of the Opposition at KUTK. (It would have been in keeping with Chinese traditions for Fu Xueli to have had various pseudonyms.) In passing, we should note the Chinese names of the others referred to – Fan Wenhui, Zhu Qingdan, Li Ping, An Fu, Bian Fulin, and Ji Waifang. Interestingly, Li Ping makes no mention of Ji Dacai, of whom Wang Fanxi had such vivid recollections. And finally, he gives a different version of the composition of the leadership trio, naming Li Ping, An Fu, and Ji Waifang. So what was the truth of the matter? We can refer here to the testimony of An Fu named by both Wang Fanxi and Li Ping as a member of the committee. This is his testimony, taken from the report of an interrogation which took place on February 12, 1930: "After the departure of a number of old Oppositionists for China, a leadership troika was chosen consisting of (1) myself, Vitin (An Fu), (2) Lektorov (Li Ping), and (3) Dorodny (Ji Waifang). This took place in September 1928. It was in essence the first properly organized leadership committee of the underground Trotskyist organization."[182] It is worth pointing out that yet another Trotskyist activist, Zhao Yanqing, referred in January 1930 to the same three persons – An Fu, Li Ping, and Ji Waifang – as making up the leadership trio, the so-called General Committee.[183]

The initial meeting of activists, apart from electing a leadership committee, also discussed tactics. According to Li Ping, An Fu proposed the following approach: "We have suffered a defeat and it is necessary to make a tactical retreat. We must begin discussions with students who are not members of the organization on questions such as their dissatisfaction with the courses and living conditions, not forgetting to raise the problems that apply to particular regional groups. Then we can move on to political questions, show people Radek's speech on Sun Yat-sen,[184] Lenin's testament, and so on, and then material on the defeat of the Chinese revolution and on the USSR. We must listen to people's opinions and get them involved."[185] This proposal was accepted without opposition, since in practice it reflected the current activity of the Chinese Trotskyists among their fellow students and among officials of the CCP who were in Moscow in particularly large numbers in the summer of 1928 for the Sixth Congress of their party. The student Oppositionists were able to make contact during that period with Wang Ruofei, Guan Xiangying, Luo Zhanglong, and Zhang Guotao.[186] The Trotskyists, especially Liu Renjing, who as a founder-member of the CCP felt at case dealing with the party leadership, introduced CCP leaders to some of Trotsky's writings, above all his article "The Chinese Revolution and the Theses of Comrade Stalin." Having read the articles, neither Zhang Guotao, Luo Zhanglong, nor Guan Xiangying showed any great interest in the Opposition, but to their credit they did not betray the people who had given them the literature.[187] Their short-lived contact with the Opposition came to light as a result of the interrogation of some Chinese Trotskyists during an investigation into the activities of the Trotskyist underground begun in February 1930. The Chinese delegation to the ECCI denounced these revelations as a "provocation" as did the Soviet party's Central Committee and the CCP Central Cornmittee. Nevertheless, Zhang Guotao was forced to appear before the ECCI and the Control (i.e., purge) Commission to deny "rumors" that he had received Opposition material from Liu Renjing. "Perhaps these rumors arose because of my links with [Liu Renjing], a longtime party member who had previously cooperated with us against Chen Duxiu," he floundered, attempting to extricate himself. "Xiang Zhongfa[188] told me at the Sixth Congress that [Liu Renjing], although not a true Trotskyist, was strongly influenced by Trotskyist ideology; he himself supported the proposal that he be sent ... to do practical work."[189]

As regards Wang Ruofei, after reading Trotsky, especially the articles in which he described the relation of forces within China following the defeat of the CCP and the establishment of GMD authority, he continued to have serious doubts for some time. He later confessed that "in 1928, when we discussed the Chinese question in the Eastern Secretariat of the ECCI, I held some incorrect opinions – that the bourgeoisie and the *kulaks* [rural bourgeoisie] were the main social bases on which the Nanjing government rested, that the Nanjing government might achieve a measure of stability and, with the help of foreign capital, begin to develop capitalism in China."[190] Such manifestly "Trotskyist" views earned Wang Ruofei a strict rebuke on May 22, 1930 from a special commission jointly organized by the Control commissions of the Comintern and the Soviet Communist Party."[191] This punishment was enough to deter him from any further alliance with Trotsky's ideas.

But in 1928, Wang Ruofei not only shared some of the views of the Opposition but also extended real material aid to it. He allowed Wang Fanxi to use his hotel room to complete the translation of a major article by Trotsky, written in June 1928, "A Criticism of the Basic Points of the Program of the Communist International."[192] This document, like many others, including the "Trotskyist Platform,"[193] was given to the Chinese Oppositionists by Polyakov, a former teacher at UTK and now a member of the underground organization of Bolshevik-Leninists in Moscow. According to An Fu, Polyakov used to attend the meetings of the General Committee as an associate member.[194] He and other Russian Trotskyists were in regular contact with An Fu, Wang Fanxi, Li Ping, Xu Yunzuo, and Liu Renjing. After Polyakov's arrest at the end of 1928, the links with the Russian Oppositionists, were carried on via the widow of A. A. Joffe, Maria Mikhailovna, who, apparently, also replaced Polyakov on the General Committee.[195] These links were brought to an abrupt end by the destruction of the Bolshevik-Leninist group in Moscow and the arrest of Maria M. Joffe.

Acquaintance with Trotsky's work "A Criticism of the Basic Points of the Program of the Communist International" had a particular impact on the Chinese Oppositionists. In this article, along with "The Chinese Question After the Sixth Congress," written in October 1928,[196] Trotsky presented a systematic exposition of his new tactical line for the Chinese Communist movement following the defeat in the National revolution.[197] His concept can be summarized as follows: the Communist movement in China had suffered a powerful defeat. (Trotsky spoke about a defeat of the Chinese revolution, but from his further reasoning it become clear, that he only assumed a CCP's rout.) The crisis in the revolutionary movement would likely be a protracted one, and under these circumstances the revolutionary situation is being "converted" into a "bourgeois stabilization." Consequently, Trotsky stated, the slogan of Soviets should be temporarily dropped as inappropriate in a period of ebb. After all, according to the experience of revolutionary Russia, the Soviets could be formed only during the rise of the mass movement, but not at its fall. In lieu of this slogan the Chinese Communists should put forward a program of deep democratic reforms, the key point of which should be the call for a National Constituent Assembly. Since the CCP accepted this minimal program, it should take into account that the struggle for reforms during the period of stabilization of the capitalist regime is dictated by nature and is only a part of the tactics of retreat. A true purpose of the proletarian vanguard, however, is to prepare the necessary conditions for a new revolutionary tide, which the Chinese Communists should be ready to lead from the very beginning in order to establish the dictatorship of the working class in their country. It is only this dictatorship that will be capable of dealing with democratic as well as socialist problems of the Chinese revolution.

Here is, for example, what Trotsky wrote on this occasion in his first letter to Preobrazhensky:

> To be sure, the Chinese revolution has "passed into a new and higher phase" – but this is correct not in the sense that it will begin surging upward tomorrow or the next day . . . Many things bespeak

the fact that the next period in China will be a period of revolutionary reflux, a slow process of assimilating the lessons of the cruelest defeats, and consequently, the weakening of the direct influence of the Communist Party. Thence flows the necessity for the latter to draw profound conclusions in all questions of principles and tactics.[198]

Of all these questions, Trotsky maintained in the second letter, it was first necessary to understand that

[I]n no case would there be such a special epoch in the Chinese revolution as an epoch of the democratic dictatorship of the proletariat and peasantry, because incomparably fewer preconditions exist there than in our own country, and as experience, and not theory, has already shown us, the democratic dictatorship of the proletariat and peasantry as such failed to materialize in our country.[199]

He emphasized that the Guangzhou insurrection led by the CCP against the GMD (December 11–13, 1927) that already "showed . . . the complete lack of vitality and the reactionary character of the slogan of the democratic dictatorship of the proletariat and the peasantry, opposed to the slogan of the dictatorship of the proletariat drawing the poor peasants behind it." The Guangzhou insurrection was directed by the ECCI, which considered it, along with the so-called "autumn harvest uprisings" in the Chinese countryside, the beginning of a new revolutionary high tide in China, now aimed against the "counterrevolutionary" regime of the GMD. All these rebellions were defeated. Trotsky assessed the Guangzhou insurrection as an adventurist attempt of the CCP, "conceived and executed contrary to the course of development of the revolution."[200] He concluded that such adventurism could only ruin the Chinese revolution before it was able to experience a new revolutionary "high tide." A call for the Soviets, in his opinion, would be a slogan of the next Chinese revolution, that should be directed against bourgeoisie, however, for the slogan that "flowed" out of the Communists' defeat in the 1925–27 revolution would be a call for convoking the National Assembly.

The material the Chinese Trotskyists translated or wrote themselves was not all destined for distribution among their fellow students. Some was sent to China, along with sums of money, financed for the most part by voluntary contributions from those who could afford them and from membership dues. The latter, it must be said, were negligible – between 30–50 kopecks[201] – and were often topped up by special levies of 70 kopecks. The money was either sent via the university secretary, who was naturally unaware of the purpose of these transfers, or via Russian Trotskyists. On occasion money would be given to students who had well-to-do relatives at home on condition that they write to their parents directing them to deliver a corresponding sum of money to such and such an address.[202] Some money was spent on subscriptions to official publications which were then dispatched to China. For example, according to Jiang Hua'an,[203] Li Ping sent *Pravda* to China every day.[204] The remaining sums were used for stationery, stamps, and so on, as the Oppositionists carried on an active correspondence not only with supporters in China but also with Trotskyist groups in third countries, for example, the United States and Germany.[205]

In the final analysis, all their work was directed toward laying the foundations for subsequent opposition activity in China. The future struggle against Stalinism in China would require great resources and the young Chinese Oppositionists did all in their power to lay the basis for it in advance. They paid great attention to the development of their tactical line. The elaboration of the line was the main business of a new meeting of activists which took place in March or April of 1929.[206] It was held in the student accommodation block of the Moscow Artillery School. The meeting consisted of the members of the General Committee, plus Wang Fanxi, Fan Wenhui, Bian Fulin, and many other representatives of Chinese Trotskyist groups which, by this time, existed at KUTK, the International Lenin School, the Artillery School, the Military Engineering School, and the Infantry School.[207] The delegates discussed the tasks facing them on their return to China. For many this question assumed an immediate practicality since at the end of the semester they would be finishing their studies and leaving for home. Some indeed, including Wang Fanxi, did all in their power to bring forward the date of their departure, so eager were they to return to practical work in China. By a majority of votes the meeting decided to forbid those returning to China to take any steps toward the formation of a new, independent political party, ordering them to conduct their activities within the framework of a secret faction inside the CCP. In the event of their expulsion, they were to work within the already existing opposition organization. (They had in mind the *Womende hua* [Our Word] group which had been set up by the former UTK students who had taken part in the demonstration in Red Square on November 7, 1927.) According to Wang Fanxi, only one person spoke out against this policy. This was Liu Renjing, who declared that he did not want to waste energy working within the Communist Party and that on his return he intended to immediately begin oppositional work outside the CCP. Only time would tell, he said, whether he would cooperate with the ten "milksops" who had returned home before him.[208]

Such an intervention from Liu Renjing was not entirely unexpected. He had always played the role of dissident within the Trotskyist organization and the majority already regarded him as a "right-wing liquidationist." This was because of his particular interpretation of

Trotsky's slogan, proposed in October 1928, for the calling of a National Assembly in China. Liu Renjing interpreted this as an appeal for the formation of parliamentary structures whereas the majority, in militant mood, saw in Trotsky's idea only a tactical maneuver to arouse the masses during a period of counterrevolutionary advance and, in the final analysis, as part of the preparation for a new uprising.[209] The meeting also re-elected the General Committee, choosing on this occasion Fan Wenhui, Bian Fulin, and Tan Boling (a KUTK student).[210]

While preparing for the struggle in China, the student Oppositionists did not neglect the struggle against the Stalinists in the universities. In 1929 they formed a united front at KUTK with all those who were at odds with the university party committee. The concrete problems of the united front tactic were discussed at a third meeting of activists which took place in May or June of 1929. Like the original meeting, this took place in a wood on the outskirts of Moscow. Eleven persons were present, including Fan Wenhui, Bian Fulin, Tan Boling, An Fu, Wang Fanxi, Li Ping, Zhao Ji, and Liu Yin. There was yet another change of leadership. The leading position on the General Committee was now taken up by Zhao Yanqing, a man who, having been born in 1897, was more experienced than other members and was popular among the students at large. Li Ping was put in charge of organizational work and Wan Zhiling (alias Wan Zhuling, UTK/KUTK from November 1927) was put in charge of agitation and propaganda.[211] In addition to the General Committee, a new body, the "Struggle Committee," was established. Its task was to coordinate the joint struggle of the Trotskyists and other disaffected elements against the Stalinists in the universities. It was made up of five persons – Liu Yin, Zhao Ji, Wang Fanxi, Ji Dacai, and Zeng Jianqian, a student at KUTV. The most significant result of the Struggle Committee's discussions with other student groups came at a general meeting of the university party branch in June 1929 when, in the presence of Qu Qiubai and Zhang Guotao, members of the Chinese delegation to the ECCI, and of the Khamovnicheskii regional secretary of the Soviet Communist Party, the Oppositionists and their allies made fierce and sustained criticisms of the KUTK party leadership.[212] This stormy meeting lasted several days but ended in defeat for the Opposition. It proved impossible to overturn the Stalinist majority in the student body. Not long after this, in mid-August, Wang Fanxi, Liu Yin, and Zhao Ji left the university and returned to China. With their departure the Struggle Committee ceased to exist.[213]

Shortly before this, apparently at the end of July, the membership of the General Committee was increased to five, with the co-option of Hu Pengju (KUTK) and Li Guangji (alias Zhong Yongcang, KUTK).[214] This was not the end of the reorganization. On the contrary, after Wang Fanxi, Liu Yin, Zhao Ji, and thirteen other activists left the university at practically the same moment,[215] the atmosphere within the Chinese Left Opposition began to overheat. A number of activists began to talk of the necessity for a new change in the leadership. As a result, a small group of between five and eight leading members met in September or October 1929, and replaced the five-member General Committee with a new three-member committee consisting of Fu Xueli who became secretary, Li Guangji, and Wan Zhiling.[216] This committee only functioned for two or three weeks, collapsing in October or early November. A large number of students returning at this time from holidays in the Crimea simply refused to recognize its authority since it had been elected by such a narrow group of activists. It was decided to form a new general committee consisting of the newly elected secretaries of the course committees. The current situation was that Li Guangji was secretary of the first-year course committee, Jia Zongzhou of the second-year, and Bian Fulin of the third-year course committee.[217] At the end of December, however, new elections to the course committees were already being prepared, although in fact only that for the second year proceeded. This resulted in Jia Zongzhou being replaced by Qiu Zhicheng.[218]

These frequent shakeups in the leadership reflected real political differences emerging among the Chinese Oppositionists. The first signs of these differences appeared after the unsuccessful intervention at the ten-day-long party general meeting. The root of the conflict was disagreement over the tactical line to pursue in the struggle against the party committee at KUTK. The sharpest clash came after a small group of leaders met in autumn 1929 and decided, on the recommendation of Jia Zongzhou and Li Guangji, to downgrade the struggle against the Stalinists in the party bureau and to break with the united front which had been built up with other disaffected students. Absent from the meeting were An Fu, Li Ping, Bian Fulin, Fan Wenhui, and Wang Jingtao all of whom resolutely opposed what they considered an opportunist switch in policy and wanted to continue the anti-bureaucratic struggle. According to Jia Zongzhou, by November 1929 a de facto split had taken place in the organization. An Fu and his supporters went so far as to produce a pamphlet which they called "Two Tactics" directed against the group of "Trotskyist opportunists," who in their turn accused An Fu of leftism.[219]

The internal dispute had extremely negative consequences for the underground organization whose ranks, however, were still growing in number toward the beginning of 1930. Evidence from a number of sources points to a membership of about eighty around this time.[220] In addition, there were scores of sympathizers and waverers.[221] The Trotskyists accounted for more than 20 percent of the total number of Chinese students in Moscow. But in conditions of continual feuding, the dangers of disintegration of such a comparatively large organization were acute. To prevent this, Jia Zongzhou proposed that the internal structures of the Trotskyist faction be strengthened. Until then, the Chinese Left

Opposition had been a fairly amorphous body. The only active body within it, apart from the short-lived Struggle Committee, was the General Committee which directed all the work of the membership. There was no real primary organization in the real meaning of the term.[222] On Jia Zongzhou's recommendation, a reorganization was carried out in the autumn of 1929. The basic unit of organization within the faction was to be a three-person cell. The leaders of each cell would, in turn, form another layer of cells – in Jia Zongzhou's words, "party troikas" – with roughly one for each study circle. These cells would, in turn, be subordinated via the appropriate course committee to the General Committee.[223] This organizational structure only extended to the Trotskyists at KUTK. In practical terms, Oppositionists in other colleges, despite the existence of formal links, were autonomous. The biggest of the groups outside KUTK at this time consisted of ten to fifteen Oppositionists at the Moscow Infantry School led by Lu Yeshen. There were also groups of Trotskyists at the Military Engineering and Artillery schools and at the International Lenin School, where, following the departure of Liu Renjing, the major role was played by Ma Yuansheng.[224] Contacts between these groups and the General Committee were organized by a special body known as the "Secretariat" whose members were Jia Zongzhou, Li Ping, and Hu Chonggu.[225]

But special measures taken to improve the security of the organization by making it more rigorously conspiratorial could do no more than postpone what was to be a tragic denouement. By the time the discussions on reorganization were taking place, the OGPU and the ECCI had at their disposal solid information on the individual membership of the Trotskyist organization at KUTK and were simply waiting for a suitable moment to deal the organization a shattering blow. In the archives of the Chinese delegation to the ECCI, of the Comintern International Control Commission, and of KUTK itself, there are innumerable documents including denunciations, intercepted letters, statements of the university authorities to the OGPU and the ECCI, files of the Chinese ECCI delegates, etc., which prove incontestably that the destruction of the Chinese Left Opposition on the territory of the USSR was inevitable. Of course, it might not have been as devastating as it turned out to be, since the authorities did not possess compromising material on all the members of the organization. In the event, what there was in the dossiers of the secret police and the Comintern was quite enough.

On June 26, 1929, a certain student, belonging to one of the disaffected groups with which the Trotskyists had cultivated close links, wrote to the rector of KUTK, Veger: "In our university there are Trotskyists and comrades who are under the influence of Trotskyism. They all have close links with the Trotskyist organization in China and are acting as mouthpieces for the counterrevolution."[226] There follows a list of thirty-three surnames. Not all of those named were indeed Trotskyists and it appears that the author of the letter may have been settling a few personal scores. Nevertheless, the majority on the list were correctly identified as Trotskyists and included Wang Fanxi, Wang Wenhui, Wang Xingeng, Wang Jingtao, Liu Yin, Zhao Ji, Fan Wenhui, Ji Waifang, Tan Boling, Gao Heng, Lu Mengyi, Li Cailian, Qi Shugong, and Xie Ying.[227] For reasons not fully understood, perhaps it got mislaid in the rectory or in transit, the letter was passed on to the authorities only after a number of the students mentioned in it had already returned home to China in mid-August. Eventually, copies were sent to the KUTK purge commission, one of whose leading members was Berzin, which began its work on October 20, 1929, and to the OGPU.

At a meeting held on October 1, 1929, the Chinese Commission of the Eastern Secretariat of the ECCI assembled and summarized all the information at its disposal concerning the activities of the Trotskyists at KUTK, acquired from its own or other sources. It adopted a resolution, the salient points of which were:

(1) We consider it a matter of urgency to remove from the university Nekrasov [Qi Shugong] (he is a hostile element and a Trotskyist), Oberg [real name Wang Xinheng] (a Trotskyist with links to the third party[228]), and Istomin [Huang Ju] (a Trotskyist with links to the third party) – all three of whom were formerly translators at KUTK. (2) To verify the links between the Trotskyists and the following persons: Dragunov [Cai Zemin], Klementieva [Liu Qianyu], Forel [Fan Wenhui], Loza [Shao Shigui], Zonin [Xiong Changchun], Devyatkin [Ji Dacai], Dontsov [Wang Jingtao], and Knizhnik [Wang Jianqiu]. (3) To note the influence of the Trotskyists on the following group: Ogloblin [Zhang Chongde], Lukashevich [Fang Shaoyuan], Slonova [Zhu Zimu], Muklevich [Qin Long, alias Qin Biao], Fazanov [Liu Hesheng], Gutman [Liao Pengming], Kobzar [Yu Jitang], Klyaz'min [Guan Erkang], Klubov [Pan Shuren], and Musin [Tan Boling]. (The first four are definitely influenced by the Trotskyists, the second four less definitely, and on the final two there is no precise information.) This entire group must be re-examined. This task is to be assigned to Comrade Tokin [a party secretary]. If our information proves correct, it will be necessary to immediately expel those concerned from the university on the same grounds as those mentioned in paragraph 1.[229]

The information was indeed correct. Those mentioned were either members of the Trotskyist organization or sympathizers. It is difficult to say whether the authorities at KUTK, in particular Tokin, were aware of this. What is certain is that no serious effort was made to verify the information they received from the Chinese Commission of the ECCI. After only three days Veger and Tokin gave the following report to the Eastern Department of the ECCI and the Chinese delegation to the ECCI:

> At a meeting of the Chinese Commission of the Eastern Secretariat of the ECCI which took place on October 1, 1929, it was proved [!] that the following members of KUTK were either members of a Trotskyist organization or sympathizers of the Trotskyists, or had links with Trotskyists or a third party. [There followed a list of names of the persons referred to in the resolution of the Chinese Commission]. Our own investigations at the university confirm the political estimate of the said Chinese Commission. We therefore consider it necessary to immediately remove these persons from the student body and send them to Vladivostok from where they will be deported to China without the secret rendezvous necessary for their continued activity as members of a clandestine party.[230]

The evidence suggests, however, that a decision was taken to hold back from taking action against those mentioned in the resolutions. For the time being they remained at liberty in Moscow and no restrictions were placed on them. The authorities continued to play a waiting game, hoping for more information to emerge. At the end of October, the KUTK secretary Yeshchenko informed the OGPU that Xu Yunzuo who, as described above, had already been expelled from the Komsomol and KUTK for membership in the Opposition but had been detained within the borders of the USSR, had approached him and, in the course of a conversation, had, through carelessness, let him see a note received from Qi Shugong concerning the latter's opposition activities.[231]

The OGPU and ECCI gathered great quantities of information during the so-called clean-up of the KUTK party organization. At the outset of this operation, which began in October, someone, referred to in the documents as Kirsanov (apparently Kirsanova, the rector of the International Lenin School and a member of the Berzin commission), received a denunciation from a KUTK student considered by the Trotskyists to be one of their closest and most serious allies in the united front against the bureaucracy. This student submitted evidence on eighty-one persons,[232] dividing his list into three parts. In the first, which consisted of twelve names, he listed those people whose membership in the Trotskyist organization he could demonstrate from an abundance of documentary evidence at his disposal. The second group consisted of thirteen persons whose membership in the organization could be supported by concrete testimony. (He deemed the documents concerning their underground activities insufficient.) In the final part of his list, consisting of fifty-six names, were those he suspected of Trotskyism without having clear evidence. Among those he listed were the leaders of the Chinese Opposition, namely, An Fu, Bian Fulin, Fan Wenhui, Ji Dacai, Hu Pengju, Fu Xueli, Wang Jingtao, Ji Waifang, Tan Boling, Wan Zhiling, Zhao Yanqing, Qi Shugong, Wang Wenhui, Huang Ju, and many others. This denunciation was forwarded to the CCP delegation to the ECCI where Deng Zhongxia, a member of the delegation, used it to draw up precise instructions to the party purge commission at KUTK on January 10, 1930:

> We must pay particular attention to the growth of Trotskyist groups at KUTK ... we must ask the OGPU to supply the college purge commissions[233] with detailed information. Those who, after examination, turn out to be Trotskyists must be expelled from the party and the entire membership informed of this so as to provide an example to the masses. Those elements whose membership in the Trotskyist organization is attested by a number of sources, or who are actually leaders of the Trotskyist group, although we as yet have no up-to-date information on this, must be arrested and sent under supervision to a suitable place on Soviet territory. As regards the remainder, suspected of Trotskyism but not considered to have played a major role, we must also raise the question of expelling them and, at a suitable moment, returning them to China, having first supplied the Central Committee with their names and a short biography of each to prevent them clandestinely rejoining our party.[234]

Clearly, sentence had already been pronounced, despite the fact that no proper investigation had yet been carried out. Penalties were doled out according to the classification of the names in the denunciation. Deng Zhongxia introduced only one elaboration. The same punishment was to be meted out to those who "according to many reports" were Trotskyists but about whom there was no documentary evidence, as to those who were undoubtedly Trotskyists. It was simply a matter of contacting the OGPU who would then make up the deficit in documentation.

The secret agents of the busy-body lecturers at KUTK had also by this time amassed enough information to give them a clear picture of the underground activity of the Trotskyists at the university. A list they compiled around this time, of Trotskyists and of persons "siding with them," contained seventy-seven names.[235]

The Chinese Left Opposition was living through its last days on Soviet territory. The purge of the party organization at KUTK acquired an ever more determined and single-minded character as the commission struggled to flush out all the Trotskyist conspirators. A number of the Oppositionists sensed that the net was closing around them and tension within the organization began to rise. Jia Zongzhou later admitted that some individuals considered the possibility of dissolving the organization and even of volunteering confessions.[236] The first person to crack under the pressure was Zhao Yanqing (Donbasov). According to Jia Zongzhou,

> [H]e seemed to fall ill with persecution fever. He was, in a way, mad. If he heard somebody whispering it seemed to him they were saying, 'There goes Donbasov the Trotskyist'; and if someone looked at him he became afraid that they were shadowing him in order to kill him. He remained in the organization. Although he wanted to resign, he hesitated to do so. Several times he broke down, crying that there was no way out. He went to see a doctor on a number of occasions.[237]

Finally, on January 21, 1930, he handed in a statement to Ignatov, the newly appointed secretary of the party branch at KUTK.[238] According to Wang Fanxi, Zhao Yanqing was under a lot of pressure from his close friend Logov[239] (a certain Fang Tingzhen[240] appears under this pseudonym in the KUTK records), who was a secret agent of the Stalinists within the Trotskyist organization. Xu Yunzuo and Yao Binghui who later escaped from Siberia to China affirm that Wang received this information from either Song Fengchun or Xiao Changbin. Zhao first confessed to Sheng Yueh who was at that time a member of the party committee. Sheng then arranged a meeting between Zhao and Ignatov in the latter's apartment.[241]

Ignatov handed Zhao Yanqing's statement to Veger, the rector of KUTK, who sent out several copies – to Stalin, Kaganovich, and Stetsky at the Central Committee, to Yaroslavsky at the Control Commission, and to Bauman and Kogan at the Moscow City Committee.[242] Zhao Yanqing was then interrogated by the CCP delegation to the ECCI and by the OGPU. From his statements and from notes found in one of his exercise books, the authorities were able to confirm, or in many cases discover for the first time, the membership of the underground organization of about sixty persons.[243] Six of these – Wang Fanxi, Liu Yin, Jiang Defang, Zhao Ji, Yuan Fan, and Xiao Zhenhan – had already returned to China.[244] Zhao Yanqing also described how Trotskyism had taken root in the International Lenin School, where he betrayed Ma Yuansheng, and in the Moscow Infantry School, where he named Lu Yeshen and a certain Li Xiaosheng. He unmasked the entire General Committee and all the course committees at KUTK and gave information about the bloc between the Trotskyists and other discontented elements.[245] Having completed his betrayal, this utterly demoralized man took his own life on January 28.[246]

The death of Zhao Yanqing was a profound shock to the members of the Trotskyist organization, all the more so since news soon leaked out about his treachery. In fact, the party committee convened a special general meeting at which Sheng Yueh made a statement about the matter.[247] The aim of the Stalinists in calling the meeting was evidently to terrify the underground Oppositionists into confessing. They succeeded in doing so. Soon afterwards, Li Ping unexpectedly cracked[248] and gave evidence on eighty-eight Trotskyists, sympathizers, and others who were influenced by Trotskyism. He did not fail to mention certain people about whose sympathies he was merely uncertain.[249]

After this the OGPU decided to waste no more time. On February 8 and 10 (and according to some reports, also 13), arrests took place at KUTK. Twenty-five persons were put behind bars, including An Fu, Bian Fulin, Wan Zhiling, Tan Boling, Qiu Zhicheng, Hu Chonggu, Li Guangji, Hu Pengju, Fan Wenhui, Ji Dacai, Jia Zongzhou, and Wang Wenhui; in other words, practically the entire leadership of the underground organization. In the following three months, another eleven activists of the Chinese Left Opposition followed them to the cellars of the Lubyanka, among them Wang Jingtao, Huang Ju, Pan Shuren, and Ma Yuansheng.[250]

The investigators kept to a punishing schedule. All-night interrogations followed one after the other[251] and by March 8, 1930 they had amassed material on 171 "Chinese Trotskyists in the USSR."[252] This figure is so large that we can safely assume a large part of the evidence was fabricated, which would be entirely in keeping with the methods of the OGPU. The prisoners, as well as giving evidence about their own group, gave information on Trotskyists in China, naming about seventy persons and revealing a large number of addresses and secret rendezvous.[253]

Immediately after the first arrests, there was a wave of voluntary confessions from those Oppositionists who remained at liberty. Activists surrendered to the party purge commissions of KUTK, the International Lenin School, and the Infantry and Artillery schools. By this time there were no longer any supporters of Trotsky at the Moscow Military Engineering School. Interestingly, these confessions were not always motivated by fear. Some activists saw them as a maneuver to permit them to stay in the party, return to China, and there take up the struggle once more under the slogans of the Opposition. This ruse, however, was quickly uncovered by their interrogators,[254] merely exposing them to even more severe punishment.

The Chinese Left Opposition on Soviet territory then ceased to exist, sharing the fate of the Russian Bolshevik-Leninists. On July 20, 1930 a special commission of the International Control Commission made up of Solts (chairman), Angaretis (secretary), Trilisser, Berzin, and Artuzov, the latter three being officials of the OGPU, with Kirsanova present as an observer, met to consider the fate of thirty-six arrested Chinese Trotskyists. They decided to "isolate" twenty-four of them; that is, to send them to concentration camps or into exile. Three others were later added to this group. Three individuals, including Jia Zongzhou and Li Guangji, were sent to work in factories in the Moscow area. The remainder were expelled from the USSR.[255]

The commission also decided to clear up some unfinished business by formally expelling from the party nine persons who for some unknown reasons had not been expelled at the time of the initial purge.[256] In only six days, Angaretis, Artuzov, Berzin, Kirsanova, Solts, and Trilisser, who only met on this one occasion to consider the matter of those arrested, arrived at their predetermined conclusion.[257] On September 13 their colleagues in the OGPU pronounced sentence: Qiu Zhicheng, Li Cibai, Zhao Yifan, Fang Shaoyuan, Fan Wenhui, Liu Hanping, Hu Pengju, and Liu Hesheng each received a sentence of five years in a camp. Jiang Hua'an, Zhang Chongde, Rong Li, and Li Shile each received three years. Various terms of imprisonment were handed down to An Fu, Tan Boling, Ma Yuansheng, Wang Jingtao, Li Yifan, Tang Youzhang, and Jiang Yimu. Several persons were sent to Ivanovo, including Wan Zhiling and Hu Chonggu. Huang Ju and Ji Dacai were sent to Nizhnii Novgorod.[258]

The majority of those former Trotskyists who were not imprisoned were sent to work in various Moscow factories as a punishment. It was intended that they should "learn from the proletariat." Some were sent back to China. The overwhelming majority were expelled from the party, although a few such as Li Ping who had "sincerely repented his mistakes" were treated leniently and got away with a reprimand and a severe warning. In Li Ping's case, this was in recognition of the fact that he had "helped to unmask the entire Trotskyist organization at KUTK, the military schools, and even in China itself."[259]

Some former leaders of the Trotskyist organization, in particular Lu Yeshen and Fu Xueli, were sent into industry. These, unlike many of their former comrades who were striving to "expiate their guilt through honest work," banded together with some like-minded people and in the early part of 1931 took the first steps toward relaunching the activities of the Left Opposition. Their base of operations was a Chinese workers' hostel.[260] But their efforts did not last long. In May 1931 they were arrested with seventeen other Oppositionists and sent to the OGPU's Butyrsky "isolator" (a jail).[261] They were soon convicted and sentenced.[262]

With this the story of the Chinese Trotskyist movement in the USSR reaches its conclusion. As they left the political scene, however, the Chinese Trotskyists did not disappear completely. Their activities gave a powerful stimulus to the emergence and growth of the Left Opposition in China itself. It is true that their theoretical achievements were meager and that they left no powerful organization as their legacy. But the Chinese Oppositionists in Russia exerted enormous influence on the internationalist wing of the Communist movement in China. Their activities gave a strong stimulus to the emergence and growth of the Left Opposition in China itself. In this way, they acted as a genuine link between Russian and Chinese Trotskyism.

Conclusion

The penetration of Bolshevism into China after the October coup d'état in Russia, coupled with the defeat of the CCP in the National Revolution of 1925–27, marked the first period in the development of communist thought on Chinese soil. The political processes then taking place in the CCP reflected the situation inside the Bolshevik party and the Comintern. The Chinese Communists slavishly followed the ideological lead of their Russian idols, directly borrowing their theoretical experience. Only at the start of their movement in 1920–22 did they disobey ECCI instructions concerning their tactical course. That is why the 1919–27 history of Bolshevism in China can be divided into three sub-periods which mirror the transformation of the Russian Communist leadership's views on the Chinese revolution.

The first sub-period was from 1918–1919 to the autumn of 1922. At this time it was Trotskyism, primary component of post-February 1917 Bolshevism in terms of the tactics and strategy of the revolutionary movement, that dominated Chinese Communist philosophy. A principal factor in the initial popularity of Trotsky's theory of permanent revolution in China was the acute crisis of world capitalism provoked by the First World War and the Bolshevik triumph in Russia. This created the illusion among many Communists that a quick breakthrough of the world revolution was possible.

When the global economic recovery dashed these hopes, a concomitant weakening of Trotskyist political influence ensued. It came during the second sub-period, from the end of 1922 until 1925, when Trotskyism was enfeebled by the renewed authority of the orthodox Leninist theory that called for the revolutionary democratic dictatorship of the proletariat and peasantry. Lenin's theory, however, was now renovated due to the peculiar conditions in China, a semi-colonial, backward country, as a concept of an anti-imperialist united front.

The third sub-period, commencing with Stalin's assumption of leadership over Bolshevik China policy in 1925, saw the replacement of Leninism with the Stalinist doctrine of the Chinese revolution. The continuing dependence of the CCP on Soviet financial aid predisposed the Chinese Communist leadership to follow Stalin, whose seizure of control over Comintern policy would lead the CCP to catastrophic defeat.

The three Bolshevik concepts of the Chinese revolution differed sharply, and a fierce ideological struggle within the AUCP(B) accompanied their elaboration. To be sure, the disagreements concerned tactics rather than strategy. All Bolshevik leaders tried their best to lead the Chinese Communists to a victory aimed at transforming China into a socialist or "non-capitalist" state. That is why the political clashes on tactical problems were of the greatest importance.

At the beginning of the first sub-period of Bolshevism's spread in China in 1919–20, all Comintern activists, including Lenin, held essentially Trotskyist views on the revolutionary process in that country. The ultimate victory of the world proletarian revolution seemed to them so close that any obstacles in its path including the lack of a working class, economic backwardness, semi-colonial status of the country, and the absence of a civil society, appeared insignificant. The world revolution was considered the natural continuation of the Civil War in Russia. The unreality of this policy soon became obvious to Lenin as even the most active Chinese workers proved more nationalist than socialist. That forced the Bolshevik leader to quickly change Comintern tactics. For the Chinese Communists, however, as well as for many other Comintern members including Trotsky, comprehension of the shift took time.

Lenin's new tactical line was neither "utopian" nor "adventurist." It was, of course, leftist, but Lenin never tried to hide that; he declared his program openly at a number of Comintern forums and in the early 1920s it began to bring results. Perhaps he hoped deep in his soul for an immediate socialist takeover in Asian and African countries. He might even have dreamed of a Red Army invasion of China. It is no secret that, in spite of his sharp polemic with Roy at the Second Comintern Congress, he enthusiastically supported Soviet intervention in Central Asia and the Caucasian Republics in 1920–21 and in Mongolia in 1921. He seriously considered the possibility of implementing plans for capturing Constantinople in 1921 and did not oppose Soviet aggression in Persia.[1] Nevertheless, there is no evidence of such extremism in China. Lenin did acknowledge the nationalist character of the Chinese revolution and urged the CCP to support the national bourgeoisie of their country. Of course, he remained an International Communist and as such demanded the Comintern defend the interests of the CCP within the national revolutionary movement in China. He had never been a moderate. He insisted on placing conditions on the alliance which would allow the CCP to retain political and organizational independence in the bloc with the GMD and to remain in that bloc only as long as it was in no position to act as a mass political party in its own right, sole leader of the national revolution. His Chinese policy, in sum, was a maneuver aimed at helping unsophisticated Communist activists to use their potential foes temporarily for their own purposes. After all, unlike Central Asia, the Caucasus, Persia, or Mongolia, China had never been under Russian political control or cultural influence. A frontal attack would not work there and indeed had not worked even in Persia. The crucial factors in China, according to Lenin's logic, were the attitude of the masses toward the Communist party and the ability of the Communists to stir up the popular revolutionary movement, skillfully exploiting the nationalist mood.

Stalin broke with this position, perhaps unconsciously convincing himself that he was simply developing Lenin's line. Nevertheless he did revise it and in so doing made it irrational. Stalin's concept was also leftist, even extreme leftist. Many of his ideas concerning the socio-economic development of the Asian countries were even closer to Roy than to Lenin. Their revolutionary impulse, however, was crippled by Stalin's adherence to the concept of a "multi-class party" that Stalin armed himself with at the beginning of 1925. In practice this theory led to intra-party collaboration of the CCP with a bourgeois political organization which for both the CCP and Stalin acquired a transcendent significance. Logically speaking, in accordance with this concept the Communists had to pursue one of two tactical lines inside the Guomindang: either offensive – with differing degrees of force – or defensive, depending upon circumstances. In the first instance, i.e., in more favorable circumstances, they had to take advantage of their presence in the Guomindang to make that organization as "leftist" as possible, namely, change it into a "workers' and peasants' party." They were supposed to do this by ousting the representatives of the bourgeoisie from leadership positions and then purging them from the party. Following this, they had to gain influence over their "petite bourgeois" allies in order to establish the "hegemony of the proletariat" in China, not directly via the Communist party but via the Guomindang. In the second instance, when the Nationalists turned out to be stronger than the Communists, the CCP had the duty of making concessions, in essence limiting its own autonomy and political independence for the sake of safeguarding the Communist party inside the Guomindang – the "people's" party.

This very concept was bureaucratic by nature, based almost wholly on arm-chair calculations in regard to power relations within the Guomindang. Extremely skillful in everything that concerned the intra-party struggle behind the scenes, Stalin, who at the time was removing his own main antagonists in the Bolshevik party from the leadership, must have been confident of the ultimate success of such a policy. Nonetheless, it was not effective in a China embroiled in a popular national revolution. Unlike the degenerating AUCP(B), the Guomindang of 1925–27 was a revolutionary party whose anti-Communist military faction enjoyed popularity among not only the officer corps but also among a considerable portion of Chinese society. One could not simply oust members of such a group from their own political organization.

Objectively speaking, the Chinese Communists turned out to be hostages of Stalin's line. On the one hand, the obligation to preserve intra-party cooperation with the Nationalists inevitably led to the suppression of any questions concerning the price of such collaboration. On the other hand, from its position inside the Guomindang the CCP was unable to struggle successfully for hegemony. No matter how cautious, any step in that direction, any attempt to take the offensive risked conflict with what was in fact a much stronger partner, one which relied, among other things, on its own armed forces. A clash would lead either to the splitting up of the "multi-class" party or simply to the expulsion of the Communists from the Guomindang. In this regard, the events of March 20 and April 12 were a serious warning to the CCP.

Finding itself a prisoner of Stalin's paradigm, the Communist party condemned itself to constant retreat in the face of its ally irrespective of what particular directives it received from Moscow. It was impossible to implement the orders to communize the Guomindang without risking the breakup of the united front. Leaving the GMD would mean burying any hope of turning it into a "workers' and peasants'" party. In essence, Stalin himself was being trapped in a cul-de-sac. In this situation, no matter which way he turned he would have to be satisfied merely with the Guomindang's anti-imperialism until the end of June 1927. His policy was bankrupt.

Trotsky did not immediately realize the real meaning of Stalin's reversal of course, and until April 1926 he fully supported the Comintern's China policy. Only the change in the power balance inside the GMD in favor of the Guomindang "centrists" and "rightists" after the March 20 events made him rethink this policy. At first reluctant, but from the autumn of 1926 persistent and energetic, Trotsky finally found himself involved in a new struggle against the Stalinists. All that he was then trying to do was to persuade the Bolshevik party leadership to revive the revolutionary impetus of Leninist theory. Through the end of the Chinese National Revolution he had struggled against the Stalinists under the banner of orthodox Leninism having concluded that it was time for the CCP to withdraw from the GMD and act in its own right, i.e., more independently, a co-leader of the national popular revolution, on the basis of inter-party collaboration with the Guomindang. He rejected self-serving bureaucratic maneuvers.

Would Trotsky's policy have been effective in China in that concrete situation? It is impossible to say. During his polemic with the Stalinists, most of the time Trotsky could not even express his Leninist views openly due to disagreements on China with his opponents inside the Opposition, Zinoviev and Radek, whose policy was quite contradictory. On the one hand, they constantly emphasized the importance of the mass revolutionary movement and the independence of the CCP within the GMD. On the other hand, they were inclined to make some bureaucratic maneuvers inside the GMD. At the same time they unconditionally refused to accept Stalin's frequent retreats before the strong Nationalists. Thus their position was even more senseless than that of Stalin. They could have led the CCP into a cul-de-sac and provoked a rout of the Communists even more quickly than Stalin did. Their ultimate acceptance of Trotsky's concept in June 1927 could not change the situation. The Stalinists did not want to discuss seriously any of the Opposition's proposals, and anyway it was too late.

The disaster which overlook the CCP the next month, and the inexorably approaching defeat of Trotsky and the Opposition in the Bolshevik party and the Comintern, led Trotsky in the autumn of 1927 to revive his pre-1922 ideas of the permanent revolution in regard to China. His views, however, could no longer win over a majority of the Chinese Communists, and only a tiny group followed him. Most of the CCP were compelled to obey Stalin, who in September 1927 was finally obliged to order his puppets to withdraw from the GMD.

The Stalinists' victory in the Bolshevik party and the Comintern created grotesquely unequal conditions for competition between leadership and opposition factions within the CCP. Not only did the leadership benefit from massive Soviet aid, but they also could rely on Stalin's ruthless police machine against their opponents in Soviet Russia. They could also appeal in their mass propaganda to the achievements of the Soviet Union in economic construction, in spite of the capitalist encirclement, to justify their own political program. By contrast the Opposition could propose only the abstraction of a future world revolution or, from late 1928, the democratic reconstruction of the Chinese military-bureaucratic regime, which had no potential for capability of reform. In a society still under the influence of absolutism, the idea of democracy was simply inapplicable. Of course, the Oppositionists made political capital from the mistakes of the ECCI and CCP during the 1925–27 revolution, the almost complete subordination of the CCP to the Russian Stalinists, the growth of bureaucracy and social inequality in the USSR, and the repressive nature of the Stalinist regime. Their ideas were effective in winning over some intellectual dissidents and internationalists from within the CCP, but in the long run they were incapable of swaying the masses, not least because those ideas coincided with much of the GMD's anti-Communist propaganda.

The tragedy of the first Chinese Trotskyists in Soviet Russia foreshadowed the ultimate collapse of the Communist Opposition in China itself. A small Trotskyist party of China – 483 members[2] – would be organized in 1929–31, only to be smashed in 1932 by the GMD secret police. Subsequent attempts to revive it would fail. Pure Trotskyism was doomed to defeat in China.

Lenin's concept of the Chinese revolution, however, survived. During the second united front of 1937–45, and the final Civil War with Chiang Kai-shek in 1946–49 the Chinese Communists actually turned back to that concept and made it the foundation of their tactical course. The situation, of course, was now completely different. The CCP acted as a mass party and was completely independent, capable of establishing its hegemony over a relatively broad coalition of anti-imperialist national forces. This time the Communist fight was successful. Mainland China fell under the CCP's dictatorship.

Notes

Introduction

1 See Harold R. Isaacs, *The Tragedy of the Chinese Revolution*, London: Secker & Warburg, 1938.

2 See Isaac Deutscher, *The Prophet Unarmed: Trotsky: 1921–1929*, Oxford: Oxford University Press, 1989.

3 "Under Lenin's Banner," in Yuri Felshtinsky, ed., *Kommunisticheskaya Oppozitsiya v SSSR: 1923–1927: Iz Arkhiva L'va Trotskogo* (The Communist Opposition in the USSR: 1923–1927: From Leon Trotsky's Archives), 4 vols., vol. 3, Benson, VT: Chalidze Publ., 1988, p. 191. A few other oppositionists also accused the Stalinists of that time as being national communists. See N. Bukharin, *Partiya i oppozitsionnyi blok. Doklad aktivu Leningradskoi organizatsii VKP(b) 28 iyulia 1926* (The Party and the Opposition Bloc. A Report to Active Functionaries of the Leningrad AUCP(B) Organization on July 28, 1926), Leningrad: Priboi, [1926], p. 64.

4 *Sotsialisticheskii vestnik* (The Socialist Herald), 1927, no. 8, p. 4.

5 Louis Fischer, "China – Seen from Moscow," *The Nation*, 1927, vol. CXXV, no. 3256, p. 613.

6 See Conrad Brandt, *Stalin's Failure in China, 1924–1927*, Cambridge, Mass.: Harvard Univ. Press, 1958.

7 See Robert C. North, *Moscow and Chinese Communists*, Stanford: Stanford Univ, Press, 1953, p. 99.

8 Leon Trotsky, "On the History of the Left Opposition," in George Breitman and Evelyn Reed, eds., *Writings of Leon Trotsky (1938–9)*, New York: Merit Publ., 1969, pp. 61–62.

9 See V. I. Lenin, "Preliminary Draft Theses on National and Colonial Questions. For the Second Congress of the Communist International," in V. I. Lenin, *Collected Works*, vol. 41, pp. 144–151; Lenin, "The Second Congress of the Communist International. July 19 – August 7, 1920. Report of the Commission on the National and Colonial Questions, July 26," ibid., pp. 240–245; Lenin, *PSS*, vol. 41, pp. 437–438, 457, 458–461, 513; Lenin, *Sochineniya* (Collected Works), 3rd ed., vol. XXV: *1920*, Moscow: Partizdat TsK VKP(b), 1937, p. 287; *Vestnik 2-go kongressa Kommunisticheskogo Internatsionala* (Bulletin of the Second Congress of the Communist International), no. 1, July 27, 1920, p. 2; *Voprosy Istorii KPSS* (Questions of the History of the CPSU), Moscow, 1958, no. 2, p. 16; *Leninskii sbornik* (Lenin Collection), vol. XXXVIII, Moscow: Politizdat, 1975, p. 321. See also A. B. Reznikov, "V. I. Lenin o natsional'no-osvoboditel'nom dvizhenii" (V. I. Lenin on the

National Liberation Movement), *Kommunist* (Communist), Moscow, 1967, no. 7, pp. 91–102.

10 Lars T. Lih et al., eds., *Stalin's Letters to Molotov: 1925–1936*, New Haven and London: Yale University Press, 1995, p. 130. Hankou was then the capital of Left Guomindang China.

11 See Breitman and Reed, *Writings of Leon Trotsky (1938–9)*, p. 352; Trotsky, *My Life. An Attempt at an Autobiography*, New York: Pathfinder Press, 1970, p. 530.

12 See, for example, Chen Zaifan, *Gongchan goji yu Zhongguo geming* (The Comintern and the Chinese Revolution), Wuhan: Huazhong shifan daxue chubanshe, 1987; Huang Xiurong, *Gongchan goji yu Zhongguo geming guanxishi* (History of Relationships between the Comintern and the Chinese Revolution), 2 vols., Beijing: Zhongguo zhongyang dangxiao chubanshe, 1989; Xiang Qing, *Gongchan goji yu Zhongguo geming guanxi lunwenji* (A Collection of Articles on the Relationship between the Comintern and the Chinese Revolution), Shanghai: Shanghai renmin chubanshe, 1986; Xu Yuandong et al., eds., *Zhongguo gongchandang lishi jianghua* (Lectures on History of the CCP), Beijing: Zhongguo qingnian chubanshe, 1982; *Jindai shi yanjiu*, 1985, no. 1, pp. 68–100; no. 2, pp. 111–126.

13 V. I. Glunin, *Kommunisticheskaya partiya Kitaya nakanune i v period Natsional'noi revolyutsii 1925–1927 gg.* (The Chinese Communist Party on the Eve and During the National Revolution of 1925–1927), 2 vols., Moscow: Institute of the Far Eastern Studies Press, 1975; L. P. Delyusin, *Agrarno-krest'ianskii vopros v politike KPK (1921–1928 gg.)* (Agrarian and Peasant Questions in the Policy of the CCP [1921–1928]), Moscow: Nauka, 1972; M. A. Persits, *Revolutionaries of India in Soviet Russia: Mainsprings of the Communist Movement in the East*, Moscow: Progress Publ., 1983, pp. 124–170; A. B. Reznikov, *The Comintern and the East: Strategy and Tactics in the National Liberation Movement*, Moscow: Progress Publ., 1984; M. F. Yuriev, *Revolyutsiya 1925–1927 gg. v Kitaye* (The Revolution of 1925–1927 in China), Moscow: Nauka, 1968; R. A. Ulyanovsky, ed., *Komintern i Vostok: Bor'ba za leninskuyu strategiyu i taktiku v national'no-osvoboditel'nom dvizhenii* (The Comintern and the East: The Struggle for a Leninist Strategy and Tactics in the National Liberation Movement), Moscow: Nauka, 1969. The latter book contains articles by Glunin, Persits, and Reznikov; Ulyanovsky was a deputy head of the CPSU CC department who supervised the work on this collection. An English translation was published in 1979 by Progress Publishers.

14 Glunin, *Kommunisticheskaya partiya Kitaya nakanune i v period Natsional'noi revolyutsii 1925–1927 gg.*, pp. 105–108, 163, 299–300; *Komintern i Vostok*, pp. 292–296; V. N. Nikiforov, *Sovetskiye istoriki o problemakh Kitaya* (Soviet Historians on China Problems), Moscow: Nauka, 1970, pp. 155–156, 180, 209–210; *Problemy Dalnego Vostoka*, 1990, no. 2, pp. 148–156.

15 Grigoriev had belonged to the same group of Soviet liberal historians, but through the early 1990s had mostly studied the CCP history of the post-1927 period. Glunin at present is a member of his department. Another well-respected historian in this group is K. V. Sheveliev.

16 In Russian historiography the words "adventurist" and "unrealistic" are used as synonyms for "leftist." In this book I use the word "leftist" (or "left-wing") in its original meaning, as an antonym of "rightist" ("right-wing".)

17 See A. M. Grigoriev, "Bor'ba v VKP(B) i Kominterne po voprosam politiki v Kitaye (1926–1927)" (The Struggle in the AUCP(B) and the Comintern on the Questions of China Policy [1926–1927]), *Problemy Dalnego Vostoka*, 1993, nos. 2, 3; M. L. Titarenko et al., eds., *VKP(B), Komintern i natsional'no-revolyutsionnoye dvizheniye v Kitaye: Dokumenty* (AUCP(B), the Comintern and the National Revolutionary Movement in China: Documents), 2 vols., Moscow: AO "Buklet", 1994, 1996. Titarenko is a director of the Institute of Far Eastern Studies where Grigoriev's group works.

18 Trotsky, "On the History of the Left Opposition," p. 262.

216

19 Titarenko et al., *VKP(B), Komintern i natsional'no-revolyutsionnoye dvizheniye v Kitaye*, vol. 1, p. 16.
20 Only one of them, namely the Russian Center for the Preservation and Study of Records of Modern History (RTsKhIDNI, hereafter Russian Center), preserves more than 1.5 million written documents, nine thousand three hundred photographs, and eight thousand six hundred meters of movie tapes which are concentrated in five hundred fifty-one thematic collections. This Center is the largest depository of documents on the International Communist movement and, of course, on the history of the Communist party of the Soviet Union.
21 See L. Kosheleva et al., eds., *Pis'ma I. V. Stalina V. I. Molotovu: 1925–1936 gg.: Sbornik Dokumentov* (J. V. Stalin's Letters to V. I. Molotov: 1925–1936: A Collection of Documents), Moscow: Rossiya Molodaya, 1995; Titarenko et al., *VKP(B), Komintern i natsional'no-revolyutsionnoye dvizheniye v Kitaye*.

Part I

1 It is a matter of factions inside the Russian Social Democratic Labor Party (RSDLP). This Marxist organization was founded in 1898 and split a few years later.
2 For example, see V. I. Lenin, "Two Tactics of Social-Democracy in the Democratic Revolution," in *Collected Works*, vol. 9, pp. 15–140.
3 Trotsky started to develop the idea of permanent revolution in the beginning of 1905 along with another active participant of the Russian revolutionary movement, Aleksandr L. Parvus.
4 Leon Trotsky, *Itogi i perspektivy. Dvizhushchiye sily revolyutsii* (Results and Prospects. Motive Forces of the Revolution), Moscow: "Sovetskii mir", 1919, pp. 34–35.
5 Ibid., pp. 39–40.
6 V. I. Lenin, "Report on the Unity Congress of R.S.D.L.P. A Letter to the St. Petersburg Workers," in *Collected Works*, vol. 10, pp. 334–335.
7 The slogan which called for the repartition of landlord land, supported by the majority of peasants, was not aimed at the development of capitalist relations. If the poor that constituted the majority of the rural population in Russia were really "keen" on capitalism, they would instinctively wish the repartition of the communal allotments as well. After all, on the eve of the First Russian revolution the latter constituted about 50% of all arable land in European Russia (see Leon Trotsky, *The History of the Russian Revolution*, Ann Arbor, MI: The Univ. of Michigan Press, n.d., p. 45.) However, the poor were only eager to take the land of landlords. Why? Because they only wanted to settle the problem of their landlessness. They needed the extra land in order to properly run their self-sufficient economy. A few years later, in the beginning of the New Economic Policy, Lenin and the Bolsheviks faced "the old Russian, semi-aristocratic, semi-muzhik and patriarchal mood,.. supreme contempt for trade," that was typical of the significant part of the Russian population (for example, see V. I. Lenin, "The Importance of Gold Now and After the Complete Victory of Socialism," in *Collected Works*, vol. 33, p. 115.)
8 Trotsky, *Itogi i perspektivy*, p. 40.
9 V. I. Lenin, "Fourth Anniversary of the October Revolution," in *Collected Works*, vol. 33, p. 54.
10 See Alexander Pantsov, "Lev Davidovich Trotsky," *Soviet Studies in History*, 1991, vol. 30, no. 1, pp. 7–43; Pantsov, "The New School of Falsification," in Marilyn Vogt-Downey, ed., *The USSR: 1987–1991: Marxist Perspectives*, Atlantic Highlands, NJ: Humanities Press, 1993, pp. 317–330.
11 See V. I. Lenin, "Letters from Afar," in *Collected Works*, vol. 23, pp. 295–342; Lenin, "The Tasks of the Proletariat in the Present Revolution," ibid., vol. 24, pp. 19–26; Lev Trotsky, *Sochineniya* (Collected Works), vol. III, part 1, Moscow: Gosizdat, 1924, pp. 3–23. In this respect, it is surprising that Volkogonov stated that two months after the February Revolution Trotsky "himself could not formulate his

thoughts yet" (Dmitrii Volkogonov, *Trotsky. Politicheskii portret* (Trotsky: A Political Portrait), book 1, Moscow: APN, 1992, p. 122.)

12 Joffe's letter was published by Yuri Felshtinsky as an appendix to Trotsky's speeches on Joffe's death (see Lev Trotsky, *Portrety* (Portraits), Benson, VT: Chalidze Publ., 1984, pp. 229–241.) For the cited sentences see pp. 240–241.

13 Nicolas Berdyaev, *The Origin of Russian Communism*, Ann Arbor, MI: The Univ. of Michigan Press, 1960, p. 105.

14 Ibid., pp. 95, 104.

15 For details see ibid., pp. 114–157. The Russian poet Sergei A. Esenin, for example, sensed this Russian poor peasant character of Bolshevism. In his poem *Anna Snegina*, describing his visit to a ruined village Krivushi where only the poor people lived, he writes about his talks with the peasants. They asked him many questions, the last was on Lenin. (The talks took place in the spring or summer of 1917, and Lenin for all people was a symbol of Bolshevism.) The author replied simply, "He is you all" (Sergei Esenin, *Sobraniye sochinenii* [Collected Works], vol. 3, Moscow: Sovetskii pisatel, 1967, p. 284.)

16 The detailed study of Weber's thoughts on Russia is from A. Kustariev. See his article in the journal *Voprosy filosofii* (Questions of Philosophy) (1990, no. 8, pp. 119–130).

17 See V. I. Lenin, "Dnevnik Zasedanii II s'ezda RSDRP: 17 (30) iyulia – 7 (20) avgusta 1903 g." (Diary of Proceedings of the Second RSDLP Congress), in V. I. Lenin, *PSS*. Vol. 7, Moscow: Politizdat, 1961, pp. 403–421.

18 On Lenin's concept of the party see M. S. Voslensky, *Nomenklatura. Gospodstvuyushchii klass Sovetskogo Soyuza* (Nomenklatura. The Ruling Class of the Soviet Union), Moscow: MP "Oktyabr", "Sovetskaya Rossiya", 1991, pp. 41–82.

19 V. I. Lenin, "What is to Be Done? Burning Questions of Our Movement," in *Collected Works*, vol. 5, p. 480.

20 N. Trotsky, *Nashi politicheskiye zadachi. Takticheskiye i organizatsionniye voprosy* (Our Political Tasks. Tactical and Organizational Questions), Geneva: RSDLP Press, 1904, pp. 54, 62.

21 Letter from F. Engels to K. Marx, February 13, 1851, in Karl Marx and Frederick Engels, *Collected Works*, vol. 38, New York: International Publ., 1982, pp. 289–290.

22 Lenin's party at the time still formally acted as the Bolshevik faction of the Russian Social Democratic Labor Party (RSDLP[B]). It would change its name in March 1918 to the Russian Communist party (Bolsheviks) – RCP(B), and late in 1925 to the All-Union Communist party (Bolsheviks) – AUCP(B).

23 Interview with N. A. Joffe at Moscow, Russia, June 5, 1991.

24 L. Trotsky, *Stalin*, vol. 2, Benson, VT: Chalidze Press, 1985, p. 140.

25 See V. I. Lenin, "Letter to P. A. Zalutsky, A. A. Solts and All Members of the Political Bureau re the Party Purge and the Conditions of Admission into the Party," in *Collected Works*, vol. 33, p. 138.

26 Letter from L. D. Trotsky to V. I. Lenin, December 21, 1921, Russian Center, 5/2/152/3.

27 See V. I. Lenin, "Comments on the Draft Resolution for the Eleventh Conference of the R.C.P.(B) on the Party Purge," in *Collected Works*, vol. 42, pp. 369–370.

28 "Pis'mo L. D. Trotskogo chlenam Tsentral'nogo Komiteta i Tsentral'noi Kontrol'noi Komissii RKP(b) ot 8 oktyabrya 1923 g." (Letter from L. D. Trotsky to Members of the RCP(B) Central Committee and the Central Control Commission, October 8, 1923), *Izvestiya TsK KPSS* (Proceedings of the CPSU CC), 1990, no. 5, pp. 170, 173.

29 Ibidem.

30 Karl Marx, "Capital. A Critique of Political Economy," vol. 1, in Karl Marx and Frederick Engels, *Collected Works*, vol. 35, New York: International Publ., 1996, p. 79.

31 See in detail A. V. Pantsov, *Iz istorii ideinoi bor'by v kitaiskom revolyutsionnom dvizhenii 20–40–kh godov* (On the History of Ideological Struggle in the Chinese Revolutionary Movement of 1920–40s), Moscow: Nauka, 1985, pp. 12–25.

32 See V. I. Glunin and A. S. Mugruzin, "Krest'yanstvo v kitaiskoi revolyutsii" ("The Peasantry in the Chinese revolution"), in R. A. Ulyanovsky, ed., *Revolyutsionnyi protsess na Vostoke. Istoriya i sovremennost'* (The Revolutionary Process in the East: History and the Present), Moscow: Nauka, 1982, p. 151.

33 The figures are from V. G. Gel'bras, *Sotsial'no-politicheskaya struktura KNR. 50–60–e gody* (Social and Political Structure of the PRC: 1950–60s), Moscow: Nauka, 1980, pp. 27, 33–34, 38.

34 Cited in Department of Marx and Lenin Writings of Beijing Library, ed., *Makesi, Engesi zhuzuo zhongyiwen zonglu* (Catalogue of Chinese Translations of Marx and Engels's Works), Beijing: Shumu wenxian, 1988, p. 1119.

35 Ibid., pp. 1120–1121.

36 On the penetration of socialism into China prior to 1917 see Martin Bernal, *Chinese Socialism to 1907*, Ithaca: Cornell Univ. Press, 1976; L. N. Borokh, *Obshchestvennaya mysl' Kitaya i sotsializm (nachalo XX v.)* (Social Thought of China and Socialism [the Beginning of the Twentieth Century]), Moscow: Nauka, 1984; M. A. Persits, "O podgotovitel'nom etape Kommunisticheskogo dvizheniya v Azii" (On the Preparatory Period of the Communist Movement in Asia), in Ulyanovsky, *Revolyutsionnyi protsess na Vostoke*, pp. 38–76.

37 Mao Zedong, "'Qida' gongzuo fangzhen" (The Seventh Congress's Course of Work), *Hongqi* (Red Banner), 1981, no. 11, p. 4.

38 See in detail Lee Feigon, *Chen Duxiu: Founder of the Chinese Communist Party,* Princeton, NJ: Princeton Univ. Press, 1983, pp. 138–146.

39 See Chow Tse-tsung, *The May Fourth Movement: Intellectual Revolution in Modern China*, Cambridge, Mass.: Harvard Univ. Press, 1960; Yu. M. Garushyants, *Dvizheniye 4 maya 1919 goda v Kitaye* (The May Fourth movement of 1919 in China), Moscow: Nauka, 1959; L. P. Delyusin, ed., *Dvizheniye "4 maya" 1919 g. v Kitaye* (The "May Fourth" Movement of 1919 in China), Moscow: Nauka, 1971. The Chinese labor movement originated at the end of the nineteenth century. Between 1895 and the end of 1918 in China it was estimated there were 152 strikes, some of which even had a political character. However, before 1919 the economic and political manifestations of Chinese workers were disunited; one could say more about workers' individual participation in the country's political life than about the aggregate actions of the working class (see Jean Chesneaux, *Le Mouvement Ouvrier Chinois de 1919 – 1927*, Paris: Mouton, 1962, chapter 6.)

40 See Xu Yuandong et. al., *Zhongguo gongchandang lishi jianghua* (Lectures on History of the Chinese Communist Party), Beijing: Zhongguo qingnian chubanshe, 1982, pp. 8–15; Chang Kuo-t'ao, *The Rise of the Chinese Communist Party: An Autobiography*, vol. 1, Lawrence etc.: Kansas Univ. Press, 1971, p. 83.

41 Li Dazhao, *Izbrannye proizvedeniya* (Selected Works), Moscow: Nauka, 1989, p. 204.

42 Mao Zedong, *O diktature narodnoi demokratii* (On the Dictatorship of People's Democracy,) Moscow: Gospolitizdat, 1949, pp. 5–6.

43 Leon Trotsky, "Perspektivy i zadachi na Vostoke" (Perspectives and Tasks in the East), in Leon Trotsky, *Zapad i Vostok. Voprosy mirovoi politiki i mirovoi revolyutsii* (The West and the East. Questions of World Politics and World Revolution), Moscow: Krasnaya nov', 1924, pp. 37, 39.

44 *Minguo ribao*, May 19, 1917.

45 See *The Bolsheviki and World Peace*, New York: Boni & Liverwright Publ., 1918.

46 See Li Dazhao, *Izbranniye proizvedeniya*, p. 160.

47 See ibid., pp. 328–329; *Li Dazhao wenji* (Li Dazhao Collected Works), vol. 2, Beijing: Renmin chubanshe, 1984, p. 482; *Wusi shiqide shetuan* (Societies of the "May Fourth" Period), vol. 2, Beijing: Shenghuo, dushu, xinzhi sanlian shudian, 1979, p. 279. Li Dazhao gives the name of the Trotsky's book in the Chinese translation – *Eguo shi*, that is *History of the Russian revolution*, apparently, assuming London edition of the Trotsky's brochure, which was entitled *History of the Russian Revolution to Brest-Litovsk* (London: Leo & Unwin Publ., 1919.)

48 N. Lenin and Leon Trotzky, *The Proletarian Revolution in Russia*, New York: The Communist Press Publ., [1918].

49 *Renmin chubanshe* (People's Publishing house) was established September 1, 1921, in Shanghai, at 625 Fude alley. Its editor was Li Da, a chief of the propaganda department of the Central Bureau (at that time acted as the Central Executive Committee) of the CCP. The Publishing house scheduled publication of 48 Marxist books, fifteen of which were printed in one year. Taking into account the demands of conspiracy, all of these books bear the information that they were printed in Guangzhou. See *Xin shiqi* (New Epoch), 1981, no. 12, p. 19; *Shanghai diqu jiandang huodong yanjiu ziliao* (Study Documents on Party-Building Activity in Shanghai District), Shanghai: Shanghai shi diyi renmin jincha xuexiao, 1986, pp. 69–71.

50 This translation was made following the first publication of Trotsky's speech, which appeared on April 24, 1924 in a KUTK newspaper *Under the Banner of Ilich* (see *Zheng Chaolin huiyilu* [Zheng Chaolin's Memoirs], Hong Kong, 1982, p. 78.)

51 See *Makesi, Engesi zhuzuo zhongyiwen zonglu*, pp. 1121, 1122; *Zhonghuazhi zui zhishi shouci* ("Most of Most" in China), Nanchang: Jiangxi jiaoyu chubanshe, 1987, pp. 1–2; *Die Werke von Karl Marx und Friedrich Engels in China: Katalog und Auswahlbibliographie*, Trier: Karl-Marx-Haus, 1984, S. 122–123).

52 On the Chinese translations of various political terms see V. G. Gel'bras, "Klass: mif ili real'nost?" (Class: Myth or Reality?), *Rabochii klass i sovremennyi mir* (The Working Class and the Contemporary World), 1974, no. 2, pp. 130–141; A. A. Krushinsky, "Smysl vyrazheniya "geming" v sovremennykh politicheskikh tekstakh" (The Gist of the "Geming" Expression in Modern Political Texts), *Odinnadtsataya nauchnaya konferentsiya "Obshchestvo i gosudarstvo v Kitaye." Tezisy i doklady* (The Eleventh Scientific Conference "Society and State in China". Theses and Presentations), part 3, Moscow: IV AN SSSR, 1980, pp. 199–205; A. V. Pantsov, "K diskussii v KPK vokrug 'idei Mao Tseduna'" ("On the Discussion in the CCP Around 'Mao Zedong Thought'," *Rabochii klass i sovremennyi mir*, 1982, no. 3, pp. 44–47; E. Yu. Staburova, *Anarkhism v Kitaye. 1900–1921* (Anarchism in China. 1900–1921), Moscow: Nauka, 1983, p. 133.

53 See Donald Klein and Anne Clark, *Biographic Dictionary of Chinese Communism. 1921–1969*, vol. 2, Cambridge, Mass.: Harvard Univ. Press, 1971, p. 961.

54 See *Jiefang yu gaizao* (Liberation and Reconstruction), 1919, no. 2, pp. 53–59.

55 Ibid., p. 56.

56 See Shao Piaoping, *Xin Eguozhi yanjiu* (A Study of New Russia), n. p.: Riben daban nanqu dongying bianyishe, 1920, 140 p.

57 *Li Dazhao wenji*, vol. 2. pp. 472–489.

58 See Luosu [Russell, Bertrand], *You E ganxiang* (Impressions from the Trip to Russia), *Xin qingnian* (New Youth), 1920, vol. 8, no. 2, pp. 1–12.

59 L. P. Delyusin was the first to pay attention to this. See L. P. Delyusin, *Diskussiya o sotsializme. Iz istorii obshchestvennoi mysli v Kitaye v nachale 20–kh godov* (Dispute on Socialism. On the History of Social Thought in China in the Beginning of 1920s), Moscow: Nauka, 1970, pp. 31–34.

60 As Russell recalled many years later, he long hesitated before making the final decision to publish his book on Russia (it was called *Practice and Theory of Bolshevism*.) He did not want "to play into the hands of reaction" but at the same time could not refrain from speaking out against the Bolsheviks' violation of human rights (see *The Autobiography of Bertrand Russell. 1914–1944*, Boston & Toronto: Little, Brown & Co., 1956, p. 185.)

61 Ibid., pp. 191, 192.

62 Li, *Izbranniye proizvedeniya*, p. 160.

63 Ibid., pp. 160, 161.

64 K. V. Sheveliev, *Iz istorii obrazovaniya Kommunisticheskoi partii Kitaya* (On the History of the Formation of the Chinese Communist Party), Moscow: Institute of Far Eastern Studies Press, 1976, p. 39.

65 Shi Cuntong, "Makeside gongchanzhuyi"(Marx's Communism), *Xin qingnian*, 1921, vol. 9, no. 4, p. 10.

66 Li, *Izbranniye proizvedeniya*, pp. 218–219. See also *Li Dazhao wenji*, p. 46.

67 Chen Duxiu, "Shehuizhuyi piping" ("Critiques of Socialism"), *Xin qingnian*, 1921, vol. 9, no. 3, pp. 11, 13.

68 Li Da, "Makesi huanyuan" ("Marx's Revival"), *Xin qingnian*, 1921, vol. 8, no. 5, pp. 1, 8.

69 Some of the supporters of communism in China (Chen Duxiu, Zhang Tailei, Shi Cuntong) did for a time recognize the possibility of a bourgeois revolution in their country. See Sheveliev, *Iz istorii obrazovaniya Kommunisticheskoi partii Kitaya*, pp. 78–80.

70 For instance, see their selected works of that time included in the following collections: *Makesizhuyi zai Zhongguo – Cong yingxiang chuanru dao chuanbo* (Marxism in China – From the Influence to the Spread), vol. 2, Beijing: Qinghua daxue chubanshe, 1983; *Gongchan xiaozu* (Communist nucleus), 2 vols., Beijing: Zhonggong dangshi ziliao chubanshe, 1987.

71 C. Martin Wilbur, ed., *The Communist Movement in China: An Essay Written in 1924 by Ch'en Kung-po*, New York: Octagon Books, 1960, p. 102.

72 Ibidem.

73 Ibid., p. 105.

74 Chen Pan-tsu [Chen Tanqiu], "Reminiscences of the First Congress of the Communist Party of China), *The Communist International*, 1936, no. 14, p. 1364. K. V. Sheveliev was the first to pay attention to this fact. See K. V. Sheveliev, "Pred"istoriya edinogo fronta v Kitaye i Uchreditel'nyi s"ezd KPK" (A Pre-history of the United Front in China and the Constituent CCP Congress), in *Kitai: traditsii i sovremennost'* (China: Traditions and the Present), Moscow: Nauka, 1976, p. 203.

75 Li, *Izbranniye proizvedeniya*, p. 322.

76 Shi Cuntong, "Women yao zemyang gan shehui geming" (How We Will Carry Out a Social Revolution), *Gongchandang* (The Communist), 1921, no. 5, p. 13.

77 See Wang Jianying, ed., *Zhongguo gongchandang zuzhi shi ziliao huibian – lingdao jigou yange he chengyuan minglu* (Collection of Documents on History of the CCP Organizations – the Evolution of Leading Organs and Their Personal Composition), Beijing: Hongqi chubanshe, 1983, p. 2.

Part 2

1 V. I. Lenin, "Address to the Second All-Russia Congress of Communist Organizations of the Peoples of the East, November 22, 1919," in *Collected Works*, vol. 30, p. 162.

2 Ibid., p. 159.

3 Lenin, "The Second Congress of the Communist International," pp. 244–245.

4 See Introduction, endnote 9.

5 Only three voters abstained. See *Der Zweite Kongress der Kommunistischen Internationale. Protokoll der Verhandlungen vom 19. Juli in Petrograd und vom 23. Juli bis 7. August 1920 in Moscau*, Hamburg: Verlag der Kommunistischen Internationale, 1921, pp. 224–232. For the English translation see Jane Degras, ed., *The Communist International. 1919–1943. Documents*, vol. 1, London: Oxford Univ. Press, 1956, pp. 139–144.

6 See M. N. Roy, "Supplementary Theses on the National and Colonial Questions," State Archives, 5402/1/488/13–14; *The Communist International*, 1920, no. 13, pp. 2416–2418. There is no data on the results of its voting.

7 See [M. N. Roy], "Manifest revolyutsionnoi partii Indii. Vozzvaniye k britanskomu proletariatu" (Manifesto of the Revolutionary Party of India. An Appeal to the British Proletariat), *Zhizn' national'nostei* (Life of the Nationalities), July 26, 1920; Roy, "Revolyutsionnoye dvizheniye v Indii" (The Revolutionary Movement in

India), *Kommunisticheskii Internatsional*, 1920, no. 12, pp. 2163–2172; *Vestnik 2–go kongressa Kommunisticheskogo Internatsionala*, no. 1, July 27, 1920, pp. 1–2.

8 See Persits, *Revolutionaries of India in Soviet Russia*, pp. 124–152.

9 Roy, "Supplementary Theses on the National and Colonial Questions," 13, 14; *The Communist International*, 1920, no. 13, pp. 2417, 2418. Emphasis added.

10 Persits, *Revolutionaries of India in Soviet Russia*, pp. 152–158.

11 The text of Sun Yat-sen's telegram to Moscow has not been found. For the Soviet government's reply see Xenia J. Eudin and Robert North, *Soviet Russia and the East: 1920–1927: A Documentary Study*, Stanford: Stanford Univ. Press, 1957, p. 217.

12 Jiang Yihua, *Guomindang zuopaide qizhi – Liao Zhongkai* (The Banner of the Left Guomindang – Liao Zhongkai), Shanghai: Shanghai renmin chubanshe, 1985, p. 69.

13 Ibidem.

14 A. Potapov, "O doktore Sun Yat-sene, byvshem pervom prezidente Kitaiskoi respubliki" (On Doctor Sun Yat-sen, the Former First President of the Chinese Republic), Russian Center, 514/1/6/35.

15 G. Voitinsky, "Moi vstrechi s Sun Yat-senom" (My Meetings with Sun Yat-sen), *Pravda*, March 15, 1925. For an abridged English translation see Eudin and North, *Soviet Russia and the East*, pp. 218–219.

16 See Jiang, *Guomindang zuopaide qizhi – Liao Zhongkai*, pp. 69–70.

17 Eudin and North, *Soviet Russia and the East*, pp. 220–221.

18 Zhang Ji, who in the beginning of 1920 participated in establishing Sun Yat-sen's contacts with the Communists, in 1923 moved to sharply anti-Communist positions.

19 See Russian Center, 514/1/20/85–91; Harold Isaacs, "Documents on the Comintern and the Chinese Revolution," *The China Quarterly*, 1971, no. 45, pp. 103–104; Lin Hongnuan, "Zhang Tailei", in *Zhonggongdang shi renwu zhuan* (Biographies of the CCP Historical Activists), vol. 4, Xian: Shenxi renmin chubanshe, 1982, pp. 81–82; *Zhang Tailei wenji* (Zhang Tailei's Collected Works), Beijing: Renmin chubanshe, 1981, p. 330; *Zhongguo geming shi jiangyi* (Lectures on the History of the Chinese Revolution), vol. 1, Beijing: Zhongguo renmin daxue chubanshe, 1983, p. 98. Some publications erroneously refer to this meeting as having taken place in August and September 1921. See Li Xin, "Li Dazhao," in *Zhonggongdang shi renwu zhuan* (Biographies of the CCP Historical Activists), vol. 2, Xian: Shenxi renmin chubanshe, 1981, p. 20; *Zhongguo xinminzhuzhuyi geming shiqi tongshi* (General History of the Period of the Neo-Democratic Revolution in China), vol. 1, Beijing: Gaodeng jiaoyu chubanshe, 1959, p. 149.) Nevertheless, it is known from Maring's own report to the ECCI that he and his interpreter Zhang Tailei set off for Shanghai to meet Sun Yat-sen only on December 10, 1921. They went the way via Hankou, Changsha, and Guangzhou. (See Russian Center, 514/1/20/85; *Zhonggong "sanda" ziliao* [Materials of the CCP Third Congress], Guangzhou: Guangdong renmin chubanshe, 1985, p. 12; Tony Saich, *The Origins of the First United Front in China: The Role of Sneevleit (Alias Maring)*, 2 vols., vol. 1, Leiden: Brill, 1991, p. 317.)

20 Saich, *The Origins*, vol. 1, p. 323.

21 Jiang Huaxuan even writes that Maring's proposal was discussed in all CCP organizations, which unanimously voted against it. See Jiang Huaxuan, "Dangde minzhu geming ganglingde tichu he guogong hezuo celüede jige wenti" (A Few Issues Concerning the Raise of the Party Program of the Democratic Revolution and Strategy of the Guomindang/CCP Alliance), *Jingdai shi yanjiu* (Modern History Studies), Beijing, 1985, no. 2, p. 115.) This is apparently an exaggeration. Summing up the results of the debate in his letter to Voitinsky of April 6, 1922, Chen Duxiu said nothing about any discussions on this issue in the Shandong, Zhengzhou, and Sichuan organizations of the CCP. Nor did he mention whether any disputes had taken place among Chinese Communists who lived abroad. See V. I. Glunin, "Komintern i stanovleniye kommunisticheskogo dvizheniya v Kitaye (1920–1927)" (The Comintern and the Foundation of the Chinese Communist Movement

[1920–27]), in Ulyanovsky, *Komintern i Vostok*, p. 252; Saich, *The Origins*, vol. 1, pp. 256, 257.)

22 See Jiang, "Dangde minzhu geming ganglingde tichu he guogong hezuo celüede jige wenti," p. 116.

23 Russian Center, 514/1/19/7–8. While adopting this decision, the Comintern Executive Committee was apparently not informed that by that time power in Guangzhou had been seized by Chen Jiongming, who in June organized a coup d'état against Sun Yat-sen, compelling him to escape to Shanghai. The CCP CEC would move temporarily to Guangzhou in the spring of 1923, after the restoration of Sun Yat-sen's power.

24 When this document was passed by the Comintern Executive Committee is not clear. Most scholars, including myself, have believed that it happened in early August 1922. (For instance, see Alexander Pantsov and Gregor Benton, "Did Trotsky Oppose Entering the Guomindang 'From the First'?" *Republican China*, 1994, vol. XIX, no. 2, p. 52.) However, newly opened Russian archives make it evident that it was at least written by Radek not long before July 29, 1922 (see Letter from K. B. Radek to J. V. Stalin and L. D. Trotsky Concerning Instructions to A. A. Joffe, Russian Center, 326/2/24/1), so it could be adopted by the Comintern Executive Committee right in the very end of July.

25 Different versions of Radek's instructions exist in Russian, English and German. Fragments and abstracts from the Russian text were published for the first time in 1969 by A. I. Kartunova, then a senior researcher at the Institute of Marxism-Leninism of the Central Committee of the CPSU. However, Kartunova's fragments and abstracts were replete with distortions and careless errors. (See A. I. Kartunova, "Komintern i nekotoriye voprosy reorganizatsii gomindana" [The Comintern and Some Questions Concerning the Reorganization of the Guomindang], in Ulyanovsky, *Komintern i Vostok*, pp. 302–303.) Unfortunately, four years later, in 1973, Dov Bing took them as an accurate rendering of the original Russian text, and translated them into English (See Dov Bing, "Was there a Sneevlietian Strategy?" *The China Quarterly*, 1973, no. 54, p. 351.) In 1980 Kartunova's publication was reproduced in a Russian collection of Comintern documents, "The Communist International and the Chinese revolution." (See M. L. Titarenko, *Kommunisticheskii Internatsional i kitaiskaya revolyutsiya: dokumenty i materialy* (The Communist International and the Chinese Revolution: Documents and Materials), Moscow: Nauka, 1986, pp. 25–26.) Tony Saich, in his annotations of the publication of Maring's China archive and of the CCP documents (see Saich, *The Origins*, vol. 1, p. 328; Saich, ed., *The Rise to Power of the Chinese Communist Party. Documents and Analysis*, Armonk: M. E. Sharpe, 1996, p. 98), still regards Kartunova's text as largely reliable, thus reproducing Bing's original mistake. At the same time, Saich was the first to publish the English text of this instruction (see Saich, *The Origins*, vol. 1, pp. 328–329.) Saich noted only "slight differences" between Kartunova's and his own text, but actually the differences between them, and between Kartunova's version and the original Russian text, are striking, and touch on fundamental questions concerning the CCP's tactical line in the Guomindang. These differences result from Kartunova's falsification of Radek's directive.

The main instance of this falsification concerns the idea that the CCP should stay in the Guomindang as long as the Communists lacked sufficient strength to act independently. Besides a number of distortions of the original document, Kartunova deleted from the text two essential sentences where this idea is expressed, together with various other passages, for example Sections V and VI of the instruction (the documents, thereby, was reduced to four sections instead of six.) An English translation of the original Russian text was published for the first time in 1994 in the American journal *Republican China* (see Pantsov and Benton, "Did Trotsky Oppose Entering the Guomindang 'From the First'", pp. 61–63.)

26 See Degras, *The Communist International*, vol. I, pp. 383–393.

27 See A. B. Reznikov, "Razrabotka IV kongressom Kominterna problem natsional'no-osvoboditel'nogo dvizheniya" (The Comintern Fourth Congress's Elaboration of Problems of the National Liberation Movement), in *Chetvertyi kongress Kominterna: Razrabotka kongressom strategii i taktiki kommunisticheskogo dvizheniya v novykh usloviyakh. Politika edinogo fronta* (The Fourth Congress of the Comintern: The Congress's Elaboration of Strategy and Tactics of the Communist Movement in New Conditions: The Policy of the United Front), Moscow: Politizdat, 1980, p. 198.

28 For an analysis of Roy's presentation at the October 28 meeting see ibid., pp. 198–199.

29 See *Byulleten IV kongressa Kommunisticheskogo Internatsionala* (Bulletin of the Fourth Congress of the Communist International), no. 19, December 1, 1922, pp. 22–27; *Protokoll des Vierten Kongress der Kommunistischen Internationale: Petrograd-Moskau vom 5. November bis 5. December 1922*, Hamburg: Verlag der Kommunistischen Internationale, 1923, pp. 590–598. For a precise brief exposition of Roy's presentation see *Der Bolschewik*, no. 14, November 23, 1922, p. 4.

30 *Byulleten IV kongressa Kommunisticheskogo Internatsionala*, p. 23. The precise brief exposition contains a declaration that Roy only referred to the fact that Eastern countries were "at various levels of social and economic development" (*Der Bolschewik*, no. 14, p. 4).

31 *Byulleten IV kongressa Kommunisticheskogo Internatsionala*, p. 23.

32 Ibidem.

33 Ibid., pp. 22, 26.

34 Ibid., p. 24.

35 Ibid., p. 26.

36 Lenin drew up initial guiding lines for the further analysis of Eastern societies, but he himself acknowledged that he and other members of the Comintern had no "extensive" experience in dealing with the Orient. See Lenin, "The Second Congress of the Communist International," p. 243. He could not devote much attention to the revolutionary movement in the East, being overwhelmed by other work. At the time he also began suffering from his progressing sickness. See in detail P. M. Shastitko, *Leninskaya teoriya natsional'no-kolonial'nogo voprosa (istoriya formirovaniya)* (Lenin's Theory of National Colonial Question [The History of Its Formation]), Moscow: Nauka, 1979, pp. 214–230; M. A. Cheshkov, "Analiz sotsial'noi struktury kolonial'nykh obshchestv v dokumentakh Kominterna (1920–1927)" (The Analysis of Social Structure of Colonial Societies in the Comintern Documents [1920–1927]), in Ulyanovsky, *Komintern i Vostok*, p. 215.

37 *Byulleten IV kongressa Kommunisticheskogo Internatsionala*, p. 26.

38 It has been already noted by Robert North and Xenia Eudin in their *M. N. Roy's Mission to China: The Communist-Kuomintang Split of 1927* (Berkeley: Univ. of California Press, 1963, p. 17.) These well-respected authors, however, came to this correct conclusion on the basis of only one passage from the "General Theses" which they unfortunately wholly misinterpreted. Here is this phrase: "The dominant classes in the colonies and the semicolonial countries are unable and unwilling to lead the struggle against imperialism as this struggle is converted into a revolutionary mass movement." (See Degras, *The Communist International*, vol. I, pp. 384–385.) At the same time, it is clear from the context of the document, that the Congress here assumed a reactionary aristocracy (feudal and patriarchal upper strata) of Eastern countries (as for China, it referred to her military governors), but not at all the national bourgeoisie.

39 This idea is in keeping with Trotsky's thesis from his "Manifesto of the Communist International to the Proletariat of the Entire World," adopted by the First Comintern Congress.

40 Degras, *The Communist International*, vol. 1, pp. 383, 384, 387, 390, 392. Emphasis added.

41 See above, p. 62.

42 Titarenko et al., *VKP(b), Komintern i natsional'no-revolyutsionnoye dvizheniye v Kitaye. Dokumenty*, vol. I, pp. 149–150. For another variant of the English translation see Saich, *The Origins*, vol. 1, pp. 377–378.

43 See Shen Dachun and Tian Haiyan, "Zhongguo gongchandang 'yida' de zhuyao wenti" (Essential Questions Concerning the First Congress of the Chinese Communist Party), *Renmin ribao*, June 30, 1961.

44 See "Kongress Kommunisticheskoi partii v Kitaye" (A Congress of the Communist Party in China), *Narody Azii i Afriki* (Peoples of Asia and Africa), 1972, no. 6, pp. 151–152.

45 See above, pp. 46–47.

46 Some authors believe that the Congress opened in early January 1922 in Irkutsk and then transferred to Moscow. (See Lin, "Zhang Tailei," p. 75; *Kommunist*, 1959, no. 17, p. 86.) The Soviet Sinologist G. S. Kara-Murza wrote that it was convened in Irkutsk in November 1922. See G. S. Kara-Murza, "Kitai v 1918–1924 gg." (China in 1918–1924), *Istorik-marksist* (Historian-Marxist), 1939, no. 5–6, p. 155. However, the former NKID commissioner in Siberia and Mongolia B. Z. Shumyatsky, who was in charge of the preparation of the Congress, later recollected that in Irkutsk they undertook only preparatory work which was completed by December 25. See B. Shumyatsky, "Iz istorii komsomola i kompartii Kitaya (Pamyati odnogo iz organizatorov komsomola i kompartii Kitaya tov. Zhang Tai-leya) (On History of the Communist Youth League and the Communist Party of China [Dedicated to the Memory of One of the Organizers of the Communist Youth League and the Communist Party of China, Comrade Zhang Tailei]), *Revolyutsionnyi Vostok* (The Revolutionary East), 1928, no. 4–5, pp. 222–227.

47 This Congress is known in historiography under various names: the First Congress of Workers of Far Eastern Countries (V. I. Lenin, *PSS*, vol. 44, p. 702); Congress of Workers of the Far East (*Bol'shaya sovetskaya entsiklopediya* [Large Soviet Encyclopedia], vol. 47, 2nd ed., Moscow: "BSE", 1957, p. 9); Conference of Peoples of the Far East (S. Kalachev [S. N. Naumov], "Kratkii ocherk istorii Kitaiskoi Kommunisticheskoi partii" [A Brief History of the Chinese Communist Party], *Kanton* [Canton], 1927, no. 1 (10), p. 42); Congress of Representatives of Communist parties of Far Eastern Countries (*Kommunist*, 1959, no. 17, p. 80); the Congress of the Toilers of the Far East (Chang, *The Rise of the Chinese Communist Party*, vol. 1, pp. 159–162, 175, 177–218.) Historians of the People's Republic of China use another name – the First Congress of Communist Parties and National Revolutionary Organizations of Far Eastern Countries, which was used in the first Chinese translation of the Manifesto accepted by the Congress. (See *Xianqu* [Pioneer], 1922, no. 10. p. 10; *Zhongguo xiandai shi* [Contemporary History of China], 1983, no. 10, pp. 35–42; Xu et al., *Zhongguo gongchandang lishi jianghua*, p. 28.) Most Western specialists call it the First Congress of the Toilers of the Far East (see, for example, Eudin and North, *Soviet Russia and the East*, pp. 145–147, 153, 221–231, 268–272.) Referring to the name displayed on the delegates' mandates, Kartunova calls it the First Congress of Communist and Revolutionary Organizations of the Far East. See A. I. Kartunova, *Politika kompartii Kitaya v rabochem voprose nakanune revolyutsii 1925–1927 godov* (Policy of the Chinese Communist Party in the Worker Question on the Eve of the Revolution of 1925–1927), Moscow: Nauka, 1983, p. 155. I use the name borrowed from a work by a Soviet specialist G. Z. Sorkin who analyzed the history of convocation of the forum in a great detail. See G. Z. Sorkin, "S"ezd narodov Dalnego Vostoka" (Congress of Peoples of the Far East), *Problemy Vostokovedeniya* (Problems of Oriental Studies), 1960, no. 5, pp. 76–86.) The ECCI officials Voitinsky and Sergei A. Dalin, who actively participated in the Congress, also called it the Congress of Peoples of the Far East. See Russian Center, 495/65a/38; 2474.

48 According to different estimations, the Chinese delegation counted 44 persons (39 with decisive and 5 with consultative votes) or 54 persons. (Sorkin, "S"ezd narodov Dalnego Vostoka," p. 79; Kara-Murza, "Kitai v 1918–1924 gg.," p. 155;

Shumyatsky, "Iz istorii komsomola i kompartii Kitaya," p. 224; Lin, "Zhang Tailei," p. 75; Kartunova, *Politika kompartii Kitaya v rabochem voprose nakanune revolyutsii 1925–1927 godov*, p. 156.)

49 See "Yuandong geguo gongchandang ji minzu geming tuanti diyici dahui xuanyan" (Manifesto of the First Congress of Communist Parties and National Revolutionary Organizations of Far Eastern Countries), *Xianqu*, Beijing, 1922, no. 10, p. 4.

50 There are different opinions concerning He Shuheng's participation in the Congress. Sheveliev, for instance, believes that he was absent there. See Sheveliev's chapter in M. L. Titarenko, ed., *Noveishaya istoriya Kitaya. 1917–1927* (Modern History of China. 1917–1927), Moscow: Nauka, 1983, pp. 85–86. However, Chinese historians consider He as the participant. See, for example, Wang Xinggang and Fang Daming, "He Shuheng," in *Zhonggongdang shi zhuan*, vol. 4, p. 17.)

51 See Kalachev, "Kratkii ocherk istorii Kitaiskoi Kommunisticheskoi partii," p. 42; Titarenko, *Noveishaya istoriya Kitaya*, p. 106; Sorkin, "S"ezd narodov Dalnego Vostoka", pp. 78–80; *Zhongguo geming shi jiangyi*, p. 82.

52 See Xiao Jingguang, "Fu Su xuexi qianhou (Before and After Study in the USSR), *Geming shi ziliao* (Materials on Revolutionary History), Beijing, 1981, no. 3, p. 12; *Zhongguo xiandai shi*, 1983, no. 10, p. 39.

53 There is a widespread view that Zhang Tailei actively participated in the Congress from the very beginning. Lin Hongnuan even writes that when Zhang Tailei arrived in Moscow from Irkutsk – where he allegedly attended the opening session of the Congress – he was received by Lenin, who asked him whether they should continue the Congress with the participation of national revolutionaries and non-party members or transform it into a forum of Communist parties of all Far Eastern countries. See Lin, "Zhang Tailei," p. 75. Nevertheless, it is known that at the beginning of January 1922 Zhang Tailei was in Guangzhou and took part in three meetings between Maring and Chen Jiongming. Zhang also attended a meeting of Guangzhou and Hailufeng region youths. See *Zhang Tailei wenji*, pp. 330–331. Only then did he leave for Soviet Russia via Shanghai, where he had time to discuss some issues with the CP leaders. At that time the way from Guangzhou to Moscow would have taken no less than three weeks. That means that Zhang Tailei could only have attended the concluding sessions of the Congress of Peoples of the Far East. It may be the reason why Kartunova, who worked with the Congress archives, could not find any data on him as a delegate.

54 This statement is taken from the speech at the Congress of the Comintern Executive Committee chairman Zinoviev. For the English translation see Hélène Carrère d'Encausse and Stuart R. Schram, eds., *Marxism and Asia*, London:The Penguin Press, 1969, p. 215.

55 See V. I. Lenin, *PSS*, vol. 44, p. 702; Chang, *The Rise of the Chinese Communist Party*, vol. 1, pp. 207–209.

56 For an abridged English translation see Eudin and North, *Soviet Russia and the East*, pp. 230–231.

57 Chang, *The Rise of the Chinese Communist Party*, vol. 1, p. 220.

58 *Zhongguo xiandai shi*, 1983, no. 10, p. 40.

59 Chang, *The Rise of the Chinese Communist Party*, vol. 1, p. 218.

60 "Zhongguo gongchandang duiyu shijude zhuzhang" (Statement of the CCP on the Current Situation," *Xianqu*, 1922, no. 9, p. 2. For another variant of the English translation see Saich, *The Rise to Power of the Chinese Communist Party*, p. 35.

61 See in detail Titarenko, *Noveishaya istoriya Kitaya*, pp. 108–109.

62 "Zhongguo gongchandang duiyu shijude zhuzhang", pp. 2, 3.

63 Ibid., p. 2.

64 Cited in Glunin, "Komintern i stanovleniye kommunisticheskogo dvizheniya v Kitaye (1920–1927), p. 252; Jiang, "Dangde minzhu geming ganglingde tichu he guogong hezuo celüede jige wenti," p. 116.

65 See *Zhongguo gongchandang jiguan fazhan cankao ziliao* (Reference Materials on the History of the CCP Organs' Development), vol. 1, Beijing: Zhonggong dangxiao chubanshe, 1983, p. 149.

66 Ibid., p. 38.

67 The name of this revolution, appended in English translation to an MA thesis by Chen Gongbo, is given incorrectly – "The Decision Concerning the Nationalist Joint Battle Line." See Wilbur, *The Communist Movement in China*, p. 119.) The resolution is indeed called "On the 'Democratic United Front'" (*Guanyu "minzhuzhuyi lianhe zhanxian" de yijuean.*) See *Zhonggong "sanda" ziliao*, p. 5.

68 See *Zhongguo gongchandang wunian laizhi zhengzhi zhuzhang* (Political statements of the Chinese Communist Party for the Past Five Years), Guangzhou: Guoguang shuju, 1926, pp. 1–23; *Zhonggong "sanda" ziliao*, pp. 5–7; Wilbur, *The Communist Movement in China*, pp. 105–117.)

69 The Communists considered as poor peasants (*pinnong*) all small peasant proprietors, tenants and farm wage-laborers, that is, 95% of the rural population.

70 Wilbur, *The Communist Movement in China*, p. 114.

71 Glunin was the first to notice this.

72 "Minquan yundong datongmeng xuanyan" (The Declaration of the Alliance of Movements for Republicanism), *Xianqu*, 1922, no. 20, pp. 1–2.

73 *Zhonggong "sanda" ziliao*, p. 7.

74 Jiang, "Dangde minzhu geming ganglingde tichu he guogong hezuo celüede jige wenti," p. 116.

75 See *Lin Boqu zhuan* (Lin Boqu's Biography), Beijing: Hongqi chubanshe, 1986, p. 75.

76 Chang, *The Rise of the Chinese Communist Party*, vol. 1, p. 250.

77 Most historians believe that the meeting took place on August 29–30. See Zimei, "Xihu huiyi shijian kao" (Verification of the Time Period of Xihu Meeting), *Zhonggong yanjiu ziliao*, 1983, no. 4, pp. 326–328. However, a number of Chinese authors refer to the second decade of August, and some even indicate a precise date – August 17 or August 17–18. See *Zhang Tailei wenji*, p. 332; Lin, "Zhang Tailei," p. 84; Li, "Li Dazhao," p. 21.

78 There are different opinions as to whether Li Dazhao was a CCP CEC member at the time of this meeting. Some deny that he was. See Xu et. al., *Zhongguo gongchandang lishi jianghua*, p. 30; *Zhongguo gongchandang jiguan fazhan cankao ziliao*, vol. 1, p. 3. Others believe that he was a CEC alternate member. See *Cihai. Lishi fenci. Zhongguo xiandaishe* (Dictionary Cihai. History Division. Modern Chinese History), Shanghai: Shanghai cishu chubanshe, 1984, p. 131; *Zhongguo gongchandang zuzhi shi ziliao huibian* (Collection of Materials on the History of the CCP Organizations' Development), Beijing: Hongqi chubanshe, 1983, p. 9. However, in his famous "Open Letter to All Comrades" of December 10, 1929, Chen Duxiu listed Li Dazhao among five members of the CCP CEC elected at the Second Party Congress. See Wang Jianmin, *Zhongguo gongchandang shigao* (Outline History of the CCP), vol. 1, Taipei: Author Press, 1965, p. 94. Li Xin and Glunin also consider Li a CEC full member. See Li, "Li Dazhao," p. 20; *Problemy Dalnego Vostoka*, 1972, no. 3, p. 128.

79 This is clear from a comparison of two documents, the CCP CEC report to the Third Party Congress (June 1923) and Chen Duxiu's "Open Letter to All Comrades" (December 1929.) If Chen recalled that all CEC members who attended the meeting voted against Maring's proposal, the report claimed that only "the overwhelming majority" of participants opposed it.

80 See Wang, *Zhongguo gongchandang shigao*, vol. 1, p. 94.

81 See Kalachev, "Kratkii ocherk istorii Kitaiskoi Kommunsticheskoi partii," p. 51.

82 *Li Dazhao wenji*, vol. 2, p. 890.

83 See Dov Bing, "Sneevliet and the Early Years of the CCP," *The China Quarterly*, 1971, no. 48, pp. 690–691.

84 See Jiang, *Guomindang zuopaide qizhi – Liao Zhongkai*, p. 71.
85 See Titarenko, *Noveishaya istoriya Kitaya*, p. 136; *Zhongguo gongchandang lishi jianghua*, p. 36.
86 See Jiang, *Guomindang zuopaide qizhi – Liao Zhongkai*, p. 72.
87 See S. L. Tikhvinsky, *Sun Yat-sen. Vneshnepoliticheskiye vozzreniya i praktika (Iz istorii natsional'no-osvoboditel'noi borby kitaiskogo naroda. 1885–1925)* (Sun Yat-sen. His Foreign Policy Views and Practice. [On history of the National Liberation Struggle of the Chinese People. 1885–1925]), Moscow: Mezhdunarodniye otnosheniya Publ., 1964, pp. 266–267.
88 See Zou Lu, *Zhongguo guomindang shigao* (Outline History of the Chinese Guomindang), Changsha: Minzhi shuju, 1931, pp. 345–348.
89 Eudin and North, *Soviet Russia and the East*, p. 141.
90 *Zhongguo gongchandang disici quanguo daibiaodahui yijiean ji xuanyan* (Resolutions and Statements of the Fourth All-China Congress of the CCP), n.d., 1925, p. 23. For an English translation see Saich, *The Rise to Power of the Chinese Communist Party*, p. 132.
91 Kalachev, "Kratkii ocherk istorii Kitaiskoi Kommunisticheskoi partii," p. 49. For another version of the English translation see C. Martin Wilbur and Julie Lian-ying How, *Missionaries of the Revolution: Soviet Advisers and Nationalist China. 1920–1927*. Cambridge, Mass.: Harvard Univ. Press, 1989, p. 459.
92 *Zhongguo gongchandang jiguan fazhan cankao ziliao*, vol. 1, p. 41.
93 Cai Hesen, "Istoriya opportunizma v Kommunisticheskoi partii Kitaya (The History of Opportunism in the Chinese Communist Party), *Problemy Kitaya* (Problems of China), 1929, no. 1, p. 4.
94 See *Byulleten IV kongressa Kommunisticheskogo Internatsionala*, no. 20, November 29, 1922, p. 18.
95 Jane Degras, ed., *The Communist International: 1919–1943: Documents*, vol. II, London: Oxford Univ. Press, 1960, pp. 5–6.
96 *Zhonggong "sanda" ziliao*, pp. 81, 82. This resolution was first published in Russian translation in 1973 by Glunin (see *Problemy Dalnego Vostoka*, 1973, no. 3, pp. 131–132.) For the English translation see Saich, *The Rise to Power of the Chinese Communist Party*, pp. 77–78.) Both translations, however, stray slightly from the Chinese text.
97 "Zhongguo gongchandang disanci quanguo dahui xuanyan" (The Statement of the Third All-China Congress of the CCP), *Xiangdao zhoukan* (Guide Weekly), 1923, no. 30, p. 228.
98 See Chang, *The Rise of the Chinese Communist Party*, vol. 1, p. 308; *Problemy Dalnego Vostoka*, 1973, no. 3, pp. 130, 132.
99 Since June 1922 *Xianqu* was a central organ of the Central Executive Committee of the Chinese Socialist Youth League.
100 See "Zhongguo gongchandang duiyu shiju zhi zhuzhang" (Statement of the Chinese Communist Party on the Current Situation), *Xianqu*, 1923, no. 24, p. 2.
101 *Zhongguo "sanda" ziliao*, p. 103.
102 Ibid., pp. 103–104. For an English translation of the whole text of the report which slightly differs from mine see Saich, *The Rise to Power of the Chinese Communist Party*, pp. 84–86.
103 See Glunin, "Komintern i stanovleniye kommunisticheskogo dvizheniya v Kitaye," p. 260.
104 *Zhonggong "sanda" ziliao*, p. 295–297.
105 See Glunin, "Komintern i stanovleniye kommunisticheskogo dvizheniya v Kitaye," p. 260.
106 *Zhongguo gongchandang disici quanguo daibiaodahui yijuean ji xuanyan*, p. 24. For the English translation see Saich, *The Rise to Power of the Chinese Communist Party*, p. 133. At the same time the delegates to the Congress, many of whom were quite leftist, pointed out that "rightist mistakes were more dangerous and widespread

than leftist ones." This contention, however, is not confirmed by other Party documents.

107 *Stenograficheskii otchet VI s"ezda Kommunisticheskoi partii Kitaya* (Stenographic Record of the Sixth Congress of the Chinese Communist Party), Book 1, Moscow: Institute of Chinese Studies Press, 1930, p. 69.

108 See R. A. Mirovitskaya, "Mikhail Borodin (1884–1951)," in M. I. Sladkovsky, ed., *Vidniye sovetskiye kommunisty – uchastniki kitaiskoi revolyutsii* (Prominent Soviet Communists – Participants of the Chinese Revolution), Moscow: Nauka, 1970, p. 24.

109 For archival documents concerning this visit see Titarenko et al., *VKP(b), Komintern i natsional'no-revolyutsionnoye dvizheniye v Kitaye*, vol. I, pp. 255–314.

110 This resolution was first published in 1969. See *Kommunist*, 1969, no. 4, pp. 12–14.

111 On the activity of Soviet advisers in China see Wilbur and How, *Missionaries of the Revolution*; A. V. Blagodatov, *Zapiski o kitaiskoi revolyutsii 1925–1927* (Notes on the Chinese Revolution of 1925–1927), 3rd ed., Moscow: Nauka, 1979; A. I. Cherepanov, *Zapiski voennogo sovetnika v Kitaye* (Notes of a Miliary Adviser in China), 2nd ed., Moscow: Nauka, 1976; V. V. Vishniakova-Akimova, *Two Years in Revolutionary China, 1925–1927*, trans. Steven I. Levine, Cambridge, Mass.: Harvard Univ. Press, 1971.

112 See *Dokumenty vneshnei politiki SSSR* (Documents on Foreign Policy of the USSR), vol. 6, Moscow: Gospolitizdat, 1962, pp. 435–436.

113 See in detail A. V. Pantsov and M. F. Yuriev, "Ustanovleniye sotrudnichestva mezhdu KPK i Sun Yat-senom v 1921–1924 gg." (The Establishment of Cooperation between Chinese Communist Party and Sun Yat-sen, 1921–1924), S. L. Tikhvinsky, ed., *SunYat-sen, 1866–1986. K 120–letiyu so dnya rozhdeniya: Sbornik statei, vospominanii, dokumentov i materialov* (SunYat-sen, 1866–1986. On the Occasion of His 120th Birthday: A Collection of Articles, Memoirs, Documents, and Materials), Moscow: Nauka, 1987, pp. 129–171.

114 Sun Yatsen, *Izbranniye proizvedeniya* (Selected Works), 2nd supplemented and revised ed., Moscow: Nauka, 1985, p. 327.

115 *Zhongguo "sanda" ziliao*, p. 120. For another variant of the English translation see Saich, *The Rise to Power of the Chinese Communist Party*, p. 90.

116 Saich, *The Rise to Power of the Chinese Communist Party*, pp. 90–91.

117 *Zhongguo "sanda" ziliao*, p. 125.

118 See *Lin Boqu zhuan*, p. 84.

119 On the First GMD Congress see in detail Yuriev, *Revolyutsiya 1925–1927 gg. v Kitaye*, pp. 17–28.

120 "Guomindang yi da dangwu baogao xuanzai" (Selected Reports on Party Affairs, Submitted to the First Guomindang Congress), *Geming shi ziliao* (Materials on the Revolutionary History), 1986, no. 2, pp. 29–30.

121 This number looks possible given that in mid-June 1923 the CCP counted 432 members. See Wang Jianying, *Zhongguo gongchandang zuzhi shi ziliao huibian – lingdao jigou yange he chengyuan minglu* (Collection of Documents on History of the CCP Organizations – the Evolution of Leading Organs and Their Personal Composition), Beijing: Hongqi chubanshe, 1983, p. 17.

122 See Zou Lu, *Zhongguo guomindang shigao*, p. 317; Zheng Canhui, "Zhongguo guomindang diyici quanguo daibiaohui" (The First All-China Congress of the Chinese Guomindang), *Geming shi ziliao*, 1986, no. 1, p. 113.

123 *Li Dazhao wenji*, vol. 2, p. 704. For the English translation see Ellsworth Tien-wei Wu, *The Chinese Nationalist and Communist Alliance, 1923–1927*, PhD Dissertation, [College Park]: Univ. of Maryland, 1965, pp. 751–752.

124 Cherepanov, *Zapiski voennogo sovetnika v Kitaye*, p. 99.

125 Zheng Canhui, "Zhongguo guomindang diyici quanguo daibiaohui," pp. 119–120.

126 Cited in Cherepanov, *Zapiski voennogo sovetnika v Kitaye*, p. 99.

127 See for instance *Zhongshan quanji* (Collected Works of Zhongshan [Sun Yat-sen]), vol. 2, Shanghai: Lianyou tushuguan inshuai gongsi, 1931, pp. 1171–1173.

128 The Borodin's role in the process was revealed by Voitinsky in his letter to Fyodor Raskolnikov (Petrov), at the time head of the ECCI Eastern department, of April 21, 1924. See Titarenko et al., *VKP(b), Komintern i natsional'no-revolyutsionnoye dvizheniye v Kitaye*, pp. 446.

129 See in detail Glunin, *Kommunisticheskaya partiya Kitaya nakanune i vo vremya Natsional'noi revolyutsii 1925–1927 gg.*, vol. 1, pp. 148–154.

130 See "Gongchandang zai Guomindang neide gongzuo wenti yijuean" (Statement on the Question of CP work in the GMD), *Dangbao* (Party Newspaper), 1924, no. 3. pp. 1–3; *Zhongguo gongchandang disici quanguo daibiaodahui yijuean ji xuanyan*, p. 25.

131 See *Xianqu*, 1922, no. 1, pp. 3–4.

132 This brochure was printed several times; at my disposal there was its third edition. See *Disan guoji yi'an ji xuanyan* (Resolutions and Manifestos of the Third International), 3rd ed., Guangzhou: Renmin chubanshe, 1926.

133 See A. A. Shiik, ed., *Rezolyutstii II-go kongressa Kominterna* (Resolutions of the Second Comintern Congress), Moscow: KUTK Press, 1928, pp. 58–77. (The text is in Chinese.)

134 See "Disan guoji dierci dahui guanyu minzu yu zhimindi wentide yi'an" (Resolutions of the Second Congress of the Third International on National and Colonial Questions), *Xin qingnian*, 1924, no. 4, pp. 67–74. Jiang was also the one who translated Lenin's report on behalf of the commission of the Second Congress on national and colonial questions (see ibid., pp. 63–67.) As for Lenin's "Preliminary Draft Theses," no translation appeared in China until 1946.

135 See ibid., 1923, no. 1, pp. 76–86. Yihong was perhaps a pseudonym.

136 See in detail A. V. Pantsov, "Dokumenty II i IV kongressov Kominterna po natsional'no-kolonial'nomu voprosam i ikh rasprostraneniye v Kitaye (1920–1924)" (Documents of the Second and Fourth Congresses of the Comintern on the National and Colonial Questions and Their Dissemination in China), in R. A. Ulyanovsky, ed., *Natsionalniye i sotsialniye dvizheniya na Vostoke: istoriya i sovremennost* (National and Social Movements in the East: History and the Present), Moscow: Science Press, 1986, pp. 23–58.

137 *Xin qingnian*, 1924, no. 4. p. 71. Emphasis added.

138 *Di san guoji yi'an ji xuanyan*, pp. 113.

139 V. M. Alekseev, "Printsypy perevodov sochinenii V. I. Lenina na kitaiskii yazyk" (Principles of Translation of V. I. Lenin's Works into Chinese), *Zapiski Instituta vostokovedeniya AN SSSR* (Notes of the USSR Academy of Sciences Institute of Oriental Studies), vol. 3, Leningrad, 1935, p. 5.

Part 3

1 V. I. Lenin, "Extraordinary Seventh Congress of the R.C.P.(B). March 6–8, 1918," in Lenin, *Collected Works*, vol. 27, p. 95.

2 Ibidem.

3 See, for example, V. I. Lenin, "Several Theses. Proposed by the Editors," in Lenin, *Collected Works*, vol. 21, pp. 403–404.

4 According to the Julian calendar then in use in Russia, the negotiations started on November 20. According to the Gregorian calendar, adopted by the Bolshevik government early in 1918, on December 3.

5 See in detail A. V. Pantsov, "Brestskii mir" (The Brest Peace), *Voprosy istorii* (Questions of History), 1990, no. 2, pp. 60–79.

6 V.I. Lenin, "Politicheskii otchet TsK RKP(b). Stenogramma vystupleniya na IX Vserossiiskoi konferentsii RKP(B). 22 sentyabrya 1920 g." ("Political Report of the RCP(B) CC. Stenogram of the Speech at the Ninth All-Russia Conference of the RCP(B). September 22, 1920"), *Istoricheskii arkhiv* (Historical Archive), 1992, no. 1, p. 21.

7 See ibid., pp. 16, 17, 22, 24–27. See also Lenin, "Zaklyuchitel'noye slovo v preniyakh po Politicheskomu otchetu TsK RKP(b) na vtorom zasedanii IX

Vserossiiskoi konferentsii RKP(b), 22 sentyabrya 1920" (Concluding Speech During the Debates on the Political Report of the RCP(B) CC at the Second Session of the Ninth All-Russian Conference of the RCP(B), September 22, 1920), ibid., pp. 27–28.

8 Lenin, "Politicheskii otchet TsK RKP(b). Stenogramma vystupleniya na IX Vserossiiskoi konferentsii RKP(B). 22 sentyabrya 1920 g.", pp. 25, 26, 27.

9 See Edward Carr, *A History of Soviet Russia: The Bolshevik Revolution: 1917–1923*, vol. 3, London: Macmillan, 1953, pp. 215–216.

10 See Volkogonov, *Trotsky*, vol. 1, p. 341.

11 Lenin, *PSS*, vol. 45, p. 19.

12 *Pravda*, January 27, 1923.

13 See in detail Karl August Wittfogel, *Oriental Despotism: A Comparative Study of Total Power*, New Haven & London: Yale Univ. Press, 1957.

14 These were Stalin, Bukharin, Jan E. Rudzutak, Aleksei I. Rykov, Mikhail P. Tomsky, Mikhail I. Kalinin, Kamenev, Zinoviev, Kliment E. Voroshilov, Anastas I. Mikoyan, Lazar M. Kaganovich, Georgii K. Ordzhonikidze, Grigorii I. Petrovsky, Valerian V. Kuibyshev, Nikolai A. Uglanov, and certain others.

15 V. Nadtocheev, "'Troika', 'semerka', Stalin" (Triumvirate, Group of Seven, Stalin), *Nedelya* (A Week), 1989, no. 1, p. 15.

16 L. Trotsky, *K sotsializmu ili kapitalizmu? (Analiz sovetskogo khozyaistva i tendentsii ego razvitiya)* (Towards Socialism or Capitalism? [An Analysis of the Soviet Economy and the Directions of Its Development]), 2nd ed., Moscow: "Planovoye Khozyaistvo", 1926, p. 64.

17 *Puti mirovoi revolyutsii. Sed'moi rasshirennyi plenum Ispolnitel'nogo Komiteta Kommunisticheskogo Internatsionala. 22 noyabrya – 16 dekabrya 1926. Stenograficheskii otchet* (Ways of the World Revolution. The Seventh Enlarged Plenum of the Communist International Executive Committee. November 22 – December 16, 1926. Stenographic Record), vol. 2, Moscow-Leningrad: Gosizdat, 1927, p. 102.

18 L. Trotsky, "Teoriya sotsializma v otdel'noi strane" (Theory of Socialism in a Particular Country), in Felshtinsky, *Kommunisticheskaya oppozitsiya v SSSR*, vol. 2, pp. 142, 146.

19 Trotsky, *K sotsializmu ili kapitalizmu?* pp. 66, 68.

20 See in detail Stephen Cohen, *Bukharin and the Bolshevik Revolution. A Political Biography. 1888–1938*, New York: Alfred A. Knopf, 1973, pp. 146, 158–159, 187–188; Robert Tucker, *Stalin as Revolutionary. 1879–1929. A Study in History and Personality*, New York, W. W. Norton, 1973, pp. 372–374.

21 See J. V. Stalin, *Works*, vol. 6, Moscow: Foreign Languages Publishing house, 1953, pp. 374–420.

22 N. I. Bukharin, *Izbranniye proizvedeniya* (Selected Works), Moscow: Politizdat, 1988, p. 78.

23 V. I. Lenin, "On the Slogan for a United States of Europe," in Lenin, *Collected Works*, vol. 21, p. 342.

24 V. I. Lenin, "Speech at a Plenary Session of the Moscow Soviet, November 20, 1922," ibid., vol. 33, p. 443.

25 V. I. Lenin, "On Co-operation," ibid., p. 468.

26 See V. I. Lenin, "Better Fewer, But Better," ibid., pp. 498–502.

27 On "already victorious socialism", see V. I. Lenin, "The Military Programme of the Proletarian Revolution," ibid., vol. 23, p. 79.

28 Lenin, "Speech at a Plenary Session of the Moscow Soviet, November 20, 1922," p. 436.

29 Lenin, "On Co-operation," p. 474.

30 *XV konferentsiya Vsesoyuznoi Kommunisticheskoi partii (b). 26 oktyabrya – 3 noyabrya 1926. Stenograficheskii otchet* (The Fifteenth Conference of the All-Union Communist Party [B]. October 26 – November 3, 1926. Stenographic Record), Moscow-Leningrad: Gosizdat, 1927, p. 528.

31 J. V. Stalin, "Reply to the Discussion on the Report on 'The Social-Democratic Deviation in Our Party', November 3, 1926," in Stalin, *Works*, vol. 8, Moscow: Foreign Languages Publishing house, 1954, p. 318.

32 V. I. Lenin, "Preliminary Draft Theses on the National and Colonial Questions. For the Second Congress of the Communist International," p. 148.

33 J. V. Stalin, "Joint Plenum of the Central Committee and Central Control Commission of the C.P.S.U (B.), July 29 – August 9, 1927," in Stalin, *Works*, vol. 10, Moscow: Foreign Languages Publishing house, 1954, pp. 53–54.

34 Albert Resis, ed., *Molotov Remembers. Inside Kremlin Politics. Conversations with Felix Chuev*, Chicago: Ivan R. Dee, 1993, p. 8.

35 Tucker, *Stalin as Revolutionary*, p. 389.

36 L. Trotsky, "Teoriya sotsializma v otdel'noi strane," p. 145.

37 Berdyaev, *The Origin of Russian Communism*, p. 8.

38 Letter from G. N. Voitinsky to L. M. Karakhan, April 22, 1925, Russian Center, Collection of non-filed documents. Borodin was the political advisor to the Guomindang Central Executive Committee and the Comintern's representative in China, 1923–1927.

39 Grigorii Voitinsky, "Tendentsii revolutsionnogo dvizheniya v Kitaye i Gomindan" (Trends in the Revolutionary Movement in China and the Guomindang), *Kommunisticheskii Internatsional* (The Communist International), 1925, no. 3, pp. 153–158; Voitinsky, "Sun Yatsen i osvoboditel'noye dvizheniye v Kitaye" (Sun Yat-sen and the Liberation Movement in China), *Bol'shevik* (The Bolshevik), 1925, no. 5–6, pp. 44–52.

40 This idea was not discussed beforehand in the Central Committee of the RKP(B). See Russian Center, 492/1/73/14,15; *Pyatyi Vsemirnyi kongress Kommunisticheskogo Internatsionala. 17 iyunya – 8 iyulya 1924 goda. Stenograficheskii otchet* (The Fifth World Congress of the Communist International. June 17–July 8, 1924. Stenographic Record, vol. 1, Moscow-Leningrad: Gosizdat, 1925, pp. 592, 593, 618. Also see materials of the Fifth Congress Commission on national and colonial questions, and Stalin's letter to Manuilsky of July 31, 1924 (Russian Center, 492/1/209–219; 558/1/2633/1–2.) In his secret July 1922 report to the ECCI, two years before the Fifth Comintern Congress, Maring portrayed the GMD as a "bloc of various classes." However, at the time his interpretation did not lead the Comintern Executive to the creation of a special theory of "workers' and peasants' (or people's) party." The Comintern continued to consider the GMD and other national parties in Asia as bourgeois or petite bourgeois.

41 Russian Center, 492/1/73/15.

42 *Pyatyi Vsemirnyi kongress Kommunisticheskogo Internatsionala: 17 iyunya–8 iyulya 1924 goda: Stenograficheskii otchet*, vol. 1, p. 618.

43 Russian Center, 492/1/219/12.

44 Letter from J. V. Stalin to D. Z. Manuilsky, July 31, 1924, Russian Center, 558/1/2633/1.

45 Russian Center, 495/163/177/1–4.

46 Grigorii Voitinsky, "Kolonial'nyi vopros na rasshirennom plenume IKKI" (The Colonial Question at the ECCI Enlarged Plenum,) *Kommunisticheskii Internatsional*, 1925, no. 4, p. 64.

47 Russian Center, 558/1/2714/17; *Pravda*, May 22, 1925. My translation is from the texts in J. V. Stalin, *Works*, vol. 7, Moscow: Foreign Languages Publishing house, 1954, pp. 149–150 and Les Evans and Russel Block, eds., *Leon Trotsky on China*, New York: Monad, 1976, p. 328. Two years later, when Stalin's China policy went bankrupt, the words "after the model of the Kuomintang" would be removed from the text of his speech. It would not be reproduced again, ever in Stalin's *Works*. The editors of *Leon Trotsky on China* were the first to make public mention of it.

48 J. V. Stalin, "The Results of the Work of the Fourteenth Conference of the R.C.P. (B.). Report Delivered at a Meeting of the Active of the Moscow Organization of the R.C.P. (B.), May 9, 1925," in Stalin, *Works*, vol. 7, p. 108.

49 Ibid., p. 16.
50 Ibid., p. 107.
51 Ibid., p. 108.
52 At the Fifth Comintern Congress Roy acted as a chairman of the colonial subcommission of the Comintern commission on national and colonial questions. See Russian Center, 492/1/209/2.
53 "Rezolyutsiya po kolonial'nomu voprosu" (Resolution on Colonial Question), ibid, 215/6.
54 Russian Center, 492/1/218/105, 106, 108–109, 110, 112. Among historians Reznikov was the first to pay attention to this amendment. See Reznikov, *Strategy and Tactics of the Comintern in National and Colonial Questions*, p. 135.)
55 Letter from Stalin to Manuilsky, July 31, 1924, 2. Stalin would continue to rely on Roy's formulas concerning the social and economic situation in Eastern countries. In May 1927 he would even openly maintain that the CCP should bear in mind not Lenin's theses on National and Colonial Questions, but Roy's "Supplementary Theses." See Stalin, *Works*, vol. 9, Moscow: Foreign Languages Publishing house, 1954, p. 266.
56 Russian Center, 495/164/16/91.
57 The reference was to the political strikes by Chinese workers in Shanghai and Hong Kong-Guangzhou which began in May and June 1925.
58 Titarenko, *Kommunisticheskii Internatsional i kitaiskaya revolyutsiya*, pp. 58, 61. Emphasis added.
59 *Shestoi rasshirennyi plenum Ispolkoma Kominterna (17 fevralya – 15 marta 1926 g.). Stenograficheskii otchet* (The Sixth Enlarged Plenum of the Comintern Executive Committee [February 17–March 15, 1926]. Stenographic Record), Moscow-Leningrad: Gospolitizdat, 1927, p. 8.
60 Russian Center, 514/1/168/219.
61 See ibid., 505/1/65/21; Leon Trotsky, "Stalin i kitaiskaya revolyutsiya. Fakty i dokumenty" (Stalin and the Chinese Revolution: Facts and Documents,) *Byulleten oppozitsii (bol'shevikov-lenintsev)*, 1930, nos. 15–16, p. 8.
62 See Russian Center, 514/1/171/7–9; see also 168/219; 505/1/65/33.
63 The chairman of the Commission was the chief of the Main Political Administration of the Red Army A.S. Bubnov (Ivanovsky). His reports and letter of instructions to Borodin about the March 20 events, preserved in the Russian Center, were recently published. See Titarenko et al., *VKP(b), Komintern i natsional'no-revolyutsionnoe dvizheniye v Kitaye*, pp. 139–152, 157–162, 208–227.
64 See Russian Center, 495/165/71/4.
65 These demands were introduced at the Guomindang Central Executive Committee Plenum by Chiang Kai-shek. The text of Chiang's demands, with changes introduced by participants in the plenum, are in Russian Center, Collection of non-filed documents. For the text of the corresponding resolution adopted by the plenum, see *Zhongguo guomindang diyi, dierci quanguo daibiaodahui huiyi shiliao* (Historical Materials of the First and Second Guomindang Congresses), 2 vols., vol. 2, Nanjing: Jiangsu guji chubanshe, 1986, pp. 53–54.
66 See for example Brandt, *Stalin's Failure in China*, pp. 71–83; Peng Shu-tse [Peng Shuzhi], "Introduction," in Evans and Block, *Leon Trotsky on China*, pp. 53–54.
67 Rafes's admission in the statement he made several months after the coup gives some idea of the level of information concerning the events of March 20 then available in Moscow: "When we arrived in China [mid-June 1926], everything we learned from our comrades concerning the March 20 events in Guangzhou and Chiang Kai-shek's military demonstration against the left Guomindang and the Communists was completely news to us. In Moscow we really had no idea of what had occurred in Guangzhou on March 20. We had no idea of how far these actions had gone or how profound were their consequences." Russian Center, 495/165/71/2.

68 See "Extract from the Protocol of the Eighteenth Session of the Politburo of the CC AUCP(B), April 1, 1926," Russian Center, Collection of non-filed documents.
69 See Titarenko et al., *VKP(b), Komintern i natsional'no-revolyutsionnoye dvizheniye v Kitaye*, pp. 163–164, 170.
70 See Russian Center, 17/2/317/1/139.
71 It is impossible to give a more precise date until such time as the Presidential Archive of the Russian Federation is opened. However, it is quite clear that Trotsky made his notion before April 29. He did not attend this day Politburo meeting that was the last in April.
72 Titarenko et al., *VKP(b), Komintern i natsional'no-revolyutsionnoe dvizheniye v Kitaye*, p. 188.
73 [Grigorii Zinoviev,] "Zayavleniye k stenogramme Ob"edinennogo plenuma TsK i Tsentral'noi Kontrol'noi Komissii" (Statement to Stenogram of the Joint Plenum of the Central Committee and Central Control Commission), Trotsky Papers, Russ 13T, 886, p. 2. Zinoviev mistakenly referred to this Politburo meeting as taking place in May 1927. On his authorship of the document see Russian Center, 495/166/189/2.
74 Russian Center, 17/162/3/55. Emphasis added.
75 Ibid., 59, 74.
76 Titarenko et. al., *VKP(b), Komintern i natsional'no-revolyutsionnoye dvizheniye v Kitaye*, p. 231.
77 Aleksandr Martynov, "Komintern pered sudom likvidatorov" (The Comintern Before the Court of the Liquidationists), *Kommunisticheskii Internatsional*, 1927, no. 30, p. 10.
78 Russian Center, 17/162/4/10.
79 From June 1926 to January 1927 Voitinsky headed the ECCI Far Eastern Bureau in Shanghai using the pseudonym Sergei.
80 See Titarenko et al., *VKP(b), Komintern i natsional'no-revolyutsionnoye dvizheniye v Kitaye*, pp. 485–486.
81 Stalin, *Works*, vol. 10, p. 18.
82 See Russian Center, 17/2/317/1/83–84; It is true, however, that the two comrades-in-arms did not see eye-to-eye in their appraisal of the directive in question. Stalin believed it was "unquestionably a mistake," while Voroshilov deemed it irreproachably correct.
83 See Russian Center, 495/165/71/27–31.
84 See *XV konferentsiya Vsesoyuznoi Kommunisticheskoi Partii (b)*, pp. 27–28, 86–87, 99.
85 Russian Center, 495/165/67/45. See also ibid., 68/40–49. After the discussion of this draft in the Chinese commission of the Comintern Executive Committee, Raskolnikov together with Bubnov introduced some insignificant changes into the text. A new draft was prepared called "The Bubnov-Petrov Theses." At the same time, Manuilsky presented his theses, which differed little in essentials from Raskolnikov's draft. Italics added.
86 Russian Center, 495/165/67/49, 50–51. Italics added.
87 Gentry was how Soviet literature on China then were referred to the *shenshi*, traditional Chinese literati.
88 Russian Center, 495/165/69/7, 8.
89 Stalin, *Works*, vol. 8, pp. 373–374.
90 Ibid., p. 384.
91 Ibid., p. 382. See also Russian Center, 495/165/267/103.
92 Stalin, *Works*, vol. 8, p. 382; Russian Center, 495/165/267/103.
93 Stalin, *Works*, vol. 8, p. 385.
94 Ibid.
95 See Russian Center, 495/165/273/14; 495/165/273/278.
96 Titarenko, *Kommunisticheskii Internatsional i kitaiskaya revolyutsiya*, pp. 92–93.
97 Ibid., p. 93.
98 Ibid., pp. 97–98.
99 Ibid., pp. 99, 94, 96.

100 Russian Center, 17/162/4/34.
101 See ibid., 514/1/233/61–72; 514/1/240/1.

Part 4

1 I could not find any other works by him at that time in which he expressed his views on Eastern problems; most likely they do not exist. In the begiining of the 1920s Trotsky as a member of the ECCI was engaged most of that time in elaborating answers to the problems posed by the Communist movement in France and Germany. In the "Manifesto of the Second Congress of the Communist International" Trotsky devoted only a few general phrases to the East.

2 Leon Trotsky, *The First Five Years of the Communist International*, 2 vols., vol. 1, New York: Pioneer Publ., 1945, p. 223.

3 See Trotsky, *Problems of the Chinese Revolution*, p. 19.

4 Actually, Trotsky's letter was addressed to the *Womende hua* ("Our Word") group of Trotskyists in China. The original of the message sent by this group to Trotsky on November 15, 1929 and signed "Pyotr", from Shanghai is in the Trotsky archives in Harvard University's Houghton Library (Russ 13.1, 1057); it was published in *Byulleten oppozitsii (bol'shevikov-lenintsev)*, no. 9 (February-March, 1930), pp. 9–10.

5 L[eon] Trotsky, "Kitaiskoi levoi oppozitsii" (To the Chinese Left Opposition), ibid., no. 19 (March, 1931), p. 27; the English translation is from the text in Evans and Block, *Leon Trotsky on China*, pp. 492–493.

6 Leon Trotsky, *The Stalin School of Falsification*, New York: Pathfinder Press, 1972, pp. 188, 197–198.

7 L. D. Trotsky, "Doklad na zasedanii kommunisticheskoi fraktsii X s"ezda Sovetov s uchastiem bespartiinikh delegatov" ("The Report to the Session of the Communist Fraction of the Tenth Soviet Congress, with the Participation of Non-Party Delegates"), in L. D. Trotsky, *Pyat' let Kominterna* (Five Years of the Comintern), 2nd ed., Moscow-Leningrad: Gosizdat, 1925, pp. 538–539.

8 L. D. Trotsky, "Mysli o partii" (Thoughts About the Party), *Pravda*, March 20, 1923.

9 L. D. Trotsky, "Zadachi XII s"ezda RKP (Doklad t. Trotskogo na zasedanii VII Vseukrainskoi konferentsii 5 aprelya 1923 g.)" (Tasks of the Twelfth RCP Congress [Comrade Trotsky's Report at a Session of the Seventh All-Ukrainian Conference, April 5, 1923]), *Pravda*, April 11, 1923.

10 *Pravda*, April 12, 1923.

11 L[eon] Trotsky, "Perspektivy i zadachi na Vostoke. (Doklad t. Trotskogo na trekhletnem yubileye Kommunisticheskogo Universiteta Trudyashchikhsya Vostoka 21 aprelya 1921goda)" (Prospects and Tasks in the East. [Comrade Trotsky's Speech at the Third Anniversary of the Communist University of the Toilers of the East, April 21, 1921]), in L[eon] Trotsky, *Zapad i Vostok. Voprosy mirovoi politiki i mirovoi revolyutsii* (West and East. Questions of World Politics and the World Revolution), Moscow: Gosizdat, 1924, pp. 33, 35.

12 Ibid., pp. 35, 41.

13 See L[eon] Trotsky, "SSSR i Yaponiya (interv'yu korrespondentu 'Osoka Mainiti', 24 aprelya 1924 goda) (The USSR and Japan [An Interview with a Correspondent of *Osoka Mainiti*, April 24, 1924]), *Izvestiya*, April 24, 1924; Trotsky, "Pervoye maya na Zapade i Vostoke. K tridtsat' pytoi godovshchine Pervomaiskogo prazdnika. (Rech na torzhestvennom zasedanii plenuma Moskovskogo Soveta 29 aprelya 1924 g.) (The First of May in the West and East. On the Thirty Fifth Anniversary of the May 1 Holiday. [Speech at the Ceremonial Plenary Session of the Moscow Soviet, April 29, 1924]), in Trotsky, *Zapad i Vostok*, pp. 42–65; Trotsky, "Sovetsko-yaponskiye vzaimootnosheniya. Interv'yu, dannoye t. Trotskim predsedatelyu o[bshchest]va Nichiro Soofukai tov. Tomizi Naito (Soviet-Japanese Mutual Relations. An Interview Given by Comrade Trotsky to Chairman of Society "Nichiro Soofukai" Comrade Tomizi Naito), *Pravda*, June 18, 1924.

14 See Letter from Trotsky to the Politburo and Narkomindel, January 20, 1923, Russian Center, 325/1/410/57.

15 Letter from L. D. Trotsky to A. A. Joffe, January 20, 1923, ibid., 325/1/410/54.

16 Letter from L. D. Trotsky to G. V. Chicherin, copied to Stalin, November 2, 1923, ibid., 325/1/415/3.

17 Letter from L. D. Trotsky to K. B. Radek, June 26, 1926, ibid., 326/2/24/108.

18 Evans and Block, *Leon Trotsky on China*, p. 114.

19 These Trotsky letters for the first time were published in Chinese translation by Wang Fanxi in *Shiyue pinglun* (October Review), 1991, no. 6.

20 Letter from L. D. Trotsky to H. R. Isaacs, November 1, 1937, Trotsky Papers, bMs Russ, 13.1, 8558, p. 1, 2.

21 Letter from L. D. Trotsky to H. R. Isaacs, November 29, 1937, ibid., 13.1, 8559, p. 1.

22 See L[eon] Trotsky, "SSSR na storone ugnetennogo Kitaya" (The USSR is on the Side of Oppressed China), *Pravda*, September 23, 1924; Trotsky, "Moskovskii dukh" (The "Moscow Spirit"), idid., June 6, 1925. (For an English translation of latter article see Evans and Block, *Leon Trotsky on China*, pp. 99–101.)

23 See "Doklad tov. L. D. Trotskogo na VI gubernskom s"ezde tekstilshchikov 29 yanvarya 1926 g." (Comrade L. D. Trotsky's Speech at the Sixth Gubernia Congress of Textile Workers, January 19, 1926), *Pravda*, January 31, 1926; "Godovshchina smerti Sun Yatsena. (Vystupleniye L. D. Trotskogo i drugikh deyatelei VKP(b) na mitinge, posvyashchennom godovshchine so dnya smerti Sun Yatsena)" (The Anniversary of Sun Yat-sen Death. [L. D. Trotsky's Speech and Speeches of Other AUCP(B) Activists at a Meeting Commemorated to Sun Yat-sen Death Anniversary]), idid., March 14, 1926. Besides, in the given period Trotsky reported on Soviet-Chinese relations on March 12, 1926 at a Moscow club, *Red October*, but the text of his speech "China and We. Dedicated to Sun Yat-sen" has not been found. (For the mention of this speech see Russian Center, 325/1/529/10.)

24 Deutscher, *The Prophet Unarmed*, pp. 321–322.

25 See L. D. Trotsky, "Konspekt k zasedaniyu Politburo 18 marta 1926 g." (Synopsis to the Meeting of the Politburo, March 18, 1926), Russian Center, Collection of non-filed documents. Also see Trotsky's letters on this matter written between January and the middle of March 1926 to the AUCP(B) Central Committee Politburo, Secretariat, Stalin, and Chicherin, ibid.

26 See "Vypiska iz protokola N 16 zasedaniya Politburo ot 18 marta 1926 g." (Extract From the Minutes no. 16 of the Meeting of the Politburo, March 18, 1926), ibid.

27 Trotsky, "Konspekt k zasedaniyu Politburo 18 marta 1926 g." Also see L[eon] Trotsky, "Rech o kitaiskoi revolyutsii" (Speech on the Chinese Revolution), in L[eon] Trotsky, *Kommunisticheskii Internatsional posle Lenina* (The Communist International After Lenin), ed. by Yu. [G.] Felshtinsky (manuscript), pp. 476–477.

28 See "Protokol N 16 zasedaniya Politburo TsK VKP(b) ot 18 marta 1926 g." (Minutes no. 16 of the Meeting of the AUCP(B) CC Politburo, March 18, 1926), Russian Center, 17/3/552/1; Letter from L.D. Trotsky to the AUCP(B) CC Secretariat, March 19, 1926, ibid, Collection of non-filed documents.

29 Trotsky also proposed Leonid Serebryakov as a member of the commission, given that the Politburo on March 18, 1926 decided to send the latter to Manchuria in the near future to negotiate with Zhang Zuolin. See Letter from L. D. Trotsky to the AUCP(B) CC Secretariat, March 19, 1926. His proposition, however, was not accepted.

30 This is evident from Trotsky's letter to Chicherin, Voroshilov, Rudzutak, Serebryakov, and Trilisser of March 22, 1926. See Russian Center, Collection of non-filed documents.

31 See "Proekt reshenii komissii, predstavlennyi Trotskim v Politburo TsK VKP(b) 25 marta 1926 g." (Draft Decisions of the Commission Submitted by Trotsky to the AUCP(B) CC Politburo on March 25, 1926), ibid.

32 "Vypiska iz protokola N 17 zasedaniya Politburo TsK VKP(b) ot 25 marta 1926 g." (Extract From the Minutes no. 17 of the Meeting of the AUCP(B) CC Politburo, March 25, 1926), ibid. On March 27 this decision was confirmed by questioning Politburo members. See "Protokol N 18 zasedaniya Politburo TsK VKP(b) ot 1 aprelya 1926 g." (The Minutes no. 18 of the Meeting of the AUCP(B) CC Politburo, April 1, 1926), Russian Center, 17/3/554/8.

33 "Vypiska iz protokola N 18 zasedaniya Politburo TsK VKP(b) ot 1 aprelya 1926 g." (Extract From the Minutes no. 18 of the Meeting of the AUCP(B) CC Politburo, April 1, 1926), ibid., Collection of non-filed documents.

34 See ibidem. Also see Felshtinsky, *Kommunistcheskaya oppositsiya v SSSR*, vol. 1, pp. 174–181.

35 L. D. Trotsky, "Konspekt k zasedaniyu Politburo 18 marta 1926."

36 See "Ob"edinennyi plenum TsK i TsKK VKP(b), 14–23 iyulya 1926 g. Stenograficheskii otchet, vol. 1, p. 15.

37 For an English translation see Evans and Block, *Leon Trotsky on China*, pp. 102–110.

38 G[rigorii] Zinoviev and L[eon] Trotsky, "Fakty i Dokumenty, kotoriye dolzhny stat dostupny proverke kazhdogo chlena VKP(b) i vsego Kominterna. Khronologicheskaya spravka" (Facts and Documents that Must Be Available for Checking by Every Member of the AUCP(B) and by the Entire Comintern: A Chronological Note), Russian Center, 495/166/189/2.

39 See "Ob"edinennyi plenum TsK i TsKK VKP(b), 14–23 iyulya 1927 g. Stenograficheskii otchet," vol. 1, p. 15. Bukharin would return to the issue at the July-August (1927) Plenum of the CC and CCC. See "Ob"edinennyi plenum TsK i TsKK VKP(b), 29 iyulya – 9 avgusta 1927 g. Stenograficheskii otchet," vol. 1, p. 40.

40 "Ob"edinennyi plenum TsK i TsKK VKP(b), 14–23 iyulya 1927 g. Stenograficheskii otchet," vol. 1, p. 75. Stalin once again reminded his colleagues about the Oppositionists' proposal of April 1926 to immediately withdraw from the Guomindang at the joint meeting of the ECCI Presidium and International Control Commission on September 27, 1927, which discussed a question of Trotsky's and Vujo Vujovič's "factional activity." (See "Ob"edinennoe zasedaniye Prezidiuma Ispolkoma Kominterna i Mezhdunarodnoi kontrol'noi komissii, 27 sentiabrya 1927 g.," p. 28; J. V. Stalin, *Works*, vol. 10, pp. 159–160.)

41 Russian Center, 17/162/3/55.

42 *Shestoi rasshirennyi plenum Ispolkoma Kominterna*, p. 613.

43 "Otchet komissii Hu Hanminya po voprosam, otnosyashchimsya k III Internatsionalu" (An Account of Hu Hanmin's Commission on the Questions Related to the Third International), Russian Center, 514/1/233/33.

44 See ibid., p. 30.

45 Special Files contained the most secret decisions of the AUCP(B) CC Politburo.

46 Lih et al., *Stalin's Letters to Molotov*, pp. 113–114.

47 See ibid., 17/3/561/1; "Ob"edinennyi plenum TsK i TsKK VKP(b), 29 iyulya – 9 avgusta 1927 g.," vol. 1, pp. 136–137. Trotsky did not attend the meeting; he was on vacation in Berlin. See Trotsky, *My Life*, pp. 522–526.

48 Trotsky assumes the May 31, 1924 Beijing agreements between the USSR and China concerning the Chinese Eastern Railway.

49 For an English translation of Trotsky's speech see Trotsky, *Problems of the Chinese Revolution*, pp. 97–98.

50 "Protokol N 3 zasedaniya plenuma TsK i TsKK VKP(b), 14–15 iyulya 1926 g." (The Minutes no. 3 of the Session of the AUCP(B) CC and CCC Plenum, July 14–15, 1926), p. 4.

51 [Zinoviev,] "Zayavleniye k stenogramme Ob"edinennogo plenuma TsK i Tsentral'noi Kontrol'noi Kommissii."

52 In 1924 and early 1925, Radek, motivated by personal interest, began to study China. After the defeat of the Hamburg uprising of 1923, in which he played a prominent role, he was in effect removed from all functions in the Comintern. Only

in the spring of 1925 did he again receive a real assignment; he was appointed to a commission – together with Broido and Voitinsky – to organize the Sun Yat-sen University in Moscow. See G. N. Voitinsky's letters of June 4, 1924, and April 22, 1925 to L. M. Karakhan, Russian Center, Collection of non-filed documents.

53 See, for example, "Imperialisticheskaya interventsiya i grazhdanskaya voina v Kitaye. Doklad t. Radeka v Bolshom teatre" (Imperialist Intervention and Civil War in China. Comrade Radek's Report at Bolshoi Theater), in *Kitai v ogne voiny* (China in the Fire of War), Moscow: "Rabochaya Moskva," 1924, pp. 23–61 (this report delivered by Radek on September 22, 1924 was reprinted in a collection of articles *Ruki proch ot Kitaya!* [Hands off China!]); Radek, "Vozhd' kitaiskogo naroda" (A Leader of the Chinese People), *Pravda*, March 14, 1925; Radek, "Voprosy kitaiskoi revolyutsii" (Questions of the Chinese Revolution), *Krasnyi Internatsional Profsoyuzov* (Red International of Labor Unions), 1925, no. 10, pp. 26–42; Radek, "Mezhdu-narodnoye obozreniye. Itogi shankhaiskikh sobytii" (International Survey: Balance Sheet of the Shanghai Events), *Izvestiya*, October 11, 1925; Radek, "Chto nado govorit' krest'yanstvu o kitaiskoi revolyutsii" (What Needs to Be Said to the Peasantry About the Chinese Revolution), *Sputnik Agitatora (Dlya derevni)* (An Agitator's Companion [For the Countryside]), 1925, no. 2 (21), pp. 19–24; Radek, "Sotsial'no-politicheskiye idei Sun Yat-sena" (The Social and Political Ideas of Sun Yat-sen), *Pravda*, March 12, 1926; Radek, "Porazheniye narodnykh armii v Kitaye" (Defeat of the People's Armies in China), *Pravda*, March 26, 1926; Radek, "Istoricheskoye znacheniye shankhaiskikh sobytii. (Vmesto predisloviya)" (Historical Meaning of the Shanghai Events [In Lieu of a Preface]), in Pavel Mif, *Uroki shankhaiskikh sobytii* (Lessons of the Shanghai Events), Moscow: Gosizdat, 1926, pp. 3–6; Radek, "Zhizn' i delo Sun Yat-sena" (The Life and Work of Sun Yat-sen), in Sergei Dalin, *V ryadakh kitaiskoi revolyutsii* (In the Ranks of the Chinese Revolution), Moscow-Leningrad: Moskovskii rabochii, 1926, pp. 3–24.

54 Karl Radek, "Voprosy kitaiskoi revolyutsii," p. 39. This article was written in August, but published in October 1925. While making comments on the article almost two years later, Trotsky would say, "Radek in 1925 wrote about it given the false and optimistic official statements" (Trotsky, "Rech o kitaiskoi revolyutsii," pp. 476–477.) So would Radek do himself in March 1927, "I was led by the Comintern officials to the belief that there was a worker-peasant government in Canton [Guangzhou]. Now I know the facts and will not believe even the *Comintern*'s journal editorial" ("Zaklyuchitel'noye slovo tov. Radeka" (Comrade Radek's Speech Closing the Debate [on the Chinese Revolution at the Communist Academy: A Stenographic Record]," Russian Center, 326/2/32/181.) In the beginning of May 1927 he would even develop this statement, "The profound disinformation and the decoration of reality typical of Comintern reports were the source of my erroneous assessment of the class character of the Canton government. While relying on the reports of the Comintern Eastern functionaries, confirmed by the proclamations of the Guomin-dang, I thought that the Canton government was indeed a "model of the real revolutionary and democratic construction," i.e., a workers' and peasants' govern-ment" (Karl Radek, "'Izmena' kitaiskoi krupnoi burzhuazii natsional'nomu dvizheniyu' [The Chinese Big Bourgeoisie's "Betrayal" of the National Movement.] Ibid., Collection of non-filed documents.)

55 Karl Radek, "Ob osnovakh kommunisticheskoi politiki v Kitaye" (Fudamentals of Communist Policy in China), Russian Center, 326/2/24/105.

56 Radek, "Istoricheskoye znacheniye shankhaiskikh sobytii," p. 4. Also see Karl Radek, "God kitaiskoi revolyutsii" (The Year of the Chinese Revolution), *Pravda*, May 30, 1926.

57 Radek, "Porazheniye narodnykh armii v Kitaye." Radek's contention, in essence, echoed Voitinsky's first reation. (See Grigorii Voitinsky, "Peregruppirovka sil v Kitaye" [The Regrouping of Forces in China]. *Pravda*, March 24, 1926.)

58 Radek, "Ob osnovakh kommunisticheskoi politiki v Kitaye," 105.

59 Ibid., 104–105, 106.
60 Letter from L. D. Trotsky to K. B. Radek, June 26, 1926, ibid., 108–108 riverside.
61 Evans and Block, *Leon Trotsky on China*, p. 111.
62 This shows that Conrad Brandt was in error when he suggested that until early March 1927 Trotsky paid little attention to Chinese affairs. (See Brandt, *Stalin's Failure in China*, p. 156.)
63 Felshtinsky, *Kommunisticheskaya oppozitsiya v SSSR*, vol. 2, p. 57. In *Leon Trotsky on China*, p. 111, instead of "must be proved," the translation given is "must be demonstrated," which seems inadequate.
64 Evans and Block, *Leon Trotsky on China*, p. 111.
65 See Letter from K. B. Radek to the Secretariat of the AUCP(B) CC, August 31, 1926, Russian Center, 530/1/10/79.
66 Evans and Block, *Leon Trotsky on China*, p. 111–112.
67 Ibid., p. 113.
68 The information about the scale of the mass movement in China available to the Comintern and Soviet media was not always in keeping with reality. See in detail L. P. Delyusin, A. S. Kostyaeva, *Revolyutsiya 1925–1927 gg. v Kitaye: problemy i otsenki* (The Revolution of 1925–1927 in China: Problems and Assessments), Moscow: Nauka, 1985; A. S. Kostyaeva, *Krest'yanskiye soyuzy v Kitaye (20–e gody XX veka)* (Peasant Unions in China in the 1920s), Moscow: Nauka, 1978; M. L. Titarenko, *Noveishaya istoriya Kitaya. 1917–1927*, p. 251–265.
69 Evans and Block, *Leon Trotsky on China*, p. 113.
70 Ibid., pp. 113–114, 115.
71 See ibid., pp. 115–120; L. D. Trotsky, "K pyatnadtsatoi partiinoi konferentsii" (On the Fifteenth Party Conference), in Felshtinsky, *Kommunisticheskaya oppozitsiya v SSSR*, vol. 2, p. 98.
72 Evans and Block, *Leon Trotsky on China*, p. 119.
73 Ibid., pp. 118, 119; Trotsky, "K pyatnadtsatoi partiinoi konferentsii", p. 98.
74 Trotsky, "K pyatnadtsatoi partiinoi konferentsii", p. 105.
75 See Trotsky, *Problems of the Chinese Revolution*, p. 98.
76 It refers to the CCP declaration adopted by the Party Central Executive Committee Plenum on July 12, 1926.
77 Letter from K. B. Radek to the Politburo of the AUCP(B) CC, September 28, 1926, Russian Center, 530/1/10/87–88. This letter for the first time was quoted by Vujovič at the ECCI Eighth Plenum. See Russian Center, 495/166/191/28. For the English translation of Vujovič's speech (he spoke in French) see Trotsky, *Problems of the Chinese Revolution*, pp. 382–396.
78 Sun Yat-sen University was planning to publish six such collections dealing with general problems of the workers' movement in China; the Shanghai events of 1925; the agrarian question and the peasants' movement; political groupings in China; and fundamental themes in Chinese history. Only the first collection was published, however.
79 See Karl Radek, "Voprosy kitaiskoi revolyutsii" (Questions of the Chinese Revolution), in Karl Radek, ed., *Voprosy kitaiskoi revolyutsii. Tom 1: Polozheniye proletariata i razvitiye rabochego dvizheniya* (Questions of the Chinese Revolution. Vol. 1: Conditions of the Proletariat and Development of the Workers' Movement), Moscow-Leningrad: Gospolitizdat, 1927, pp. 233–256.
80 See *Pyatnadtsataya konferentsiya Vsesoyuznoi partii (b). 26 oktyabrya – 3 noyabrya 1926 g. Stenograficheskii otchet*, p. 87.
81 See Karl Radek, *Istoriya revolyutsionnogo dvizheniya v Kitaye. Kurs 1926–27 gg.* (History of the Revolutionary Movement in China. A course given in 1926–27). Lectures 1–17, Moscow: UTK Press, 1926–1927.
82 See Mikhail Zhakov, *Otrazheniye feodalizma v "Men-tsi"* (The Reflection of Feudalism in "Mencius"), Moscow: UTK Press, 1927.
83 See "Doklad tovarishcha Radeka" (A Presentation of Comrade Radek), ARAN, 377/2/2a/2–28.

84 Specialists taking part in the discussion included Vladimir Gorev, Mikhail Zhakov, Mikhail Pokrovsky, Rubach, and Georgii Fridlyand.
85 That is why, ironically, he noted in his response to the discussion at the Society of Historians-Marxists, "One cannot go to work studying Chinese history without a hypothesis. And I made bold to put forward this hypothesis in spite of the fact that in 20 years I would might be shot for this incorrect hypothesis" (ibid, 57.) Indeed he was not shot, but knifed after having been sentenced by Stalin's court to 10 years in prison. It happened earlier than 20 years, in 1939.
86 See Karl Radek, "Lenin i kitaiskaya revolyutsiya" (Lenin and the Chinese Revolution), *Pravda*, January 21, 1927. Radek apparently presented the same ideas at Sverdlov University and at several conferences, according to Vujo Vujovič. (For a reference to these conferences, see Russian Center, 495/166/191/28–29.)
87 See Karl Radek, "Novy etap v kitaiskoi revolyutsii" (A New Period in the Chinese Revolution), *Novy Mir*, 1927, no. 3, pp. 146–159.
88 See Karl Radek, "Tezisy po kitaiskomu voprosu" (Theses on the Chinese Question), in Felshtinsky, *Kommunisticheskaya Oppositsiya v SSSR*, vol. 2, pp. 192–193.
89 See, for example, Grigorii Zinoviev, "Nabrosok o zadachakh nashei vneshnei politiki pered litsom ukhudsheniya mezhdunarodnogo polozheniya SSSR" (A Draft Note on the Tasks of Our Foreign Policy in Regard to Deterioration of the International Status of the USSR), ibid., pp. 156–158; Zinoviev, "Neskol'ko tezisov o kitaiskoi revolyutsii" (Several Theses on the Chinese Revolution), Russian Center, 324/1/348/1–8.
90 L. D. Trotsky, "On China," ibid., 325/1/531/126.
91 Evans and Block, *Leon Trotsky on China*, p. 121–124.

Part 5

1 Russian Center, 17/162/4/ 64.
2 Ibid., 71–72.
3 Ibid., 83.
4 Voitinsky informed Moscow of Chiang Kai-shek's putschist intentions in late February 1927. See ibid., 514/1/240/12–13.
5 Ibid., 17/162/4/90–93.
6 Ibid., 532/4/311/32.
7 *Pravda*, March 15, 1927.
8 Radek's presentation was included into the agenda of the Communist Academy meeting dedicated to the second anniversary of Sun Yat-sen's death on March 10, 1927. The Bureau of the Academy Presidium which made the decision unwisely authorized Radek to present his report on behalf of the Academy (see ARAN, 350/1/103/29.) On the next day *Pravda* reported Radek's forthcoming presentation.
9 Carr (*A History of Soviet Russia: Foundations of a Planned Economy: 1926–1929*, vol. 1, London: Macmillan, 1971, p. 132) mistakenly states that Voroshilov was among Radek's opponents in the debates at the Communist Academy. It was actually Voroshilov's secretary for foreign political affairs, S. S. Joffe, who took part in the debates.
10 Radek erred. Lenin expressed this idea in his "Report of the Commission on the National and Colonial Questions" as follows: "We, as Communists, should and will support bourgeois-liberation movements in the colonies only when they are genuinely revolutionary, and when their exponents do not hinder our work of education and organizing in a revolutionary spirit the peasantry and the masses of the exploited." (Lenin, "Report of the Commission on the National and Colonial Questions, July 26," p. 242.)
11 Karl Radek, "Dvizhushchiye sily kitaiskoi revolyutsii" (Motive Forces of the Chinese Revolution [A Presentation to the Communist Academy: A Stenographic Record]), Russian Center, 326/2/32/145, 146, 147; "Zaklyuchitel'noye slovo tov. Radeka" (Concluding Speech of Comrade Radek), ibid., 177–178.

12 Radek, "Dvizhushchiye sily kitaiskoi revolyutsii," 153.
13 Russian Center, 532/4/311/26, 32.
14 In keeping with his socio-economic analysis of Chinese society of that time he included in the Chinese bourgeoisie all big landlords.
15 K. Radek, "Vo vtoruyu godovshchinu smerti Sun Yatsena" (On the Second Anniversary of Sun Yat-sen's Death), *Izvestiya*, March 11, 15, 1927.
16 See S. Dalin, "Sun Yatsen. Ko 2–i godovshchine ego smerti (12 marta 1925 g.) (Sun Yat-sen. On the Second Anniversary of His Death [March 12, 1925]), *Pravda*, March 12, 1927.
17 See Zinoviev and Trotsky, "Fakty i Dokumenty," 2.
18 "Revolyutsiya v Kitaye i gomindan" (The Revolution in China and the Guomindang), *Pravda*, March 16, 1927.
19 See *Pravda*, March 31, 1927. See also Stalin, *Works*, vol. 9, pp. 196–204.
20 Leon Trotsky, "A Brief Note (March 22, 1927)," in Evans and Block, *Leon Trotsky on China*, pp. 125–126.
21 See M. Alsky, *Kanton pobezhdaet ...* (Canton Victorious ...), Moscow: Communist Academy Press, 1927, p. 141. For an English translation of the citation from this book see Evans and Block, *Leon Trotsky on China*, p. 128.
22 Leon Trotsky, "Letter to Alsky (March 29, 1927)," in Evans and Block, *Leon Trotsky on China*, pp. 128–132.
23 See G. Zinoviev, "Theses on the Chinese Revolution," in Trotsky, *Problems of the Chinese Revolution*, pp. 313–381.
24 [Zinoviev], "Neskol'ko tezisov o kitaiskoi revolyutsii," 4, 5.
25 Leon Trotsky, "To the Politburo of the AUCP(B) Central Committee (March 31, 1927)," in Evans and Block, *Leon Trotsky on China*, pp. 123–135.
26 This article ("Class Relations in the Chinese Revolution"), like many others, was denied publication at the time. For its English translation see ibid., pp. 136–148.
27 See Trotsky's notes on the Chinese revolution, written on April 5 and 6 (Russian Center, Collection of non-filed documents.)
28 The Bureau of the Party's Moscow Committee had planned to hold this meeting as early as March 21, but because Bukharin was sidelined by illness, it was postponed. (See Russian Center, 1/20/194/94, 100.)
29 "Doklad N. I. Bukharina o kitaiskoi revolyutsii aktivu Moskovskoi organizatsii 4 aprelya 1927 g." (N. I. Bukharin's Report on the Chinese Revolution to the Moscow Party Activists, April 4, 1927), ibid., 324/1/353/5, 6. Later this report, was published in a significantly revised form as "Problems of the Chinese Revolution" in a collection of articles entitled *Voprosy kitaiskoi revolyutsii* (Questions of the Chinese Revolution), Moscow-Leningrad: Gosizdat, 1927, pp. 57–122. Another edited version of the report was published in *Pravda* on April 19, 1927.
30 "Doklad Bukharina o kitaiskoi revolyutsii," 2–4, 5.
31 This speech was never published, and the official stenogram was not distributed. Attempts by Trotsky and other Oppositionists to obtain the text from the Central Committee Secretariat, Stalin's and Bukharin's secretaries, and the Moscow Committee, were unsuccessful. See Russian Center, 589/3/4307/1/215; 495/166/189/3. The most complete version of the speech was provided by the Serbian Communist Vujo Vujovič who cited his "exact notes" at the Eighth Plenum of the Comintern Executive Committee. He misdated Stalin's speech, however. See ibid, 495/166/191/31–32. Vujovič's speech was translated into English and published by Max Shachtman in Trotsky's *Problems of the Chinese Revolution* (pp. 382–396.) Stalin's unwillingness to make his speech broadly accessible is understandable. The course of events in China undermined his basic conclusions so quickly that it would not have been possible to correct the stenogram. With Martynov's help, Stalin tried to prepare at least some brief theses on the basis of his speech, but at the end he withheld them also from publication. See J. V. Stalin, "Tezisy o kitaiskom voprose" (Theses on the Chinese Question), ibid., 558/1/2848/1–8.

32 Trotsky, *Problems of the Chinese Revolution*, pp. 388–390.
33 On Radek's speech see Zinoviev and Trotsky, "Fakty i Dokumenty," 3.
34 A. Martynov, "Problema kitaiskoi revolyutsii" (A Problem of the Chinese revolution), *Pravda*, April 10, 1927.
35 See Russian Center, Collection of non-filed documents. This work was first published in a German translation. See Leon Trotzki, *Schriften*, Bd. 2: *Über China*, part 1, [Hamburg]: Rasch und Rohring, 1990, p. 155–157.
36 Grigorii Zinoviev, "K urokam kitaiskoi revolyutsii: Po povodu stat'i tov. A. Martynova" (On the Lessons of the Chinese Revolution: On Comrade A. Martynov's Article), Russian Center, 495/166/188/2–20.
37 Letter from V. D. Kasparova and G. L. Shklovsky to the AUCP(B) CC and CCC, After April 12, 1927, ibid., 17/71/78/4–5.
38 L. Trotsky, "Fighting Against the Stream. April 1939," in Breitman and Reed, *Writings of Leon Trotsky (1938–9)*, p. 352. The same ideas are contained in his autobiography. See Trotsky, *My Life*, p. 530.
39 Max Shachtman, who published Zinoviev's *Theses* for the first time, mistakenly dated this letter April 15, 1927. See Trotsky, *Problems of the Chinese Revolution*, p. 313.
40 It was not until the morning of April 14 that information about the Shanghai events reached the general public.
41 Grigorii Zinoviev, "Proekt rezolyutsii aprel'skogo (1927 g.) plenuma TsK VKP(b)" (The Draft Resolution of the April (1927) Plenum of the AUCP[B] CC), Russian Center, 495/166/187/156–163.
42 See Russian Center, 17/2/284/23. It has not been possible to ascertain the decisions of the Party's highest organ on which Rykov reported. Judging by the archival protocols, there were no Politburo meetings between April 7 and 16. Perhaps the reference is to the intention to make a loan of three million dollars to the Wuhan Guomindang government, Chiang Kai-shek's main opponent. The Politburo adopted a resolution in this regard on April 16. See ibid., 162/4/102.
43 *Pravda*, April 19, 1927.
44 See Zinoviev and Trotsky, "Fakty i Dokumenty," 3.
45 See "Vozzvaniye Ispolkoma Kominterna v svyazi s kontrevolyutsionnym perevorotom Chan Kai-shi" (ECCI Proclamation Concerning the Counterrevolutionary Coup by Chiang Kai-shek), in Titarenko, *Kommunisticheskii Internatsional i kitaiskaya revolyutsiya*, pp. 110–113. See also the editorial in *Pravda*, April 15, 1927.
46 As Carr correctly guessed, the author of this article was Martynov. See Carr, *A History of Soviet Russia: Foundations of a Planned Economy: 1926–1929*, vol. 1, p. 145.
47 See *Kommunisticheskii Internatsional*, 1927, no. 16 (90), pp. 3–10.
48 Leon Trotsky, "On the Slogan of Soviets in China," in Evans and Block, *Leon Trotsky on China*, p. 149.
49 Ibid., p. 151.
50 For the original of this document, see "Pis'mo T. G. Mandalyana, N. M. Nasonova, N. A. Fokina i A. E. Albrekhta v russkuyu delegatsiyu IKKI ot 17 marta 1927 g." (Letter of T. G. Mandalyan, N. M. Nasonov, N. A. Fokin, and A. E. Albrekht to the Russian Delegation of the ECCI, March 17, 1927), Russian Center, 508/2/11/19–44. This letter was subsequently used by both Oppositionists and Stalinists in the continuing struggle between them. Oddly, neither side ever mentioned Mandalyan as one of the letter's authors. His name is also missing from the archival copies I have seen, and the text of the letter published in English does not include Mandalyan's name. See Leon Trotsky, *Problems of the Chinese Revolution*, pp. 391–426.
51 See Leon Trotsky, "Polozheniye v Kitaye posle perevorota Chan Kai-shi i perspektivy" (The Situation in China After Chiang Kai-shek's Coup d'état and Perspectives), Russian Center, 589/3/4307–2/118–114.
52 The Institute of Red Professors educated future Soviet professors of social science and party and state officials. Founded in 1921, it was divided into several schools in 1930–31.

53 See Leon Trotsky, "Ne nado musoru!" (We Don't Need This Rubbish!), Russian Center, 17/785/34/83–90.

54 "V Politburo, Prezidium TsKK," (To the Politburo, CCC Presidium), in Felshtinsky, *Kommunisticheskaya oppozitsiya v SSSR*, vol. 2, p. 234. Felshtinsky made an error: he failed to indicate that the letter was signed by Trotsky as well as Zinoviev. He also erred in dating the text, assigning it to "the beginning of April 1927."

55 See Leon Trotsky, "The Chinese Revolution and the Theses of Comrade Stalin," in Evans and Block, *Leon Trotsky on China*, p. 158.

56 See J. V. Stalin, "Questions of the Chinese Revolution: Theses for Propagandists, Adopted by the AUCP(B) CC," in Stalin, *Works*, vol. 9, pp. 224–234.

57 See J. V. Stalin, "Concerning Questions of the Chinese Revolution: Reply to Comrade Marchulin," ibid., pp. 236–242; Stalin, "Talk with Students of the Sun Yat-sen University, May 13, 1927," ibid., pp. 243–273; Stalin, "The Revolution in China and the Tasks of the Comintern: Speech Delivered at the Tenth Sitting, Eighth Plenum of the E.C.C.I., May 24, 1927," ibid., pp. 288–318.

58 See "O tezisakh Zinovieva po kitaiskomu voprosu" (On Comrade Zinoviev's Theses on the Chinese Question), Russian Center, 17/3/634/16–32.

59 Trotsky, "The Chinese Revolution and the Theses of Comrade Stalin," pp. 168–169.

60 Ibid., pp. 171–172.

61 Ibid., pp. 174–178.

62 Ibid., pp. 162–180.

63 See Radek, "'Izmena' kitaiskoi krupnoi burzhuazii natsional'nomu dvizheniyu."

64 Letter from L. D. Trotsky to K. B. Radek, May 14, 1927, Russian Center, 325/1/359/113.

65 See Russian Center, 324/1/350/14–18, 43, 48–50, 51a.

66 For a fairly rough preliminary draft of this article, see Russian Center, 324/1/350/1–68.

67 Grigorii Zinoviev, "Vynuzhdennyi otvet" (An Obligatory Reply), ibid., 508/1/107/35–79.

68 See ARAN, 350/2/150/45–64.

69 Grigorii Zinoviev, "Eshche k urokam kitaiskoi revolyutsii: Potryasayushchii dokument" (Once More on Lessons of the Chinese Revolution. A Shocking Document), Russian Center, 324/1/346/3–25.

70 See Tan Pingshan, *Puti razvitiya kitaiskoi revolyutsii* (Directions of Development of the Chinese Revolution), Moscow-Leningrad: Gosizdat, 1927.

71 Trotsky, *Problems of the Chinese Revolution*, p. 119.

72 See "Pis'mo G. E. Zinovieva N. K. Krupskoi ot 16 maya 1927 g." (Letter from G. E. Zinoviev to N. K. Krupskaya, May 16, 1927), in *Izvestiya TsK KPSS* (CPSU CC News), 1989, no. 2, pp. 206–207; "Pis'mo L. D. Trotskogo N. K. Krupskoi k voprosu o 'samokritike', 17 maya 1927 g." (Letter from L. D. Trotsky to N. K. Krupskaya Concerning a Question of "Self-Criticism", May 17, 1927), in Felshtinsky, *Kommunisticheskaya oppozitsiya v SSSR*, vol. 3, pp. 57–59.

73 "Protokol no. 101 zasedaniya Politburo TsK VKP(b) ot 12 maya 1927 g." (Minutes No. 101 of the AUCP(B) CC Politburo Session of May 12, 1927), Russian Center, 17/3/63/6–7.

74 Ibid., 2.

75 See Evans and Block, *Leon Trotsky on China*, pp. 210–214.

76 See "Protokol no. 101 zasedaniya Politburo TsK VKP(b) ot 12 maya 1927 g.," 33–36.

77 See A. Svechin, "Voennoye iskusstvo v budushchei voyne" (Military Art in a Future War), *Pravda*, May 1, 1927.

78 See "Protokol no. 101 zasedaniya Politburo TsK VKP(b) ot 12 maya 1927 g.," 1–2.

79 See *Pravda*, May 13 and 17, 1927. Zinoviev argued that the meeting only consisted of party members.

80 Letter from the AUCP(B) CC Politburo to M. M. Borodin, M. N. Roy, and Lyuks [O. Yu. Pliche], May 30, 1925, Russian Center, 17/162/5/30.

81 Ibid., 8–9.

82 See the letter of the AUCP(B) CC Politburo to the Comintern Executive of May 19, 1927, Russian Center, 17/3/635/15–17.

83 See Leon Trotsky, "The Communist Party and the Kuomintang [Guomindang]," Evans and Block, *Leon Trotsky on China*, pp. 199–203.

84 The two latter documents have not been found in the archives.

85 See Russian Center, 495/166/189/2–7.

86 See "V Tsentral'nyi komitet VKP(b). 'Zayavleniye 83–kh'" (To the AUCP(B) Central Committee. Declaration of the Eighty-Three), ibid., 17/71/88/39–45.

87 See ibid., 324/1/361/1–55.

88 See Evans and Block, *Leon Trotsky on China*, pp. 216–248.

89 At that time the CCP periodicals were issued no more than once a week.

90 Leon Trotsky, "It Is Time to Understand, Time to Reconsider, and Time to Make A Change," in Evans and Block, *Leon Trotsky on China*, p. 242.

91 See Titarenko, *Kommunisticheskii Internatsional i kitaiskaya revolyutsiya*, pp. 116–133. Bukharin wrote the resolution on China.

92 See Russian Center, 17/162/5/8–9, 29–30, 33–34, 36–38, 42, 49–51.

93 Ibid., 46. Cited in Stalin, *Works*, vol. 10, p. 35.

94 Russian Center, 17/162/5/54.

95 "Rezolyutsiya o vystuplenii tt. Trotskogo i Vuiovicha na plenarnom zasedanii IKKI" (Resolutions on the Activity of Comrades Trotsky and Vujovič at the Plenary Session of the ECCI), ibid., 495/166/71/1–8.

96 For Zinoviev's and Trotsky's explanations at the Commission of the AUCP(B) Central Control Commission see ibid., 589/2/4307–1/280–189.

97 Lih et al., *Stalin's Letters to Molotov*, p. 135.

98 Isaac Deutscher incorrectly gives the date for this session as "July 24." Apparently following Deutscher, Evans and Block give the same incorrect date. (See Deutscher, *The Prophet Unarmed*, p. 341; Evans and Block, *Leon Trotsky on China*, p. 632.)

99 See Leon Trotsky, "Ot Chan Kai-shi k Wan Tsin-weyu: O nyneshnem etape kitaiskoi revolyutsii" (From Chiang Kai-shek to Wang Jingwei: On the Current Period of the Chinese Revolution), Russian Center, 324/1/354/1–12 or 326/2/95/165–176.

100 See Zinoviev's note on the question of withdrawal from the Guomindang, ibid., 324/1/351/5–8. See also Zinoviev's criticism of Trotsky's statement in ibid., 324/1/354/1–12.

101 See Leon Trotsky, "Why Have We Not Called for Withdrawal from the Kuomintang [Guomindang] Until Now," in Evans and Block, *Leon Trotsky on China*, pp. 249–250.

102 See Radek's notes in regard to Trotsky's statement in Russian Center, 326/2/95/165–176.

103 See "Pis'mo G. E. Zinovieva, L. D. Trotskogo, K. B. Radeka i G. E. Yevdokimova v Politburo TsK VKP(b), v Prezidium TsKK, v Ispolkom Kominterna ot 25 iyunia 1927 g.," (Letter of G. E. Zinoviev, L. D. Trotsky, K. B. Radek, G. E. Yevdokimov to the AUCP(B) CC Politburo, CCC Presidium, and the Comintern Executive, June 25, 1927), in Felshtinsky, *Kommunisticheskaya oppozitsiya v SSSR*, vol. 3, pp. 131–132.

104 See Grigorii Yevdokimov, Grigorii Zinoviev, Karl Radek, Georgii Safarov, Leon Trotsky, "Novy etap kitaiskoi revolyutsii: Ot Chan Kai-shi k Wan Tsin-weyu" (The New Period of the Chinese Revolution: From Chiang Kai-shek to Wang Jingwei), Russian Center, 17/71/88/1–29.

105 Letter from Grigorii Yevdokimov, Grigorii Zinoviev, and Leon Trotsky to the AUCP(B) CCC and the Politburo of the AUCP (B) CC, July 4, 1927, ibid., 30–31.

106 For the original letter see ibid., 495/3/25/69. This letter was first published by Evans and Block (*Leon Trotsky on China*, p. 251), who did not indicate a precise date for the document.

107 Lih et al., *Stalin's Letters to Molotov*, pp. 136–137.

108 Kosheleva et al., *Pis'ma I.V. Stalina V.I. Molotovu*, p. 104. This phrase was translated incorrectly in the American edition of the Stalin's letters. (See Lih et al., *Stalin's Letters to Molotov*, pp. 137.)
109 See Nikolai Bukharin, "Tekushchii moment kitaiskoi revolyutsii" (The Current Moment in the Chinese Revolution), *Pravda*, June 30, 1927.
110 Lih et al., *Stalin's Letters to Molotov*, p. 138.
111 Russian Center, 17/162/5/65–66.
112 Lih et al., *Stalin's Letters to Molotov*, p. 139.
113 Ibid., p. 143.
114 See V. I. Stalin, "Notes on Contemporary Themes," in Stalin, *Works*, vol. 9, pp. 328–369.
115 Lih et al., *Stalin's Letters to Molotov*, pp. 140, 141, 142.
116 See Russian Center, 324/1/34/1–24.
117 See Lih et al., *Stalin's Letters to Molotov*, p. 138.
118 Osinsky, Manuilsky, Bauman, Molotov, Milyutin, Voroshilov, Lozovsky, Stalin, Krupskaya, Bubnov, and Rykov took part in the discussion as part of the AUCP(B) majority.
119 For the stenographic record of the Plenum see Russian Center, 17/2/317.
120 Zinoviev emphasized this point, which he had set forth in "Events in China", "Our International Situation and the Danger of War", and "Contours of the Forth-coming War and Our Tasks". See Russian Center, 324/1/34/1–24; 357/1–38; Felshtinsky, *Kommunisticheskaya oppozitsiya v SSSR*, vol. 3, pp. 131–132. Zinoviev sent the latter article to the Politburo asking for its distribution to Central Committee members. It was later attached as an appendix to the first volume of the Plenum's stenographic record. See Russian Center, 17/2/317–1/168–178.
121 See *Vsesoyuznaya Kommunisticheskaya partiya (bol'shevikov) v rezolyutsiyakh i resheniyakh s"ezdov, konferentsii i plenumov TsK* (The All-Union Communist Party [Bolshevik] in Resolutions and Decisions of Congresses, Conferences and CC Plenums), 2 parts, part 2, 6th ed., Moscow: Gospolitizdat, 1941, pp. 170–179, 189–193.
122 Lih et al., *Stalin's Letters to Molotov*, p. 140.
123 Ibid., p. 143.
124 Ibid., pp. 139, 143.
125 See, for example, Stalin, "Talk with Sun Yat-sen University Students on May 13, 1927," pp. 261–263. In 1918–23 the revolutionary Mustapha Kemal led an anti-imperialist, anti-monarchical movement in Turkey. He had the assistance of the Soviet government, which viewed him at least until 1921 as a left-wing nationalist leader and through 1923 sought to guide him. Kemal, however, did not become a Soviet puppet. The Turkish republic proclaimed in 1923 was a bourgeois state. To forestall opposition to the course he was taking, in 1921 Kemal massacred Turkish Communists. Soviet leaders used the phrases "Kemalist way" and "Kemalism" to describe the pursuit of a bourgeois or capitalist path of development in a former colonial or semi-colonial country.
126 Russian Center, 17/2/317–1/167.
127 See *Pravda*, July 25, 1927.
128 See Russian Center, 17/2/317–1/61, 66, 142.
129 *Pravda*, September 30, 1927.
130 See Leon Trotsky, "New Opportunities for the Chinese Revolution, New Tasks, and New Mistakes," in Evans and Block, *Leon Trotsky on China*, pp. 256–269.
131 Russian Center, 325/1/489/5. For the English translation of a large portion of this letter, see Evans and Block, *Leon Trotsky on China*, pp. 279–287.
132 Leon Trotsky, "Zametki ot 25 iyunya 1927 g." (Notes, June 25, 1927), in Felshtinsky, *Kommunisticheskaya oppozitsiya v SSSR*, vol. 3, pp. 132–133.
133 Ibid, p. 134.
134 Evans and Block, *Leon Trotsky and China*, pp. 264–265.

135 Ibid., p. 266.
136 See Trotsky Papers, document T3091, pp. 1–10.
137 See Letter from L. D. Trotsky to G. E. Zinoviev of September 22, 1927, in Felshtinsky, *Kommunisticheskaya oppozitsiya v SSSR*, vol. 3, pp. 132–134.
138 Ibid., vol. 4, p. 160.
139 Russian Center, 495/3/36/3.
140 See ibid., 505/1/65/1–33.
141 See *Vsesoyuznaya Kommunisticheskaya partiya (bol'shevikov) v rezolyutsiyakh i resheniyakh s"ezdov, konferentsii i plenumov TsK*, p. 220.
142 See Felshtinsky, *Kommunisticheskayi oppozitsiya v SSSR*, vol. 4, pp. 250–266.
143 See *XV s"ezd Vsesoyuznoi Kommunisticheskoi partii (b). Stenograficheskii otchet* (Fifteenth Congress of the All-Union Communist Party [B]: Stenographic Record), Moscow-Leningrad: Gosizdat, 1928, pp. 1337, 1338.
144 Ibid., pp. 1317–1319.
145 Ibid., pp. 1266–1267.

Part 6

1 *Pravda*, June 30, 1920.
2 *2-i kongress Kommunisticheskogo Internatsionala: Stenograficheskii otchet* (Stenographic Record of the Second Congress of the Communist International), Moscow: The Comintern Press, 1921, pp. 165–166.
3 *Pod Znamenem Ilicha*, May 8, 1926. On April 18, 1924, with the abolition of Narkomnats, KUTV was placed under the direction of the Central Executive Committee of the USSR. From 1929 to 1937 (when it was restructured), it was managed by the Scientific Research Association for the Study of National and Colonial Problems. In 1937–38, it was under the control of the Presidium of the Central Executive Committee of the USSR. It was closed down in 1938.
4 *Zhizn' Natsional'nostei*, May 15, 1921; *Sobranie uzakonenii i rasporyazhenii rabochego i krestyanskogo pravitel'stva* (The Statutes and Orders of the Workers' and Peasants' Government), 1921, no. 36, p. 194; *Pod Znamenem Ilicha, May 8, 1926.*
5 *Zhizn' Natsional'nostei*, May 14, 1921.
6 Ibid., May 22, 1921; *Pod Znamenem Ilicha*, May 8, 1926. It should be noted that when KUTV was opened, there were already a number of general educational establishments giving training in Marxism-Leninism to members of the national liberation and Communist movements of the Near and Middle East. For example, there was a Socialist Academy of the East. See *Kommunist* (The Communist) [Baku], October 15, 1920. In mid-January 1921, the first students graduated from the "shock" courses in Soviet activity and propaganda in the East (see *Zhizn' Natsional'nostei*, March 17, 1921). But KUTV was the first school dedicated to the systematic education of revolutionaries from the major countries of the East, including China.
7 This decision was taken by the Organization Bureau of the AUCP(B) Central Committee (see Russian Center, 530/1/27.) The internal reorganization of UTK into a Communist institution (by re-working the study program, altering the basis for the selection of students, and reinforcing party-political work) dragged on until the start of the 1929–30 academic year. See G. V. Efimov, "Iz istorii Kommunisticheskogo universiteta trudyashchikhsya Kitaya" (Episodes in the History of the Communist University of the Toilers of China), *Problemy Dalnego Vostoka*, 1977, no. 2, p. 173.
8 *Gongchan zazhi*, 1929, no. 1, p. 5.
9 See N. N. Timofeeva, "Kommunisticheskii universitet trudyashchikhsya Vostoka (KUTV) (1921–1925)" (The Communist University of the Toilers of the East [KUTV] [1921–25]) [hereafter cited as "KUTV, 1921–25"], *Narody Azii i Afriki*, 1976, no. 2, p. 52.
10 See M. A. Persits, "Vostochniye internatsionalisti v Rossii i nekotoriye voprosy natsional'no-osvoboditel'nogo dvizheniya (1918–iyul 1920)" (Eastern Internationalists

in Russia and Some Questions of the National Liberation Movement [1918–July 1920]), in Uliyanovsky, *Komintern i Vostok*, p. 89.

11 See N. N. Timofeeva, "Kommunisticheskii universitet trudyashchikhsya Vostoka (KUTV) v 1926–1938 gg." (The Communist University of the Toilers of the East [KUTV] in 1926–38) [hereafter cited as "KUTV, 1926–38"], *Narody Azii i Afriki*, 1976, no. 5, p. 40.

12 Sheng Yueh, *Sun Yat-sen University and the Chinese Revolution: A Personal Account*, Lawrence, KS: Kansas University Press, 1971, p. 66.

13 A. M. Grigoriev, *Revolyutsionnoye dvizheniye v Kitaye v 1927–1931 gg. (Problemy strategii i taktiki)* (The Revolutionary Movement in China in 1927–1931 [Problems of Strategy and Tactics]), Moscow: Nauka, 1980, p. 271.

14 See Russian Center, 532/l/41.

15 Cited in R. A. Mirovitskaya, "Sovetskii Soiuz i KPK (konets 20–kh – nachalo 30–kh godov" (The Soviet Union and the CCP at the End of the 1920s and the Start of the 1930s), in M. L. Titarenko, ed., *Opyt i uroki istorii KPK: K 60–letiyu obrazovaniya partii* (Experience and Lessons from the History of the CCP: On the Sixtieth Anniversary of the Party Founding), Moscow: Institute of the Far Eastern Studies Press, 1981, p. 202.

16 Ibidem.

17 Qiwu Laoren (Bao Huiseng), "Do i posle obrazovaniya Kommunisticheskoi partii Kitaya" (Before and After the Formation of the Communist Party of China), *Rabochii klass i sovremennyi mir*, 1971, no. 2, p. 120; *Renmin ribao*, August 14, 1983; Xiao, "Fu Su xuexi qianhou," p. 6; Klein and Clark, *Biographical Dictionary*, vol. 1, p. 241; vol. 2, p. 982.

18 See Xiao, "Fu Su xuexi qianhou," p. 6.

19 Ibidem.

20 Klein and Clark, *Biographical Dictionary*, vol. 2, p. 983.

21 See Qiwu Laoren, "Do i posle obrazovaniya," p. 121.

22 The remaining graduates of the school's first intake (among them Peng Shuzhi) arrived in Moscow in the second half of September.

23 See Russian Center, 532/l/393/69–72.

24 See Jiang Kanghu, *Xin E youji* (A journey to the New Russia), Shanghai: Shangwu yinshuguan, 1923, p. 35; Russian Center, 532/l/393/22–29, 61–64.

25 See Russian Center, 495/225/730; 532/1/393/5, 17; *Zheng Chaolin huiyilu*, p. 59.

26 *Pod Znamenem Ilicha*, April 26, 1924.

27 The "comparative predominance of the intelligentsia at the start of the movement was observed everywhere," wrote Lenin. See V. I. Lenin, "How V. Zasulich Fights Liquidationism," in Lenin, *Collected Works*, vol. 24, p. 22.

28 Sheng, *Sun Yat-sen University*, p. 16.

29 See Russian Center, 530/2/35.

30 Sheng, *Sun Yat-sen University*, p. 16.

31 Calculated according to Russian Center, 530/1/3; 530/l/42/79.

32 Our best information is that the last group of this intake (seventy-five persons) arrived at UTK on September 22, 1926. See Russian Center, 530/l/42.

33 Russian Center, 530/1/42/68.

34 See Sheng, *Sun Yat-sen University*, pp. 21–22.

35 See Russian Center, 495/225/874; 532/1/393/5, 10, 15, 21, 30; *Zheng Chaolin huiyilu*, pp. 54–55, 62.

36 See Russian Center, 532/1/393/14, 18, 70.

37 Ibid., 43.

38 Sheng, *Sun Yat-sen University*, p. 102; Jiang Zemin, "Zai Faguo, Bilishi qingong jianxuede rizi (Days of Diligent Work and Economical Study in France and Belgium), *Geming shi ziliao*, 1981, no. 3, p. 84.

39 See Russian Center, 530/1/9/11; S. A. Dalin, *Kitaiskie Memuary: 1921–1927* (Chinese memoirs: 1921–27), Moscow: Nauka, 1975, p. 176.

40 Russian Center, 530/1/42; Sheng, *Sun Yat-sen University*, pp. 30, 137–38, 147.

41 Calculated according to Russian Center, 530/l/42.

42 Ibid., 530/1/16.

43 Calculated according to Russian Center, 530/l/42/79–61. About fifty GMD members remained at UTK, many of whom expressed a desire to join the Komsomol or Communist Party. See ibid., 530/2/26.

44 See also Russian Center, 530/l/33.

45 Calculated according to Russian Center, 530/1/42/79–61.

46 See ibid., 532/1/69/4–9; Sheng, *Sun Yat-sen University*, p. 42.

47 Calculated from Russian Center, 530/1/75.

48 Calculated from Klein and Clark, *Biographical Dictionary*, vol. 2, pp. 1056–57.

49 Liu Shaoqi, "Rech na mitinge moskvichei vo Dvortse sporta 7 dekabria 1960 g." (Speech at a Meeting Held in the Moscow Palace of Sports, December 7, 1960), *Pravda*, December 8, 1960.

50 Sheng, *Sun Yat-sen University*, p. 63.

51 The name of the second author of *The ABC of Communism*, it is true, was never mentioned. See, for example, Russian Center, 495/225/401, 1100, 1629 and other sources.

52 Wang Fanxi, *Shuangshan huiyilu* (Memoirs of Shuangshan), Hong Kong: Zhou Publisher, 1977, p. 34.

53 This institute was founded in autumn 1921 by Chinese anarchists as part of the program of "diligent work, economical study" in France. For more details, see Staburova, *Anarkhizm v Kitaye*, pp. 111–112. More than one hundred Chinese studied there.

54 The University of Labor at Charleroi was formed by Belgian socialists for the children of Belgian workers. However, the administration opened its doors to young Chinese also, giving them free accommodation and setting up special courses for them. For details, see Jiang, "Zai Faguo, Bilishi qingong jianxue rizi," pp. 74–84. Among others, Nie Rongzhen and Liu Bojian followed training courses here.

55 *Pod Znamenem Ilicha*, April 26, 1924; Efimov, "Iz istorii Kommunisticheskogo universiteta trudyashchikhsya Kitaya," p. 172.

56 Russian Center, 495/225/1629; Sheng, *Sun Yat-sen University*, p. 69.

57 According to other reports, Sleptsov (Russian Center, 495/225/31).

58 Russian Center, 530/1/40, 75, 530/l/76/2, 7, 9, 20, 27; Yang Zilie, *Zhang Guotao furen huiyilu* (Memoirs of Madame Zhang Guotao), Hong Kong: Zilian chubanshe, 1970, p. 216.

59 Both Qu Qiubai and Li Zongwu arrived in Moscow in January 1921 as correspondents of the Beijing newspaper *Chen bao* (Morning Post). See Xiao, "Fu Su xuexi qianhou," p. 11; Jiang, *Xin E youji*, p. 35; and Klein and Clark, *Biographical Dictionary*, vol. 1, p. 241.

60 Russian Center, 530/l/16.

61 Ibid., 532/l/37/5; Timofeeva, "KUTV, 1921–25," p. 50; *Pod Znamenem Ilicha*, May 8, 1926; Wang, *Shuangshan huiyilu*, p. 53; *Qianjin bao*, December 18, 1925; Sheng, *Sun Yat-sen University*, p. 61.

62 See Timofeeva, "KUTV, 1921–25," p. 50, and "KUTV, 1926–38," p. 34.

63 Russian Center, 530/l/16, 68.

64 See *Zheng Chaolin huiyilu*, p. 63.

65 This discipline was an introduction to the social sciences, history, political economy, and philosophy for those students with only a slight acquaintance with Marxism. See Dalin, *Kitaiskie Memuary*, p. 176.

66 See Russian Center, 530/1/16. According to Sheng Yueh, the UTK students also studied one Western language, English, German, or French. See Sheng, *Sun Yat-sen University*, p. 61.

67 See Russian Center, 530/1/16.

68 See Sheng, *Sun Yat-sen University*, p. 75.

69 This was extremely characteristic of Radek who, until 1927, as argued earlier, taught a general course on the history of the revolutionary movement in China. We have the testimony of several persons that he was deeply revered and loved by the majority of students. See, in particular, Russian Center, 530/2/29, 32.

70 For details, see Meng Qingshu, *Vospominaniya o Van Mine* (Memories of Wang Ming). (Manuscript), Moscow, n. d., pp. 66–67.

71 See Russian Center, 530/2/29.

72 Ibid., 530/1/4.

73 Ibid., 530/1/30/124; 532/1/10/3.

74 Ibid., 530/l/16.

75 Timofeeva, "KUTV, 1926–38," p. 30.

76 Ibid., p. 40.

77 See G. Broido, "Kommunisticheskii universitet trudyashchikhsya Vostoka" (The Communist University of the Toilers of the East), *Zhizn' Natsional'nostei*, January 26, 1921.

78 Some translators, on graduating from UTK and returning home, published translations of the lectures under their own names. One of these was Han Liangxian for whose work the famous GMD activist Hu Hanmin wrote introduction. See Sheng, *Sun Yat-sen University*, p. 56.

79 See Timofeeva, "KUTV, 1921–25," p. 54.

80 See Timofeeva, "KUTV, 1926–38," p. 35.

81 See Efimov, "Iz istorii Kommunistichskogo universiteta trudyashchikhsya Kitaya," p. 175.

82 See Russian Center, 530/l/9.

83 See Nikiforov, *Sovetskie istoriki o problemakh Kitaya*, p. 127.

84 See Russian Center, 530/l/28.

85 One of those who began to study the question of reforming the Chinese script at UTK and at the China Institute was Wu Yuzhang (see his biographical sketch).

86 Sheng, *Sun Yat-sen University*, p. 4; Russian Center, 530/l/29.

87 Such terminology was used, in particular, at the Sixth Congress of the CCP. See *Stenograficheskii otchet VI s"ezda Kommunisticheskoi partii Kitaya*, book 4, p. 27.

88 "Song Liang tongzhi gei [Liu] Shaoqi tongzhide xin" (Letter from Song Liang [Sun Yefang] to [Liu] Shaoqi), in Liu Shaoqi, *Lun dang* (On the Party), Dalian: Dazhong shudian, 1947, p. 345.

89 For a full test of the document translated into English, see Wilbur and How, *Missionaries of the Revolution*, pp. 527–529.

90 Ibid., p. 527.

91 Cited in Karl Marx and Frederick Engels, "The Alliance of Socialist Democracy and the International Working Men's Association," in Karl Marx and Frederick Engels, *Collected Works*, vol. 23, New York: International Publ., 1988, pp. 545.

92 See Russian Center, 530/l/42; *Zhonggong dangshi ziliao* (Materials on the History of the CCP), 1982, no. 1, pp. 180–83.

93 Russian Center, 530/l/5–8.

94 Meng, *Vospominaniya o Van Mine*, pp. 66–67.

95 See Russian Center, 530/l/28; 530/2/29, 40; 514/l/1012/2–11; Chiang Ching-kuo, *My Days in Soviet Russia*, Taipei, 1963, p. 8.

96 UTK was situated at no. 16 Volkhonka Street.

97 See Testimony of Comrade Nekrasov, Russian Center, 514/l/1012/3, 4–5.

98 See Testimony of a Student, ibid., 12.

99 More precisely, Sun Yat-sen University of the Toilers of China.

100 This refers to the Hong Kong-Canton (Guangzhou) strike.

101 Testimony of Comrade Nekrasov, 2.

102 On August 5, 1927, Bei Yunfeng, Gao Heng, Dong Rucheng, Xu Yunzuo, and Qi Shugong were sent to KUTV and on the military-political courses as translators. See Russian Center, 530/l/42/71; Testimony of Comrade Nekrasov, 3, 4.

103 See Wang Pingyi. "Liu E qianhou" (Before and After [My] Visit to Russia), *Liushi nian lai Zhongguo liu E xuesheng zhi fengxiang diaoku* (Chinese Students' Reminiscences of [Their] Visit to Russia Sixty Yeas Ago), Taipei: Zhonghua shuju chubanshe, 1988, pp. 19–26; Wu K'un-jung, "The Left Opposition Faction in the Chinese Communist Party" (Part 1), *Issues & Studies* , vol. 10, no. 6 (March 1974), p. 80.

104 See Russian Center, 495/225/327, 2411; 505/l/22/10; 514/l/1031/13–14; 530/1/16, 34, 56, 62; 530/2/26, 41, 42; Testimony of Comrade Nekrasov, 3, 4; Wang, *Shuangshan huiyilu*, pp. 63, 80, 145; *Zheng Chaolin huiyilu*, p. 290; Meng, *Vospominaniya o Van Mine*, p. 69; *Pravda*, November 16, 1927.

105 Interview with Wang Fanxi at Leeds, England, July 25, 1992.

106 See, for example, Wang, *Shuangshan huiyilu*, 64, 80; *Zheng Chaolin huiyilu*, 290; Liu Renjing tan tuoluociji zai Zhongguo" (Liu Renjing on Trotskyists in China), *Zhonggong dangshi ziliao*, 1982, no. 1, p. 248; Ming Yuan, "Qiuxiaopaide xingcheng ji qi molo" (The Rise and Fall of the Group of Liquidationists), *Shehui xinwen* (Social News), 1933, vol. 3, no. 23, p. 323.

107 Calculated from Russian Center, 530/l/42.

108 Ibid., 530/2–32. That in summer 1927 there were no less than fifteen Oppositionists at the university was also mentioned at one of the meetings of the UTK party committee. Ibid., 530/2/26.

109 Ibid., 495/327.

110 No such person as Lu Yen figures in the register of students at UTK.

111 Sheng, *Sun Yat-sen University*, 166.

112 See Russian Center, 495/225/1532, 1816, 2129, 2185, 2226.

113 Ibid., 530/2/26.

114 Ibid., 530/2/41.

115 See Testimony of Comrade Nekrasov, 2.

116 Ibid., 3.

117 Conversation between Comrades Kotelnikov and Khabarov, Russian Center, 514/ 1/1031/13.

118 See Testimony of Comrade Nekrasov, 4–5.

119 Russian Center, 530/l/37.

120 Ibid., 530/2/29.

121 Ibid., 530/2/41.

122 See Statement of Nekrasov to the Purge Commission, ibid., 495/225/362; Conversation between Comrades Kotelnikov and Khabarov, November 21, 1936, ibid., 495/225/1036/12–13.

123 See Minutes no. 9 of the Soviet Communist Party branch bureau at UTK, November 9, 1927. Ibid., 530/2/26.

124 One of the documents referred to states that the Opposition banner had written on it, "Long live the leaders of the world revolution: Zinoviev, Radek, Preobrazhensky, etc." (Russian Center, 530/2/26). Naturally, the word "etc." would never appear on a banner. Most probably, Trotsky's name appeared alongside those of the other "leaders."

125 Russian Center, 530/2/24, 26.

126 Louis Fischer. *Men and Politics: An Autobiography*, New York: Puell, Sloan and Pearce, 1941, p. 88.

127 Vincent Sheean. *A Personal History*. Garden City, N. Y.: Doubleday, Doran & Co., 1935, p. 284.

128 See Minutes no. 8 of the AUCP(B) branch bureau at UTK, November 9, 1927. Russian Center, 530/2/26.

129 Apart from these, Xiao Changbin was also present at the meeting.

130 See Minutes no. 9 of the AUCP(B) branch bureau at UTK, November 9, 1927. Russian Center, 530/2/26.

131 Miller was the pseudonym or Hu Jiansan, a UTK student and member of the party cell bureau.

132 Brandler was the pseudonym of He Shangzhi, a UTK student and member of the party cell bureau.

133 Golubev, i.e., Chen Shaoyu (Wang Ming), was at this time a member of the party cell bureau at UTK.

134 Yevgenii Proletariev was the pseudonym of Bu Shiqi, a translator and teacher at UTK and an alternative member to the party cell bureau.

135 Doronin was the pseudonym of the UTK student Pan Wenyu.

136 Mikhailov was the pseudonym of Xiao Changbin.

137 In fact, Xiao Changbin joined the CCP in December 1925. See Russian Center, 495/225/1963.

138 See Minutes no. 9 of the AUCP(B) branch bureau at UTK, November 9, 1927.

139 Zhu Huaide was a member of both the Party and the Komsomol simultaneously.

140 In reality, of course, there were no real right GMD members left at UTK. This was merely a political label which the administration applied from time to time to those GMD members who remained at the university after the July coup carried out by Wang Jingwei in China.

141 See Russian Center, 530/l/16; *Pravda*, November 16, 1927.

142 See Minutes no. 4 of a Meeting of the UTK Management, November 10, 1927. Russian Center, 530/1.

143 *Pravda*, November 16, 1927.

144 See Extracts from Minutes no. 46 of a Meeting of the Presidium of the Khamovnicheskii District Committee, November 22, 1927. Russian Center, 530/2/24.

145 Ibid., 530/l/42/52, 53, 55, 59, 70.

146 Interview with Wang Fanxi at Leeds, England, August 4, 1992. On the meeting between Trotsky and Liang Ganqiao, see also Pu Qingquan [Pu Dezhi], "Zhongguo tuopaide changsheng he meiwang" (The Birth and Death of the Chinese Trotskyists), *Chen Duxiu pinglun xuanbian* (Collection of Critical Articles on Chen Duxiu), vol. 2, Zhengzhou: Henan renmin chubanshe, 1982, p. 388.

147 Russian Center, 495/225/327.

148 On this, see the letter sent from Vladivostok by Lu Yuan to Chen Qi and Wen Yue, ibid., 530/l/57.

149 See E. M. Landau, *Stranitsi proshlogo* (Pages of the Past). (Manuscript). Moscow, n. d., pp. 125, 131.

150 Testimony of Comrade Nekrasov, 2.

151 There are differing reports concerning Dong Yixiang. In February – March 1930, during the interrogation of Chinese Trotskyists arrested by OGPU, several persons referred to him as "sympathizing" with the Opposition after 1927. See Russian Center, 514/1/1010/53. I am not inclined, however, to believe such information concerning Dong Yixiang, first, because it is not supported by other sources and second, because we have information concerning the close link between him and one of the leaders of the anti-Trotskyist struggle at UTK in 1927, Zhou Dawen. Moreover, there is evidence that the accusation of "Trotskyism" leveled at Dong Yixiang served the purposes of his personal enemies Wang Ming and Pavel Mif, who had once removed him, along with Zhou Dawen, Yu Xiusong, and other UTK students, from leading work in the university party organization and subsequently took any opportunity to settle accounts with them. Finally, Wang Ming, by the end of 1931 the leader of the CCP delegation to the ECCI, engineered the execution in 1938, in the USSR, of Dong Yixiang, Zhou Dawen, and Yu Xiusong as "members of the anti-Soviet bloc of rightists and Trotskyists." In August 1957, they were rehabilitated. On this, see Russian Center, 495/225/932, 1048; Interview with Wang Fanxi at Leeds, England, July 27, 1992.

152 Russian Center, 495/225/1341; 495/225/2411; 505/l/22/13; 530/2/41; 530/2/46; Testimony of Comrade Nekrasov, 6–7; Conversation between Comrades Kotelnikov and Khabarov, 13–14.

153 We can make a judgment on this on the basis that on his return to China (toward October 1929) Xiao Changbin immediately became involved in oppositional activity. See Russian Center, 495/225/2129; 530/246; Wang, *Shuangshan huiyilu*, p. 145.

154 See Testimony of Comrade Nekrasov, 3, 5. We have no information concerning Bei Yunfeng's position. Dong Rucheng left the USSR around this time.

155 Russian Center, 530/2/41.

156 Ibid., 494/225/547; Conversation between Comrades Kotelnikov and Khabarov, 13–14.

157 Russian Center, 530/1/34.

158 Ibid. Feng Fufa, the sister of Feng Hongguo and Feng Funeng, left with them. She also studied at UTK under the pseudonym Sobinova. See also ibid., 495/225/1341, 2034.

159 Ibid., 495/225/56.

160 Wang, *Shuangshan huiyilu*, p. 80.

161 Russian Center, 495/225/2226.

162 According to other sources, admittedly undocumented, one of them was shot crossing the frontier. See Wang, *Shuangshan huiyilu*, p. 139.

163 Russian Center, 514/1/1010/54, 55; 530/1/56.

164 Ibid., 514/1/1010/56; 530/1/56, 57.

165 The former Chinese Trotskyist Pu Dezhi (alias Pu Qingquan) indicated in an article that Xu Yunzuo was active in the Trotskyist organization in China in 1930–31. See Pu, "Zhongguo tuopaide changsheng he meiwang," p. 392. This is patently untrue. As regards Yao Binghui, shortly after his return to China, he was arrested by the GMD secret police and capitulated, going over to the side of the Nationalists. In 1937 he became a secret agent for the GMD guard. Interview with Wang Fanxi at Leeds, England, July 25, 1992.

166 Testimony of Comrade Nekrasov, 10. It is curious that the next time Qi Shugong met Radek, they hardly spoke. "When we met," reports Qi, "he stated that the Soviet Communist Party line was correct, and that he himself had been mistaken. 'There is no point whining on, admitting your mistakes. You just have to rejoin the ranks of the party and carry on with your work'. I didn't manage a reply – he loved to hear his own voice and never listened to others. He was called away somewhere and left, bidding me farewell."

167 See Testimony of Comrade Nekrasov, 6.

168 Russian Center, 532/2/40/108, 109.

169 Ibid., 530/2/26.

170 Ibid.

171 This refers to the disarming in the summer 1927 of working class pickets in Wuhan.

172 Wang, *Shuangshan huiyilu*, p. 57.

173 I have no reason to consider this and other denunciations and statements about Hu Chonggu entirely without foundation. Hu became an active member of the Chinese Trotskyist organization in the USSR.

174 Russian Center, 495/225/543.

175 Ibid.

176 Wang, *Shuangshan huiyilu*, p. 63.

177 Calculated from ibid., 72, 80, 83. Russian Center, 495/225/57, 1100, 1116; 505/1/22/10; 530/1/62; Li Ping, "Yu Mo huiqude fanduipai fenzi, yijiusanshi ba qi" (Oppositionists Returned from Moscow, August 7, 1930), ibid., 530/1/62; Testimony of a Student, 12–13; Testimony of Comrade Nekrasov, 6, 7. Wang Fanxi maintains, however, that "without exaggeration" more than nine-tenths of the students transferred from KUTV to UTK in autumn 1928 were already Trotskyists. See Wang, *Shuangshan huiyilu*, p. 83. This implies a membership of at least 123 which seems completely unbelievable, the more so since there is no documented evidence to support this in the archives. According to other reports, there were about thirty members of the organization in January 1929. See Testimony of a Student, 14.

178 See Russian Center, 495/225/1114, 2129; Testimony of a Student, 14; Wang, *Shuangshan huiyilu*, p. 145.
179 Russian Center, 495/225/1153, 1157, 2050; 530/l/64; Li, "Yu Mo huiqude fanduipai fenzi, yijiusanshi ba qi," 1; Interview with Wang Fanxi at Leeds, England, July 25, 1992.
180 Wang, *Shuangshan huiyilu*, p. 83.
181 Testimony of a Student, 13, 14.
182 From the Testimony of Vitin, Russian Center, 514/l/1012/26.
183 See Record of Communication between the Student Donbasov and a Member of the CCP Delegation, Comrade Deng Zhongxia. Ibid., 514/l/1010/99. From July 1927 to June 1928, Zhao Yanqing attended the military-political course at KUTV under the pseudonym Mamashkin (hence his nickname "Mama" by which he was known at KUTV and UTK/KUTK and as which he is referred to in several memoirs).
184 This probably refers to Radek's article "Sun Yat-sen." See Karl Radek, *Portrety i pamflety* (Portraits and Pamphlets), Moscow and Leningrad: Gosizdat, 1927, pp. 156–64. This work was translated into Chinese and published by UTK during the first half of 1927. It is also very probable that this refers to Radek's article "On the Second Anniversary of Sun Yat-sen's Death."
185 Testimony of a Student, 14.
186 According to various sources, the Chinese Oppositionists had specific hopes regarding Guan Xiangying, going so far as to regard him as their candidate for the post of Central Committee secretary at the forthcoming CCP Congress. See Li, "Yu Mo huiqude fanduipai fenzi, yijiusanshi ba qi," 1, 2.
187 Testimony of a Student, 14; Conversation between Comrades Kotelnikov and Nekrasov, 7; From the Testimony of Vitin, 29; Russian Center, 514/l/1010/51; Wang, *Shuangshan huiyilu*, pp. 90–92; "Liu Renjing tan tuoluocijipai zai Zhongguo," p. 242.
188 Xiang Zhongfa was elected general secretary of the Central Committee at the first plenum of the CCP's Sixth CC.
189 Russian Center, 495/225/3078.
190 "Zayavleniye I. Nemtsova v IKK Kominterna ot 10 iunya 1931 g." (Declaration of I. Nemtsov to the International Control Commission, June 10, 1931), ibid., 495/225/874.
191 "Vypiska iz protokola zasedaniya Sekretariata IKK Kominterna ot 10 iunya 1931 g." (Extracts from the Minutes of the International Control Commission Secretariat, June 10, 1931). Ibid.
192 See Wang, *Shuangshan huiyilu*, p. 91. For Trotsky's "Critics" see Russian Center, 325/1/174/1–115. For the English translation of a part of this article devoted to China ("Summary and Perspectives of the Chinese Revolution") see Evans and Block, *Leon Trotsky on China*, pp. 291–341.
193 An Fu, who mentioned a "Trotskyist Platform" in his testimony, evidently had in mind the "Draft Platform of the Bolshevik Leninists (Opposition) for the Fifteenth Congress of the Communist Party of the Soviet Union (Bolshevik) [The Crisis in the Party and the Way to Overcome It]," which was submitted to the Politburo by thirteen members of the Central Committee in September 1927.
194 From the Testimony of Vitin, 30.
195 See Wu, "The Left Opposition in the Chinese Communist Party" (Part 1), 80. It is curious that, according to An Fu, Maria M. Joffe gave a letter to Liu Renjing to pass on to Trotsky as the former was about to return to China via Europe and intended to visit Trotsky at Prinkipo. See From the Testimony of Vitin, 28. What the letter contained, however, is unknown. The Trotsky archives at Harvard and Liu Renjing's own memoirs record neither its receipt by Liu nor its delivery to Trotsky. Wang Fanxi, who was close to Liu Renjing in the late 1920s and early 1930s, recalls that Liu never mentioned this letter. "Even if such a letter existed," Wang says, "it

was probably some sort of a recommendation, which Joffe might have given to Liu Renjing who had an intention to visit Trotsky. But most likely no letter ever existed. Joffe was a clever woman and would not have sent Trotsky a letter. It was too risky." Interview with Wang Fanxi at Leeds, England, July 27, 1992.

196 See Evans and Block, *Leon Trotsky on China*, pp. 345–397. This article was also well-known among the Chinese Oppositionists.

197 For the first time Trotsky shaped a new tactical line for the CCP in his three letters to Preobrazhensky which were written in March-April 1928 in Alma-Ata, but there are no evidence that the Chinese Oppositionists were familiar with this correspondence. For the first two original letters by Trotsky see Russian Center, 325/1/489/1–2, 5–7. For an English translation of the first one and the huge part of the second one see Evans and Block, *Leon Trotsky on China*, pp. 276–287. The original of the third letter was not found in archives. For an English translation see ibid., pp. 287–290.

198 Ibid., p. 279.

199 Ibid., p. 280.

200 Ibid., p. 356.

201 Apparently per month. See Russian Center, 495/225/2045; Testimony of a Student, 14.

202 See Russian Center, 495/225/1446; 503/1/22/3; Testimony of the Student Lugovoi – Minutes of Interrogation, February 9, 1930, ibid., 514/1/1012/23; Testimony of Comrade Nekrasov, 9.

203 Jiang Hua'an arrived in the USSR at the end of September 1927 and studied on the military-political course at KUTV until the summer of 1928, then until February 1930 at KUTK. His pseudonym was Andrei Vasilievich Namietkin.

204 Russian Center, 495/225/2045.

205 From the Testimony of Vitin, 29; Testimony of the Student Lugovoi, 23.

206 From the Testimony of Vitin, 26; Testimony of a Student, 15.

207 Wang, *Shuangshan huiyilu*, p. 102; Testimony of Comrade Nekrasov, 9–10.

208 Wang, *Shuangshan huiyilu*, p. 102.

209 Ibid., 94–95.

210 See Russian Center, 505/1/22/7; From the Testimony of Vitin, 26; Testimony of a Student, 15–16; Record of Communication between the Student Donbasov and a Member of the CCP Delegation, Comrade Deng Zhongxia, 99.

211 Russian Center, 505/1/22/90; From the Testimony of Vitin, 26; Testimony of a Student, 17.

212 For a stenographical record of this meeting, see Russian Center, 530/1/7071.

213 Ibid., 530/1/56, 64; From the Testimony of Vitin, 26–27, 32–33; Testimony of a Student, 17.

214 See Record of Communication between the Student Donbasov and a Member of the CCP Delegation, Comrade Deng Zhongxia, 99; From the Testimony of Vitin, 26; Testimony of a Student, 16.

215 They were sent as part of a group of twenty-six who left Moscow in four parties on August 13, 14, 16, and 18. Apart from Wang Fanxi, Liu Yin, and Zhao Ji, the group included the following Trotskyists – Wang Xingeng, Gao Heng, Ye Ying (alias Ye Yin, the wife of Wang Fanxi who was known as Nevskaya while studying on the military-political course at KUTV, October 1927–June 1928, and later, at KUTK, had the pseudonym Anna Dunaeva), Li Cailian, Lu Mengyi, Pu Dezhi, Xie Ying, Huang Liewen, Xie Shuda, Jiang Defang, Zhou Qiheng, Zhou Qingchong, and Yuan Fan. See Russian Center, 530/1/56; 530/1/64.

216 See Testimony of a Student, 16; Testimony of the Student Lugovoi, 20–21.

217 From the Testimony of Vitin, 27; Testimony of a Student, 17; Testimony of the Student Lugovoi, 21; Record of Communication between the Student Donbasov and a Member of the CCP Delegation, Comrade Deng Zhongxia, 99.

218 See Testimony of the Student Lugovoi, 22; Russian Center, 495/225/1891.

219 See Testimony of the Student Lugovoi, 21; Testimony of a Student, 16–17.

220 From the Testimony of Vitin, 28; Testimony of a Student, 17; Letter from V. I. Veger to the AUCP(B) CC Addressed to L. M. Kagonovich, A. I. Stetsky; AUCP(B) Moscow Committee, K. Ya. Bauman, Kogan, April 25, 1930," Russian Center, 530/1/71.

221 See List of Trotskyists at the Communist University of the Toilers of China, Russian Center, 514/1/1010/38; List of Chinese Trotskyists in the USSR, ibid., 514/1/1010/44–56.

222 Interview with Wang Fanxi at Leeds, England, July 25, 1992.

223 Testimony of the Student Lugovoi.

224 Record of Communication between the Student Donbasov and a Member of the CCC Delegation, Comrade Deng Zhongxia, 99; Testimony of the Student Lugovoi, 22; From the Testimony of Vitin, 28; Testimony of Comrade Nekrasov, 9–10; Russian Center, 514/1/1010/48, 52, 54; 530/1/62.

225 See Testimony of the Student Lugovoi, 22; Testimony of a Student, 17.

226 Russian Center, 514/1/1010/42, 43.

227 Ibid.

228 Refers to the Chinese Revolutionary Party formed at the start of 1928 in Shanghai on the initiative of Tan Pingshan and some other former Communists. The party raised liberal democratic slogans.

229 "Postanovleniye kitaiskoi kommissii Vostochnogo sekretariata IKKI ot 1 oktyabrya 1929 g." (Resolution of the Chinese Commission of the Eastern Secretariat of the ECCI, October 1, 1929), Russian Center, 530/1/48.

230 "Letter from Veger and Tokin to the Eastern Department of the ECCI," Russian Center, 530/1/56. To be sent to China without a party rendezvous was equivalent to being expelled from the party, with the corresponding loss of the income which went along with the status of a professional Communist revolutionary.

231 Russian Center, 530/1/56.

232 I have discovered three versions of this document. The most complete, entitled "List of Trotskyists," contains information on eighty-one persons. The other two refer to seventy-nine and sixty-eight persons respectively (the last version has pages missing). The lists tally almost perfectly with each other with only a couple of names not matching up. See Russian Center, 514/1/1010/25–35, 77–81, 87–90. The document is not signed. I managed to identify its author by comparing it with other material stored alongside it in the archives. See, for example, Russian Center, 495/225/1106, 1891, 2411.

233 Another commission, chaired by Appen, was set up to assist the Berzin commission shortly after the latter commenced work.

234 Deng Zhongxia, "Nekotoriye soobrazheniya otnositel'no partiinoi chistki vuz[ovskoi] yacheiki v KUTK" (Some Considerations concerning the Party Purge of the College Cell at KUTK), Russian Center, 514/1/1010/1. Deng Zhongxia evidently used a fourth version of the denunciation referred to above: he speaks of seventy-four Trotskyists and "sympathizers."

235 See the list of Chinese students at KUTK who, according to the OGPU, were Trotskyists or Oppositionists linked with them. Russian Center, 514/1/1010/57–66.

236 See Testimony of the Student Lugovoi.

237 Ibid. Sheng Yueh describes the condition of Zhao Yanqing at this time in similar terms. See Sheng, Sun Yat-sen University, pp. 175–76.

238 I have been unable to locate the text of the declaration. As to its existence, see Russian Center, 530/1/71.

239 Interview with Wang Fanxi at Leeds, England, July 25, 1992.

240 Russian Center, 530/1/75.

241 Sheng, Sun Yat-sen University, p. 175.

242 Russian Center, 530/1/71.

243 Wang Fanxi writes that Zhao Yanqing betrayed between 200 and 300 Chinese Trotskyists. (See his Shuangshan huiyilu, p. 111). This, however, could not be true since there were simply not that many Chinese Trotskyists in the USSR.

244 See Members of the Trotskyist Organization at KUTK (according to Donbasov), Russian Center, 514/l/1010/17; List of Trotskyist students at KUTK named by the student Donbasov in His Testimony and Statements, ibid., 18; Supplement, ibid., 80; Record of Communication between the Student Donbasov and a Member of the CCP Delegation, Comrade Deng Zhongxia, 99.

245 See Supplement, 80; Record of Communication between the Student Donbasov and a Member of the CCP Delegation, Comrade Deng Zhongxia, 99.

246 Russian Center, 514/l/1010/46.

247 Sheng, *Sun Yat-sen University*, p. 176.

248 Ibid., 176–77; Testimony of the Student Lugovoi, 24.

249 See Testimony of a Student, 17–18.

250 See OGPU on the List of Students Arrested at KUTK, Russian Center, 514/1/1010/36–37; 530/l/62; List of those arrested by the OGPU on February 8 and 19, 1930, ibid., 514/l/1010/73–74; ibid., 495/225/1100.

251 Sheng Yueh later described how some of these interrogations were conducted (during this period he acted as translator for one of the investigators). See Sheng, *Sun Yat-sen University*, pp. 178–80. On the life of Chinese Trotskyists in Soviet prisons, see Ma Yuansheng, *Liu Su jishi* (Notes on Life in the USSR), Beijing: Qunzhong chubanshe, 1987, pp. 124–44; Tang Youzhang, *Geming yu liufang* (Revolution and Exile), Changsha: Hunan renmin chubanshe, 1988.

252 List of Chinese Trotskyists in the USSR, 44–56.

253 See List of Foreign Trotskyist Addresses and Rendezvous in China, Russian Center, 514/l/1010/91; List of Trotskyists in China, ibid., pp. 92–97; List of Trotskyists who were Former Members of the Party Cell at KUTK, ibid., 530/l/39; Li, "Yu Mo huiqude fanduipai fenzi, yijiusanshi ba qi," 1; Testimony of the Student Lugovoi, 23.

254 See Qu Weituo [Qu Qiubai] and Deng Zhongxia, "Nashe mneniye o KUTK" (Our Views on KUTK), sent to the ECCI, AUCP(B) CC, and CCP CC from the CCP Delegation to the ECCI, Russian Center, 530/1/68.

255 Five persons were deported from the USSR, including Bian Fulin and Wang Wenhui.

256 See Russian Center, 505/1/22/2–14; 505/2/23; 514/1/1010/36–37; 530/l/62.

257 See Minutes no. 1 of the meeting of the commission examining the activities of Chinese students at KUTK, concerning the purge relating to the fifth group, June 26, 1930. Ibid., 505/l/23.

258 See OGPU on the List of Students Arrested at KUTK, 36–37; Supreme Court of the USSR, Ruling no. 4N-013598/57, Russian Center, 495/225/1100; ibid., 495/225/ 543; 495/225/1106, 1116, 1384, 2045.

259 Characteristics of the KUTK students sent to work in industry, ibid., 530/1/73.

260 The hostel was located at no. 51 Ulitsa Herzena (Herzen Street).

261 See Russian Center, 514/1/1014/1–15.

262 What became of the majority of former members of the Chinese Trotskyist organization active in the USSR is unknown. We do, however, know a few facts about some of them. For example, Qiu Zhicheng and Hu Pengju managed to escape from the USSR, in 1933 and 1934 respectively, but sometime between 1937 and 1939 they were arrested by the Xinjiang government (apparently they were then shot). Of those who were subject to repression, fifteen persons were finally rehabilitated on March 8, 1958. Their names were: Liu Hesheng, Li Zibai, Zhao Yifan, Liu Hanping, Rong Li, Jiang Hua'an, Zhang Chongde, Li Shile, Wang Wenhui, Li Weimin, Jin Hongdi, Chen Fang, Cheng Bing, and also Qiu Zhicheng and Hu Pengju (who were partially rehabilitated). It is unclear which, if any, of them was still alive at the time of their rehabilitation. According to the information in the archives, we can be sure of the survival through it all of less than ten persons, who included Wan Zhiling and Fan Wenhui. This was despite the fact that the former was arrested and sentenced three times and the latter twice. In 1955 Fan

Wenhui and his family were finally allowed to leave the USSR for the People's Republic of China. And in 1956 Wan Zhiling and several other former Chinese Trotskyists left for the PRC. See Russian Center, 495/225/1018, 1116; Supreme Court of the USSR, Ruling no. 4N-013598/57.

Conclusion

1 See in detail M. A. Persits, *Zastenchivaya interventsiya. O sovetskom vtorzhenii v Iran. 1920–1921 gg.* (A Shamefaced Intervention. On the Soviet Invasion of Iran. 1920–1921), Moscow: "AIRO-XX", 1996.

2 See Report no. 1 of the Secretariat of the CCP Left Opposition to the International Secretariat of International Left Opposition and L. D. Trotsky, May 9, 1931, Trotsky Papers, bMs Russ, 13.1, 1068, p. 1.

Bibliography

Primary Sources

Archival Sources

Russian Center for the Preservation and Study of Records of Modern History (RTsKhIDNI, Russian Center)

Collection 5, Inventory 2, Secretary of Chairman of Council of People's Commissars and Council of Labor and Defense Vladimir Ilich Lenin: 1917–1923: Documents on Party and Public Activity of Vladimir Ilich Lenin.

Collection 17, Inventory 2, Plenums of the Central Committee of RCP(B) and AUCP(B): 1918–1941.

Collection 17, Inventory 3, Minutes of Sessions of the Politburo of the Central Committee of RCP(B) and AUCP(B): 1919–1941.

Collection 17, Inventory 20, Department of Leading Party Organs: Sector of the Information: Party organizations of Russia: 1926–1937.

Collection 17, Inventory 71, Documents of the Internal Opposition in the AUCP(B). (1921–1937.)

Collection 17, Inventory 85, Secret Department of the AUCP(B) CC: 1918–1926.

Collection 324, Grigorii Evseevich Zinoviev.

Collection 325, Leon Davidovich Trotsky.

Collection 326, Karl Bengardovich Radek.

Collection 492, The Fifth Congress of the Communist International.

Collection 495, Inventory 3, Political Secretariat of the Executive Committee of the Communist International.

Collection 495, Inventory 65a, Personal Files of Employees of the Executive Committee of the Communist International Apparatus.

Collection 495, Inventory 154, Eastern Secretariat of the Executive Committee of the Communist International.

Collection 495, Inventory 163, The Fifth Enlarged Plenum of the Executive Committee of the Communist International.

Collection 495, Inventory 164, The Sixth Enlarged Plenum of the Executive Committee of the Communist International.

Collection 495, Inventory 165, The Seventh Enlarged Plenum of the Executive Committee of the Communist International.

Collection 495, Inventory 166, The Eighth Plenum of the Executive Committee of the Communist International.

Collection 495, Inventory 225, Personal Files of the Members of the Chinese Communist Party.

Collection 505, International Control Commission of the Communist International.

Collection 508, Delegation of the AUCP(B) to the Executive Committee of the Communist International.

Collection 514, The Central Committee of the Chinese Communist Party.

Collection 530, The Communist University of the Toilers of China.

Collection 532, The Communist University of the Toilers of the East and the Research Institute of National and Colonial Problems.

Collection 558, Joseph Vissarionovich Stalin.

Collection 589, Inventory 3, Committee of Party Control at the Central Committee of the Communist Party of the Soviet Union (1952 – 1991): Personal Files of Communists.

Collection of N. Tolmachev Military Political Academy.

Collection of non-filed documents.

State Archive of the Russian Federation
(GARF, State Archives)
Collection 3415, The Communist Academy.
Collection 5402, Mikhail Pavlovich Pavlovich.

Archive of the Russian Academy of Sciences
(ARAN)
Collection 350, The Communist Academy.
Collection 354, Institute of World Economy and International Politics of the Communist Academy.
Collection 377, Society of Historians-Marxists.

Former Party Archive of Sverdlov Oblast
(PASO)
Collection 10, Organizational and Distributive Department.
Collection 153, The Ural Machine Plant.
Collection 161, The Ural Machine Plant's Newspaper *Za tyazheloye mashinostroeniye* (For Heavy Mechanical Engineering).

The Houghton Library at Harvard University
Trotsky Papers.

Bureau of Investigation of the Ministry of Legislation on Taiwan
Miscellaneous papers on Chinese Communist movement.

Private archives
Archives of Meng Qingshu.
 Meng Qingshu. *Vospominaniya o Van Mine* (Memoirs of Wang Ming). (Manuscript). Moscow, n. d.
Archives of Wang Fanxi.
 Miscellaneous papers.
Archives of Ephraim Moiseevich Landau.
 Landau, E. M. *Stranitsy proshlogo* (Pages of the Past). (Manuscript). Moscow, n. d.
Archives of Yuri Felshtinsky.
 Trotsky, Leon. *Tretii Internatsional posle Lenina* (The Third International After Lenin). Ed. Yuri Felshtinsky. (Manuscript).

Printed Documents

The Bolsheviki and World Peace. New York: Boni & Liverwright Publ., 1918.

Bukharin, N. I. *Izbranniye proizvedeniya* (Selected Works). Moscow: Poiltizdat, 1988.

——. *Partiya i oppozitsionnyi blok: Doklad aktivu Leningradskoi organizatsii VKP(b) 28 iyulya 1926 g.* (The Party and the Oppositionist Bloc: Presentation to a Meeting of the Leningrad AUCP(B) Branch, July 28, 1926). Leningrad: Priboi, [1926].

——. *Problemy kitaiskoi revolyutsii* (Problems of the Chinese Revolution). Moscow: Pravda, 1927.

——. *Problemy kitaiskoi revolyutsii* (Problems of the Chinese Revolution). In *Voprosy kitaiskoi revolyutsii* (Questions of the Chinese Revolution). Moscow-Leningrad: Gosizdat, 1927, pp. 57–122.

——. "Tekushchii moment kitaiskoi revolyutsii" (The Current Moment in the Chinese Revolution). *Pravda* (The Truth). June 30, 1927.

Chen Duxiu, "Shehuizhuyi piping" ("Critiques of Socialism"). *Xin qingnian* (New Youth). 1921, vol. 9, no. 3, pp. 1–13.

Chen Duxiu wenzhang xuanbian (Selected Articles of Chen Duxiu). 2 vols. Beijing: Shenghuo, dushu, xinzhi sanlian shudian, 1984.

D'Encausse, Hélène Carrère and Stuart R. Schram, eds. *Marxism and Asia.* London: The Penguin Press, 1969.

Degras, Jane, ed. *The Communist International: 1919–1943: Documents.* 3 vols. London: Oxford University Press, 1960.

II Congres de la III Internationale Compte Rendu Stenographique, Petrograd, 17 juillet, Moscou 23 juillet – 7 aout 1920. Petrograd: Edition de l'International Communiste, 1920.

"Disan guoji dierci dahui guanyu minzu yu zhimindi wentide yi'an" (Resolution of the Second Congress of the Third International on National and Colonial Questions). *Xin qingnian.* 1924, no. 4, pp. 67–74.

Disan guoji yi'an ji xuanyan (Resolutions and Manifestos of the Third International). Guangzhou: Renmin chubanshe, 1922.

Disan guoji yi'an ji xuanyan (Resolutions and Manifestos of the Third International). 3rd ed. Guangzhou: Renmin chubanshe, 1926.

"Doklad tov. L. D. Trotskogo na VI gubernskom s"ezde tekstilshchikov 29 yanvarya 1926 g." (Comrade L. D. Trotsky's Speech at the Sixth Gubernia Congress of Textile Workers, January 19, 1926). *Pravda.* January 31, 1926.

Dokumenty vneshnei politiki SSSR (Documents of Foreign Policy of the USSR). Vol. 6. Moscow: Gospolitzdat, 1962.

Eudin, Xenia J. and Robert C. North. *Soviet Russian and the East: 1920–1927: A Documentary Survey.* Stanford: Stanford University Press, 1957.

Evans, Les and Russell Block, eds. *Leon Trotsky on China.* New York: Monad, 1976.

Felshtinsky, Yuri, ed. *Kommunisticheskaya Oppozitsiya v SSSR: 1923–1927: Iz Arkhiva L'va Trotskogo* (The Communist Opposition in the USSR: 1923–1927: from Leon Trotsky's Archives). 4 vols. Benson, VT: Chalidze Publ., 1988.

Gao Jun et al., eds., *Zhongguo xiandai zhengzhi sixiang shi ziliao xuanji* (A Collection of Historical Documents Concerning Political Ideologies of Modern China). 2 vols. Chengdu: Sichuan renmin chubanshe, 1986.

"Godovshchina smerti Sun Yat-sena. (Vystupleniye L. D. Trotskogo i drugikh deyatelei VKP(b) na mitinge, posvyashchennom godovshchine so dnya smerti Sun Yat-sena)" (Sun Yat-sen Death Anniversary. [L. D. Trotsky's Speech and Speeches of Other AUCP(B) Activists at a Meeting Commemorated to the Anniversary of Sun Yat-sen Death]). *Pravda.* March 14, 1926.

"Gongchandang zai Guomindang neide gongzuo wenti yijuean" (Statement on the Question of CP work in the GMD). *Dangbao* (Party Newspaper). 1924, no. 3. pp. 1–3.

Gongchanzhuyi xiaozu (Communist nuclei). 2 vols. Beijing: Zhonggong dangshi ziliao chubanshe, 1987.

"Guomindang yi da dangwu baogao xuanzai" (Selected Reports on Party Affairs, Submitted to the First Guomindang Congress). *Geming shi ziliao* (Materials on the Revolutionary History). 1986, no. 2, pp. 28–35.

Ho Chi Minh, ed. *Zhongguo yu Zhongguo qingnian* (China and Chinese Youth). Moscow: KUTV Press, 1923.

"Imperialisticheskaya interventsiya i grazhdanskaya voina v Kitaye. Doklad t. Radeka v Bolshom teatre" (Imperialist Intervention and Civil War in China. Comrade Radek's Report at Bolshoi Theater). In *Kitai v ogne voiny* (China in the Fire of War). Moscow: "Rabochaya Moskva," 1924, pp. 23–61.

Isaacs, Harold, "Documents on the Comintern and the Chinese Revolution." *The China Quarterly*. 1971, no. 45, pp. 103–112.

Joffe, A. A. "Pis'mo L. D. Trotskomu ot 10 noyabrya 1927 g." (Letter to L. D. Trotsky, November 10, 1927). In Leon Trotsky. *Portrety* (Portraits). Benson, VT: Chalidze Publ., 1984, pp. 229–241.

Kamenev L. B., ed. *Leninskii sbornik* (Lenin Collection). Vol. XXXVIII. Moscow: Politizdat, 1975.

Kongress Kommunisticheskoi partii v Kitaye (Congress of the Communist Party in China). *Narody Azii i Afriki* (Peoples of Asia and Africa). 1972, no. 6, pp. 151–155.

Kosheleva, L. et al., eds. *Pis'ma I. V. Stalina V. I. Molotovu: 1925–1936 gg.: Sbornik Dokumentov* (J. V. Stalin's Letters to V. I. Molotov: 1925–1936: A Collection of Documents). Moscow: Rossiya Molodaya, 1995.

Kun, Bela, ed. *Komintern v rezolyutsiyakh* (The Comintern in Resolutions). 2nd ed. Moscow: Ya. M. Sverdlov Communist University Press, 1926.

——, ed. *Kommunisticheskii Internatsional v dokumentakh: Resheniya, tezisy i vozzvaniya kongressov Kominterna i plenumov IKKI. 1919 – 1932* (The Communist International in Documents: Decisions, Theses and Statements of Congresses of the Comintern and Plenums of the ECCI. 1919 – 1932). Moscow: Partizdat, 1933.

Lenin lun dongfang geming (Lenin on the Revolutions in the East). Moscow: KUTK Press, 1929.

Lenin lun minzu zhimindi wenti (Lenin on National and Colonial Questions). N.p.: Jiefangshe, 1946.

Lenin, N. (Ulyanov V.) *Sobraniye sochinenii* (Collected Works). Vol. XIX: *Natsional'nyi vopros (1919–1920 gg.)* (National Question [1919–1920]). Moscow: Gosizdat, 1921.

Lenin, N. and Leon Trotzky. *The Proletarian Revolution in Russia*. New York: The Communist Press Publ., [1918].

Lenin, V. I. *Collected Works*. 45 vols. Moscow: Foreign Languages Publ. House/Progress Publ., 1963–1977.

——. "Politicheskii otchet TsK RKP(b): Stenogramma vystupleniya na IX Vserossiiskoi konferentsii RKP(b), 22 sentyabrya 1920 g." (Political Report of the RCP(B) CC: Stenogram of the Presentation at the Ninth All-Russia Conference of the RCP(B), September 22, 1920). *Istoricheskii arkhiv* (Historical Archives). 1992, no. 1, pp. 14–27.

——. *Polnoye sobraniye sochinenii* (Complete Collected Works). 55 vols. Moscow: Politizdat, 1963–1978.

——. *Sochineniya* (Collected Works). 3rd ed. Vol. XXV: *1920*. Moscow: Partizdat TsK VKP(b), 1937.

——. "Zaklyuchitel'noye slovo v preniyakh po Politicheskomu otchetu TsK RKP(b) na vtorom zasedanii IX Vserosiiskoi konferentsii RKP(b): 22 sentyabrya 1920 g." (Concluding Speech During the Debates on the Political Report of the RCP(B) CC at the Second Session of the Ninth All-Russia Conference of the RCP(B), September 22, 1920). *Istoricheskii arkhiv*. 1992, no. 1, pp. 27–29.

Li Da. "Makesi huanyun" (Marx's Revival). *Xin qingnian*, 1921. Vol. 8, no. 5, pp. 1–8.

Li Dazhao. *Izbranniye proizvedeniya* (Selected Works). Moscow: Nauka, 1989.

Li Dazhao wenji (Collected Works of Li Dazhao). 2 Vols. Beijing: Renmin chubanshe, 1984.

Lih, Lars T. et al., eds. *Stalin's Letters to Molotov. 1925–1936*. New Haven and London: Yale University Press, 1995.

Liu Fa qingong jianxue yundong (The "Diligent Work and Economical Study" Movement in France). 2 vols. Shanghai: Shanghai renmin chubanshe, 1986.

Makesi zai Zhongguo – cong yingxiang chuanru dao chuanbo (Marxism in China – From the Ideological Penetration to the Spread). Vol. 1. Beijing: Qinghua daxue chubanshe, 1983.

Mao Zedong, "'Qida' gongzuo fangzhen" (The Seventh Congress's Course of Work). *Hongqi* (Red Banner). 1981, no. 11, pp. 1–7.

Maring, H. "Revolyutsionno-natsionalisticheskoye dvizheniye na yuge Kitaya" (The Revolutionary National Movement in Southern China). *Kommunisticheskii Internatsional* (The Communist International). 1922, no. 22, pp. 5803–5816.

Martynov, A. "Komintern pered sudom likvidatorov" (The Comintern Before the Court of the Liquidationists). *Kommunisticheskii Internatsional*. 1927, no. 30, pp. 9–21.

——. "Problema kitaiskoi revolyutsii" (A Problem of the Chinese Revolution). *Pravda*. April 10, 1927.

Meijer, J., ed. *The Trotsky Papers: 1917–1922*. 2 vols. London, The Hague, Paris: Mouton, 1971.

Mif, Pavel, ed. *Strategiya i taktika Kominterna v natsional'no-kolonial'noi revolyutsii na primere Kitaya* (Strategy and Tactics of the Comintern in the National and Colonial Revolution on China's Example). Moscow: IWEIP Press, 1934.

Mosike Zhongshan daxue "Guoji pinglun" (1926–1927) (Moscow Zhongshan [Sun Yat-sen] University's *Guoji pinglun* [1926–1927]). Beijing: Zhonggong zhongyang dangxiao chubanshe, 1981.

"Na trudnom perevale – ot gomindana k sovetam" (On the Difficult Passing – from the Guomindang towards Soviets). *Kommunisticheskii Internatsional* (The Communist International). 1927, no. 41 (115), pp. 3–7.

North, Robert and Xenia Eudin, *M. N. Roy's Mission to China: The Communist-Kuomintang Split of 1927*. Berkeley: University of California Press, 1963.

"Minquan yundong datongmeng xuanyan" (The Declaration of the Alliance of Movements for Republicanism). *Xianqu* (Pioneer). 1922, no. 20, pp. 1–2.

"Minzu yu zhimindi wenti. Lenin zai dierci guoji dahui zhi yanshuo (National and Colonial Questions. Lenin's Speech on the Second Congress of the International). *Xin qingnian* (New Youth). 1924, no. 4, pp. 63–67.

O kitaiskoi revolyutsii: Stat'ya N. Bukharina i postanovleniye IKKI (On the Chinese Revolution: N. Bukharin's Article and the ECCI Resolution). Irkutsk: APO Irk. Okruzhkoma of the AUCP(B), 1927.

"Pis'mo G. E. Zinovieva N. K. Krupskoi ot 16 maya 1927 g." (Letter from G. E. Zinoviev to N. K. Krupskaya, May 16, 1927). *Izvestiya TsK KPSS* (News of the CPSU CC). 1989, no. 2, pp. 206–207.

"Pis'mo L. D. Trotskogo chlenam Tsentral'nogo Komiteta i Tsentral'noi Kontrol'noi Komissii RKP(b) ot 8 oktyabrya 1923 g." (Letter from L. D. Trotsky to Members of the RCP(B) Central Committee and the Central Control Committee, October 8, 1923). *Izvestiya TsK KPSS*. 1990, no. 5, pp. 165–175.

"Politicheskaya fizionomiya russkoi oppozitsii. (Iz rechi tov. Stalina na ob"edinennom zasedanii Prezidiuma IKKI i IKK 27 sentyabrya 1927 g.)" (The Political Physiognomy of the Russian Opposition. (From the Speech of Comrade Stalin at the Joint Session of the ECCI Presidium and the ICC, September 27, 1927). *Kommunisticheskii Internatsional*. 1927, no. 41 (115), pp. 10–24.

Protokoll des Vierten der Kommunistischen Internationale: Petrograd, Moskau vom 5. November bis 5. December 1922. Hamburg: Verlag Der Kommunistischen Internationale, 1923.

Puti mirovoi revolyutsii. Sed'moi rasshirennyi plenum Ispolnitel'nogo Komiteta Kommunisticheskogo Internatsionala. 22 noyabrya – 16 dekabrya 1926 g. Stenograficheskii otchet (Ways of the World Revolution. The Seventh Enlarged Plenum of the Communist

International Executive Committee. November 22 – December 16, 1926. Stenographic Record). 2 vols. Moscow-Leningrad: Gosizdat, 1927.

XV konferentsiya Vsesoyuznoi Kommunisticheskoi partii (b): 26 oktyabrya – 3 noyabrya: Stenograficheskii otchet (The Fifteenth Conference of the All-Union Communist Party [B]): October 26 – November 3, 1926: Stenographic Record. Moscow-Leningrad: Gosizdat, 1927.

XV kongress Vsesoyuznoi Kommunisticheskoi partii (b): Stenograficheskii otchet (The Fifteenth Conference of the All-Union Communist Party [Bolsheviks]): Stenographic Record. Moscow-Leningrad: Gosizdat, 1928.

Pyatyi Vsemirnii kongress Kommunisticheskogo Internatsionala. 17 iyunya – 8 iyulya 1924 goda. Stenograficheskii otchet (The Fifth World Congress of the Communist International. June 17 – July 8, 1924. Stenographic Record. 2 vols. Moscow-Leningrad: Gosizdat, 1925.

Radek, Karl. "Chto nado govorit' krest'yanstvu o kitaiskoi revolyutsii" (What Needs to Be Said to the Peasantry About the Chinese Revolution). *Sputnik Agitatora (Dlya Derevni)* (An Agitator's Companion [For the Countryside]). 1925, no. 2 (21), pp. 19–24.

——. "Istoricheskoye znacheniye shanhaiskikh sobytii. (Vmesto predisloviya)" (Historical Meaning of the Shanghai Events. [In Lieu of a Preface]). In Pavel Mif. *Uroki shankhaiskikh sobytii* (Lessons of the Shanghai Events). Moscow: Gosizdat, 1926, pp. 3–6.

——. *Istoriya revolutsionnogo dvizheniya v Kitaye. Kurs 1926–27 gg.* (History of the Revolutionary Movement in China. A course given in 1926–27). Lectures 1–17, Moscow: UTK Press, 1926–1927.

——. "Lenin i kitaiskaya revolyutsiya" (Lenin and the Chinese Revolution). *Pravda.* January 21, 1927.

——. "Mezhdunarodnoye obozreniye. Itogi shanhaiskikh sobytii" (International Survey. Balance Sheet of the Shanghai Events). *Izvestiya.* October 11, 1925.

——. "Novy etap v kitaiskoi revolyutsii" (A New Period in the Chinese Revolution). *Novy Mir.* 1927, no. 3, pp. 146–159.

——. "Porazheniye narodnykh armii v Kitaye" (Defeat of the People's Armies in China). *Pravda.* March 26, 1926.

——. "Shanhai pal" (Shanghai Has Fallen). *Izvestiya.* March 22, 1927.

——. "Sotsial'no-politicheskiye idei Sun Yat-sena" (The Social and Political Ideas of Sun Yat-sen). *Pravda.* March 12, 1926.

——. "Sun Yat-sen." In Karl Radek. *Portrety i pamflety* (Portraits and Pamphlets). Moscow-Leningrad: Gosizdat, 1927.

——. "Vo vtoruyu godovshchinu smerti Sun Yatsena" (On the Second Anniversary of Sun Yat-sen's Death). *Izvestiya.* March 11, 15, 1927.

——. "Voprosy kitaiskoi revolyutsii" (Questions of the Chinese Revolution). *Krasnyi Internatsional Profsoyuzov* (Red International of Labor Unions). 1925, no. 10, pp. 26–42.

——. "Voprosy kitaiskoi revolyutsii" (Questions of the Chinese Revolution). In Karl Radek, ed. *Voprosy kitaiskoi revolyutsii. Tom 1: Polozheniye proletariata i razvitiye rabochego dvizheniya* (Questions of the Chinese Revolution. Vol. 1: Conditions of the Proletariat and Development of the Workers' Movement). Moscow-Leningrad: Gospolitizdat, 1927.

——. "Vozhd' kitauskogo naroda" (A Leader of the Chinese People). *Pravda.* March 14, 1925.

——. "Zhizn' i delo Sun Yat-sena" (The Life and Work of Sun Yat-sen). In Sergei Dalin, *V ryadakh kitaiskoi revolyutsii* (In the Ranks of the Chinese Revolution). Moscow-Leningrad: Moskovskii rabochii, 1926.

"Rech t. Radeka" (Comrade Radek's Speech). In *Ruki proch ot Kitaya!* [Hands off China!]). Moscow: Gosizdat, 1924, pp. 3–22.

"Rech tov. Stalina na V Vsesoyuznoi konferentsii VLKSM 29 marta 1927 g." (Comrade Stalin's Speech Delivered at the Fifth All-Union Conference of the AULCLY). *Pravda.* March 31, 1927.

"Revolyutsiya v Kitaye i gomindan" (The Revolution in China and the Guomindang). *Pravda*. March 16, 1927.

Rezolyutsii i ustav Kommunisticheskogo Internatsionala, prinyatye Vtorym kongressom Kommunisticheskogo Internatsionala (19–go iyulya – 7–go avgusta 1920 g.) (Resolutions and Charter of the Communist International, Adopted by the Second Congress of the Communist International [July 19 – August 7, 1920]). Petrograd: The Communist International Press, n. p.

"Rezolyutsiya Prezidiuma IKKI po voprosu o natsional'no-osvoboditel'nom dvizhenii v Kitaye i o partii gomindan" (The Resolution of the ECCI Presidium Concerning the National Liberation Movement in China and the Guomindang). *Kommunist* (The Communist). 1969, no. 4, pp. 12–14.

[Roy, M. N.] "Manifest revolyutsionnoi partii Indii: Vozzvaniye k britanskomu proletariatu" (Manifesto of the Revolutionary Party of India: The Appeal to the British Proletariat). *Zhizn' national'nostei* (Life of the Nationalities). July 26, 1920.

——. "Revolyutsionnoiye dvizheniye v Indii" (The Revolutionary Movement in India). *Kommunisticheskii Internatsional*. 1920, no. 12, pp. 2163–2172.

Saich, Tony. *The Origins of the First United Front in China: The Role of Sneevliet (Alias Maring)*. 2 vols. Leiden: Brill, 1991.

——, ed. *The Rise to Power of the Chinese Communist Party. Documents and Analysis*. Armonk: M. E. Sharpe, 1996.

The Second Congress of the Communist International: Proceedings of Petrograd Session of July 17 and Moscow Session of July 19 – August 7, 1920. Moscow: Publ. Office of the Communist International, 1920.

Shanghai daxue shiliao (Historical Materials on Shanghai University). Shanghai: Fudan daxue chubanshe, 1984.

Shanghai diqu jiandang huodong yanjiu ziliao (Study Documents on Party-Building Activity in Shanghai District). Shanghai: Shanghai shi diyi renmin jincha xuexiao, 1986.

Shao Piaoping. *Xin Eguozhi yanjiu* (A Study of New Russia). n. p.: Riben daban nanqu dongying bianyishe, 1920.

Shehuizhuyi sixiang zai Zhongguo chuanbo (ziliao xuanji) (Spread of Socialist Ideas in China. [Selected Documents]). Vol. 1. [Beijing]: Zhongguo zhongyang dangxiao keyan bangongshe, 1985.

Shestoi rasshirenyi plenum Ispolkoma Kominterna (17 fevralya – 15 marta 1926 g.): Stenograficheskii otchet (The Sixth Enlarged Plenum of the Executive Committee of the Communist International [February 17 – March 15, 1926]: Stenographic Record). Moscow-Leningrad: Gospolitzdat, 1927.

Shi Cuntong, "Makeside gongchanzhuyi" (Marx's Communism). *Xin qingnian*. 1921, vol. 9, no. 4, pp. 1–11.

——. "Women yao zemyang gan shehui geming" (How We Will Carry Out a Social Revolution"). *Gongchandang* (The Communist). 1921, no. 5, p. 5–13.

Shiik, A. A., ed. *Rezolyutsii II-go kongressa Kominterna* (Resolutions of the Second Congress of the Comintern). Moscow: KUTK Press, 1928. (In Chinese.)

Shirinya, K. K. et al., ed. *V. I. Lenin i Kommunisticheskii Internatsional* (V. I. Lenin and the Communist International). Moscow: Politizdat, 1970.

Sovetsko-kitaiskiye otnosheniya: 1917 – 1957 (Soviet-Chinese Relations: 1917 – 1957: A Collection of Documents). Moscow: Oriental Literature Press, 1959.

Stalin J. V. *Works*. 13 vols. Moscow: Foreign Languages Publ., 1954.

Stenograficheskii otchet VI s"ezda Kommunisticheskoi partii Kitaya (Stenographic Record of the Sixth Congress of the Chinese Communist Party). 6 books. Moscow: Institute of Chinese Studies Press, 1930.

Sun Yatsen. *Izbranniye proizvedeniya* (Selected Works). 2nd supplemented and revised ed. Moscow: Nauka, 1985.

Tan Pingshan. *Puti razvitiya kitaiskoi revolyutsii* (Directions of Development of the Chinese Revolution). Moscow-Leningrad: Gosizdat, 1927.

Titarenko, M. L., ed. *Kommunisticheskii Internatsional i kitaiskaya revolyutsiya: Dokumenty i materialy* (The Communist International and the Chinese Revolution: Documents and Materials). Moscow: Nauka, 1986.

—— et al., eds. *VKP(b), Komintern i natsional'no-revolyutsionnoye dvizheniye v Kitaye: Dokumenty* (AUCP(B), the Comintern and the National Revolutionary Movement in China: Documents). 2 vols. Moscow: AO "Buklet", 1994, 1996.

"Tov. Stalin o politicheskikh zadachakh Universiteta narodov Vostoka. (Rech na sobranii studentov KUTV 18 maya 1925 goda)" (Comrade Stalin on Political Tasks of the University of the Peoples of the East. [Speech at a Meeting of the KUTV Students, May 18, 1925]). *Pravda*, May 22, 1925.

Trotsky, Leon. *The Bolsheviki and World Peace*. New York: Boni and Livewright Publ., 1918.

——. *The First Five Years of the Communist International*. 2 vols. New York: Pioneer Publ., 1945.

——. *History of the Russian Revolution to Brest-Litovsk*. London: Leo and Unwin Publ., 1919.

——. *Itogi i perspektivy. Dvizhushchiye sily revolutsii* (Results and Prospects. Motive Forces of the Revolution). Moscow: "Sovetskii mir", 1919.

——. *K sotsializmu ili kapitalizmu? (Analiz sovetskogo khozyaistva i tendentsii ego razvitiya)* (Towards Socialism or Capitalism? [An Analysis of the Soviet Economy and the Directions of Its Development]). 2nd ed. Moscow, "Planovoye Khozyaistvo", 1926.

——. "Moskovskii dukh" (The "Moscow Spirit"). *Pravda*, June 6, 1925.

——. "Mysli o partii" (Thoughts About the Party). *Pravda*, March 20, 1923.

——. *Novy Kurs* (The New Course). Moscow: "Krasnaya nov'", 1924.

——. *Problems of the Chinese Revolution*. New York: Pioneer Publ., 1962.

——. *Problems of the Chinese Revolution*. 2nd ed. Ann Arbor: University of Michigan Press, 1962.

——. *Pyat' let Kominterna* (Five Years of the Comintern). 2nd ed. Moscow-Leningrad: Gosizdat, 1925.

——. *Schriften*. Bd. 2: *Über China*. 2 Parts. [Hamburg]: Rasch und Rohring, 1990.

——. *Sochineniya* (Collected Works). Vol. III, part 1. Moscow: Gosizdat, 1924.

——. "Sovetsko-yaponskiye vzaimootnosheniya. Interv'yu, dannoye t. Trotskim predsedatelyu o[bshchest]va Nichiro Soofukai tov. Tomizi Naito" (Soviet-Japanese Mutual Relations. An Interview Given by Comrade Trotsky to Chairman of Society "Nichiro Soofukai" Comrade Tomizi Naito). *Pravda*, June 18, 1924.

——. "SSSR i Yaponiya (interv'yu korrespondentu 'Osoka Mainiti', 24 aprelya 1924 goda) (The USSR and Japan [An Interview with a Correspondent of *Osoka Mainiti*, April 24, 1924]). *Izvestiya*. April 24, 1924.

——. "SSSR na storone ugnetennogo Kitaya" (The USSR is on the Side of Oppressed China). *Pravda*. September 23, 1924.

——. "Stalin i kitaiskaya revolyutsiya: Fakty i dokumenty" (Stalin and the Chinese Revolution: Facts and Documents), *Byulleten oppozitsii (bol'shevikov-lenintsev)* (Bulletin of the Opposition [Bolshevik Leninists]). 1930, nos. 15–16, pp. 7–19.

——. "Zadachi XII s"ezda RKP (Doklad t. Trotskogo na zasedanii VII Vseukrainskoi konferentsii 5 aprelya 1923 g.)" (Tasks of the Twelfth RCP Congress [Comrade Trotsky's Report at a Session of the Seventh All-Ukrainian Conference, April 5, 1923]). *Pravda*, April 11, 12, 1923.

——. *Zapad i Vostok. Voprosy mirovoi politiki i mirovoi revolutsii* (West and East. Questions of World Politics and the World Revolution). Moscow: Gosizdat, 1924.

Trotsky, N. *Nashi politicheskiye zadachi. Takticheskiye i organizatsionniye voprosy* (Our Political Tasks. Tactical and Organizational Questions). Geneva: RSDLP Press, 1904.

Ustav i rezolyutsii Kommunisticheskogo Internatsionala, prinyatiye na II kongresse, sostoyavshemsya v Moskve s 17 iyulya po 7 avgusta 1920 g. (Charter and Resolutions of the Communist International, Adopted at the Second congress, that was Held in Moscow from July 17 to August 7, 1920). Prague: *Pravda* Newspaper Press, 1921.

Voitinsky, Grigorii. "Kolonial'nyi vopros na rasshirennom plenume IKKI" (A Colonial Question at the ECCI Enlarged Plenum). *Kommunisticheskii Internatsional*. 1925, no. 4, pp. 64–71.

——. "Peregruppirovka sil v Kitaye" (The Regrouping of Forces in China). *Pravda*, March 24, 1926.

——. "Sun Yatsen i osvoboditel'noye dvizheniye v Kitaye" (Sun Yat-sen and the Liberation Movement in China). *Bol'shevik* (The Bolshevik). 1925, no. 5–6, pp. 44–52.

——. "Tendentsii revolutsionnogo dvizheniya v Kitaye i gomindan" (Trends in the Revolutionary Movement in China and the Guomindang). *Kommunisticheskii Internatsional*. 1925, no. 3, pp. 153–158.

Voprosy kitaiskoi revolyutsii (Questions of the Chinese Revolution). Moscow-Leningrad: Gosizdat, 1927.

Vsesoyuznaya Kommunisticheskaya partiya (bol'shevikov) v rezolyutsiyakh i resheniyakh s"ezdov, konferentsii i plenumov TsK (All-Union Communist Party [Bolsheviks] in Resolutions and Decisions of Congresses, Conferences and CC Plenums). 2 parts. 6th ed. Moscow: Gospolitizdat, 1941.

Vtoroi kongress Kominterna: Iyul' – avgust 1920 (The Second Congress of the Comintern: July – August 1920). Moscow: Partizdat, 1934.

2-i kongress Kommunisticheskogo Internatsionala: Stenograficheskii otchet (The Second Congress of the Communist International: Stenographic Record). Petrograd: The Communist International Press, 1921.

Wilbur, C. Martin, ed. *The Communist Movement in China: An Essay Written in 1924 by Ch'en Kung-po*. New York: Octagon Books, 1960.

—— and Julie Lian-ying How. *Missionaries of the Revolution: Soviet Advisers and Nationalist China, 1920–1927*. Cambridge, Mass.: Harvard University Press, 1989.

Wu Xiangxiang, ed. *Zhongguo gongchandang shi* (History of the CCP). Taipei: Wenxing shudian, 1962.

Wusi shiqide shetuan (Societies of the "May Fourth" Period). 4 vols. Beijing: Shenghuo, dushu, xinzhi sanlian shudian, 1979.

"Yuandong geguo gongchandang ji minzu geming tuanti diyici dahui xuanyan" (Manifesto of the First Congress of Communist Parties and National Revolutionary Organizations of Far Eastern Countries). *Xianqu*. 1922, no. 10, p. 4–5.

Zhang Tailei wenji (Zhang Tailei's Collected Works). Beijing: Renmin chubanshe, 1981.

Zhonggong "sanda" ziliao (Materials of the CCP Third Congress). Guangzhou: Guangdong renmin chubanshe, 1985.

Zhongguo gongchandang disanci quanguo dahui xuanyan (Statements of the Third All-China Congress of the CCP). *Xiangdao zhoukan* (Guide Weekly). 1923, no. 30, pp. 228–231.

Zhongguo gongchandang disici quanguo daibiaodahui yijuean ji xuanyan (Resolutions and Statements of the Fourth All-China Congress of the CCP). N. p., 1925.

"Zhongguo gongchandang duiyu shiju zhi zhuzhang" (Statement of the CCP on the Current Situation). *Xianqu*. 1923, no. 24, pp. 1–2.

"Zhongguo gongchandang duiyu shijude zhuzhang" (Statement of the CCP on the Current Situation). *Xianqu*. 1922, no. 9, pp. 1–3.

Zhongguo gongchandang jiguan fazhan cankao ziliao (Reference Materials on the History of the CCP Organs' Development). Vol. 1. Beijing: Zhonggong dangxiao chubanshe, 1983.

Zhongguo gongchandang wunian laizhi zhengzhi zhuzhang (Political Statements of the Chinese Communist Party for the Past Five Years). Guangzhou: Guoguang shuju, 1926.

Zhongguo Guomindang dierci diyi, dierci quanguo daibiaodahui huiyi shiliao (Historical Materials of the First and Second Guomindang Congresses). 2 vols. Nanjing: Jiangsu guji chubanshe, 1986.

Zhongshan quanji (Collected Works of Zhongshan [Sun Yat-sen]). Vol. 2. Shanghai: Lianyou tushuguan inshuai gongsi, 1931.

Der Zweite Kongress der Kommunistischen Internationale: Protokoll der Verhandlungen vom 19. Juli in Petrograd und vom 19. Juli bis 7. August 1920 in Moskau. Hamburg: Verlag der Kommunistischen Internationale, 1921.

Der Zweite Kongress der Kommunistischen Internationale: Protokoll der Verhandlungen vom 19. Juli in Petrograd und vom 19. Juli bis 7. August 1920 in Moskau. Petrograd: Verlag der Kommunistischen Internationale, 1921.

Interviews

Interviews with Rozaliya Ephraimovna Belenkaya at Moscow, Russia, November 11, 1991 and at New York City, May 16, 1998.

Interview with Nadezhda Adolfovna Joffe at Moscow, Russia, June 5, 1991.

Interview with Nikolai Semenovich Kardashev at Moscow, Russia, March 15, 1993.

Interview with Lin Ying at Moscow, Russia, March 1, 1993.

Interviews with Tatiyana Invarovna Smilga at Moscow, Russia, June 2, 5, 1991.

Interview with Ivan Yakovlevich Vrachev at Moscow, Russia, November 3, 1991.

Interviews with Wang Fanxi at Leeds, England, July 25, 27, 30, and August 1, 4, 11, 1992.

Memoirs

The Autobiography of Bertrand Russell. 1914–1944. Boston & Toronto: Little, Brown & Co., 1956.

Blagodatov, A. V. *Zapiski o kitaiskoi revolyutsii 1925–1927* (Notes on the Chinese Revolution of 1925–1927). 3rd ed. Moscow: Nauka, 1979;

Cadart, Claude and Cheng Yingxiang, eds. *Mémoires de Peng Shuzhi: L'Envol du Communisme en Chine.* Paris: Gallimard, 1983.

Chang Kuo-t'ao. *The Rise of the Chinese Communist Party. An Autobiography.* 2 vols. Lawrence, etc.: Kansas University Press, 1971.

Chen Pan-tsu [Chen Tanqiu], "Reminiscences of the First Congress of the Communist Party of China). *The Communist International.* 1936, no. 14, pp. 1363–1366.

Cherepanov, A. I. *Zapiski voennogo sovetnika v Kitaye* (Notes of a Miliary Adviser in China). 2nd ed. Moscow: Nauka, 1976.

Chiang Ching-kuo. *My Days in Soviet Russia.* Taipei, 1963.

Chiang Chungcheng (Chiang Kai-shek). *Soviet Russia in China: Summing-up at Seventy.* New York: Farrar, Straus and Co, 1957.

Dalin, S. A. *Kitaiskiye memuary: 1921–1927* (Chinese Memoirs: 1921–1927). Moscow: Nauka, 1975.

——. *V ryadakh kitaiskoi revolyutsii* (In the Ranks of the Chinese Revolution). Moscow-Leningrad: Moskovskii rabochii, 1926.

Fischer, Louis. *Men and Politics: An Autobiography.* New York: Puell, Sloan and Pearce, 1941.

Guan Suozhi. "Mosike dongfang daxue huiyi" (Memoirs of the Moscow University of the East). *Gongdang wenti yanjiu* (Study of CCP's Issues). 1980, vol. 7, no. 3, pp. 1–2; no. 8, pp. 11–13.

Guo Shaotang. *Istoriko-memuarniye zapiski kitaiskogo revolyutsionera* (Historical Memoir Notes of a Chinese Revolutionary). Moscow: Nauka, 1990.

Jiang Kanghu. *Xin E youji* (A Journey to the New Russia). Shanghai: Shangwu yingshuguan, 1923.

Jiang Zemin. "Zai Faguo, Bilishi qingong jianxuede rizi" (Days of Diligent Work and Economical Study in France and Belgium). *Gemin shi ziliao.* 1981, no. 3, pp. 71–84.

Joffe N. A. *Vremya nazad: Moya zhizn', moya sud'ba, moya epokha* (Time Goes Back: My Life, My Fate, My Epoch). Moscow: T.O.O. "Biologicheskiye nauki" Press, 1992.

"Liu Renjing tan tuoluociji zai Zhongguo" (Liu Renjing on Trotskyists in China). *Zhonggong dangshi ziliao*. 1982, no. 1, pp. 238–255.

Lu Yeshen. "Qianyan" (Preface). In Ma Yuansheng. *Liu Su jishi* (Notes on Life in the USSR). Beijing: Qunzhong chubanshe, 1987, pp. 1–4.

Luosu [Russell, Bertrand]. *You E ganxiang* (Impressions from the Trip to Russia). *Xin qingnian*. (New Youth). 1920, vol. 8, no. 2, pp. 1–12.

M. N. Roy's Memoirs. Bombey: Allied Publ., 1964.

Ma Yuansheng. *Liu Su jishi* (Notes on Life in the USSR). Beijing: Qunzhong chubanshe, 1987.

Qiwu Laoren [Bao Huisen]. "Do i posle obrazovaniya Kommunisticheskoi partii Kitaya" (Before and After the Formation of the Communist Party of China), trans. Yu. M. Garushyants. *Rabochii klass i sovremennyi mir* (The Working Class and the Contemporary World). 1971, no. 2, pp. 117–127.

Pu Qingquan [Pu Dezhi]. "Zhongguo tuopaide changsheng he meiwang"(The Birth and Death of the Chinese Trotskyists). In *Chen Duxiu pinglun xuanbian* (Collection of Critical Articles on Chen Duxiu). Vol. 2. Zhengzhou: Henan renmin chubanshe, 1982, pp. 383–405.

Ren Zhuoxuan. "Liu E ji gui guo houde huiyi" (Memoirs of [My] Visit to Russia and of What Happened After [My] Return Home). In *Liushi nian lai Zhongguo liu E xuesheng zhi fengxiang dioaku* (Chinese Students' Reminiscences of [Their] Visit to Russia Sixty Yeas Ago). Taipei: Zhonghua shuju chubanshe, 1988, pp. 73–113.

Resis, Albert, ed. *Molotov Remembers. Inside Kremlin Politics. Conversations with Felix Chuev.* Chicago: Ivan R. Dee, 1993.

Roy, Manabendra Nath. *My Experiences in China.* 2nd ed. Bombey: Renaissance Publ., 1945.

Sheean, Vincent. *Personal History.* Garden City, N.Y.: Doubleday, Doran and Co, 1935.

Sheng Yueh. *Sun Yat-sen University in Moscow and the Chinese Revolution: A Personal Account.* Lawrence, KS: Kansas University Press, 1971.

"Song Liang tongzhi gei [Liu] Shaoqi tongzhide xin" (Letter from Song Liang [Sun Yefang] to [Liu] Shaoqi). In Liu Shaoqi. *Lun dang* (On the Party). Dalian: Dazhong shudian, 1947, pp. 345–346.

Sun Yefang. "Guanyu Zhongguo Mo zhibu" (On Moscow Branch of the CCP). *Zhonggong dangshi ziliao*. 1982, no. 1, pp. 180–183.

Tang Youzhang. *Geming yu liufang* (Revolution and Exile). Changsha: Hunan renmin chubanshe, 1988.

Trotsky, Leon. "Fighting Against the Stream." In George Breitman and Evelyn Reed, eds. *Writings of Leon Trotsky (1938–9)*. New York: Merit Publ., 1969, pp. 63–65.

——. *My Life. An Attempt at an Autobiography.* New York: Pathfinder Press, 1970.

——. "On the History of the Left Opposition." In Breitman, George and Evelyn Reed, eds. *Writings of Leon Trotsky (1938–9)*. New York: Merit Publ., 1969, pp. 61–62.

Vishniakova-Akimova, V. V. *Two Years in Revolutionary China, 1925–1927*, trans. Steven I. Levine. Cambridge, Mass.: Harvard University Press, 1971.

Voitinsky, G. "Moi vstrechi s Sun Yat-senom" (My Meetings with Sun Yat-sen). *Pravda.* March 15, 1925.

Wang Fanxi. *Shuangshan huiyilu* (Memoirs of Shuangshan). Hong Kong: Zhou, 1977.

Wang Pingyi. "Liu E qianhou" (Before and After [My] Visit to Russia). In *Liushi nian lai Zhongguo liu E xuesheng zhi fengxiang diaoku* (Chinese Students' Reminiscences of [Their] Visit to Russia Sixty Yeas Ago). Taipei: Zhonghua shuju chubanshe, 1988, pp. 19–26.

Wang Xuean. *Liu E huiyilu* (Memoirs of [My] Visit to Russia). Taipei: Sanmin shudian, 1969.

Xiao Jingguang. "Fu Su xuexi qianhou" (Before and After Studies in the Soviet Union). *Geming shi ziliao* (Materials on the History of Revolution). 1981, no. 3, pp. 1–21.

Zheng Chaolin. "Chen Duxiu yu tuopai" (Chen Duxiu and Trotskyists). In *Zheng Chaolin huiyilu* (Memoirs of Zheng Chaolin). Hong Kong, 1982, pp. 246–351.

Zheng Chaolin huiyilu (Zheng Chaolin's Memoirs). Hong Kong, 1982.

Zheng Chaolin. *Ji Yin Kuan* (Memoirs of Yin Kuan). (Manuscript). [Shanghai], n. d.
Yang Zilie. *Zhang Guotao furen huiyilu* (Memoirs of Madame Chang Guotao). Hong Kong: Zilian chubanshe, 1970.

Newspapers

Chen bao (Morning). Beijing, 1919.
Dangbao (Party Newspaper). Shanghai, 1924.
Izvestiya (News). Moscow, 1917–1927.
Kommunist (The Communist). Baku, 1920.
Meizhou pinglun (Weekly Review). Beijing, 1919.
Minguo ribao (Republican Daily). Shanghai, 1917.
Nedelya (A Week). Moscow, 1989.
Pod znamenem Ilicha (Under the Banner of Ilich). Moscow, 1923–1926.
Pravda (Truth). Moscow, 1917–1930.
Qianjin bao (Forward). Moscow, 1925–1926.
Renmin ribao (People's Daily). Beijing, 1949–1984.
Shishi xinbao (Facts). Shanghai, 1917.
Vestnik 2–go kongressa Kommunisticheskogo Internatsionala (Bulletin of the Second Congress of the Communist International). Moscow, 1920.
Zhizn' national'nostei (Life of the Nationalities). Moscow, 1920–1921.

Journals

Bol'shevik (The Bolshevik). Moscow, 1925–27.
Der Bolschewik. Moscow, 1922.
Byulleten IV kongressa Kommunisticheskogo Internatsionala (Bulletin of the Fourth Congress of the Communist International). Moscow, 1922.
Byulleten oppozitsii (bol'shevikov-lenintsev) (Bulletin of the Opposition [Bolshevik Leninists]). Paris, New York, 1929–41.
Chuban shiliao (Materials on Publishing Business). Beijing, 1983.
The China Quarterly. London, 1973.
The Communist International. Moscow, 1920, 1936.
The International Press Correspondence. Berlin, 1920–27.
Dongfang zazhi (The Orient). Shanghai, 1918.
Gongchandang (The Communist). Shanghai, 1920–21.
Gongchan zazhi (Communist Journal). Moscow, 1929–30.
Gongdang wenti yanjiu (Study of CCP's Issues). Taipei, 1980–93.
Geming shi ziliao (Materials on the Revolutionary History). Beijing, 1981.
Geming shi ziliao (Materials on the Revolutionary History). Shanghai, 1986.
Guoji pinglun (International Review). Moscow, 1926–27.
Guomin (Nation). Beijing, 1919.
L'International Communiste. Moscow, 1920.
Issues & Studies. Taipei, 1974–98.
Istoricheskii arkhiv (Historical Archives). Moscow, 1992.
Istorik-marksist (Historian-Marxist). Moscow, 1925–27.
Izvestiya TsK KPSS (News of the CPSU CC). Moscow, 1989–91.
Jiefang yu gaizao (Liberation and Reconstruction). Beijing, 1919–20.
Jindai shi yanjiu (Modern Historical Studies). Beijing, 1985.
Kanton (Canton). Guangzhou, 1927.
Kommunist (The Communist). Moscow, 1969.
Kommunisticheskii Internatsional (The Communist International). Moscow, 1920–27, 1936.
Die Kommunistische Internationale. Moscow, 1920.

Krasnyi Interatsional Profsoyuzov (Red International of Labor Unions). Moscow, 1925.
Lishi yanju (Historical Studies). Beijing, 1960.
Meizhou yaolan (Weekly Cradle). Moscow, 1928–29.
Narody Azii i Afriki (People's of Asia and Africa). Moscow, 1972–76.
The Nation. New York, 1927.
Novy Mir (New World). Moscow, 1927, 1950.
Novy Mir (New World). New York, 1917.
Otechestvennyye Arkhivy (Archives of the Fatherland). Moscow, 1992.
Problemy Dalnego Vostoka (Problems of the Far East). Moscow, 1972–93.
Problemy Kitaya (Problems of China). Moscow, 1929.
Problemy Vostokovedeniya (Problems of Oriental Studies). Moscow, 1960
Rabochii klass i sovremennyi mir (The Working Class and the Contemporary World). Moscow, 1972–82.
Revolyutsionnyi Vostok (The Revolutionary East). Moscow, 1927.
Shehui xinwen (Social News). Shanghai, 1932–34.
Shiyue pinglun (October Review). Hong Kong, 1991.
Shuguan (Dawn). Beijing, 1920.
Sobraniye uzakonenii i rasporyazhenii rabochego i krest'yanskogo pravitel'stva (The Statutes and Orders of the Workers' and Peasants' Government). Moscow, 1921.
Sotsialisticheskii vestnik (The Socialist Herald). Berlin, 1927.
Sputnik agitatora (dlya derevni) (An Agitator's Companion [For the Countryside]). Moscow, 1925.
Voprosy filosofii (Questions of Philosophy). Moscow, 1990.
Voprosy istorii (Questions of History). Moscow, 1990.
Voprosy istorii KPSS (Questions of the History of the CPSU). Moscow, 1958.
Xiangdao zhoukan (The Guide Weekly). Shanghai, 1923–27.
Xianqu (The Pioneer). Beijing, 1922–23.
Xin qingnian (New Youth). Shanghai, 1920–25.
Xin shiqi (New Era). Beijing, 1981.
Xinhua wenzhai (Xinhua [New China] Digest). Beijing, 1984.
Zhonggong dangshi yanjiu (Historical Studies on the CCP). Beijing, 1989.
Zhongguo xiandai shi (Modern History of China). Beijing, 1983–93.
Zhonggong yanjiu ziliao (Materials on the CCP Studies). Beijing, 1989.
Die Zukunft (Future). New York, 1917.

Secondary Sources

Alekseev, V. M. "Printsypy perevodov sochinenii V. I. Lenina na kitaiskii yazyk" (Principles of Translation of V. I. Lenin's Works into Chinese). *Zapiski Instituta vostokovedeniya AN SSSR* (Notes of the USSR Academy of Sciences Institute of Oriental Studies). Vol. 3. Leningrad, 1935, p. 5.
Alexander, Robert. *International Trotskyism: 1919–1985: A Documented Analysis of the Movement*. Durham & London: Duke University Press, 1991.
Alsky, M. *Kanton pobezhdaet ...* (Canton Victorious ...). Moscow: Communist Academy Press, 1927.
Benton, Gregor. "Bolshevising China, From Lenin to Stalin to Mao, 1921–1944." *International Conference "The Russian Revolution and Its Aftermath."* Youngstown, OH, 1994.
———. *China's Urban Revolutionaries: Explorations in the History of Chinese Trotskyism*. Atlantic Highlands, NJ: Humanities Press, 1996.
Berdyaev, Nicolas. *The Origin of Russian Communism*. Ann Arbor, MI: The University of Michigan Press, 1960.
Bernal, Martin. *Chinese Socialism to 1907*. Ithaca: Cornell University Press, 1976.
Bing, Dov. "Sneevliet and the Early Years of the CCP." *The China Quarterly*. 1971, no. 48, pp. 687–695.

——. "Was There a Sneevlietian Stategy?" *The China Quarterly.* 1973, no. 54, pp. 349–357.

Bol'shaya sovetskaya entsiklopediya (Large Soviet Encyclopedia). Vol. 47. 2nd ed. Moscow: "BSE", 1957.

Borodin B. A. "Trotsky i Chan Kaishi" (Trotsky and Chiang Kai-shek). *Problemy Dalnego Vostoka.* 1990, no. 2, pp. 148–156.

Borokh, L. N. *Obshchestvennaya mysl' Kitaya i sotsializm (nachalo XX v.)* (Social Thought of China and Socialism (the Beginning of the Twentieth Century). Moscow: Nauka, 1984.

Brandt, Conrad. *Stalin's Failure in China.* Cambridge, Mass.: Harvard University Press, 1958.

Broido, G. "Kommunisticheskii universitet trudyashchikhsya Vostoka" (The Communist University of the Toilers of the East). *Zhizn' Natsional'nostei.* January 26, 1921.

Broué, Pierre. "Chen Duxiu and the Fourth International." *Revolutionary History.* 1990, vol. 2, no. 4, pp. 7–12.

——. *Histoire de l'Internationale Communiste. 1919–1943.* Paris: Fayard, 1997.

——. *Trotsky.* Paris: Fayard, 1988.

—— and Alexander Pantsov. "Otkrytoye pis'mo generalu D. A. Volkogonovu" (An Open Letter to General D. A. Volkogonov." *Konflikty i konsensus* (Conflicts and Consensus). 1994, no. 5, pp. 73–80.

Cai Hesen. "Istoriya opportunizma v Kommunisticheskoi partii Kitaya" (History of Opportunism in the Chinese Communist Party). *Problemy Kitaya* (Problems of China). 1929, no. 1, pp. 1–77.

Cao Zhongbin and Dai Maolin. *Mosike Zhongshan daxue yu Wang Ming* (Moscow Zhongshan [Sun Yat-sen] University and Wang Ming). Harbin: Heilongjiang renmin daxue chubanshe, 1988.

Carr, Edward. *A History of Soviet Russia: The Bolshevik Revolution: 1917–1923.* Vol. 1. London: Macmillan, 1951; Vol. 2, London: Macmillan, 1952; Vol. 3, London: Macmillan, 1953.

——. *A History of Soviet Russia: Foundations of a Planned Economy: 1926–1929.* 2 vols. London: Macmillan, 1971.

——. *A History of Soviet Russia: Socialism in One Country: 1924–1926.* Vol. 1. London: Macmillan, 1958; Vol. 2. London: Macmillan, 1960; Vol. 3. London: MacMillan, 1964.

Chen Yingjin. "Lenin zhuzuo zai Zhongguo chuanbo" (Spread of Lenin's Works in China). *Lenin shehuizhuyi jingji jianshe shilun yanjiu* (Study of Lenin's Theory of Socialist Economic Construction). Vol. 2. Tianjin: Jiefang zhengzhi xuean chubanshe, 1985, pp. 411–426.

Chen Zaifan. *Gongchan goji yu Zhongguo geming* (The Comintern and the Chinese Revolution). Wuhan: Huazhong shifan daxue chubanshe, 1987.

Cheshkov, M. A. "Analiz sotsial'noi struktury kolonial'nykh obshchestv v dokumentakh Kominterna (1920–1927)" (The Analysis of Social Structure of Colonial Societies in the Comintern Documents [1920–1927]). In R. A. Ulyanovsky, ed. *Komintern i Vostok: Bor'ba za leninskuyu strategiyu i taktiku v national'no-osvoboditel'nom dvizhenii* (The Comintern and the East: The Struggle for a Leninist Strategy and Tactics in the National Liberation Movement). Moscow: Nauka, 1969, pp. 192–216.

Chesneaux, Jean. *Le Mouvement Ouvrier Chinois de 1919–1927.* Paris: Mouton, 1962.

Chih Yu-ju. *The Political Thought of Ch'en Tu-hsiu.* Ph.D. theses. [Bloomington]: Indiana University, 1965.

Chow Tse-tsung. *The May Fourth Movement: Intellectual Revolution in Modern China.* Cambridge, Mass.: Harvard University Press, 1960.

Cihai. Lishi fenci. Zhongguo xiandaishe (Dictionary Cihai. History Division. Modern Chinese History). Shanghai: Shanghai cishu chubanshe, 1984.

Cohen, Stephen. *Bukharin and the Bolshevik Revolution. A Political Biography. 1888–1938.* New York: Alfred A. Knopf, 1973.

Dalin, Sergei. "Sun Yat-sen. Ko 2–i godovshchine ego smerti (12 marta 1925 g.)" (Sun Yat-sen. On the Second Anniversary of His Death [March 12, 1925]). *Pravda*. March 12, 1927.

Delyusin, L. P. *Agrarno-krest'yanskii vopros v politike KPK (1921–1928 gg.)* (Agrarian and Peasant Questions in the Policy of the CCP [1921–1928]). Moscow: Nauka, 1972.

——. *Diskussiya o sotsializme. Iz istorii obshchesyvennoi misli v Kitaye v nachale 20–kh godov* (Dispute on Socialism. On the History of Social Thought in China in the Beginning of 1920s). Moscow: Nauka, 1970.

——. *Diskussiya o sotsializme. Iz istorii obshchesyvennoi misli v Kitaye v nachale 20–kh godov* (Dispute on Socialism. On the History of Social Thought in China in the Beginning of 1920s). 2nd ed., Moscow: Nauka, 1980.

——, ed. *Dvizheniye "4 maya" 1919 g. v Kitaye* (The "May Fourth" Movement of 1919 in China). Moscow: Nauka, 1971.

—— and A. S. Kostyaeva. *Revolyutsiya 1925–1927 gg. v Kitaye: problemy i otsenki* (The Revolution of 1925–1927 in China: Problems and Assessments). Moscow: Nauka, 1985.

Department of Marx and Lenin Writings of Beijing Library, ed. *Makesi, Engesi zhuzuo zhongyiwen zonglu* (Catalogue of Chinese Translations of Marx and Engels's Works). Beijing: Shumu wenxian, 1988.

Deutscher, Isaac. *The Prophet Armed: Trotsky: 1879–1921*. Oxford: Oxford University Press, 1989.

——. *The Prophet Outcast: Trotsky: 1929–1940*. Oxford: Oxford University Press, 1989.

——. *The Prophet Unarmed: Trotsky: 1921–1929*. Oxford: Oxford University Press, 1989.

Deyateli SSSR i revolyutsionnogo dvizheniya v Rossii: Entsiklopedicheskii slovar' "Granat" (Activists of the USSR and the Revolutionary Movement in Russia: Encyclopedia Dictionary "Granat"). Moscow: Sovietskaya Entsiklopedia, 1989.

Dirlik, Arif. *The Origins of Chinese Communism*. New York: Oxford University Press, 1989.

Duran, Damien. "The Birth of the Chinese Left Opposition." *Revolutionary History*, 1990. Vol. 2, no. 4, pp. 3–6.

Efimov, G. V. "Iz istorii Kommunisticheskogo universiteta trudyashchikhsya Kitaya" (Episodes in the History of the Communist University of the Toilers of China). *Problemy Dalnego Vostoka*, 1977, no. 2, pp. 169–175.

Engels, Frederick. "Letter to Karl Marx, February 13, 1851." In Karl Marx and Frederick Engels. *Collected Works*. Vol. 38. New York: International Publ., 1982, pp. 289–291.

Feigon, Lee. *Chen Duxiu: Founder of the Chinese Communist Party*. Princeton, N.J.: Princeton University Press, 1983.

Fischer, Louis. "China, Seen From Moscow." *The Nation*, 1927. Vol. CXXY, no. 3256 (November 30). pp. 613–614.

Garushyants, Yu. M. *Dvizheniye 4 maya 1919 goda v Kitaye* (May Fourth Movement of 1919 in China). Moscow: Nauka, 1959.

Gel'bras, V. G. "Klass: mif ili real'nost'?" (Class: Myth or Reality?) *Rabochii klass i sovremennyi mir*. 1974, no. 2, pp. 130–141.

——. *Sotsialno-politicheskaya struktura KNR. 50–60–e gody* (Social and Political Structure of the PRC: 1950–60s). Moscow: Nauka, 1980.

Glunin, V. I. "Bor'ba za edinyi natsional'nyi front v Kitaye (k 50–letiyu III s"ezda KPK)" (The Struggle for the United Front in China [On the Occasion of the Third CCP Congress' Fiftieth Anniversary]). *Problemy Dalnego Vostoka*. 1973, no. 3, pp. 125–132.

——. "Grigorii Voitinsky (1893–1953)." In M. I. Sladkovsky, ed. *Vidniye sovetskiye kommunisty – uchastniki kitaiskoi revolyutsii* (Prominent Soviet Communists – Participants of the Chinese Revolution). Moscow: Nauka, 1970, pp. 22–40.

——. "Komintern i stanovleniye kommunisticheskogo dvizheniya v Kitaye (1920–1927)" (The Comintern and the foundation of the Chinese Communist Movement

[1920–27]). In Ulyanovsky, R. A. ed. *Komintern i Vostok: Bor'ba za leninskuyu strategiyu i taktiku v national'no-osvoboditel'nom dvizhenii* (The Comintern and the East: The Struggle for Lenin's Strategy and Tactics in the National Liberation Movement). Moscow: Nauka, 1969, pp. 242–299.

——. *Kommunisticheskaya partiya Kitaya nakanune i v period Natsional'noi revolyutsii 1925–1927 gg.* (The Chinese Communist Party on the Eve and During the National Revolution of 1925–1927). 2 vols., Moscow: Institute of the Far Eastern Studies Press, 1975.

—— and A. S. Mugruzin. "Krest'yanstvo v kitaiskoi revolyutsii" ("The Peasantry in the Chinese revolution"). In R. A. Ulyanovsky, ed. *Revolyutsionnyi protsess na Vostoke. Istoriya i sovremennost'* (The Revolutionary Process and the East: History and the Present). Moscow: Nauka, 1982, pp. 111–165.

Grigoriev, A. M. "Bor'ba v VKP(b) i Kominterne po voprosam politiki v Kitaye (1926–1927) (The Struggle in the AUCP(B) and the Comintern on the Questions of China Policy [1926–1927]). *Problemy Dalnego Vostoka.* 1993, no. 2, pp. 123–134; no. 3, pp. 112–128.

——. *Revolyutsionnoye dvizheniye v Kitaye v 1927–1931 gg. (Problemy strategii i taktiki)* (The Revolutionary Movement in China in 1927–1931 [Problems of Strategy and Tactics]). Moscow: Nauka, 1980.

Huang Xiurong. *Gongchan goji yu Zhongguo geming guanxi shi* (History of Relationships between the Comintern and the Chinese Revolution). 2 vols. Beijing: Zhonggong zhongyang dangxiao chubanshe, 1989.

Isaacs, Harold. *The Tragedy of the Chinese Revolution.* London: Secker and Warburg, 1938.

——. *The Tragedy of the Chinese Revolution.* Revised ed. Stanford: Stanford University Press, 1951.

Jacobs, Dan. *Borodin: Stalin's Man in China.* Cambridge, Mass.: Harvard University Press, 1981.

Jian. "Wu Yuzhang zai Haisanwei" (Wu Yuzhang in Vladivostok). *Shehui xinwen.* 1933. Vol. 2, no. 20, p. 276.

Jiang Huaxuan. "Dangde minzhu geming ganglingde tichu he guogong hezuo celüede jige wenti" (A Few Issues Concerning the Raise of the Party Program of the Democratic Revolution and Strategy of the Guomindang-CCP Alliance). *Jindai shi yanjiu* (Modern History Studies). 1985, no. 2, pp. 111–126.

Jiang Yihua. *Guomindang zuopaide qizhi – Liao Zhongkai* (The Banner of the Left Guomindang – Liao Zhongkai). Shanghai: Shanghai renmin chubanshe, 1985.

Jordan, Donald. *The Northern Expedition: China's National Revolution of 1926–1928.* Honolulu: University of Hawaii Press, 1976.

Kagan, Richard. *The Chinese Trotskyist Movement and Ch'en Tu-hsiu: Cultural Revolution and Policy: With an Appended Translation of Ch'en Tu-hsiu's Autobiography.* Ph.D. theses, [Philadelphia]: University of Pennsylvania, 1969.

Kalachev S. [S. N. Naumov]. "Kratkii ocherk istorii Kitaiskoi Kommunisticheskoi partii" (A Brief History of the Chinese Communist Party). *Kanton* (Canton). 1927, no. 1 (10), pp. 13–78.

Kara-Murza, G. S. "Kitai v 1918–1924 gg." (China in 1918–1924). *Istorik-marksist* (Historian-Marxist). 1939, no. 5–6, pp. 150–170.

Kartunova, A. I. "Komintern i nekotoriye voprosy reorganizatsii gomindana" (The Comintern and Some Questions Concerning the Reorganization of the Guomindang). In R. A. Ulyanovsky, ed. *Komintern i Vostok: Bor'ba za leninskuyu strategiyu i taktiku v national'no-osvoboditel'nom dvizhenii* (The Comintern and the East: The Struggle for Lenin's Strategy and Tactics in the National Liberation Movement). Moscow: Nauka, 1969, pp. 300–312.

——. *Politika kompartii Kitaya v rabochem voprose nakanune revolyutsii 1925–1927 godov* (Policy of the Chinese Communist Party on the Worker Question on the Eve of the Revolution of 1925–1927). Moscow: Nauka, 1983.

273

Klein, Donald and Anne Clark. *Biographic Dictionary of Chinese Communism: 1921–1969.* 2 vols. Cambridge, Mass.: Harvard University Press, 1971.

Knei-Paz, Baruch. *The Social and Political Thought of Leon Trotsky.* Oxford: Clarendon Press, 1978.

Kostyaeva, A. S. *Krest'yanskiye soyuzy v Kitaye (20–e gody XX veka)* (Peasant Unions in China in the 1920s). Moscow: Nauka, 1978.

Krushinsky, A. A. "Smysl vyrazhniya "geming" v sovremennikh politicheskikh tekstakh" (The Gist of the "Geming" Expression in Modern Political Texts). In *Odinnadtsataya nauchnaya konferentsiya "Obshchestvo i gosudarstvo v Kitaye."* *Tezisy i doklady* (The Eleventh Scientific Conference "Society and State in China." Theses and Presentations). Part 3. Moscow: IV AN SSSR, 1980, pp. 199–205.

Krymov, A. G. (Guo Shao-tang). *Obshchestvennaya mysl' i ideologicheskaiya bor'ba v Kitaye v 1917–1927 gg.* (Social Thought and Ideological Struggle in China in 1917–1927). Ph.D. theses, Moscow: IV AN SSSR, 1962.

Kuo, Thomas. *Ch'en Tu-hsiu (1879–1942) and the Chinese Communist Movement.* South Orange, NJ: Seton Hall University Press, 1975.

Kuo, Warren. *Analytical History of Chinese Communist Party.* Book Two. Taipei: Institute of International Relations, 1968.

Lerner, Warren. *Karl Radek: The Last Internationalist.* Stanford: Stanford University Press, 1970.

Levine, Marilyn A. *The Found Generation: Chinese Communism in Europe During the Twenties.* Seattle: University of Washington Press, 1993.

Levine, Steven. "Trotsky on China: The Exile Period." *Papers on China.* 1964, no. 18, pp. 90–128.

Li Hongnuan. "Zhang Tailei." In *Zhonggongdang shi renwu zhuan* (Biographies of the CCP Historical Activists). Vol. 4. Xian: Shenxi renmin chubanshe, 1982, pp. 70–99.

Li Xin. "Li Dazhao." In *Zhonggongdang shi renwu zhuan* (Biographies of the CCP Historical Activists). Vol. 2, Xian: Shenxi renmin chubanshe, 1981, pp. 1–41.

Li Xuanrong. *Tuoluociji pingzhuan* (Trotsky's Biography). Beijing: Zhongguo shehui kexue chubanshe, 1986.

Li Zhiqiang. "Lun Tuoluociji dui Zhongguo gemingde zhuzhang ji yingxiang" (On Trotsky's Views of and Impact on the Chinese Revolution). *Jindai shi yanjiu.* 1985, no. 1, pp. 68–100.

Lin Boqu zhuan (Lin Boqu's Biography). Beijing: Hongqi chubanshe, 1986, p. 75.

Liu Shaoqi. "Rech na mitinge moskvichei vo Dvortse sporta 7 dekabrya 1960 g." (Speech at a Meeting Held in the Moscow Palace of Sports. December 7, 1960). *Pravda.* December 8, 1960.

Luk, Michael Y. L. *The Origins of Chinese Bolshevism: An Ideology in the Making: 1921–1928.* Hong Kong: Oxford University Press, 1990.

Mao Zedong. *O diktature narodnoi demokratii* (On the Dictatorship of People's Democracy). Moscow: Gospolitizdat, 1949.

——."'Qida' gongzuo fangzhen" (The Seventh Congress's Course of Work). *Hongqi* (Red Banner). 1981, no. 11, pp. 1–7.

Marx, Karl. "Capital. A Critique of Political Economy." Vol. 1. In Karl Marx and Frederick Engels. *Collected Works.* Vol. 35. New York: International Publ., 1996.

—— and Frederick Engels, "The Alliance of Socialist Democracy and the International Working Men's Association." In Karl Marx and Frederick Engels. *Collected Works.* Vol. 23. New York: International Publ., 1988, pp. 454–580.

Meisner, Maurice. *Li Ta-chao and the Origins of Chinese Marxism.* Cambridge, Mass.: Harvard University Press, 1967.

Miller, James. *The Politics of Chinese Trotskyism: The Role of a Permanent Opposition in Communism.* Ph.D. theses, Urbana-Champaign: University of Illinois, 1979.

Ming Yuan. "Quxiaopaide xingcheng ji qi molo" (The Rise and Fall of the Group of Liquidationists). *Shehui xinwen* (Social News). 1933, vol. 3, no. 23, pp. 322–325; no. 24, pp. 338–341.

Mirovitskaya, R. A. "Mikhail Borodin (1884–1951)." In M. I. Sladkovsky, ed. *Vidniye sovetskiye kommunisty – uchastniki kitaiskoi revolyutsii* (Prominent Soviet Communists – Participants of the Chinese Revolution). Moscow: Nauka, 1970, pp. 22–40.

——. "Sovetskii Soyuz i KPK (konets 20–kh – nachalo 30–kh godov" (The Soviet Union and the CCP at the End of the 1920s and the Start of the 1930s). In M. L. Titarenko, ed. *Opyt i uroki istorii KPK: K 60–letiyu obrazovaniya partii* (Experience and Lessons from the History of the CCP: On the Sixtieth Anniversary of the Party Founding). Moscow: Institute of the Far Eastern Studies Press, 1981, pp. 200–202.

Nadtocheev, V. "'Troika,' 'Semerka,' Stalin" (Triumvirate, Group of Seven, Stalin). *Nedelya* (A Week). 1989, no. 1, pp. 15–16.

Nikiforov, V. N. *Sovetskiye istoriki o problemakh Kitaya* (Soviet Historians on China Problems). Moscow: Nauka, 1970.

Nikolaeva, K. "Kak nel'zya ponimat' edinstvo partii" (How It is Impossible to Understand the Party Unity). *Pravda*, May 17, 1927.

Pantsov, A. V. "Brestskii Mir" (The Brest Peace). *Voprosy istorii* (Questions of History). 1990, no. 2, pp. 60–79.

——. "Chinese Working-class Movement and the Influence of Socialist Ideas in the Early 20th Century." *18th International Congress of Historical Sciences*. Montréal, 1995.

——. "Dokumenty II i IV kongressov Kominterna po natsional'nomu i kolonial'nomu voprosam i ikh rasprostraneniye v Kitaye" (Documents of the Second and Fourth Congresses of the Comintern on the National and Colonial Questions and Their Disseminaton in China." In R. A. Ulyanovsky, ed. *Natsional'niye i sotsial'niye dvizheniya na Vostoke: Istoriya i sovremennost'* (National and Social Movements in the East: History and the Present). Moscow: Science Press, 1986, pp. 23–58.

——. "From Students to Dissidents: The Chinese Trotskyists in Soviet Russia." *Issues & Studies*. 1994, vol. 30, no. 3 (March), pp. 97–112; no. 4 (April), pp. 56–73; no. 5 (May), pp. 77–109.

——. *Iz istorii ideinoi bor'by v kitaiskom revolyutsionnom dvizhenii 20–40–kh godov* (On the History of Ideological Struggle in the Chinese Revolutionary Movement of 1920–40s). Moscow: Nauka, 1985.

——. "K diskussii v KPK vokrug 'idei Mao Tseduna'" ("On the Discussion in the CCP Around 'Mao Zedong Thought'," *Rabochii klass i sovremennyi mir.* 1982, no. 3, pp. 44–47.

——. "Lev Davidovich Trotsky." *Soviet Studies in History.* 1991, vol. 30, no. 1, pp. 7–43.

——. "The New School of Falsification." In Marilyn Vogt-Downey, ed. *The USSR: 1987–1991: Marxist Perspectives.* Atlantic Highlands, NJ: Humanities Press, 1993, pp. 317–330.

——. "O Marxismo na Rússia e na China: o Marxismo?" In Jorge Nóvoa, ed. *A História á Deriva: Um Balanço de Fim de Século.* Salvador-Bahia: Universidade Federal de Bahia Press, 1993, pp. 234–257.

——. "Stalin's Policy in China, 1925–27: New Light from Russian Archives," *Issues & Studies*, 1998, vol. 34, no. 1 (January), pp. 129–160.

—— and Gregor Benton. "Did Trotsky Oppose Entering the Guomindang 'From the First'?" *Republican China.* 1994, vol. XIX, no. 2 (April), pp. 52–66.

—— and M. F. Yuriev. "Ustanovleniye sotrudnichestva mezhdu KPK i Sun Yat-senom v 1921–1924 gg. (The Establishment of the Cooperation Between CCP and Sun Yat-sen from 1921 to 1924." In S. L. Tikhvinsky, ed. *Sun Yatsen: 1866–1986. K 120–letiyu so dnya rozhdeniya: Sbornik statei, vospominanii, dokumentov i materialov* (Sun Yat-sen, 1866–1986: On the Occasion of his 120th Birthday: A Collection of Articles, Memoirs, Documents, and Materials). Moscow: Nauka, 1987, pp. 129–171.

Peng Shu-tse [Peng Shuzhi], "Introduction." In Les Evans and Russell Block, eds. *Leon Trotsky on China.* New York: Monad Press, 1976, pp. 31–97.

Persits, M. A. "Iz istorii stanovleniya Kommunisticheskoi partii Kitaya: Doklad, podgotovlennyi Chzhang Tai-leem dlya III kongressa Kominterna kak istoricheskii istochnik" (On the History of the Foundation of the Chinese Communist Party: A

Report, Prepared by Zhang Tailei to the Third Comintern Congress as a Historical Source). *Narody Azii i Afriki.* 1971, no. 4, pp. 47–58.

——. "O podgotovitel'nom etape Kommunisticheskogo dvizheniya v Azii" (On the Preparatory Period of the Communist Movement in Asia). In R. A. Ulyanovsky, ed. *Revolyutsionnyi protsess na Vostoke. Istoriya i sovremennost'* (The Revolutionary Process and the East: History and the Present). Moscow: Nauka, 1982, pp. 38–76.

——. *Revolutionaries of India in Soviet Russia: Mainsprings of the Communist Movement in the East.* Moscow: Progress Publ., 1983.

——. "Vostochniye internatsionalisty v Rossii i nekotoriye voprosy natsional'no-osvoboditel'nogo dvizheniya (1918 – iyun' 1920) (Eastern Internationalists in Russia and Some Questions of the National Liberation Movement [1918 – June 1920]). In R. A. Ulyanovsky, ed. *Komintern i Vostok: Bor'ba za leninskuyu strategiyu i taktiku v national'no-osvoboditel'nom dvizhenii* (The Comintern and the East: The Struggle for Lenin's Strategy and Tactics in the National Liberation Movement). Moscow: Nauka, 1969, pp. 53–109.

——. *Zastenchivaya interventsiya. O sovetskom vtorzhenii v Iran. 1920–1921 gg.* (A Shamefaced Intervention. On the Soviet Invasion of Iran. 1920–1921). Moscow: "AIRO-XX", 1996.

Popov N. A. "Kitaiskiye proletarii v Grazhdanskoi voine v Rossii" (Chinese Proletarians in the Civil war in Russia). In N. V. Liu, ed. *Kitaskiye dobrovol'tsy v boyakh za Sovietskuyu vlsast', 1918–1922* (Chinese Volunteers in the Struggle for Soviet Power, 1918–22). Moscow: Nauka, 1961, pp. 5–37.

——. "Uchastiye kitaiskikh internatsional'nykh chastei v zashchite Sovetskoi respubliku vo vremya Grazhdanskoi voiny (1918–1920 gg.)" (The Participation of Chinese International Units in Defense of the Soviet Republic in the Period of the Civil War [1918–1920]). *Voprosy istorii.* 1957, no. 10, pp. 109–123.

Ren Jianshu and Tang Baolin. *Chen Duxiu zhuan* (Chen Duxiu's Biography). 2 vols. Shanghai: Shanghai renmin chubanshe, 1989.

Reznikov, A. B. "Bor'ba V. I. Lenina protiv sektantskikh izvrashchenii v natsional'no-kolonial'nom voprose" (V. I. Lenin's Struggle Against Sectarian Distortions in the National and Colonial Questions). *Kommunist* (The Communist). 1968, no. 5, pp. 36–47.

——. *The Comintern and the East: Strategy and Tactics in the National Liberation Movement.* Moscow: Progress Publ., 1984.

——. "Razrabotka IV kongressom Kominterna problem natsional'no-osvoboditel'nogo dvizheniya" (The Comintern Fourth Congress's Elaboration of Problems of the National Liberation Movement). In *Chetvertyi kongress Kominterna: Razrabotka kongressom strategii i taktiki kommunisticheskogo dvizheniya v novykh usloviyakh. Politika edinogo fronta* (The Fourth Congress of the Comintern: The Congress's Elaboration of Strategy and Tactics of the Communist Movement in New Conditions: The Policy of the United Front). Moscow: Politizdat, 1980, pp. 194–238.

——. "V. I. Lenin o natsional'no-osvoboditel'nom dvizhenii" (V. I. Lenin on the National Liberation Movement). *Kommunist* (Communist). Moscow, 1967, no. 7, pp. 91–102.

Shastitko, P. M. *Leninskaya teoriya natsional'no-kolonial'nogo voprosa (istoriya formirovaniya)* (Lenin's Theory of National Colonial Question [The History of Its Formation]). Moscow: Nauka, 1979.

Shen Dachun and Tian Haiyan, "Zhongguo gongchandang 'yida' de zhuyao wenti" (Essential Questions Concerning the First Congress of the Chinese Communist Party). *Renmin ribao.* June 30, 1961.

Sheveliev, K. V. *Iz istorii obrazovaniya Kommunisticheskoi partii Kitaya* (On the History of the Formation of the Chinese Communist Party). Moscow: Institute of Far Eastern Studies Press, 1976.

——. *Iz istorii obrazovaniya Kommunisticheskoi partii Kitaya* (On the History of the Formation of the Chinese Communist Party). *Problemy Dalnego Vostoka.* 1980, no. 4, 141–154.

——. "Pred"istoriya edinogo fronta v Kitaye i Uchreditel'nyi S"ezd KPK" (A Pre-history of the United Front in China and the Constituent CCP Congress). In *Kitai: traditsii i sovremennost'* (China: Traditions and the Present). Moscow: Nauka, 1976, pp. 197–209.

Shumyatsky, B. "Iz istorii komsomola i kompartii Kitaya (Pamyati odnogo iz organizatorov komsomola i kompartii Kitaya tov. Zhang Tai-leya) (On History of the Communist Youth League and the Communist Party of China [Dedicated to the Memory of One of the Organizers of the Communist Youth League and the Communist Party of China Comrade Zhang Tailei]). *Revolyutsionnyi Vostok* (The Revolutionary East). 1928, no. 4–5, pp. 194–230.

Sorkin, G. Z. "S"ezd narodov Dalnego Vostoka" (Congress of Peoples of the Far East). *Problemy Vostokovedeniya* (Problems of Oriental Studies). 1960, no. 5, pp. 76–86.

Staburova, E. Yu. *Anarkhism v Kitaye. 1900–1921* (Anarchism in China. 1900–1921). Moscow: Nauka, 1983.

Svechin, A. "Voennoye iskusstvo v budushchei voine" (Military Art in a Future War). *Pravda*, May 1, 1927.

Tang Baolin. *Zhongguo tuopai shi* (History of Trotskyist Groups in China). Taipei: Dongda tushu gongsi, 1994.

Tikhvinsky, S. L. *Sun Yat-sen. Vneshnepoliticheskiye vozzreniya i praktika (Iz istorii natsional'no-osvoboditel'noi borby kitaiskogo naroda. 1885–1925)* (Sun Yat-sen. His Foreign Policy Views and Practice [On history of the National Liberation Struggle of the Chinese People. 1885–1925]). Moscow: Mezhdunarodniye otnosheniya Publ., 1964.

Timofeeva, N. N. "Kommunisticheskii universitet trudyashchikhsya Vostoka (KUTV) (1921–1925)" (The Communist University of the Toilers of the East [KUTV] [1921–25]). *Narody Azii i Afriki*. 1976, no. 2, pp. 47–57.

——. "Kommunisticheskii universitet trudyashchikhsya Vostoka (KUTV) v 1926–1938 gg." (The Communist University of the Toilers of the East [KUTV] in 1926–38). *Narody Azii i Afriki*. 1979, no. 5, pp. 30–42.

Titarenko, M. L. ed. *Noveishaya istoriya Kitaya. 1917–1927* (Modern History of China. 1917–1927). Moscow: Nauka, 1983.

Trotsky, Leon. *The History of the Russian Revolution*. Ann Arbor, MI: The University of Michigan Press, n.d.

——. "Kitaiskoi levoi oppozitsii" (To the Chinese Left Opposition). *Byulleten oppozitsii (bol'shevikov-lenintsev)* (Bulletin of the Opposition [Bolshevik Leninists]). no. 19 (March, 1931), pp. 27–30.

——. *Portrety* (Portraits). Benson, VT: Chalidze Publ., 1984.

——. *Stalin*. 2 vols. Benson, VT: Chalidze Publ., 1985.

——. *The Stalin School of Falsification*. New York: Pathfinder Press, 1972.

Tuck, James. *Engine of Mischief: An Analytical Biography of Karl Radek*. Westport, Con.: Greenwood Press, 1988.

Tucker, Robert. *Stalin as Revolutionary. 1879–1929. A Study in History and Personality*. New York: W. W. Norton, 1973.

Ulyanovsky, R. A., ed. *The Comintern and the East*. Moscow: Progress Publ., 1979.

——, ed. *Komintern i Vostok: Bor'ba za leninskuyu strategiyu i taktiku v national'no-osvoboditel'nom dvizhenii* (The Comintern and the East: The Struggle for Lenin's Strategy and Tactics in the National Liberation Movement). Moscow: Nauka, 1969.

Ustinov, V. M. "Kitaiskiye kommunisticheskiye organizatsii v Sovetskoi Rossii (1918–1922 gg.) (Chinese Communist Organization in Soviet Russia [1918–1922]). In N. V. Liu, ed. *Kitaskiye dobrovol'tsy v boyakh za Sovetskuyu vlsast', 1918–1922* (Chinese Volunteers in the Struggle for Soviet Power, 1918–22). Moscow: Nauka, 1961, pp. 38–53.

Ven de Van, Hans J. *From Friend to Comrade: The Founding of the Chinese Communist Party: 1920–1927*. Berkeley: University of California Press, 1991.

Volkogonov, Dmitrii. *Triumf i tragediya. Politicheskii portret I. V. Stalina* (Triumph and Tragedy. A Political Portrait of J. V. Stalin). 2 books. Moscow: APN, 1989.

——. *Trotsky. Politicheskii portret* (Trotsky: A Political Portrait). 2 books. Moscow: APN, 1992.

Volobuev, P. V., ed. *Politicheskiye deyateli Rossii. 1917. Biograficheskii slovar* (Political Activist of Russia. 1917. A Biographic Dictionary). Moscow: Nauchnoiye izd. "BSE", 1993.

Voslensky, M. S. *Nomenklatura. Gospodstvuyushchii klass Sovetskogo Soyuza* (Nomenklatura. The Ruling Class of the Soviet Union). Moscow: MP "Octyabr", "Sovetskaya Rossiya", 1991.

Wang Jianmin, *Zhongguo gongchandang shigao* (Outline History of the CCP). Vol. 1. Taipei: Author Press, 1965.

Wang Jianying. *Zhongguo gongchandang zuzhi shi ziliao huibian – lingdao jigou yange he chengyuan minglu* (Collection of Documents on History of the CCP Organizations – the Evolution of Leading Organs and Their Personal Composition). Beijing: Hongqi chubanshe, 1983.

Wang Xinggang, Fang Daming, "He Shuheng." In *Zhonggongdang shi zhuan*, (Biographies of the CCP Historical Activists). Vol. 4. Xian: Shenxi renmin chubanshe, 1982, pp. 1–38.

Die Werke von Karl Marx und Friedrich Engels in China: Katalog und Auswahlbibliographie. Trier: Karl-Marx-Haus, 1984.

Wittfogel, Karl August. *Oriental Despotism: A Comparative Study of Total Power.* New Haven & London: Yale University Press, 1957.

Wu, Ellsworth Tien-wei. *The Chinese Nationalist and Communist Alliance, 1923–1927.* Ph.D. theses, [College Park]: University of Maryland, 1965.

Wu K'un-jung. "The Left Opposition Faction in the Chinese Communist Party." *Issues & Studies.* 1974, vol. X, no. 6, pp. 78–90; vol. X, no. 7, pp. 70–86.

Xiang Qing. *Gongchan goji yu Zhongguo geming guanxi lunwenji* (A Collection of Articles on the Relationship between the Comintern and the Chinese Revolution). Shanghai: Shanghai renmin chubanshe, 1986.

Xu Juezai. "Makesizhuyi zai Zhongguo chuanbo 'diyi'" (Events, Happened for the First Time During the Spread of Marxism in China). *Xin shiqi.* 1981, no. 8, p. 30; no. 9, p. 26; no. 10, p. 28; no. 11, p. 27; no. 12, p. 19.

Xu Yuandong et. al. *Zhongguo gongchandang lishi jianghua* (Lectures on History of the Chinese Communist Party). Beijing: Zhongguo qingnian chubanshe, 1982.

Ye Yongle. *Chen Boda qiren* (Chen Boda as a Person). N.p., n.d.

Yuriev, M. F. *Revolyutsiya 1925–1927 gg. v Kitaye* (The Revolution of 1925–1927 in China). Moscow: Nauka, 1968.

Zhakov, Mikhail. *Otrazheniye feodalizma v "Men-tsi"* (The Reflection of Feudalism in "Mencius"). Moscow: UTK Press, 1927.

Zhang Yihong. *Ye Qing sixiang jiuzheng* (Correction of Ye Qing's Thought). Taipei: Tianran shushe, 1964.

Zhang Yunhou. "Lenin zhuzuo zhongyiwen nianbiao (12.1919 – 3.1960)" (Chronology of Translations of Lenin's Work into Chinese [12.1919 – 3.1960]). *Lishi yanjiu.* 1960, no. 4, pp. 47–91.

Zheng Canhui, "Zhongguo Guomindang diyici quanguo daibiaohui" (The First All-China Congress of the Chinese Guomindang). *Geming shi ziliao.* 1986, no. 1, p. 113–126.

Zhimei, "Xihu huiyi shijian kao" (Verification of the Time Period of Xihu Meeting). *Zhonggong yanjiu ziliao.* 1983, no. 4, pp. 326–328.

Zhongguo geming shi jiangyi (Lectures on History of the Chinese Revolution). Vol. 1, Beijing: Zhongguo renmin daxue chubanshe, 1983.

Zhongguo xinminzhuzhuyi geming shiqi tongshi (General History of the Period of the Neo-Democratic Revolution in China). Vol. 1. Beijing: Gaodeng jiaoyu chubanshe, 1959.

Zhonghuazhi zui zhishi shouci ("Most of Most" in China). Nanchang: Jiangxi jiaoyu chubanshe, 1987.

Zou Lu. *Zhongguo Guomindang shigao* (Outline History of the Chinese Guomindang). Changsha: Minzhi shuju, 1931.

Selected Biographical List*

Akselrod, Pavel (real first name: Pinkhus) Borisovich (alias Aleksandrovich, N. D., Rabochii, Shteinberg) (1850–1928). *Land and Liberty* (Populist) group member from the early 1870s. *Emancipation of Labor* (Marxist) group member from 1883. RSDLP member from 1898. Co-leader of Mensheviks from 1903. Chairman of Menshevik Party Central Committee from August 1917. Member of Petrograd Soviet Executive Committee, 1917. Emigrated after the October Revolution.

Albrekht, Aleksandr Emel'yanovich (alias Arno, real name: Abramovich) (1888–?). RSDLP(B) member from 1908. After October Revolution, member of Petrograd, Odessa, and Sevastopol Party Committees and Odessa Soviet Presidium. Worked in ECCI from 1919. Comintern representative in China, 1926–30 (with intervals.)

Alsky, M. (real name: Viktor Moritsevich Shtein) (1890–1964). RSDLP(B) member from 1917. Soviet Sinologist. Financial advisor to GMD Nationalist Government, 1926–27. Member of Trotskyist Opposition. Expelled from Party, 1927. Imprisoned. Released. Research fellow at Institute of Oriental Studies, 1935–64.

An Fu (alias Vitin) (?–?). CCP member from 1926. AUCP(B) candidate member from 1928. Studied at KUTK, 1928–30. Co-leader of Chinese Trotskyists in Moscow, 1928–30. Repressed.

Andreev, Mikhail Georgievich (1888–1945). Russian and Soviet Sinologist. Studied and worked in China, 1913 and 1925–27. RKKA officer, 1928–45. KUTK professor, 1925 and 1927–30. Professor at Institute of Oriental Studies, 1925–31. RKKA Military Academy professor from 1928. Research fellow at IWEIP from 1933.

Angaretis, Zigmas Ionovich (alias Aleksa) (1882–1940). RSDLP(B) member from 1906. Representative of Communist Party of Lithuania to ECCI from 1921. Secretary of International Control Commission, 1926–35. Repressed.

Artuzov, Artur Khristianovich (real name: Frauchi) (1891–1943). RSDLP(B) member from 1917. Head of Cheka-OGPU Counter-intelligence Department from 1919.

Avdeev, Ivan Avdeevich (real name: Anatolii Avdeevich Divil'kovsky) (1877–1932). RSDLP member from 1901. Central Committee candidate member and Chairman of Stalingrad Provincial Economic Council, 1927. Member of Zinovievist Opposition. Expelled from Party, 1927. Repressed.

Bakaev, Ivan Petrovich (1887–1936). RSDLP(B) member from 1906. Chairman of Leningrad Provincial Control Commission, 1925–27. Member of Central Control

---

* Only the names of the more important individuals are given, and not all pseudonyms are included.

Commission, 1925–27. Member of Zinovievist Opposition. Expelled from Party, 1927. Recanted, 1928. Repressed.

Bao Huiseng (alias Huisheng, Bao Yide, Qiwu laoren) (1894–1979). Chinese Communist activist from 1920. Co-founder of CCP, 1921. Editor of *Laodong zhoukan* (Labor Weekly), 1921. Head of CCP Wuhan Regional Committee, 1923–25. Head of Political Department of Whampoa Military Academy, 1925. Participated in Northern Expedition, 1926–27. After 1925–27 Revolution left the CCP. Taught at Northern Chinese People's Revolutionary University from 1950.

Bauman, Karl Yanovich (1892–1937). RSDLP(B) member from 1907. Central Committee member, 1925–37. Politburo candidate member, 1929–30. Second, then First Secretary of Moscow Party Committee, 1928–30. Secretary of Central Committee, 1929–34. Repressed.

Berzin, Jan Karlovich (real name: Peteris Kiuzis) (1889–1938). RSDRP(B) member from 1905. Head of Intelligence Department of RKKA General Staff, 1924–35, 1937. Repressed.

Bian Fulin (alias Fyodor Alekseevich Vershinin) (1904–?). CCP member from January 1927. AUCP(B) candidate member from 1928. Studied at KUTK, 1928–30. Co-leader of Chinese Trotskyists in Moscow.

Borodin, Mikhail Markovich (alias Anglichanin, Bankir, Aleksandr Greenberg, Aleksandr Humberg, Mikhail Berg, Georg Braun, M. Braun, Jacob, Nikiforov, real name: Gruzenberg) (1884–1951). RSDLP(B) member from 1903. Worked in ECCI from 1919. Main political adviser to Guomindang Central Executive Committee and ECCI representative in China, 1923–27. Deputy Minister of Labor, Deputy Head of TASS, Editor-in-Chief of Soviet Information Bureau, 1927–32. Editor-in-chief of *Moscow News*, 1932–51. Repressed.

Brike, Simon Karlovich (alias Bestuzhev, real name: Briker) (1898–1937). Paole Zion member, 1916–18. AUCP(B) member from 1918. Head first of Eastern Propaganda Bureau, then Turkish section of ECCI Eastern Department from November 1921 through mid-1920s. Later worked in USSR Commissariat of Foreign Affairs and Asov-Black Sea Commission of Party Control. Repressed.

Broido, Grigorii Ivanovich (1885–1956). Deputy Commissar for Nationalities, 1921–23. Rector of KUTV, 1921–26. Chairman of RSFSR Gosizdat, 1926–33. Deputy Commissar of Education and Director of Partizdat, 1934–41.

Bu Shiqi (Yevgenii Andreevich Proletariev, Pu Mingying, Bu Daoming, real name: Pu Daoming (1902–1964). Chinese Communist activist from 1920, CCP member from 1921. Studied at Shanghai School of Foreign Languages (1920–21) and Moscow international schools, 1921–23, 1925–26. Co-leader of Chinese Socialist Youth League, 1923–24. Interpreter for Borodin, 1924–25, and Shao Lizi, 1926. Taught at UTK and International Lenin School, 1926–33. Arrested in China and confessed, 1933. Head of West Asian (i.e., Russian) Department of GMD Ministry of Foreign Affairs, 1944–49. Director of Institute of International Relations on Taiwan from 1961.

Bubnov, Andrei Sergeevich (alias Ivanovsky) (1885–1940). RSDLP(B) member from 1903. Central Committee candidate member, 1917, 1919–20, 1922–23, and full member, 1917–18, 1924–40. Secretary of Central Committee, 1925. Head of RKKA Political Department, 1924–26. Head of Soviet delegation to Guangzhou, 1926. RSFSR Commissar of Education, 1929–40. Repressed.

Bukharin, Nikolai Ivanovich (1888–1938). RSDLP(B) member from 1906. Central Committee member, 1917–34 and candidate member, 1934–37. Politburo candidate member, 1919–24 and full member, 1924–29. ECCI member, 1919–29. Editor-in-chief of *Pravda*, 1917–29. Member of Supreme Economic Council Presidium, 1929–32. *Izvestiya* editor, 1934–37. Repressed.

Cai Chang (Cai Tate, Rosa Nikolaeva) (1900–1990). Younger sister of Cai Hesen. Chinese Communist activist from 1922. PCF member, 1923. Studied at KUTV, 1924–25. Secretary of CCP Central Committee Women's Committee, 1937–45. Central

Committee member, 1945–82. Deputy Chairwoman of International Democratic Women's Federation, 1947–49. Chairwoman of All-China Women's Federation, 1949–78. Deputy Head of National People's Congress Standing Committee, 1975–83.

Cai Hesen (1895–1931). Activist in Chinese Communist movement from 1921. Central Committee member from 1922. Politburo member from 1927. Editor-in-chief of *Xiangdao zhoukan* from 1922. CCP representative to ECCI, 1925–27, 1928–30. CCP Central Committee Northern Bureau Secretary, 1927–28. Central Committee representative in Hong Kong from 1930.

Chen Boda (alias Chen Shangyu) (1904–1989). CCP member from 1927. Studied at UTK/KUTK, 1927–30. Communist propagandist, 1930–45. Central Committee member, 1945–73, Politburo candidate member, 1956–69, full member, 1969–73. Expelled from Party, 1973 and sentenced to 18 years in prison, 1981, for so-called "counterrevolutionary activity." Released, 1988.

Chen Changhao (alias Izumrudov) (1906–1967). Chinese Communist Youth League member from 1926. UTK/KUTK student, 1927–30. CCP member, 1930. Political Commissar of various divisions of Chinese Red Army from 1930. CCP Central Committee candidate member from 1934. Deputy Head of CCP Central Committee Propaganda Department from 1937. Translator in USSR, 1939–52. Deputy director of CCP Central Committee Bureau of translation of works of Marx, Engels, Lenin, Stalin from 1953.

Chen Duxiu (alias Old man; real name: Chen Qiansheng) (1879–1942). Leader of New Culture movement, 1915. Editor of *Xin qingnian* from 1915. Co-leader of "May Fourth" movement, 1919. Founder of Chinese Communist Party, leader of CCP, 1921–27. Expelled from Party, 1929. Leader of Chinese Trotskyists, 1929–1932. Arrested by GMD police, 1932. Paroled, 1937.

Chen Gongbo (1890–1946). Co-founder of Chinese Communist movement. First CCP Congress delegate, 1921. Left CCP and excluded from Party, 1923. GMD Central Executive Committee member from 1925. Collaborated with Japanese invaders, 1938–1945. Shot as a national traitor.

Chen Jiongming (1875–1933). Guangdong warlord. Collaborated with Sun Yat-sen, 1920–22. Guangdong governor, 1920–22. In June 1922 revolted against Sun Yat-sen. Defeated by GMD National Revolutionary Army, 1925.

Chen Qi (alias Anton Fyodorovich Soloviev) (1906–?). Chinese Communist Youth League member from 1926. UTK/KUTK student, 1926–29. Member of Trotskyist Opposition, 1927. Exiled to Azerbaijan, then to Far East. Repressed.

Chen Qiaonian (alias Krasin) (1902–1928). Chen Duxiu's second son. Joined CCP in 1923 in France. KUTV student, 1923–24. Central Committee member and Secretary of Hubei Provincial committee from 1927. Arrested by GMD police, February 1928. Executed.

Chen Shaoyu (alias Ivan Andreevich Golubev, Wang Ming) (1905–1974). CSYL member from 1924. CCP member from 1925. Studied and worked at UTK/KUTK, 1925–29. Editor of CCP Central Committee journal *Hongqi* (Red Banner), 1929–31. Politburo member, 1931–45. Head of CCP delegation to ECCI, 1931–37. ECCI Presidium member, 1932–43. ECCI Political Secretariat member, 1932–35. While in the Soviet Union closely cooperated with OGPU (NKVD), fabricated accusations against Chinese Communists. Responsible for arresting and executing many. Head of CCP Central Committee United Front Department, 1938–39. CCP Central Committee member, 1945–69. In January 1956 arrived in Soviet Union for medical treatment. Died in Moscow.

Chen Tanqiu (alias Deng, Yunxian) (1896–1943). Co-founder of CCP, 1921. Secretary of CCP Wuhan Regional Committee, 1924. CCP Central Committee candidate member from 1927. Secretary consecutively of CCP Jiangxi, Manchurian, Jiangsu, Fujian provisional Committees, 1927–34. Member of CCP delegation to ECCI, 1935–39. Party representative in Xinjiang from 1939. Arrested by a Xinjiang warlord and executed.

Chen Wangdao (1891–1977). Chinese Communist activist, 1920–21. Author of first Chinese translation of *Communist Manifesto.* Later taught at various schools.

Chen Yannian (Lin Mu, Sukhanov) (1898–1927). Chen Du-xiu's eldest son. Joined CCP in 1922 in France. Co-founder of Marxist journal *Shaonian* (Youth), 1923. KUTV student, 1923–24. Secretary of CCP Regional Committee of Jiangsu and Zhejiang, 1927. CCP Central Committee member from 1927. Arrested by GMD police, June 26, 1927. Executed.

Chen Yimou (1907–1932). Studied at UTK through 1927. Co-leader of Chinese Trotskyist movement.

Chen Yuandao (alias Nevsky) (1901–1933). CSYL member from 1923. CCP member from 1925. Studied and worked at UTK/KUTK, 1925–29. Worked in Jiangsu, Henan, Hebei Provincial Party Committees. Executed.

Chiang Ching-kuo (alias Nikolai Vladimirovich Elizarov). (1909 – 1988). Chiang Kai-shek's son. Chinese Communist Youth League member from 1925. Soviet Komsomol member from 1926. AUCP(B) candidate member, 1930–41. Studied at UTK, 1925–27 and Special Military School and Tolmachev Military-Political Academy, 1927–30. Metalworker at Moscow Dinamo plant, 1930–31. Chairman of October Revolution Collective Farm at Korovino (Moscow province), 1931. International Lenin School post-graduate student, 1931–32. Aid to a shop superintendent at Uralmash plant, Sverdlovsk, 1932–34. Deputy editor of Uralmash newspaper *Za tyazheloye mashinostroyeniye* (For Heavy Machinary Construction), 1924–27. Deputy Head of Sverdlovsk City Soviet Organizational Department, 1937. On Stalin's order sent back to China, 1937. President of Chinese Republic from 1976.

Chiang Kai-shek (alias Jiang Zhongzheng, Chiang Chungcheng) (1887–1975). GMD member from 1908. Central Executive Committee member from 1926. Head of Whampoa Military Academy from 1924. Commander-in-Chief of Guomindang National Revolutionary Army from 1926. Head of Guomindang regime from 1928.

Chicherin, Georgii Vasilievich (1872–1936). RSDLP member from 1905. Menshevik. Member of British Socialist Party, 1915–18. RSFSR/USSR Commissar of Foreign Affairs, 1918–30. Central Committee member, 1925–30. Retired.

Dai Jitao (alias Tianchou, Xiaoyuan) (1891–1949). GMD member from 1911. Sun Yat-sen's Secretary from 1911. Member of GMD Central Executive Committee from 1924. Ideologist of "Right" Guomindang. Rector of Sun Yat-sen University in Guangzhou, 1926–27. Head of Examination *yuan* (house) from 1928. Committed suicide.

Dalin, Sergei Alekseevich (1902–1985). RCP(B) member from 1919. Communist Youth International staff member, 1921–24. Member of Comintern Far Eastern Secretariat Presidium, 1921–22. Communist Youth International representative in China, 1922 and 1924. Taught at UTK, 1925–26. Sun Yat-sen University representative in China, 1926–27. Member of Trotskyist Opposition, 1927. *Isvestiya* and TASS correspondent, 1928–31. Repressed.

Dan, Fyodor Ilich (real name: Gurvich) (1871–1947). RSDLP member from 1898 and Central Committee member from 1905. Co-leader of Mensheviks. After February 1917 Revolution, Member of Executive Committee Bureau of Petrograd Soviet. Arrested, 1921, deported, 1922. Editor of *Sotsialisticheskii Vestnik*, 1922–42.

Deng Enming (1901–1931). Co-founder of CCP, 1921. Secretary of CCP Qingdao City Committee from 1922. Secretary of Shandong Regional Party Committee, 1926. Arrested by GMD police, 1928. Executed.

Deng Pei (1884–1927). CCP member from 1921. Co-organizer of Chinese labor movement. Co-leader of Tangshan and Anluan miners', and Beijing-Fengtian railroad workers' strikes, 1922. CCP Central Executive Committee candidate member from 1923. Executed.

Deng Xiaoping (alias Krezov, Ivan Sergeevich Dozorov, real name: Deng Xixian) (1904–1997). Activist in Chinese Communist movement from 1922.

Studied at KUTV, 1926–27 and UTK, 1927. Secretary of CCP CC, 1927, 1934–37. Co-leader of Soviet movement in Guangxi, 1930–31. Political Commissar of 129th division of Eighth Route Army, 1937–45. Deputy Premier of PRC, 1952–56, 1973–76, 1977–78. Central Committee General Secretary, 1956–66. Central Committee member, 1945–66, 1973–76, and from 1977. Politburo member, 1956–66, 1973–76, and from 1977, Politburo Standing Committee member, 1975–76 and from 1977. Deputy Chairman of Central Committee, 1975–76. Chairman of Central Committee Military Committee from 1981 and PRC Central Military Committee from 1983. Retired, 1990.

Deng Zeru (1869–1934). Member of Sun Yat-sen's *Revolutionary Alliance* from 1907. Head of GMD Guangdong Provincial Committee from 1922. GMD Central Control Commission member from 1924.

Deng Zhongxia (real name Deng Longbo) (1894–1933). Chinese Communist activist from 1920. Co-organizer of labor movement, 1921–22. CCP Central Executive Committee candidate member, 1923–25 and 1928–33. Politburo candidate member, 1927–28. Secretary of Jiangsu and Guangdong Provincial Party Committees, 1927–28. Member of Profintern Executive Committee from 1928. Member of CCP delegation to ECCI, 1928–30. Political Commissar of Second Army Group from 1930. Executed.

Dewey, John (1859–1952). American philosopher, psychologist, and educator.

Dong Biwu (alias Slukhov) (1886–1975). Joined Sun Yat-sen's revolutionary movement in 1911. Participated in Xinhai Revolution, 1911–12. Co-founder of CCP, 1921. Co-leader of Hubei Party organization, 1921–28. Studied at KUTK, 1928–32. Rector of Party School, 1935. Central Committee member from 1938. Chairman of Supreme Court from 1954. Politburo member from 1966.

Dong Yixiang (alias Lev Mikhailovich Orlinsky) (1899–1938). Chinese Socialist Youth League member from 1920. CCP member from 1921. Studied at UTK/ KUTK, 1925–27. Worked in NKVD in Soviet Far East, 1936–38. Repressed.

Dzerzhinsky, Feliks Edmundovich (1877–1926). RSDLP(B) Central Committee member from 1917. Politburo candidate member from 1924. Chairman of All-Russia Cheka (later OGPU), 1917–26. Commissar of Internal Affairs, 1919–23. Commissar of Transportation, 1921–24. Chairman of Supreme Economic Council from 1924.

Ehrenburg, Georgii Borisovich (1902–1967). Soviet Sinologist. Scientific Secretary of Scientific Research Institute for Chinese Studies, 1928–30. Professor at Moscow State University from 1930.

Engels, Friedreich (1820–1893). German philosopher and revolutionary. Co-founder of Marxism.

Epshtein, Bella (?-1938). Taught at UTK through 1927. Member of Trotskyist Opposition. Repressed. Shot at Vorkuta concentration camp.

Fan Wenhui (alias Fan Jinbiao, Fang Jinglu, Aleksei Makarovich Forel) (1904–1956). CCP member from 1926. AUCP(B) candidate member from 1928. Studied at UTK/KUTK, 1927–30. Co-leader of Chinese Trotskyists in Moscow, 1928–30. Arrested. Allowed to return to China, 1955.

Feng Qiang (Varsky) (?–?). CCP member and AUCP(B) candidate member. Studied at UTK, 1926–27. Member of Trotskyist Opposition. Expelled from USSR.

Feng Yuxiang (1882–1948). Chinese marshal, Commander-in-Chief of Nationalist Army from 1924. Member of Guomindang from 1926. Chairman of Guomindang Revolutionary Committee Central Committee Political Council, 1948.

Feng Ziyou (1882–1958). Member of Sun Yat-sen's *China Revival Society* from 1895. Member of *Revolutionary Alliance* from 1905. Expelled from Party for opposition to united front, 1924. Later rejoined GMD. Member of Nationalist Government from 1935.

Fokin, Nikolai Alekseevich (alias Molodoi) (1899–?). RCP(B) member from 1919. General Secretary of Turkmenistan Komsomol Central Committee and Central Asian Bureau of Komsomol Central Committee through 1924. Worked in

Communist Youth International from 1924. Secretary of Communist Youth International Executive Committee, 1924. Communist Youth International representative in China, 1926–27. Head of Eastern Department of Communist Youth International Executive Committee, 1927–30. Deputy Head of Eastern Department of Profintern, 1930–1933. Repressed.

Frunze, Mikhail Vasilievich (1885–1925). RSDLP(B) member from 1904. AUCP(B) Central Committee member from 1921. Politburo candidate member from 1925. Chairman of USSR Revolutionary Military Council and Commissar for Military and Naval Affairs, 1925.

Fu Xueli (alias Dvoikin) (?–?). Studied at KUTK, 1929–30. Co-leader of Chinese Trotskyists in Moscow. Repressed.

Gao Feng (alias Filippov) (1886–1926). Activist in Chinese Communist movement from 1922. Studied at KUTV, 1923–25. Secretary of Baoding City Party Commintee from 1925. Executed.

Gao Junyu (1896–1925). Activist in Chinese Communist movement from 1920. Secretary of Beijing Socialist Youth League, 1920–22. Editor of *Xiangdao zhoukan* and *Zhengzhi shenghuo* (Political Life), 1922–24. CCP Central Executive Committee member, 1922–23. Sun Yat-sen's secretary, 1924–25.

Geller, Lev Naumovich (alias Professor, Professionalist, Tarasov) (1875–?). RSDLP(B) member from 1904. Chairman of International Propaganda Council, 1920. Head of Profintern Eastern Department, 1922–30. Profintern representative in China, June-July 1926. Taught at International Lenin School from 1930. Repressed.

Gessen, Sergei Mikhailovich (1898–1838). RSDLP(B) member from 1916. After October Revolution, worked as Party activist in Petrograd, Samara, Yekaterinburg, and Minsk. Communist Youth International representative to ECCI, 1927. Member of Zinovievist Opposition, 1927. Expelled from Party, 1927. Recanted. Repressed.

Gingor, Semeon Vladimirovich (alias Gingorn) (1896–?). RCP(B) member from 1919. Taught history of Western revolutionary movement at UTK, February, 1926 – September, 1927. Member of Trotskyist Opposition. Repressed.

Gu Yingfen (1897–1956). GMD Central Executive Committee member from 1926. Member of Guangzhou Government Control Commission, 1925. Head of GMD CEC Youth and Agricultural Departments, 1926. Worked in Chiang Kai-shek's administration from 1931. Chinese, then Taiwanese Ambassador to Australia, 1948–51.

Guan Xiangying (alias Steklov, real names: Guaerjia [Mongolian], Guan Zhixiang [Chinese] (1902–1946). Chinese Socialist Youth League member from 1924. Studied at KUTV, 1924–25. CCP member from 1925. Central Committee member from 1928. Secretary of Chinese Communist Youth League CC, 1928–30. Political Commissar of Chinese Red Army Third Corps and of Second Army, 1932–37. Political Commissar of 120th Division of Eighth Route Army, 1937–45.

Guo Miaogen (alias Vazhnov) (1907). Studied at International Lenin School, 1928–30. Member of Trotskyist Opposition in Moscow. Repressed.

Guralsky Abram (Boris) Yakovlevich (alias Rustitko, Lepiti, Klein, Yakov, Dupon, real name: Kheifets) (1890–1960). Bund member from 1904. Latvian Region Social Democratic Party member from 1907. RSDLP(B) member from 1918. Deputy Chairman of Kiev Provincial Soviet Executive Committee, member of All-Ukrainian Central Executive Committee, ECCI representative in Germany, 1919–20 and 1921–23. Member of KPD Central Committee, Chairman of German Revolutionary Committee, 1923. KPD delegate to Fifth Comintern Congress, 1924. ECCI representative in France, 1924–1925. Head of Department at Marx and Engels Institute, 1926–1928. Member of Zinovievist Opposition. Expelled from Party, 1927. Recanted, 1928. Member of ECCI delegation in Latin America, 1930–34. Repressed.

He Shuheng (1876–1935). Co-founder of CCP, 1921. Worked in Hunan Party organization, 1921–28. Studied at KUTK, 1928–30. Commissar of Worker-Peasant Control in Chinese Soviet Government from 1931. Killed in action.

Ho Chi Minh (alias Nguyen Sinh Cung, Nguyen Ai Quoc, real name: Nguyen Tat Thanh) (1890–1969). Co-founder of French Communist Party, 1919. Studied at KUTV, 1923–24. ECCI activist, 1924–43. Co-founder of Vietnamese Communist movement, 1925. President of Democratic Republic of Vietnam from 1946.

Hu Chonggu (alias Nurin) (1902–?). CCP member from 1926. Studied at KUTV and KUTK, 1927–30. Co-leader of Chinese Trotskyists in Moscow. Repressed.

Hu Hanmin (1879–1936). Member of Sun Yat-sen's *Revolutionary Alliance* from 1905. Central Executive Committee member from 1924. Governor of Guangdong province and Minister of Foreign Affairs in Nationalist Government, 1925. Head of GMD delegation to USSR, 1925–26. After April 12, 1927, Chairman of GMD Central Executive Committee, and Head of Legislative *yuan* (house).

Hu Pengju (alias Gaevoy) (1907–?). Studied at KUTK, 1928–30. Co-leader of Chinese Trotskyists in Moscow. Repressed.

Huang Ju (alias Aleksandr Aleksandrovich Istomin) (1904–?). Studied and worked at UTK/KUTK, 1926–30. Member of Chinese Trotskyist Opposition. Repressed.

Iolk, Evgenii Sigizmundovich (alias E. Iogan, E. Ioganson, E. Barsukov, Iota, Yao Kai) (1900–1942). Soviet Sinologist. Member of Borodin's staff in China, 1926–27. Taught at various Moscow schools through 1932. Served in RKKA from 1932.

Isaacs, Harold (1910–1986). American journalist. Trotskyist from 1931. Author of *The Tragedy of the Chinese Revolution*, 1938.

Ivanov, Aleksei Alekseevich (alias Ivin) (1885–1942). Russian and Soviet Sinologist. Professor at Beijing University, 1917–27. *Pravda* correspondent in China, 1927–30. Research fellow at IWEIP, 1932–42.

James, Cyril Lionel Robert (alias Johnson, J. R. Johnson, CLR, Jimmy, Nello) (1901–1989). West Indian and American Socialist, co-founder of Pan-African movement.

Ji Dacai (alias Martynov, Devyatkin) (1903–?). CCP member from 1925. AUCP(B) candidate member from 1928. Studied at KUTV and KUTK, 1927–30. Co-leader of Chinese Trotskyists in Moscow. Repressed.

Ji Waifang (alias Dorodnyi) (?–?). Studied at KUTK, 1928–30. Co-leader of Chinese Trotskyists in Moscow. Repressed.

Jia Zongzhou (alias Kuznetsov, Stepan Lukich Lugovoy) (1903–?). CCP member from 1924. Studied at KUTV and KUTK, 1927–30. Co-leader of Chinese Trotskyists in Moscow. Repressed.

Jiang Guangci (alias Jiang Guangqi) (1901–1931). Chinese Socialist Youth League member from 1920. Studied at KUTV, 1921–24. CCP member from 1922. Taught at Shanghai University from 1924.

Joffe, Adolf Abramovich (alias V. Krymskii, Viktor, Vladimir Petrovich, Pavel Ivanovich) (1883–1927). RSDLP(B) member from July 1917. RSDLP(B) Central Committee candidate member, 1917–19. Participant in October Revolution. Deputy Commissar of Foreign Affairs and RSFSR Ambassador to Germany, 1918. Member of Defense Council and Ukrainian Commissar of State Control, 1919–20. Deputy Chairman of RCP(B) Turkestan Commission and Bureau, 1921. Head of diplomatic mission to China, 1922–24. USSR Ambassador to Austria, 1924–25. Member of Trotskyist Opposition. Committed suicide.

Joffe, Maria Mikhailovna (1896–?). Second wife of A. A. Joffe from 1920. Member of Trotskyist Opposition. Repressed, 1929. Spent 1929–57 in concentration camps and exile. Emigrated to Israel, 1975.

Joffe, Nadezhda Adolfovna (1906–1999). Daughter of A. A. Joffe. Member of Trotskyist Opposition. Repressed. Since 1991 had lived in New York City.

Joffe, Semeon Samoilovich (1895–1938) RSDLP(B) member from 1916. Co-leader of Bolshevik movement in Smolensk, 1917. Voroshilov's secretary on foreign political affairs, 1927. Repressed.

Ju Zheng (1876–1951). Member of Sun Yat-sen's *Revolutionary Alliance* from 1905. Minister of Internal Affairs in Guangzhu Government from 1922.

Kalinin, Mikhail Ivanovich (1875–1946). RSDLP member from 1898. RCP(B) Central Committee member from 1919. Politburo member from 1926. Chairman of All-Union Central Executive Committee from 1922.

Kamenev Lev Borisovich (real name: Rosenfeld) (1883–1936). RSDLP member from 1901. Central Committee member, 1917–27. Politburo member, 1919–26. Chairman of All-Russian Central Executive Committee, 1917. Chairman of Moscow Soviet, 1918–24. Deputy Chairman of Council of People's Commissars, 1922–26. Chairman of Labor Defense Council, 1924–26. Director of Lenin Institute, 1923–26. Commissar of Domestic and Foreign Trade, 1926. Soviet Ambassador to Italy, 1926–1927. Member of Zinovievist Opposition. Expelled from Party, 1927. Recanted, 1928. Repressed.

Kara-Murza, Georgii Sergeevich (1906–1945). Soviet Sinologist. Killed in aircraft crash.

Karakhan, Lev Mikhailovich (alias Mikhailov, Shakh, real name: Karakhanyan) (1889–1937). RSDLP(B) member from 1917. Secretary of Petrograd Soviet, 1917. Deputy Commissar of Foreign Affairs, 1918–20, 1927–34. Soviet Ambassador to Poland, 1921, China, 1923–26, and Turkey, 1934. Repressed.

Kasparova, Varsenika Dzhavadovna (1875–1941). RSDLP(B) member from 1904. Served in Political Department of Eleventh Red Army, 1919–1920. Co-organizer of Russian Communist women's movement from 1920. Head of Eastern Department of International Women's Secretariat, 1923–27. Member of Trotskyist Opposition. Expelled from Party, 1927. Recanted, 1934. Repressed.

Kazanin, Mark Isaakovich (1899–1972). Soviet Sinologist.

Kemal Ataturk, Pasha Mustapha (1881–1938). Turkish revolutionary. Colonel. First President of Turkish Republic, 1923–38. Established a bourgeois, pro-Western regime. In early 1920s, Bolsheviks regarded him as an anti-imperialist ally.

Kerensky, Aleksandr Fyodorovich (1881–1970). Russian Socialist Revolutionary, 1917. Minister of Justice in Provisional Government, March-May 1917. Minister of Military and Naval Affairs, May-September 1917. Prime-Minister, September–November 1917. Commander-in-Chief of Russian Army, August-November 1917. Emigrated after October Revolution.

Kirsanova, Klavdia Ivanovna (1888–1947). Wife of Ye. Yaroslavsky. RSDLP(B) member from 1904. After October Revolution, Secretary of Omsk City Party Committee, 1920–22. Rector of J. M. Sverdlov Communist University from 1922, then rector of International Lenin School. Arrested. Released, 1941.

Kolokolov, Vsevolod Sergeevich (1896–1979). Soviet Sinologist.

Kopp, Victor Leontievich (alias Tomsky) (1880–1930). RSDLP member from 1901. RSFSR Ambassador to Germany, 1919–21. Member of NKID Collegium, 1923–25. USSR Ambassador to Japan, 1925–27, and Sweden, from 1927.

Kosior, Stanislav Vikentievich (1889–1939). RSDLP(B) member from 1907. Secretary of Right-bank Regional Committee of Communist Party (Bolshevik) of Ukraine, 1918. Secretary of AUCP(B) Siberian Bureau, 1922–25. Central Committee Secretary, 1925–28. Politburo candidate member, 1927–30, full member from 1930. General Secretary of CP(B)U Central Committee, 1928–38. Repressed.

Krupskaya, Nadezhda Konstantinovna (1869–1939). Lenin's wife. RSDLP member from 1898. After October Revolution, member of Commissariat of Education Collegium. Member of Central Control Commission, 1924–27, and Central Committee from 1927. RSFSR Deputy Commissar of Education from 1929.

Kuchumov, Vladimir Nikolaevich (1900–?). Soviet Sinologist.

Kuibyshev, Valerian Vladimirovich (1888–1935). RSDLP(B) member from 1904. Central Committee Secretary from 1922. Chairman of Central Control Commission, Commissar of Worker-Peasant Inspectorate, Deputy Chairman of Council of People's Commissars, and Deputy Chairman of Labor Defense Council from 1923. Chairman of Supreme Economic Council from 1926. Chairman of State Planing Committee from 1930. Chairman of Soviet Control Commission from 1934.

286

Kuznetsova, Maria Fyodorovna (alias Nora) (?–?). Voitinsky's wife. Accompanied him to China, 1920–21. Representative of International Women's Secretariat in China, 1926–27.

Landau, Ephraim Moiseevich (1893–1977). Came to Russia from Poland after October Revolution. Served in RKKA as Chairman of Revolutionary Commission of Second Division (Baku) through May 1923. Took Centrosoyuz courses, 1923–26. Economist at Centrosoyuz, 1926–29. Member of Trotskyist Opposition. Arrested, 1929. Prisoner at Verkhne-Uralskii political isolator in Archangel, 1929–33. Released, 1933. Arrested and sentenced to 5 years in Vorkuta camps, December 28, 1936. Released, 1944. Arrested again and sent to Krasnoyarskii krai (region), January 6, 1951. Released, 1954.

Lenin, Vladimir Ilich (alias Nikolai Lenin, real name: Ulyanov) (1870–1924). Co-founder of *St-Petersburg Union of Struggle for Emancipation of Working Class*, 1895. RSDLP member from 1898. Founder of RSDLP(B). Central Committee member, 1903–24. Politburo member, 1919–24. Co-organizer of October Revolution. Chairman of Council of People's Commissars, 1917–24. Chairman of Labor Defense Council, 1922–24.

Li Da (alias G. S.) (1890–1966). Co-founder of CCP, 1921. CCP Central Bureau member in charge of propaganda, 1921–22. Left CCP, 1923. Taught at various schools. Re-joined CCP, 1949.

Li Dazhao (alias Li Shouchang, Qinhua) (1889–1927). One of first Chinese Communists, founder of Beijing Marxist nucleus, 1920. CCP member from 1921. Member of CCP Central Executive Committee, 1922–27. Leader of CCP Central Executive Committee Northern Bureau, 1921–27.

Li Fuchun (alias Grigoriev) (1900–1975). Activist in Chinese Communist movement from 1922. Studied at KUTV, 1925. Secretary of Jiangxi Party Provincial Committee, 1928–34. Minister of Heavy Industry, 1950–54. Deputy Premier and Head of State Planning Committee from 1954. Central Committee candidate member from 1934 and full member from 1945. Politburo member, 1956–69, and Politburo Standing Committee member, 1966–69.

Li Guangji (alias Plotnikov, Zhong Yongcang) (?–?). Studied at KUTK, 1929–30. Co-leader of Chinese Trotskyists in Moscow. Repressed.

Li Guangya (alias Stolbov) (?–?). Studied at UTK, 1926–27. Member of Trotskyist Opposition. Expelled from USSR.

Li Hanjun (1890–1927). Co-founder of Chinese Communist movement, 1921. Left Party, 1922. Taught at various schools, worked in GMD Hubei Government. Killed in Wuhan.

Li Ping (alias Lektorov) (?–?). Studied at KUTK, 1928–30. Co-leader of Chinese Trotskyists in Moscow. Repressed.

Li Zongwu (alias Li Zhongwu) (?–?). Correspondent of Beijing newspaper *Chen bao* (Morning) in Soviet Russia, 1920–21.

Liang Ganqiao (alias Lastochkin) (1904–194?). CCP member from 1926. Studied at Whampoa Military Academy, 1924–25, and UTK, 1926–27. Co-founder of Chinese Trotskyist movement, 1927. Expelled from Party, 1928. Joined GMD, 1931. Co-leader of Chiang Kai-shek's "Blueshirt Clique."

Liao Zhongkai (1877–1925). Member of Sun Yat-sen's *Revolutionary Alliance* from 1905. GMD Central Executive Committee member from 1924. Prominent GMD "left" member. Commissar of Whampoa Military Academy and Minister of Finance in Guangzhou Government from 1924. Assassinated.

Lin Aimin (alias Leonidov) (1906–?). Chinese Communist Youth League and Soviet Komsomol member from 1926. Studied at UTK, 1926–27. Member of Trotskyist Opposition. Expelled from USSR.

Lin Boqu (alias Lin Zuhan, Komissarov) (1885–1960). Member of Sun Yat-sen's *Revolutionary Alliance* from 1905. Participated in Xinhai Revolution, 1911–12. CCP member from November 1921. Head of GMD CEC General

Department, 1922. GMD Central Executive Committee member, 1924–26. GMD representative and Head of Political Department of NRA Sixth Corps, 1926–27. Studied at UTK/KUTK, 1927–30. Conducted Party work in Soviet Far East, 1930–32. Chairman of Communist Government in Shenxi-Gansu-Ningxia Border Region, 1937–48. Central Committee member from 1938, Politburo member from 1945. Deputy Chairman of National People's Congress Standing Committee from 1955.

Liu Bojian (alias Sherstinsky) (1895–1935). Activist in Chinese Communist movement from 1922. Studied at KUTV, 1923–26 and Military-Political and Frunze Military Academies, 1928–30. Head of General Political Department of Feng Yuxiang's Nationalist Army, 1926–27. Conducted political work in Chinese Red Army. Taken prisoner by GMD and executed.

Liu Changsheng (1904–67). Docker in Vladivostok, 1922. RCP(B) member from 1923. CCP member from 1928, CCP Central Committee candidate member, 1945–56, and full member from 1956. Deputy Chairman of Chinese labor unions, 1953–57. Killed by Red Guards.

Liu Renjing (alias Lensky, Neal Shi, Liu Ruoshui) (1902–1987). CCP member from 1921. General Secretary of Chinese Socialist (Communist) Youth League, 1923–26. Studied at International Lenin School, 1926–29. Member of Chinese Trotskyist Opposition. Expelled from Party, 1929. Theoretician of Chinese Left Opposition. Arrested, imprisoned, 1935–37 and 1952. Recanted, 1972.

Liu Renshou (alias Martyn Martynovich Khabarov) (1905–1937). Liu Renjing's brother. Chinese Communist Youth League member from 1925. Studied at UTK, 1925–27, and Military Engineering School, 1927–28. Soviet Komsomol member, 1927–30. Worked in OGPU and Foreign Languages Publishing house, 1929–35. Plumber at a factory from 1935.

Liu Shaoqi (1898–1969). CCP member from 1921. Studied at KUTV, 1921. Co-organizer of Chinese labor movement from 1921. Deputy Chairman and Secretary of All-China General Labor Union Executive Committee, 1925–27. Central Committee member from 1927. Politburo member from 1928. Secretary of Central Committee Secretariat and Deputy Chairman of Revolutionary Military Council from 1943. Deputy Chairman of Central People's Government from 1949. Chairman of Standing Committee of National People's Cougress from 1954. Politburo Standing Committee member and Central Committee Deputy Chairman from 1956. Chairman of People's Republic of China from 1959. Expelled from Party, 1968.

Liu Yin (alias Liu Ying, Kashin, Gubarev, Li Jianfang, Li Maimai) (1906–1940). Chinese Communist Youth League member from 1925. CCP member from 1928. AUCP(B) candidate member, 1928–29. Co-leader of Chinese Trotskyists in Moscow, then in China from 1928. Left Trotskyist movement in mid-1930s.

Lozovsky, A. (real name: Solomon Abramovich Dridzo) (1878–1952). RSDLP member from 1901. Central Committee candidate member, 1927–39 and full member from 1939. General Secretary of Profintern and ECCI member, 1921–37. Deputy Commissar of Foreign Affairs, 1939–46. Repressed.

Lu Yuan (alias Shou Shi, Yi Bai, Lu Yiyuan, Lu Yan) (1903–?). Chinese Communist Youth League member from 1925. Studied at Shanghai University, 1922–25 and UTK, 1925–27. Soviet Komsomol member from 1926. Co-founder of Chinese Trotskyist movement, 1927. Expelled from Party, 1928. Joined GMD, 1931.

Lunacharsky, Anatolii Vasilievich (1875–1933). Activist in Russian Social Democratic movement from 1896. Member of RSDLP(B) from 1903. Commissar of Education from October 1917. Chairman of Scientific Council at USSR Central Executive Committee, 1929–33. USSR Ambassador to Spain, 1933.

Luo Han (alias Loganov) (1898–1941). CCP member from 1922. Studied at KUTV, 1926–28. Member of Trotskyist Opposition in Moscow from 1928. Co-leader of Left Opposition in China from 1929. Killed in a Japanese air raid.

Luo Yinong (alias Bukharov) (1902–1928). Chinese Communist Youth League member from 1920. CCP member from 1921. Studied at KUTV, 1921–25. Head of Propaganda Department of Guangdong-Guangxi Party Regional Committee, 1925. Secretary of Jiangsu-Zhejiang Party Committee, 1926–27. Central Committee member from 1927. Politburo member and Head of Organizational Department, 1927–28. Executed.

Luo Zhanglong (1896–1995). Activist in Chinese Communist movement from 1920. CCP Central Executive Committee member, 1923–24, 1927–28 and candidate member, 1925–27, 1928–31. CEC Secretary and Central Executive Committee Bureau member, 1923–25. Expelled from Party for opposition to Comintern, 1931. Taught at various schools.

Ma Yuansheng (alias Petukhov, Petrov) (1906–1977). Studied at International Lenin School, 1928–30. Member of Trotskyist Opposition in Moscow. Arrested. Released and returned to China in 1950s.

Madyar, Ludwig Ignatovich (real name: Lajos Milgorf) (1891–1940). Participated in Hungarian Revolution, 1919. TASS staff member, 1922–26. Worked in China, 1926–28. Deputy Head of ECCI Eastern Secretariat, 1929–34. Repressed.

Mandalyan, Tates (Tateos) Gegamich (alias Chernyak, Professionalist) (1901–?). RSDLP(B) member from 1917. Labor Union activist in Caucasus, 1920–23. Worked in Profintern from 1923. Profintern representative in China, 1926–27. Chairman of Voronezh Labor Union Council, 1927–36. Political adviser to ECCI General Secretary Georgii Dimitrov, 1936–37.

Manuilsky, Dmitrii Zakharovich (1883–1959). RSDLP member from 1903. RSDLP(B) member from 1917. Central Committee member, 1923–52. Secretary of CP(B)U Central Committee, 1921. ECCI Presidium member, 1924–28. Secretary of Comintern Executive, 1928–43. Deputy Chairman of Council of People's Commissars and Commissar of Foreign Affairs of the Ukraine, 1944–53.

Mao Zedong (1893–1976). Co-founder of CCP, 1921. CEC (CC) candidate member, 1924–25 and 1927, full member, 1923–24, and from 1928. Politburo candidate member, 1930–34. Politburo Secretariat and Standing Committee member, 1935–43. Chairman of CCP Central Committee from 1943. GMD Central Executive Committee candidate member, 1924–27.

Maring, Hendrikus (alias Andersen, Martin Ivanovich Bergman, H. Brouwer, Mander, Philipp, Sentot, Simons, Joh van Son, real name: Sneevliet) (1883–1942). Activist in Communist movement on Java and in Holland, worked in ECCI from 1920. Secretary of Second Comintern Congress Commission on National and Colonial Questions, 1920. ECCI representative in China, 1921–23, in Germany, Austria, Holland, Norway, Sweden, and France, 1923–28. Member of Trotskyist Opposition. Expelled from Comintern, 1928. Murdered by Nazis in Amsterdam.

Martov, Yulii Osipovich (real name: Tsederbaum) (1873–1923). Co-founder of *St-Petersburg Union of Struggle for Emancipation of Working Class*, 1895. RSDLP member from 1898. Co-leader of Mensheviks. Member of All-Russia Central Executive Committee, 1918–20. Left Russia, 1920. Founder and editor of *Sotsialisticheskii Vestnik* from 1921.

Martynov, Aleksandr Samoilovich (alias Miner, Polyakov, real name: Saul Samuilovich Piker) (1865–1935). *People's Will* (Populist terrorist group) member from 1885. RSDLP member from 1899. RCP(B) member from 1923. *Kommunisticheskii Internatsional* editor from 1924.

Marx, Karl (1818–1883). German philosopher and revolutionary. Co-founder of Marxism.

Mazunin (?–?). Taught at UTK through 1927. Member of Trotskyist Opposition. Repressed.

Mencius (alias Mengzi, real name: Meng Ke) (372–289 B.C.). Chinese philosopher, Confucianist.

Meng Qingshu (alias Meng Jingsu, Rosa Vladimorovna Osetrova) (1905–1983). Chen Shaoyu's wife. Studied at UTK/KUTK, 1926–29.

Mif, Pavel (real name: Mikhail Aleksandrovich Fortus) (1901–1938). RSDLP(B) member from 1917. Pro-rector of UTK, 1925–27. Rector of UTK/KUTK, 1927–29. Deputy Head of ECCI Eastern Secretariat, 1928–35. Political adviser to ECCI General Secretary Georgii Dimitrov, 1935. Rector of KUTV, 1936. Director of Institute for Scientific Research on National and Colonial Problems, 1937. Arrested, December 11, 1937, and executed, July 28, 1938.

Molotov, Vyacheslav Mikhailovich (real name: Skryabin) (1890–1986). RSDLP(B) member from 1906. Central Committee candidate member, 1920–21, full member, 1921–57. Politburo candidate member, 1921–26, full member, 1926–57. Secretary of Donetsk Provincial Party Committee, 1919–20. Secretary of CP(B)U, 1920. Secretary of AUCP(B) Central Committee, 1921–30. Chairman of Council of People's Commissars, 1930–41. USSR Commissar of Foreign Affairs, 1939–49, and Minister of Foreign Affairs, 1953–56. Soviet Ambassador to Mongolia, 1957–60.

Muralov, Nikolai Ivanovich (1877–1937). RSDLP(B) member from 1903. Central Control Commission member, 1925–27. Commander of Moscow military district, 1921–24. Commander of North Caucasus military district, 1924–25. Member of RSFSR State Planning Committee, Rector of Agricultural Academy, 1925–27. Member of Trotskyist Opposition. Expelled from Party, 1927. Repressed.

Musin, Isaak Maksimovich (alias Iokhelis, real name: Iokhel) (1894–1927). Bund member, 1913 – October 1917. RCP(B) member from 1918. After October Revolution, worked in Commissariat of Foreign Affairs. Political reviewer and secretary of ECCI Far Eastern and Eastern Departments from 1922. TASS correspondent in China, 1925–1927. Committed suicide.

Nasonov, Nikolai Mikhailovich (alias Nazonov, Charlie, Yunosha) (1902–?). RCP(B) member from 1919. Secretary of Tambov Komsomol Provincial Committee, 1921–22. Komsomol Central Committee Far Eastern Bureau member, 1922–23. Secretary of Vladivostok Komsomol Provincial Committee, 1923–24. Secretary of Komsomol Central Asian Bureau, 1924–25. Communist Youth International representative in China, 1925–27, and USA, 1927–28. Head of Negro Section of ECCI Eastern Department, 1932–33. Repressed.

Nechaev, Sergei Gennadievich (1847–1882). Extreme left activist in Russian revolutionary movement. Arrested in Switzerland, 1872. Died in prison in St-Petersburg.

Nie Rongzhen (alias Zorin) (1899–1992). Chinese Communist Youth League member from 1922. CCP member from 1923. Studied at KUTV and Soviet Military Academy, 1924–25. Deputy Chief of Staff of Chinese Red Army, 1931–35. Deputy Commander of 115th division of Eighth Route Army, 1937–43. Central Committee member from 1945. Politburo member, 1956–69, 1977–87.

Ordzhonikidze, Georgii Konstantinovich (alias Sergo) (1886–1937). RSDLP(B) member from 1903. First Secretary of Transcaucasian and North Caucasus Regional Party Committees, 1922–26. Chairman of Central Control Commission and Commissar of Worker-Peasant Inspectorate, 1926–30. Deputy Chairman of Council of People's Commissars and Labor Defense Council. Chairman of Supreme Economic Council, 1930. USSR Commissar of Heavy Industry, 1932. Committed suicide.

Oshanin, Ilya Mikhailovich (1900–1982). Soviet Sinologist.

Parvus, Aleksandr Lvovich (real name: Helfond) (1869–1924). Activist in Russian and German Social Democratic movements. Abandoned political activity, 1918.

Peng Shuzhi (alias Ivan Petrov) (1895–1983). Activist in Chinese Communist movement from 1921. Studied at KUTV, 1921–24. Secretary of CCP Moscow branch, 1921–24. Central Executive Committee Bureau member, Head of Propaganda Department, and editor of *Xin qingnian* and *Xiangdao zhoukan*, 1925–27. CCP Central Executive Committee candidate member, 1927–29. Expelled from Party, 1929. Co-leader of Chinese Trotskyist Opposition from 1929.

Plekhanov, Georgii Valentinovich (1856–1918). Co-leader of Populist organizations *Land and Liberty*, 1875–81, and *Black Partition*, 1881–83. Founder of Russian Social Democratic movement (*Emancipation of Labor* group), 1883. Co-leader of RSDLP from 1898. Leader and theoretician of Menshevism.

Polivanov, Evgenii Dmitrievich (1891–1938). Soviet Sinologist. Repressed.

Polyakov (?–?). Taught at UTK through 1927. Member of Trotskyist Opposition. Repressed.

Potapov, A. S. (?–?). General of Imperial Russian Army. Lived in China, 1917–20. Collaborated with Soviet authorities. Taught at various Soviet schools from 1920.

Preobrazhensky, Yevgenii Alekseevich (1886–1937). RSDLP(B) member from 1903. Central Committee candidate member, 1917–18. Central Committee Organizational Bureau member, 1920–21. Secretary of Ural Regional Party Committee, 1918–19. Secretary of Central Committee, 1920–22. Chairman of Financial Committee of Party Central Committee and Council of People's Commissars from 1921. Member of Commissariat of Finance Collegium, 1921–27. Member of Trotskyist Opposition. Expelled from Party, 1927. Recanted, 1929. Repressed.

Prigozhin, Abram Grigorievich (1896–1937). RSDLP(B) member from 1918. Taught at Ural and Siberian Communist Universities, 1925–26. Taught history of Western revolutionary movement at UTK, September 1926–June 1, 1927. Member of Trotskyist Opposition. Repressed.

Qi Shugong (alias Ji Shugong, Ji Bugong, Nikolai Alekseevich Nekrasov) (1908–?). Soviet Komsomol member, 1924–30. Studied at UTK, 1925–27. Worked at KUTV and KUTK, 1927–30. Member of Trotskyist Opposition. Repressed.

Qin Bangxian (alias Pogorelov, Bo Gu) (1907–1946) CCP member from 1925. Studied and worked at UTK/KUTK, 1926–30. Head of Chinese Communist Youth League Central Committee Propaganda Department, 1930–31. Secretary of CCYL CC, 1931–34. CCP Central Committee General Secretary, 1931–35. Head of CCP Central Committee Organizational Department, 1936–37. Head of Central Committee Changjiang (Yangzi) and Southern Bureaus, 1937–41. Killed in aircraft crash.

Qiu Zhicheng (alias Vosmerkin) (1908–?). Chinese Communist Youth League member from 1926. CCP member from 1927. Studied at KUTK, 1928–30. Co-leader of Chinese Trotskyists in Moscow. Repressed.

Qu Qiubai (alias Strakhov; real name: Qu Shuang) (1899–1935). Correspondent of Beijing newspaper *Chen bao* in Moscow, 1921–22. CCP member from 1922. CCP Central Executive Committee candidate member and Editor-in-Chief of *Xin qingnian*, 1923–25. CCP CEC (CC) member from 1924. Head of CCP Central Executive Committee Propaganda Department, 1927. Politburo member, 1927–31. After Communist defeat in July 1927, Head of CCP Central Committee Provisional Politburo and Editor-in-Chief of CCP journal *Buersaiweike* (The Bolshevik). Head of CCP delegation to ECCI and member of ECCI Presidium, 1928–30. Commissar of People's Education in Chinese Soviet Government, 1931–34. Taken prisoner by GMD and executed.

Radek, Karl Berngardovich (real name: Karol Sobelsohn) (1885–1939). RSDLP(B) member from 1903. Member of Polish Social Democratic Party from 1902, and of Social Democratic Party of Poland and Lithuania from 1904. Activist in German Left Social Democratic movement from 1908. RCP(B) Central Committee member, 1919–24. ECCI Secretary, 1919–23. Rector of UTK, 1925–27. Member of Trotskyist Opposition. Expelled from Party, 1927. Recanted, 1930. Head of Central Committee International Information Bureau, 1932–36. Repressed.

Rafes, Moisei Grigorievich (alias Max) (1883–1942). Bund member from 1900. RCP(B) member from 1919. Worked in ECCI Department of Agitation and Propaganda from 1920. Secretary of ECCI Far Eastern Bureau, June-October 1926. Head of TASS Foreign Department from 1926. Repressed.

291

Rakovsky, Khristian Georgievich (alias Dragomir, Ghelengiceanu, Dionisy Grigoriev, Kh. G. Insarov, Khristiou Khristev) (1873–1941). Activist in revolutionary movements in Bulgaria, Switzerland, Germany, France, Romania, and Russia. RSDLP(B) member from 1917. Central Committee member, 1919–27. Chairman of Ukrainian Government, 1918–23. USSR Ambassador to Great Britain, 1923–25, and France, 1925–27. Member of Trotskyist Opposition. Expelled from Party, 1927. Recanted, 1934. Repressed.

Raskolnikov, Fyodor Fyodorovich (alias Petrov, real name: Il'in) (1892–1939). RSDLP(B) member from 1910. Deputy Commissar for Naval Affairs and Commander of Volga, Caspian, and Baltic fleets, 1918–21. Soviet Ambassador to Afghanistan, 1921–23. Head of ECCI Eastern Department, March 1924–February 1926. Soviet Ambassador to Estonia, Denmark, and Bulgaria, 1930–38. Emigrated, 1938. Expelled from Party, 1938. Assassinated.

Ren Bishi (alias Brinsky, Zheng Ling, real name: Ren Peiguo) (1904–1950). Activist in Chinese Communist movement from 1920. CCP member from 1921. Studied at KUTV, 1921–24. Head of Chinese Socialist (Communist) Youth League Organizational Department, 1924–27. General Secretary of CCYL CEC, 1927–28. CCP Central Committee member, 1928. Secretary of CCP Hubei Provincial Committee from 1929. CCP Central Committee Politburo member from 1931. Secretary of CCP Hunan-Jiangxi Soviet Regional Committee, 1933–34. Head of General Political Department of Communist Eighth Route Army, 1937–38. Member of CCP delegation to ECCI, 1938–40. Secretary of CCP Central Committee Secretariat from 1943.

Ren Zhuoxuan (alias Rafael, Ye Qing) (1896–1990). Activist in Chinese Communist movement from 1922. French Communist Party member, 1923–25. Studied at UTK, 1925–26. Co-leader of CCP Moscow branch. Worked in Guangdong Regional and Hunan Provincial Party Committees, 1926–27. Arrested by GMD secret police and confessed, 1927. Taught at various schools from 1940.

Robespierre, Maximilian (1758–1794). French revolutionary, co-leader of *Jacobins* club. Head of Committee of Public Safety, 1793–94.

Roy, Manabendra Nath (alias Johnson, real name: Battacharya Narendra Nath) (1892–1948). Active member of Indian and Mexican Communist movements. Worked in ECCI from 1920. ECCI member, 1927–28. Expelled from ECCI, 1928. General Secretary of Radical Democratic Party of India from September 1940.

Rudzutak, Jan Ernestovich (1887–1938). RSDLP(B) member from 1905. Central Committee member, 1920–37. Politburo member, 1926–30. Commissar of Transportation, 1924–30. Deputy Chairman of Council of People's Commissars and Labor Defense Council, 1926–37. Chairman of Central Control Commission and Worker-Peasant Inspectorate, 1931–34. Repressed.

Russell, Bertrand Arthur William, 3rd Earl (1872–1970). British philosopher and mathematician, whose emphasis on logical analysis influenced twentieth century philosophy. Nobel Prize laureate for Literature, 1950.

Rykov, Aleksei Ivanovich (1881–1938). RSDLP member from 1898. Central Committee member, 1905–07, 1917–18, 1920–30 and candidate member, 1934–37. Organizational Bureau member, 1920–24. Politburo member, 1922–30. Chairman of Supreme Economic Council, 1918–24, Council of People's Commissars, 1924–30, and Labor Defense Council, 1926–30. Commissar of Communication, 1931–36. Expelled from Party, 1937. Repressed.

Safarov, Georgii Ivanovich (alias Volodin, Egorov, Samovarchik) (1891–1942). RSDLP(B) member from 1908. Central Committee candidate member, 1921–23, 1924–25. Secretary and Head of ECCI Eastern Department, August 1921–May 1922. Editor of *Petrogradskaya Pravda*, 1922–26. First Secretary of Soviet Embassy in China, 1926–27. Member of Zinovievist Opposition. Expelled from Party, 1927. Recanted, 1928. Deputy Head of ECCI Eastern Länder Secretariat, 1929–34. Repressed.

Serebryakov, Leonid Petrovich (1890–1937). RSDLP(B) member from 1905. Member of Kostroma Soviet, 1917. After October Revolution, member of Moscow Provincial Party Committee, RCP(B) Central Committee Secretary, All-Russian Council of Labor Unions Secretary. Member of Trotskyist Opposition. Expelled from Party, 1927. Recanted, 1928. Repressed.

Shachtman, Max (alias Mikhails, Pedro, S-n, M. N. Trent) (1904–1972). Member of USA Workers Party (i.e., Communist Party), 1921–28. Co-founder of journal *Militant*, 1928. Co-founder of Communist League of America, 1929. Founder of Pioneer Publishing House, 1931. Co-founder of Socialist Workers' Party (SWP), 1937. After being expelled from SWP, co-founded Workers Party, 1940 (from 1949, Independent Socialist League.)

Shao Lizi (1882–1967). Member of Sun Yatsen's *Revolutionary Alliance* from 1905. CCP member, 1921–26. Head of Whampoa Military Academy Secretariat, 1925. GMD Central Executive Committee representative to ECCI, 1926–27. After July 1927, Head of GMD Central Executive Committee Propaganda Department, Chinese Ambassador to USSR, and National Political Consultative Conference Secretary. Resigned from GMD Government, 1949.

Shchukar, Maxim Ilich (1897–?). Soviet Sinologist. Professor at UTK/KUTV. Repressed.

Shen Dingyi (alias Shen Jianhou, real name: Shen Xuanlu) (1883–1928). One of first Chinese Communists, later an outstanding GMD activist. GMD member from 1923. GMD Central Executive Committee candidate member from 1924. Left Communist movement and expelled from CCP, 1925. Assassinated.

Shen Zemin (alias Cheng Zeren, real name: Shen Deji) (1902–1933). Younger brother of famous writer Shen Yanbing (Mao Dun). Activist in Chinese Communist movement from January 1921. Chinese Socialist Youth League Central Executive Committee member, 1922–23. Taught at Shanghai University from 1924. Studied and worked at UTK/KUTK, 1926–30. CCP Central Committee member from 1931.

Shi Cuntong (alias Shi Renrong, Fang Guochang) (1890–1970). Activist in Chinese Communist movement from 1920. Secretary of Chinese Socialist Youth League, 1922–24. Taught at various Communist schools, 1924–27. After CCP defeat in July 1927, left Party.

Shklovsky Grigorii Lvovich (alias Babushkin, Dedushkin) (1875–1937). RSDLP member from 1898. Soviet diplomat, 1918–25. Central Control Commission member, 1925–27. Member of Zinovievist Opposition. Repressed.

Shumyatsky, Boris Zakharovich (alias Andrei Chervony) (1886–1938). RSDLP(B) member from 1903. Deputy Chairman of Krasnoyarsk Soviet, Chairman of Siberian Soviet CEC, 1917. Deputy Chairman of Siberian Revolutionary Committee, 1919. Chairman of Far Eastern Republic Council of Ministers and Soviet Council of People's Commissars representative in Siberia and Mongolia, 1920–22. Soviet Ambassador to Iran, 1922–1925. Rector of KUTV, 1926–28. Head of Agitation and Propaganda Department of AUCP(B) Central Committee Central Asian Bureau, 1928–30. Chairman of Soviet Cinematographic Committee, 1930–33. Repressed.

Smirnov, Vladimir Mikhailovich (1887–1937). RSDLP(B) member from 1907. After February 1917 Revolution, member of RSDLP(B) Moscow Committee and Revolutionary Committee. RSFSR Commissar of Commerce and Industry, 1918. Expelled from Party as a leader of intra-party Democratic Centralist Group, 1927. Repressed.

Solts, Aaron Aleksandrovich (1872–1945). RSDLP(B) member from 1898. After February 1917 Revolution, editor of Bolshevik newspapers *Sotsial-Demokrat* and *Pravda*. AUCP(B) Central Control Commission member, 1920–23. Central Control Commission Presidium and International Control Commission member, 1923–34. Later worked in USSR Office of Public Prosecutor.

Song Fengchun (alias Karl Preis) (1906–?). Chinese Communist Youth League and CCP member from 1925. Studied at UTK, 1926–27. Co-leader of Trotskyist movement in China.

Stalin, Joseph Vissarionovich (alias Koba, Vasilii, Vasiliev, K. St., real name: Djugashvili) (1879–1953). RSDLP member from 1898. Central Committee member from 1917. Politburo member from 1919. Commissar for Nationalities, 1917–22. Central Committee General Secretary from 1922. Chairman of Council of People's Commissars from 1941.

Su Zhaozheng (1885–1929). CCP member from 1925. Central Committee member from 1927. Organizer of Guangzhou-Hong Kong strike, 1925–26. Chairman of All-China Federation of Labor, 1926. Minister of labor in Wuhan Government of Guomindang, March-June 1927.

Sun Chuanfang (1885–1935). Chinese warlord. Military governor of Fujian province, 1923–24. Controlled Zhejiang, Fujian, Jiangsu, Anhui and Jiangxi from 1925. Defeated by NRA, 1927. Retired, 1929. Assassinated.

Sun Ke (alias Sun Fo) (1891–1973). Sun Yat-sen's son. GMD Central Executive Committee member from 1924. Mayor of Guangzhou, 1921–22, 1923–24, 1925–27. Head of Guangdong Provincial Government, 1925–27. Member of Wuhan Government, 1927. Minister of finance of Nanjing Government from September 1927. Head of Legislative *yuan* (house), 1932–48. Left China for France and USA, 1949. Came to Taiwan to become Head of Examination *yuan*, 1965.

Sun Yat-sen (alias Sun Zhongshan, Sun Yixian, real name: Sun Wen) (1866–1925). Chinese revolutionary. Founder of Guomindang. Provisional President of Chinese Republic, 1912. President of Military Government of South China, 1917, 1920–22, 1923–25.

Svechin, Aleksandr Andreevich (1878–1938). Russian military historian and theoretician. Major-general, Head of Russian General staff, 1916. Head of Red Army General Staff after October Revolution. Professor at Frunze Military academy and General Staff Academy. Repressed.

Tan Boling (alias Musin) (1903–?). Studied at Shanghai University, 1921–25. Whampoa Military Academy cadet, 1926. CCP member from 1926. Studied at KUTK, 1928–30. Co-leader of Chinese Trotskyists in Moscow, 1928–30. Repressed.

Tan Pingshan (1886–1956). CCP member from 1921. Central Committee and Politburo member, 1926–27. Minister of agriculture in Wuhan Government of Guomindang, March-June 1927. After 1925–27 revolution, left CCP. Co-founder of Peasant-Worker Democratic Party. Served in People's Republic State apparatus from 1949.

Tan Yankai (1880–1930). GMD member from 1912. GMD Central Executive Committee member from 1924. Governor of Hunan province, 1918–20. Executive Head of Guomindang Nationalist Government, 1926–27, 1928, 1929.

Tkachev, Pyotr Nikitich (1844–1885). Extreme left activist in Russian revolutionary movement.

Tomsky, Mikhail Pavlovich (alias M.T., real name: Efremov) (1880–1936). RSDLP(B) member from 1904. Central Committee member, 1919–34 and candidate member from 1934. Politburo member, 1922–30. Chairman of Moscow Labor Unions Council, 1917–18. Chairman of All-Soviet Labor Unions Council, 1918–21, 1922–29. Deputy Chairman of Supreme Economic Council Presidium, 1929–30. Head of State Publishing House from 1932. Committed suicide.

Treint, Albert (alias Bertreint) (1889–1971). PCF Central Committee member and ECCI Presidium candidate member, 1927. Member of Zinovievist Opposition. Expelled from Party, 1928.

Trilisser, Meer Abramovich (alias Moskvin) (1883–1940). RSDLP member from 1901. Cheka official from 1921. Head of OGPU Foreign Department, February, 1926 – October, 1929. Deputy Commissar of RSFSR Commissariat of Worker-Peasant Inspectorate, 1930–34. Member of AUCP(B) Central Control Commission Presidium from 1930. Repressed.

Trotsky, Leon Davidivich (alias Pero, Nikolai Trotsky, real name: Bronshtein) (1879–1940). RSDLP member from 1898. RSDLP(B) member from July 1917. Central Committee member, 1917–27. Politburo member, 1919–26. Co-organizer of October Revolution. Commissar of Foreign Affairs, 1917–18. Chairman of Revolutionary Military Council and Commissar for Military and Naval Affairs, 1918–25. Chairman of Concessions Committee, 1925–27. Leader of Trotskyist Opposition. Expelled from Party, 1927. Exiled abroad, 1929. Assassinated.

Uglanov, Nikolai Aleksandrovich (alias Nikolai Ugryumii) (1886–1940). RSDLP(B) member from 1907. Central Committee candidate member from 1921. Central Committee member, 1923–30. Politburo candidate member and Central Committee Secretary, 1926–29. Moscow City Party Secretary, 1924–28. USSR Commissar of Labor, 1928–30. Repressed.

Veger, V. I. (?–?). Rector of KUTK, 1929–1930.

Voitinsky, Grigorii Naumovich (alias Grigorii, Grigoriev, Sergei, Sergeev, Tarasov, real name: Zarkhin) (1893–1953). RSDLP(B) member from 1918. Deputy Chairman of Aleksandrov City Revolutionary Committee in Sakhalin, 1920. RCP(B) Far Eastern Bureau Vladovostok branch representative in China, 1920–21. Head of ECCI Far Eastern Department, Deputy Head of Eastern Department, 1922. ECCI representative in China, 1925. Head of ECCI Far Eastern Bureau, 1926–27. Deputy Chairman of Fruit and Vegetable Center of All-Soviet Agriculture Cooperation, 1927–29. Secretary of Profintern Pacific Secretariat, 1932–34. Taught Chinese history at various schools from 1934.

Volin, Mikhail (real name: Semen Natanovich Belenky) (?–?). Soviet Sinologist. Director of Scientific Research Institute for Chinese Studies, 1928–30.

Volk, Yakov Ilich (?–1937). Professor at UTK/KUTK through 1929. Later, reviewer on Japan of ECCI Eastern Department. Repressed.

Voroshilov, Kliment Yefremovich (1881–1969). RSDLP(B) member from 1903. Central Committee member, 1921–61 and from 1966. Central Committee Politburo (Presidium) member, 1926–60. Chairman of Revolutionary Military Council and Commissar for Military and Naval Affairs from 1925. USSR Commissar of Defense from 1934. Deputy Chairman of Council of People's Commissars from 1940. Chairman of Supreme Soviet Presidium, 1953–60.

Vujovič, Vujo (alias Voytslav, Voyslav, Vladislav Dmitrievich) (1897–1936). Serbian RSDLP member from 1912. Active member of French and Yugoslav Communist movements, 1918–21. AUCP(B) member from 1924. Member, Secretary of Communist Youth International Executive and its representative in Germany, France, Italy, Czechoslovakia, 1921–26. Yugoslav Communist Party Deputy representative to ECCI, ECCI Presidium candidate member, 1924–26. Member of Trotskyist Opposition. Expelled from AUCP(B), 1927. Recanted, 1930. Senior research fellow at International Agrarian Institute, 1930–32. ECCI Balkan Länder Secretariat member, 1931–35. Repressed.

Wan Zhiling (alias Wan Zhuling, Vsevolod Alekseevich Korsh) (?–?). Studied at UTK/KUTK, 1927–30. Co-leader of Chinese Trotskyists in Moscow. Repressed.

Wang Dengyun (1897–1977). Member of GMD delegation to USSR, 1923. Worked at Whampoa Military Academy, 1925–26.

Wang Fanxi (alias Shuangshan, Vasilii Pavlovich Kletkin, real name: Wang Wenyuan) (1907–). CCP member from 1925. Studied at UTK/KUTK, 1927–29. Joined Chinese Trotskyist organization at KUTK, 1928. Returned to China, 1929. Expelled from CCP, 1930. Co-founder of *Shiyue she* (October Group) of Trotskyists in China, 1930. Co-founder of CCP Left Opposition, May 1931. Emigrated, 1949. At present (July 1999) lives in Leeds, England.

Wang Jiaxiang (alias Kommunard) (1906–1974). Chinese Communist Youth League member from 1925. Studied and worked at UTK/KUTK, 1925–29. CCP member from 1928. Commissar of Foreign Affairs of Chinese Soviet Government from 1931. Politburo member, 1934–45. Served as Head of Red and Eighth Route Armies General Political Departments. CCP Central Committee candidate member, 1945–56. Ambassador to USSR, 1949–51. Deputy Foreign Minister, 1951–56. Central Committee member, 1956–69 and from 1973.

Wang Jingwei (alias Wang Zhaoming) (1883–1944). Sun Yat-sen's close associate. Member of *Revolutionary Alliance* from 1905. Leader of "Left" Guomindang, Head of Guomindang Nationalist Government, Chairman of Military and Political Councils of GMD CEC, July 1925 – May, 1926. Head of Wuhan Nationalist Government, April-September 1927. Leader of GMD Reorganizationist Group. Collaborated with invading Japanese from 1938. Head of pro-Japanese collaborationist regime at Nanjing from 1940.

Wang Jinmei (real name: Wang Ruijun) (1898–1925). Co-founder of CCP, 1921. Secretary of Shandong Regional Party committee from 1921. Head of Jinan branch of Secretariat of All-China Federation of Labor from 1922.

Wang Pingyi (alias Bo Ping, Ozolin, Elizavetin) (1905?–?). Studied at UTK/KUTK, 1926–28. Co-leader of Left Opposition in China, 1930–31.

Wang Ruofei (alias Ivan Nemtsov, real name Wang Yunsheng) (1896–1946). Activist in Chinese Communist movement from 1922. PCF member, 1922. Studied at KUTV, 1923–25. Secretary of Henan-Shenxi Regional Party Committee, 1925. Later, Head of CCP Central Executive Committee Secretariat. CCP Central Committee member from 1927. Briefly sympathized with Trotskyists. Member of CCP delegation to ECCI, 1928–30. Accused as a "supporter" of Trotskyists, 1929. Sent to work in a factory, 1930. Returned to China and arrested by GMD secret police, 1931. Released on parole, 1937. Head of CCP Central Executive Committee Secretariat, 1937–45. Killed in aircraft crash.

Wang Wenhui (alias Boris Romanovich Yarotsky) (1906–?). CCP member from 1925. Studied at UTK/KUTK, 1925–30. Member of Trotskyist Opposition. Repressed.

Wang Zhihao (alias Ryutin) (1902–?). CCP member and AUCP(B) candidate member from 1926. Studied at UTK/KUTK, 1925–27. Member of Trotskyist Opposition. Deported from USSR.

Wen Yue (alias Senkevich) (1902–?). Chinese Communist Youth League member from 1927. Studied at UTK/KUTK, 1926–27. Member of Trotskyist Opposition. Repressed.

Wu Tiecheng (1888–1953). Military adviser to Sun Yat-sen's Governments from 1917. Guangzhou Chief of Police, 1923–April 1926. Later occupied various posts in GMD and Nationalist Government apparatus.

Wu Yuzhang (alias Shuren, Burenin) (1878–1966). Member of Sun Yatsen's *Revolutionary Alliance* from 1905. Participated in Xinhai Revolution, 1911–12. CCP member from 1925. GMD Central Executive Committee member, 1926–27. Studied at KUTK, 1928–30. Instructor at Chinese Lenin school in Vladivostok, Head of Chinese Department of USSR Academy of Sciences Far Eastern branch, and Head of Chinese section of movement for liquidation of illiteracy, 1930. Head of KUTV Chinese Department, 1931–34. Conducted Comintern work in France, 1935–36, 1937. Secretary of CCP Sichuan Provincial Committee, 1937–45. Chairman of Committee for Reform of Chinese script from 1955.

Xiang Jingyu (Nadezhdina, real name: Xiang Junxian) (1895–1928). Activist in Chinese Communist movement from 1922. Head of CCP Central Committee Women's Department through 1925. Studied at UTK, 1925–27. Worked in CCP Hankou City Committee, edited CCP journal *Changjiang* (Yangzi). Arrested by GMD secret police and executed.

Xiang Zhongfa (alias Te Sheng, Yang Tesheng, Zhong Fa, Ke Fa) (1880–1931). CCP member from 1922. Chairman of Wuhan Federation of Labor General Council, 1926. CCP Central Committee member from May 1927. Provisional Politburo member, 1927. Worked in Profintern, 1928. CCP Central Committee General Secretary from 1928. Arrested by GMD secret police, confessed, and executed.

Xiao Changbin (alias Zhi Qi, Naum Mikhailovich Mikhailov) (1900–?) Chinese Socialist Youth League member from 1923. CCP member from 1925. Studied at UTK/KUTK, 1926–27. Member of Trotskyist Opposition. Returned to China, 1929. Activist in Trotskyist movement in North China through 1931.

Xiao Jingguang (1903–1989). Chinese Socialist Youth League member from 1920. CCP member from 1922. Studied at KUTV, 1921–24, and Leningrad Mlitary-Political Academy, 1927–30. Commander of Twenty-Ninth Corps of Red Army, 1935–36. Central Committee candidate member, 1945–56 and full member, 1956–82.

Xiong Xiong (alias Silvestrov) (1892–1927). Activist in Chinese Communist movement from 1922. Studied at KUTV, 1923–25. Taught at Whampoa Military Academy from 1925. Executed.

Xu Teli (alias Markin) (1877–1968). CCP member from 1927. Studied at KUTK, 1928–30. Later, Deputy Head of CCP Central Committee Propaganda Department. CCP Central Committee member from 1945. After proclamation of People's Republic in 1949 became member of Central People's Government.

Xu Yunzuo (alias Yuriev) (?–?). Studied at UTK, 1925–27. Worked at KUTV and KUTK, 1927–30. Member of Trotskyist Opposition. Repressed.

Xu Zheng'an (alias Latyshev) (1899–?). CCP member from 1926. Studied and worked at UTK/KUTK, 1926–30. Member of Trotskyist Opposition. Repressed.

Yang Huabo (alias Korolenko) (1908–?). Chinese Communist Youth League and Soviet Komsomol member. Studied at UTK, 1926–27. Member of Trotskyist Opposition. Expelled from USSR.

Yang Mingzhai (alias Shmidt) (1882–1938). Arrived in Russia before fall of tsardom. After October Revolution joined RKP(B). Worked in Vladivostok Department of Far East Bureau of RKP(B), 1920. Accompanied Voitinsky to China, 1920–21. Worked and studied at UTK, 1925–27, then worked in Beiping (Beijing)-Tianjin Regional Party Organization. Editor of Chinese newspaper *Gongrenzhi lu* (Worker's Way) in Khabarovsk. Accused by Chen Shaoyu as a "Trotskyist" and arrested, 1937. Executed.

Yang Paoan (1896–1931). CCP member from 1921. Secretary of GMD Central Executive Committee Organizational Department, 1924–27. Co-leader of Hong Kong-Guangzhou strike, 1925. CCP Central Committee member, 1927–28.

Yang Shangkun (alias Saltykov) (1907–). Chinese Communist Youth League member from 1925. CCP member from 1926. Studied at UTK/KUTK, 1926–30. Central Committee candidate member, 1934–45 and full member, 1979–92. Secretary of CC Northern Bureau, 1937–41. After founding of PRC in 1949, governor of Guangdong and mayor of Guangzhou. Poliburo member, 1982–92. Chairman of PRC, 1988–93.

Yaroslavsky, Yemelian (alias Vladimir Semenovich Lapin, real name: Minei Izrailevich Gubelman) (1878–1943). RSDLP member from 1898. RCP(B) Central Committee member from 1921. RCP(B) Central Committee Secretary, 1921–22. Secretary of Central Control Commission, 1923–34. Member of Central Committee Commission of Party Control from 1934.

Ye Jianying (alias Yukhnov) (1897–1986). Taught at Whampoa Military Academy, 1924–26. CCP member from 1927. Participated in Northern Expedition, 1926–27. Studied at KUTV and KUTK, 1928–30. Chief of Staff of Red Army from 1930 and of Eighth Route Army from 1937. Member of Central Committee from 1945, of Politburo from 1966. Politburo Standing Committee member from 1973. Deputy Chairman of Central Committee, 1973–82.

Yevdokimov, Grigorii Yeremeevich (1884–1936). RSDLP(B) member from 1903. Central Committee member, 1919–25. Chairman of Petrograd Labor Unions, Secretary of Leningrad Party Provincial Committee, 1920–25. Central Committee Secretary and Organizational Bureau member, 1925–27. Member of Zinovievist Opposition. Expelled from Party, 1927. Recanted, 1928. Repressed.

Yin Kuan (alias Ryazanov) (1897–1967). Activist in Chinese Communist movement from 1922. Studied at KUTV, 1923–24. Secretary of CCP Shandong Party Committee, 1924–25. Secretary of Jiangsu-Zhejiang Regional Party Committee and Anhui Provincial Committee, 1925. Member of Trotskyist Opposition. Expelled from Party, 1929. Served about 20 years in GMD and Maoist prisons.

Yu Shude (1894–1982). CCP member from 1921. GMD Central Executive Committee member, 1924–27. After Communist defeat in July 1927, left CCP. Taught at various schools.

Yu Xiusong (alias Narimanov) (1899–1938). Activist of Chinese Communist movement from 1920. Secretary of Shanghai Socialist Youth League, 1920–21. CSYL Central Executive Committee member, 1922–25. Studied at UTK and International Lenin School, 1925–33. Conducted Party work in Soviet Far East, 1933–35. Worked in Xinjiang Party Committee from 1935. Accused by Chen Shaoyu as a "Trotskyist", arrested by a Xingjiang warlord and sent to USSR, 1937. Executed.

Yun Daiying (1895–1931). Activist in Chinese Communist movement from 1920. CCP member from 1921. Head of Chinese Socialist Youth League Propaganda Department, 1923–24. GMD Central Executive Committee member, 1926–27. CCP Central Executive Committee member from 1928. Editor of CCP journal *Hongqi* (Red Banner) and newspaper *Hongqi ribao*, 1928–31. Arrested by GMD secret police, 1930, executed.

Zalutsky Pyotr Antonovich (1888–1937). RSDLP(B) member from 1907. Member and Secretary of All-Russia Central Executive Committee Presidium, 1921, then Secretary of Ural and Petrograd Provincial Party Committee, and RCP(B) Central Committee Central Western Bureau. Central Committee candidate member, 1920–23, full member, 1923–25. Member of Zinovievist Opposition. Expelled from Party, 1927. Recanted, 1928. Chairman of Lower Volga Regional Sovnarkhoz, 1928–32. Arrested, 1934. Sentenced to five years in prison, January 16, 1935. Executed.

Zasulich, Vera Ilinichna (1849–1919). Activist in Russian revolutionary movement from 1868. *Land and Liberty* group member from early 1877. *Emancipation of Labor* group member from 1883. RSDLP member from 1898. Co-leader of Mensheviks from 1903.

Zhakov, Anatolii Petrovich (1895–?). M. P. Zhakov's younger brother. Taught at UTK through 1927. Member of Trotskyist Opposition. Repressed.

Zhakov, Mikhail Petrovich (?–?). RCP(B) member from 1923. Taught at UTK through 1927. Leader of Left Opposition in Khamovnicheskii district of Moscow. Repressed.

Zhang Guotao (alias Amosov, Popov, Spiridonov, Kotelnikov) (1897–1979). Co-founder of CCP. Member of CCP Central Committee, 1921–23, 1925–38. Politburo member, 1928–38. GMD CEC candidate member, 1924–26. Secretary of Jiangxi and Hubei Party Committees, 1926–27. Member of CCP delegation to ECCI, 1928–30. Deputy Chairman of Chinese Soviet Government, 1931–36. Expelled from Party, 1938. Emigrated, 1949.

Zhang Ji (1882–1947). GMD activist. Central Control Commission member from 1924.

Zhang Qiubai (?–?). GMD activist. Participated in Congress of Peoples of Far East, 1922.

Zhang Tailei (real name: Zhang Zengrang) (1898–1927). Activist in Chinese Communist movement from 1920. Secretary of Chinese Section of Comintern Far Eastern Secretariat, 1921. Maring's interpreter, 1921–22. Chinese Socialist Youth League representative to Communist Youth International, 1924. CCP Central Executive Committee candidate member, 1925–27. Borodin's interpreter, 1925–26. Chinese Communist Youth League Central Executive Committee General Secretary, 1925. Politburo candidate member and Secretary of CCP Hubei and Guangdong Provincial Party Committees, 1927. Killed in action.

Zhang Wentian (alias Izmailov, Luo Fu, Si Mai) (1900–1976). CCP member from 1925. Studied and worked at UTK/KUTK and Institute of Red Professors, 1925–28. Head of CCP Central Committee Propaganda Department, 1930–33. Politburo member, 1931–56, candidate member, 1956–59. Secretary of Central Committee Secretariat, 1934–35. General Secretary of CCP CC, 1935–38. Ambassador to USSR, 1951–55. First Deputy Foreign Minister from 1955. Dismissed from office for his criticism of Mao Zedong's policy, 1959.

Zhang Zuolin (1875–1928). Head of Fengtian (Shenyang) clique of militarists, controlled Beijing Government, 1920–22 and 1924–28. Defeated by NRA, 1928. Assassinated.

Zhao Ji (alias Lyalin, Dinamin) (1903–?). Chinese Communist Youth League member from 1922. CCP member from 1924. Served at NRA during Northern Expedition. AUCP(B) candidate member from 1928. Studied at KUTV and KUTK, 1928–29. Co-leader of Chinese Trotskyists in Moscow and in China from 1928.

Zhao Shiyan (alias Sutin) (1901–1927). Activist in Chinese Communist movement from 1922. Studied at KUTV, 1923–24. Secretary of Beijing Party Committee, Head of Central Committee Northern Bureau Propaganda Department, 1924. Head of Jiangsu-Zhejiang Party Regional Committee Organizational Department, 1926. CCP Central Committee member, Secretary of Jiangsu Party Provincial Committee, 1927. Executed.

Zhao Yanqing (alias Mamashkin, Mama, Donbasov) (1897–1930). CCP member from 1926. AUCP(B) candidate member. Studied at KUTV and KUTK, 1927–30. Co-leader of Chinese Trotskyists in Moscow. Committed suicide.

Zheng Chaolin (alias Marlotov) (1901–1998). Activist in Chinese Communist movement from 1922. Studied at KUTV, 1923–24. Editor of *Xiangdao zhoukan*, 1924. Member of Hubei Provincial Party Committee, 1925–27. Expelled from Party, 1929. Co-leader of Chinese Trotskyist Opposition from 1929. Served 30–odd years in GMD and Maoist prisons.

Zhou Dawen (alias Zhou Daming, Di Yi, Luo Fu, Vladimir Vasilievich Chugunov) (1903–1938). CCP member from 1923. Chairman of All-Chinese Student Union, 1924. Studied and worked at UTK and International Lenin School, 1925–27. Instructor of political economy at International Lenin School, 1931–32. Editor-in-Chief of Chinese newspaper *Gongrenzhi lu* in Khabarovsk from 1932. Accused by Chan Shaoyu as a "Trotskyist" and arrested, 1937. Executed.

Zhou Enlai (alias Moskvin, Chen Guang, Wu Hao) (1898–1976). Activist in Chinese Communist movement from 1922. Secretary of European branches of Chinese Communist Youth League and CCP, 1922–24. Head of Political Department of Whampoa Military Academy, 1924–26. Secretary of CCP Central Executive Committee Military Department, 1926–27. Politburo member from 1927 and Politburo Standing Committee member from 1928. Head of CCP Central Committee Organizational Department and Secretary of Central Committee Military Commission, 1928–30. Head of CCP delegation to ECCI, 1930. Later, occupied various leading posts in CCP Central Committee apparatus. Premier of People's Republic of China from 1949. Deputy Chairman of CCP CC, 1956–69.

Zhu De (alias Danilov, real name: Zhu Daizhen) (1886–1976). CCP member from 1922. Studied at KUTV and a Soviet secret military school, 1925–26. Co-founder of Soviet movement in China, 1927–28. Commander-in-Chief of Chinese Communist Military Forces through 1949. Deputy Chairman of People's Central Government, 1949–54. Chairman of National People's Congress Standing Committee from 1959. CCP Central Committee candidate member from 1930. Politburo member from 1934 and Politburo Standing Committee member from 1973. Deputy Chairman of Central Committee, 1956–69.

Zhu Huaide (alias Okunev) (1905–?). Chinese Communist Youth League and CCP member from 1925. Soviet Komsomol member and AUCP(B) candidate member from 1926. Studied at UTK, 1926–27. Member of Trotskyist Opposition. Expelled from USSR.

Zhu Zhixin (alias Shi Shen, Zhu Dafu) (1885–1920). Guomindang activist. Killed by Guangxi warlords.

Zinoviev, Grigorii Evseevich (real name: Ovsei-Hersh Aronovich Radomyslsky) (1883–1936). RSDLP member from 1901. RSDLP(B) member from 1903. Central Committee member, 1907–27. Politburo candidate member, 1919–21, full member, 1921–26. Chairman of Petrograd Soviet, 1917–26. Chairman of Comintern, 1919–26.

Leader of Zinovievist Opposition. Expelled from Party, 1927. Recanted, 1928. Repressed.

Zou Lu (real name: Deng Sheng) (1885–1954). Member of Sun-Yat-sen's *Revolutionary Alliance* from 1905. Participated in Xinhai Revolution, 1911–12. Rector of Guangdong University from 1923 and Zhongshang [Sun Yat-sen] University from 1937.

Zuo Quan (alias Rogozin, real name Ji Quan) (1905–1942). CCP member from 1925. Studied at UTK/KUTK through 1930. Later, Chief of Staff of Communist First Front Army, Deputy Chief of Staff of Eighth Route Army. Killed in action.

Zurabov (?–?). Taught at KUTV through 1927. Member of Trotskyist Opposition. Repressed.

Index

article, 153; and the AUCP(B) CC and
CCC July–August 1927 Plenum,
153–154, 245; and the Fiftheenth
AUCP(B) Congress, 158; expelled
from the Party CC, 159; expelled from
Party, 159; his self-"disarming",
159–160; mentioned, 31, 84, 114, 139,
140, 163, 179, 181, 183, 234, 242,
243, 250

Zinovievists. *See* Left Opposition in Russia
Zonin. *See* Xiong Changchun
Zou Lu: biographical sketch, 301;
mentioned, 58
Die Zukunft (Future), 15
Zuo Quan: biographical sketch, 301;
mentioned, 170
Zurabov: biographical sketch, 301;
mentioned, 178